REVOLUTION POLITICKS

Daniel Finch, Seventh Earl of Winchilsea and
Second Earl of Nottingham

Reproduced by permission of the Trustees of the
National Portrait Gallery

REVOLUTION
POLITICKS

The Career of Daniel Finch
Second Earl of Nottingham, 1647–1730

BY

HENRY HORWITZ

Assistant Professor of History
University of Iowa

CAMBRIDGE
AT THE UNIVERSITY PRESS
1968

Published by the Syndics of the Cambridge University Press
Bentley House, P.O. Box 92, 200 Euston Road, London, N.W.1
American Branch: 32 East 57th Street, New York, N.Y. 10022

Library of Congress Catalogue Card Number: 68–11284
Standard Book Number: 521 0 53404

Printed in Great Britain
at the University Printing House, Cambridge
(Brooke Crutchley, University Printer)

CONTENTS

Preface   *page* vii

Abbreviations   xi

Note on Dates and Style   xii

1   The Making of the Man: 1647–72   1

2   The Apprentice Parliamentarian: 1673–9   8

3   At the Admiralty Board: 1679–84   20

4   The Defence of the Church: 1685–8   39

5   Counsel for the Constitution: 1688–9   64

6   The Contest for the King's Favour: 1689–90   86

7   Defeat at Sea: 1690–3   118

8   In the Wilderness: 1693–1702   147

9   The Promised Land: 1702–4   167

10 The High Churchman at Bay: 1704–11   200

11 Peace and the Protestant Succession: 1711–16   230

12 The Closing Years: 1716–30   251

13 Conclusion   258

Select Guide to Sources   275

List of Works Cited   280

Index   289

To W.T.M.
teacher and friend

PREFACE

It is a commonplace of English history that while the seventeenth century was 'the century of revolution', the eighteenth century was 'the classical age of the constitution'. The earlier period was an era of 'great parties' divided on far-reaching issues of principle, the latter one of 'small parties' distinguished by only 'small divisions'.[1] And as Professor Mansfield has recently reminded us, it was the 'hesitant concensus' of 1689 that eventually transformed the character of English politics by uniting, in the words of the Toleration Act, 'their Majesties' protestant subjects in interest and affection'.[2]

The author of the Toleration Act of 1689 was Daniel Finch, second Earl of Nottingham, whose career as parliamentarian and minister spanned the half-century from the stormy years of the 1670s to the calmer days of the 1720s. First Commissioner of the Admiralty during the Exclusion crisis, Secretary of State under William III and again under Queen Anne, and President of the Council under George I, Nottingham was deservedly ranked by Sir Keith Feiling among 'the first flight' of later Stuart political leaders.[3] But despite his prominence, Nottingham's career has never been accorded detailed treatment, either in his own day or in ours. Early in George I's reign, John Oldmixon did begin to prepare a vindication of and apologia for Nottingham with the earl's consent. However, when he saw the manuscript, Nottingham objected so strenuously to his treatment at Oldmixon's hands that he had the work suppressed.[4] More recently, Professor

---

[1] For this distinction, see H. C. Mansfield, 'Party Government and the Revolution of 1688', *American Political Science Review*, LVIII (1964), 933–47.

[2] *Ibid.* p. 940.

[3] K. G. Feiling, *A history of the Tory party 1640–1714* (Oxford, 1924), p. 5.

[4] *The conduct*, p. 19; LRO, Finch MSS. Correspondence, box VI, bundle 24, E. Southwell to Nottingham, 13 Dec. 1716; *ibid.* box VII, bundle 25, E. Curll to E. Southwell, 24 May and 15 June 1717; National Maritime Museum, Southwell MSS., vol. XV, Nottingham to E. Southwell, 15 Dec. 1716.

W. A. Aiken of Lehigh University was contemplating a biography of Nottingham, but service in the Second World War and his premature death intervened.[1] It is the aim of this study to redress the balance, in the hope that by tracing Nottingham's course and analysing his political position a better understanding may be gained not only of the man and the views that he epitomized, but also of the character of the 'Revolution politicks' which link the seventeenth and eighteenth centuries.

If those objectives have been at least partially realized in this work, much of the credit is due to Dr G. V. Bennett of New College, Oxford, who presided over its birth as a doctoral dissertation in the University of Oxford between 1959 and 1963. His guidance and his insight into Nottingham and his times have furnished me with invaluable guideposts.

In preparing this study, I have incurred many other obligations which I can only acknowledge here. Three fellow workers in later Stuart political history, Mr G. Holmes of Glasgow University, Dr W. Speck of the University of Newcastle-on-Tyne, and Professor H. Snyder of the University of Kansas have generously shared with me the fruits of their researches in countless discussions during the past eight years and I have profited greatly from those exchanges.

Others whose help I received while working on my dissertation were Mr K. Thomas of St John's College, Oxford, who first suggested this topic to me; Professor H. Habakkuk of All Souls College, Oxford, who gave me the benefit of his knowledge of the Finch family's circumstances; Rev. R. Thomas, formerly

[1] Professor Aiken did complete an M.Litt. thesis at Cambridge University in 1933 entitled 'The Administration of Daniel Finch, second earl of Nottingham, as secretary of state under Queen Anne, 1702–4' and an essay 'The Admiralty in Conflict and Commission, 1679–1684' published posthumously in *Conflict in Stuart England: Essays in honour of Wallace Notestein*, ed. W. A. Aiken and B. D. Henning (London, 1960). He also assembled and edited a collection of Nottingham's and other contemporaries' memoirs and papers under the title of *The Conduct of the Earl of Nottingham*. His papers have been deposited in the Yale University Library, and I am grateful to Mrs W. A. Aiken for extending her permission to me to see them before I embarked upon my own researches.

Librarian of Dr Williams' Library, who guided me through the byways of Dissenting history; and Mr F. Bickley, editor of the Finch papers for the Historical Manuscript Commission, who introduced me to the intricacies of Nottingham's hand.

In the later stages of preparation, the criticism and encouragement I received from Professors C. Robbins of Bryn Mawr College, B. Henning of Yale University, D. Lacey of the United States Naval Academy, my colleague in the University of Iowa R. Colie, and M. H. Curtis and my fellow-members of the first Folger Shakespeare Library post-doctoral seminar in Tudor-Stuart history was most valuable.

Throughout my researches, I have benefited greatly from the assistance so willingly given me by the staffs of the various libraries and repositories upon whose resources I have drawn. Especial thanks are due to those who went beyond the normal limits of professional service in furthering my inquiries: Mr R. Ellis, Secretary of the Historical Manuscript Commission; the late Miss D. Coates, Librarian at Longleat; Mr S. Arthur of the British Museum; and Mr P. King, County Archivist of Northamptonshire.

For permitting me to use documents in their possession, I am most grateful to the Duke of Buccleuch and Queensberry, the Duke of Devonshire and the Trustees of the Chatsworth Settlements, the Duke of Marlborough, the Duke of Portland, the Marquess of Bath, the Marquess of Downshire, the Earl Spencer, Colonel James Hanbury, and Mr O. R. Bagot. I should also like to thank the National Portrait Gallery for permission to publish the frontispiece.

I gratefully acknowledge, too, the financial support afforded me by the United States Government under the Fulbright Act during my first two years as a doctoral candidate between 1959 and 1961 and by the Folger Shakespeare Library under its first post-doctoral programme during the summer of 1964.

Some of the material in chapters 3, 11 and 13 first appeared in articles in the *Journal of Ecclesiastical History* in 1964 and the *Journal of British Studies* in 1966. I wish to thank the editors of those journals for permission to use that material in this work.

Finally, I want to thank my research assistants Mrs M. Gessell and Mr W. Rohrer for their help in checking the footnotes, reading the proofs, and compiling the index.

ABBREVIATIONS

(Full details of manuscript sources quoted will be found in the
Select Guide to Sources, pp. 275–9)

BRO   Berkshire Record Office

BM   British Museum

BIHR   *Bulletin of the Institute of Historical Research*

Burnet   *Bishop Burnet's History of His Own Time* (Oxford, 1833)

CJ   *Journals of the House of Commons*

CSPD   *Calendar of State Papers Domestic*

CTB   *Calendar of Treasury Books*

Clarendon correspondence   *Correspondence of Henry Hyde, Earl of Clarendon, and of his brother, Laurence Hyde, Earl of Rochester*, ed. S. W. Singer (London, 1828)

The conduct   *The Conduct of the Earl of Nottingham*, ed. W. A. Aiken (New Haven, 1941)

DNB   *Dictionary of National Biography*, ed. L. Stephen (London, 1885–1900)

Dalrymple   *Memoirs of Great Britain and Ireland*, ed. Sir J. Dalrymple (London, 1771–3)

EHR   *English Historical Review*

FSL   Folger Shakespeare Library

GEC   G. E. Cokayne, *The Complete Peerage*, ed. V. Gibbs (London, 1910–59)

Grey   A. Grey, *Debates of the House of Commons from the Year 1667 to the Year 1694* (London, 1769)

HMC   Publications of the Historical Manuscript Commission

Hatton correspondence   *Correspondence of the family of Hatton being chiefly letters addressed to Christopher first Viscount Hatton A.D. 1601–1704*, ed. E. M. Thompson (Camden Society, London, 1878)

KAO   Kent Archives Office

LJ   *Journals of the House of Lords*

LRO   Leicestershire Record Office

Luttrell	N. Luttrell, *A brief historical relation of state affairs from September 1678 to April 1714* (Oxford, 1857)
Morrice	'The Entring Book' of Roger Morrice, Dr Williams' Library
NRO	Northamptonshire Record Office
PH	*Cobbett's Parliamentary History of England. From the Norman Conquest in 1066, to the Year 1803* (London, 1806–20)
PRO	Public Record Office
Tindal	Rapin de Thoyras, *The History of England*, and N. Tindal, *The Continuation of Mr. Rapin's History of England From the Revolution to the Present Times* (London, 1757–9)
WSL	William Salt Library

NOTE ON DATES AND STYLE

Throughout the text of this study, *Old Style* dates have been used, though with the year taken to begin on 1 January. However, in the footnotes contemporary letters dated *New Style* in the original have been cited under both *Old* and *New Style* dates.

In transcripts from manuscript, abbreviations have been extended and contractions filled in. Otherwise, the style and spelling of the manuscript material has not been altered.

CHAPTER I

THE MAKING OF THE MAN

1647–72

On thursday the 30th of July 1646...Mr Heneage Finch...was maryed to Mistress Elizabeth Harvey...By her hee had his eldest sonne borne the 2 of July 1647 being fryday about a quarter of an hour after 8 a clock in the morning or somewhat more which was Christened...the 8th day of the said month of July and called Daniel.[1]

Daniel's family heritage, in the unpropitious year of 1647, was the moderate royalism and Anglicanism of Kent whence the Finches had taken their rise in the later fifteenth century.[2] Service to the crown, coupled with a series of advantageous marriages, had provided the basis for a gradual enhancement of the family's position during the sixteenth and early seventeenth centuries. From what were apparently modest squirearchical origins, the main branch of the family in the person of the widow of Sir Moyle Finch (1551–1614) had bought its way into the peerage during the early Stuart 'inflation of honours', with Lady Finch, *née* Heneage, being made first Viscountess of Maidstone in 1623 and then Countess of Winchilsea in 1628.[3]

Daniel's own grandfather, the first Heneage Finch, was only a younger son of Sir Moyle and the new Countess of Winchilsea, but his legal training and a lucrative second marriage had enabled him to establish his own family on a solid footing before his death in 1631.[4] His eldest son Heneage was also trained for the law, by

[1] BM Add. MSS. 34177, fos. 16–17.
[2] Feiling, *Tory party*, p. 16; A. Everitt, *The community of Kent and the great rebellion 1640–60* (Leicester, 1966), pp. 45–55, 116–24.
[3] For a somewhat fanciful account of the family's origins, see B. I'Anson, *The history of the Finch family* (London, 1933), esp. pp. 12–21, 52–5.
[4] *DNB*, 'Heneage Finch'. At his grandmother's death in 1634, the second Heneage Finch also inherited valuable estates in Buckinghamshire and Northamptonshire (H. J.

way of Westminster School, Christ Church and the Inner Temple. Called to the bar in 1645, his royalist sympathies do not seem to have hindered him during the interregnum from building up a lucrative practice or from acquiring the reputation of a skilful and eloquent pleader. And when the restoration of the Stuart house came in 1660, his legal acumen and his services as one of the leading royalist spokesmen in the Convention parliament were quickly rewarded with a knighthood, a baronetcy, and the post of Solicitor-General to Charles II.[1]

A year after his first appearance at the bar, Heneage married Elizabeth, the daughter of Daniel Harvey—a prosperous London merchant, associated chiefly with the Levant trade, 'of very eminent loyaltie, prudence, integritie, & generositie'.[2] Little survives to shed much light upon the boyhood of Daniel Finch, the eldest child of their alliance, save for the aura of affection and devotion that pervades the family correspondence in later years and that suggests the loving concern with which Daniel was brought up. Admitted to the Inner Temple early in 1658, it is unlikely that he began to study law at such a young age, though he must have been intimately familiar with the precincts of the Inns of Court since the family resided for a time close by Heneage Finch's chambers.[3] A few months later, following in his father's footsteps, Daniel entered Westminster School where he lived as a boarder for over three years in the house of Dr Richard Busby, the headmaster and his father's former tutor at Christ Church.[4] The fervid Anglicanism and rigorous curriculum of Westminster were, no doubt, important influences on Daniel's character, while some of the friendships he formed (particularly with George

Habakkuk, 'Daniel Finch, 2nd Earl of Nottingham: his house and estate', *Studies in social history*, ed. J. H. Plumb (London, 1955), p. 142.

[1] GEC, 'Heneage Finch' [first Earl of Nottingham]; *Lord Nottingham's chancery cases*, ed. D. E. C. Yale (Selden Society, London, 1957), I, xiii–xvi; J. R. Jones, 'Political groups and tactics in the convention of 1660', *Historical Journal*, VI (1963), 169.

[2] GEC, 'Heneage Finch'; KAO, Dering MSS. U275, A3, an unpaginated autobiographical fragment of another of Harvey's sons-in-law, Sir Edward Dering.

[3] *The Records of Old Westminsters*, ed. G. F. R. Barker and A. H. Stenning (London, 1928), I, 328.   [4] *Ibid.*

THE MAKING OF THE MAN

Legge) were of lasting significance. But it is only after he matriculated at Christ Church as a Gentleman Commoner on 26 July 1662 that we can first perceive something of his personality.[1]

The University, and Christ Church in particular, had not escaped the Restoration reaction which swept aside Puritan notions of conduct.[2] But the dissoluteness of some of Daniel's fellow collegians seems to have had but little effect on his own way of life, shepherded as he was by his tutor Benjamin Woodruff and also by Richard Allestree (soon to be made Regius Professor of Divinity).[3] Even in his youth, Daniel seems to have displayed the family traits of gravity and temperateness, for his father (now Sir Heneage) felt confident, even as he dispatched to him 'a large treatise of good counsell' which had been drawn up by his Uncle John's friend, Dr Thomas Baines, that it would not be needed.[4] Although apparently the butt of derision from some of his acquaintances, Daniel showed a commendable devotion to his studies. Indeed, the excellence of some of his early efforts even roused his father's suspicion of their authenticity.[5] Yet in the main, Sir Heneage felt justified in writing in April 1663 to Daniel (with a characteristic combination of advice and praise), 'loose not the reputation which I am told you have gayn'd of diligence and sobriety'.[6]

Daniel, in fact, would seem to have been in more danger of succumbing to self-complacency than to dissipation or indolence, though on occasion his father did express some uneasiness about his behaviour. 'It was never your mother's meaning nor mine that you should lose an hours study for him', he cautioned Daniel when informed that his dancing master had been entertained of a morning.[7] The purpose of an Oxford education, Sir Heneage made clear, was not to teach Daniel how to be 'that which the town calls a fine gentleman being to my understanding rather a

[1] J. Foster, *Alumni Oxonienses: 1500–1714* (London, 1891–2), II, 496.
[2] See, for example, *The life and times of Anthony Wood*, ed. A. Clark (Oxford Historical Society, Oxford, 1892), II, 2.   [3] *HMC Finch*, I, 208, 212, 245, 249, and *passim*.
[4] *Ibid.* pp. 211–12.   [5] *Ibid.* pp. 236–7.   [6] *Ibid.* p. 249.   [7] *Ibid.* p. 244.

3   I-2

libell than a commendation'.[1] Rather, he encouraged and exhorted him to develop that steadiness of judgment and loyalty to the Church that were the hallmarks of his own life. Only a month after Daniel's arrival in Oxford, his father was reminding him 'to frequent the publique prayers, and study to reverence and defend, as well as to obey, the Church of England'.[2] Again, urging Daniel to prepare himself carefully for his first Easter away from home, he advised him that 'Nothing can make you truly wise but such a religion as dwells upon your heart and governs your whole life'.[3]

Daniel's health was another frequent concern of his parents. He would seem to have been a somewhat delicate, if not sickly youth, and only a fortnight after he first went up to Oxford his father permitted him to journey with his tutor to Bath partly, at least, for reasons of health.[4] What complaints he suffered from is not entirely clear, though he was prone to frequent infections, but, as Sir Heneage later recalled to him, 'All your former studyes were full of payns and difficultys and the close pursuit of them might impayr your health'.[5] Perhaps it was for this reason that Daniel left Oxford without taking a degree. A continental tour was proposed for him, and, after a tearful family farewell at Dover, he left England late in the summer of 1665 accompanied by his younger brother Heneage who 'in Jest... wayt[s] upon his brother over seas as farr as Bruxels'.[6]

Daniel's eventual destination, by way of Frankfurt, Munich and Venice, was Florence, where his uncle Sir John Finch was now serving as English Resident at the court of the Grand Duke of Tuscany.[7] His 'chiefest study' at Florence, as his father observed to him soon after his arrival, was to be 'conversation and to understand men'.[8] But he was also to avail himself of this oppor-

[1] HMC Finch, I, 244. [2] Ibid. p. 212. [3] Ibid. p. 249. [4] Ibid. p. 208.
[5] Ibid. pp. 401, 403; LRO, Finch MSS., uncalendared section of Sir Heneage's letter of 15/25 Nov. 1665.
[6] KAO, Dering MSS. U 350, C/2/116, Sir Heneage to [Robert Southwell], 3 Sept. 1665.
[7] LRO, Finch MSS., Literary papers 16, a diary in Latin kept by Daniel Finch on his trip to Florence; A. Malloch, Finch and Baines, a seventeenth century friendship (Cambridge, 1917), pp. 32–45. [8] HMC Finch, I, 403.

tunity to master those 'outward accomplishments' that denoted
good breeding in later seventeenth-century England. Thus, we
hear once again of the employment of a dancing master and also
of a master of arms.[1] Still, there was ample time for travel too—
to Naples, Rome and Venice usually in the company of Dr
Baines.[2]

In this fashion, Daniel spent almost two years in Italy before
the first summons came to return home. Congratulating him on
his twentieth birthday in July 1667, his father expressed his great
desire to see him once again and remarked that it was 'now high
time you should return and settle yourselfe'.[3] It was at first
proposed that he journey home in the company of his uncle, but
the delay in obtaining Sir John's recall and Daniel's own wish to
spend some time in France eventually moved his father to permit
him to stay the following winter there. A few months in France,
Sir Heneage thought, would be 'time enough to make you master
of the French tongue, as farr as will be necessary for conversation,
and to instruct or perfect your fencing, riding, and dauncing,
without inconvenience to your health'.[4]

Daniel's sojourn in France was, however, to be extended beyond
his father's original expectation. Arriving in Paris in the early
autumn, his stay seems to have been uneventful at first. But early
in February 1668, John Trevor, who bore the character of Envoy
Extraordinary to Louis XIV, reached Paris. Trevor, so Sir Heneage
wrote his son, was highly esteemed by the English Court and it
was rumoured that he would soon be advanced to a secretaryship
of state 'so that it will be a happy circumstance of your travells,
to be made known to him abroad'.[5] All proceeded as he had
hoped; Daniel was introduced to the envoy and his father
permitted him to extend his term in Paris so that he might
return with Trevor's party.[6] Finally in June 1668, almost

[1] Ibid. p. 404.
[2] Ibid. pp. 414–15; Conway Letters, ed. M. H. Nicolson (New Haven, 1930), pp. 284–5.
[3] HMC Finch, I, 469.   [4] Ibid. p. 479.
[5] Ibid. p. 493.   [6] Ibid. p. 509.

three years after his tour had begun, he set foot once again in England.[1]

Daniel was now twenty-one and, as his cousin Sir Roger Twysden wrote in compliment to his father, 'every body speaks him a very fine gentleman, and one you and your lady are likely to have much comfort in'.[2] Unfortunately, it is at this time that he is almost completely lost to view; virtually nothing is known of his activities for over four years save that he was made a Fellow of the Royal Society shortly after his return—an indication that in some small measure he may have shared his former tutor's and his uncle's interests in 'natural philosophy'.[3] It may be conjectured that at least part of this period was spent in studying law, for among his personal papers which seem to date from this time are to be found numerous notes on, and extracts from, lawbooks.[4] He also appears to have been assisting Sir Heneage in the management of his official and family affairs.[5]

But if these were his chief activities in the years after his return from the continent, no doubt both he and his father must have regarded them merely as preliminaries to his own 'settlement' in marriage and the world of affairs. Thanks to Sir Heneage's continued advancement—the Attorney-Generalship in 1670 and the Lord Keepership in 1673—he was eventually able to make a very fortunate match for Daniel with Lady Essex Rich, co-heiress of the third Earl of Warwick. Her guardian, the Countess of Warwick, had previously rejected a number of prospective husbands for her niece 'because the young men were not viceless'.[6] But when Finch was proposed to her, probably by Lord Halifax late in 1673, she gave her approval to his suit 'upon the assurance I had from all the persons that knew him, that he was an extraordinary both

---

[1] Second series of the catalogue of the collection of...Alfred Morrison; the Bulstrode papers (London, 1897), I, 46.   [2] HMC Finch, I, 510.
[3] The records of the Royal Society of London (4th ed. London, 1940), p. 381; Malloch, Finch and Baines, pp. 31–2; DNB, 'Benjamin Woodruff'.
[4] LRO, Finch MSS., Legal papers 9.   [5] HMC Finch, II, 19–20; CSPD, 1670, p. 508.
[6] Autobiography of Mary, Countess of Warwick, ed. T. C. Croker (Percy Society, London, 1848), p. 35.

ingenuous and civil person (which upon my own knowledge of him, I afterwards found to be true)'.[1] By mid-April 1674, Daniel was reported to be 'a very close suitor to my Lady Essex', and her own consent was soon won.[2] On 16 June 1674 the couple was wed in the chapel of Lady Warwick's house at Lees, Essex, by her chaplain Thomas Woodroff, with the Lord Keeper (newly ennobled as Baron Finch of Daventry) making a handsome financial settlement on his son.[3] The marriage was to vindicate fully Lady Warwick's judgment; Lady Essex, as the few extant letters to her reveal, was beloved by her husband and doted upon by her father-in-law.[4]

Even before his marriage, however, Daniel had made his entry into politics. In the winter of 1672–3, he had become a candidate for the parliamentary seat at Great Bedwyn, Wiltshire, vacated by the death of Sir John Trevor. Bedwyn was a burgage borough under the influence of the lords of the manor, the Seymour Dukes of Somerset (relations of the Finches by marriage).[5] But Daniel's success, even though he was probably sponsored by the Dowager Duchess, was by no means assured since the individual burgage owners (some eighty in number) had not yet been bought out by the lords of the manor.[6] Indeed, before he was elected late in January 1673, Daniel had been put to the charge of a new town hall for Bedwyn.[7] On 4 February, then, he took his place for the first time in the House of Commons at the opening of the tenth session of the Cavalier parliament of 1661–78.

[1] *Ibid.* p. 36. See also *HMC Finch*, II, 17.   [2] *CSPD*, 1673–5, pp. 227–8.
[3] P. Finch, *History of Burley-on-the-Hill* (London, 1901), I, 176; *HMC Finch*, II, 16–19.
[4] See, for example, *ibid.* pp. 24–6.
[5] B. Willis, *Notitia Parliamentaria*, III (London, 1750), pt. I, p. 63; S. T. Bindoff, 'Parliamentary history 1529–1688', *A history of Wiltshire* (The Victoria History of the Counties of England, London, 1957), v (ed. R. B. Pugh and E. Crittal), 159 and n. 31. The Duchess was the mother-in-law of Sir Heneage's cousin, the second Earl of Winchilsea. Sir Heneage and Daniel later served as trustees of her will.
[6] Willis, *Notitia*, III, pt. I, p. 63; *A history of Wiltshire*, v, 159.
[7] Bodl. Willis MSS. 15, fos. 78–9. However, his election (and all other by-elections ordered by Lord Chancellor Shaftesbury during the parliamentary recess) was adjudged void by the Commons when they met, but Daniel was successful when the election was re-run early in February (*Members of parliament* (Return to the House of Commons, London, 1878), I, 530 and note).

CHAPTER 2

THE APPRENTICE PARLIAMENTARIAN

1673–9

In Parliament, (my first publick appearance in the year 1672/3) I alwaies
thought the limits of the Prerogative of the Crown and the liberties and rights
of the people so well Settled, that those landmarks ought not to be remov'd...I
did not think it a breach of Trust, with which every member is vested, to
gratify King Charles 2 with little summs, whose revenue for all services was not
above 1,200,000 pounds...I was alwaies against Impeachments...because there
is not an instance of any prosecution by impeachment...that was carryd on by
legal Steps in matter and form, rage and violence overruling Law...[and]
because the opinion of the declaratory power...which is so universally received
and believ'd...is most certainly false and this is plain even to a demonstration
...I have allways been for some Indulgence in Those, who differ'd in Religion
from the Establisht Church, so far as was consistent with the safety of the
Church and peace of the state.[1]

So wrote Daniel Finch in the 1720s, recounting for the benefit of
his children his early years as a member of the Cavalier parliament.
The tone of these recollections was undoubtedly affected by his
experiences of the intervening half-century, but they do accord
with much of what can be gleaned from other sources about his
attitudes and activities as a young member of parliament.

Finch's desire to balance the claims of prerogative and liberty
was exemplified, on the one hand, in his opposition to efforts made
in the Commons to usurp the royal prerogative in the shaping of
foreign policy and the conduct of military operations. In the 1677
session, he spoke out against proposals to word a Commons'
address on foreign policy in a way which would effectively have
tied the king's hands in his choice of allies, and in the first 1678
session he objected also to the proposed appointment by parlia-

[1] LRO, Finch MSS., Political papers 148, pp. 1–2.

ment of commissioners to oversee the management of the war then being mooted against France.[1] On the other hand, his apparent opposition in 1673 to the king's unilateral suspension of the penal statutes against recusants and Protestant dissenters, as well as his support in 1677 for a Habeas Corpus bill, illustrate his readiness to reject extreme prerogative claims and his concern for the liberty of the subject.[2]

His inclination to favour Court requests for supply is also amply attested to in surviving accounts of the Commons' proceedings between 1673 and 1678. On virtually every occasion when proposals for supply were before the House, Finch is recorded as having urged their adoption.[3] His record on impeachments is marked by a similar consistency. Not surprisingly, his strongest words were reserved for those few instances when his father came under fire.[4] But he also opposed impeachment proceedings begun against the Earl of Arlington in 1674 and against the Earl of Danby in 1675 and 1678.[5]

Again, though Finch's most notable labours to secure some alleviation of the dissenters' position were to be undertaken after 1679, there is confirmation in contemporary sources of his interest in a relaxation of the penal laws as they applied to Protestants even in these early years. During the 1674 session, he prepared a speech in support of a proposal to modify on their behalf the Oath of Supremacy.[6] Again, during the spring session of 1675, he reminded the House of its earlier discussion of schemes of indulgence and sought to persuade his fellow members of the wisdom of easing the plight of 'so considerable a part of the nation' for reasons both of 'charity and prudence'.[7]

But faithful as is the account given in Finch's fragmentary memoir to many of the positions he adopted in his first years in

[1] App. F6, G1.
[2] LRO, Finch MSS., Political papers 148, p. 2, and Political papers 42, p. 22.
[3] App. E2, F1, F3, F7, G3.   [4] App. F2, G7, H2.
[5] App. C1, D1, H8. See also App. B1, G4, G6, H7.
[6] App. C2.   [7] Grey, III, 163.

parliament, it would be misleading to view them solely through the spectacles of his old age. They need also to be placed in their immediate setting—the years of Charles II's reign from the fall of the Cabal to the meeting of the first Exclusion parliament.

From this perspective, it would appear that the course which the young member of parliament steered through the shifting political sands of the 1670s closely paralleled that of his father, save perhaps for Finch's early interest in indulgence. With the collapse of the Cabal, Attorney-General Finch—accounted a friend of Secretary Arlington since Clarendon's fall—drew closer to the new Lord Treasurer, Sir Thomas Osborne (soon to be made Earl of Danby).[1] And it was the Treasurer and his ally Sir Edward Seymour, the Speaker, who were the chief movers of the elder Finch's promotion, after the dismissal of the Earl of Shaftesbury, to the Lord Keepership on 10 November 1673.[2] For a time, however, the new Lord Keeper tried to keep a foot in each camp by remaining on friendly terms with the Secretary.[3] It could well be, then, that the defence of Arlington made by Daniel in the following session was prompted by his father's ties to the Secretary, though he may also have been influenced by the surprisingly adept self-vindication Arlington made when he appeared before the Commons in January 1674.[4]

However, by the beginning of the next parliamentary session in April 1675, the Lord Keeper had cast off his remaining links with Arlington, and he and Danby were now working hand-in-glove.[5] This was clearly reflected in his son's behaviour in the Commons.

---

[1] For the elder Finch's connections with Arlington, see *CSPD*, 1667–8, p. 258; PRO, PRO 31/3/129, Colbert au Roi, 10/20 Nov. 1673; KAO, Dering MSS. U350, C2/121, Sir Heneage Finch to Sir Edward Dering, 12 Aug. 1669. For Sir Heneage's connections, before the fall of the Cabal, with Osborne (chiefly through Finch's brother-in-law, Viscount Conway), see *CSPD*, 1671, p. 510; *HMC Lonsdale*, p. 95; *Conway letters*, p. 365.

[2] *Essex Papers*, ed. O. Airy, 1 (Camden Society, London, 1890), 140.

[3] *Ibid. Letters addressed from London to Sir Joseph Williamson while plenipotentiary at the Congress of Cologne in the years 1673 and 1674*, ed. W. D. Christie (Camden Society, London, 1874), II, 92. Cf. *Essex Papers*, I, 141–2, 150.

[4] App. C 1. For Arlington's speech, see Grey, II, 275–80.

[5] *Essex Papers*, I, 228; A. Browning, *Thomas Osborne Earl of Danby and Duke of Leeds 1632–1712* (Glasgow, 1944–51), I, 136–7.

As Daniel himself explained in a letter to his Uncle John (now English Ambassador in Constantinople), when Danby's impeachment was moved by several cronies of Arlington,

I...mov'd that we might rather...proceed to examine how far these matters [alleged against Danby] were Criminal before wee went about to hear proofes ...I moved this because I thought it in itselfe the most naturall method, And I meant it as a service to my Lord Treasurer (and so my Lord Conway tells mee hee tooke it.) Not that I have any Obligations to my Lord Treasurer but because hee professed a friendship to my father.[1]

It would seem, then, that while Finch did not count himself a personal adherent of Danby, both his father's position and his own inclinations led him to side with the Court on most issues during the life of the Cavalier parliament, and he does indeed figure as a probable Court supporter and spokesman on the various parliamentary working lists drawn up for Danby between 1675 and 1678.[2] Certainly, he repeatedly backed Court-inspired motions for supply and also spoke out against a variety of opposition measures.[3] Among these was the Place bill of 1675 which he attacked in what one historian has characterized as a 'remarkably able' speech.[4]

Nevertheless, Daniel was prepared to take an independent line on certain issues. Not only did he support the abortive Habeas Corpus bill of 1677 (though he thought it poorly drafted); he also spoke out in favour of providing relief for the dissenters both in 1674 and 1675 though such proposals ran directly counter to Danby's avowed policy of a close alliance with the Anglican hierarchy.[5] But despite his father's support of this tactic of the Lord Treasurer, Daniel was much more disturbed—as were many other members of parliament in the middle and later 1670s—by the danger to the established order posed by Catholic influence

[1] LRO, Finch MSS., Political papers 37, *sub* 26 April.
[2] Browning, *Osborne*, III, 64, 76, 94, 115, 118.
[3] See above, p. 9, n. 3; also App. D3, G1, G5, H1.
[4] Feiling, *A history of the Tory party*, p. 159 and n. 3; App. D2.
[5] App. C2, D4; Browning, *Osborne*, I, 146–9 and *passim*.

than he was by the dissenting 'threat', particularly as the chances of James's succession to the throne grew. Thus, he wholeheartedly backed two unsuccessful measures brought forward in the 1677 session, one to assure the exclusion of Catholics from the Commons, the other (sponsored by Danby who was now shifting his own ground) to limit the powers of any Catholic successor in the making of clerical appointments.[1] Moreover, his father (who was made Lord Chancellor late in 1675) seems at first to have been convinced of the veracity of the witnesses to the existence of the popish plot, and their disclosures spurred the younger Finch on during the autumn session of 1678.[2] Besides advocating a successful bill which disabled all Catholics but the Duke of York from sitting in either House,[3] Daniel himself proposed and subsequently drafted a measure which would have made it treason for anyone to take up a military position without first having taken the oaths and complied with the other provisions of the first Test Act.[4] Furthermore, when the king, following Danby's advice while ignoring the counsel of the Lord Chancellor, rejected the Militia bill late in November, Finch openly questioned on the floor of the House the wisdom of those who had advised the royal veto.[5] Consequently, as he himself noted, his speech of 21 December 1678 against the new impeachment charges brought against Danby seems to have come as a surprise to 'my Lord Treasurer and all his relations and friends, who I fancy did not expect me for an advocate for him'.[6] In this instance, however, his principal reason for opposing the proposed articles of impeachment was that he did not believe the charges, though serious, amounted to treason. The same day, then, that he made a lengthy speech questioning the legal basis of the impeachment, he also

---

[1] LRO, Finch MSS., Political papers 42, p. 4; App. F97.
[2] LRO, Finch MSS., Political papers 58.
[3] App. H4. Finch did, however, oppose the motion for the removal of the Duke from Court (App. H1).
[4] LRO, Finch MSS., Political papers 57(ii), p. 33; CJ, IX, 542. Drafts of the bill are in LRO, Finch MSS., Political papers 54.
[5] App. H6. [6] LRO, Finch MSS., Political papers 57(ii), p. 68.

voted against a motion made by Danby's adherents to recommit the articles, explaining later in a letter to his uncle that 'I would not play a trick to serve a turn'.[1]

Despite Finch's closely argued legal objections to the impeachment of December 1678, sentiment against the Lord Treasurer was now too great and the articles were eventually carried in the Commons. The success of Danby's enemies reflected, in large measure, the fears of Catholic and French influence at Court which had troubled English politics since the early 1670s; the apprehensions that had been aroused by Charles's policies during the days of the Cabal and by the disclosure of James's conversion to Catholicism had never been laid to rest. As one unsympathetic contemporary later commented,

There were two things, which, like Circe's Cups, bewitched Men, and turned them into Brutes, viz. Popery and French Interest: and if either of these happened to be whispered in the House of Commons, they...ran immediately into Clamour and high Debates.[2]

The crux of the problem was that the tack to which Charles had gradually shifted after the wreck of his 'Grand Design' upon the rock of stubborn Dutch naval resistance in the third Anglo–Dutch War had done little to remove the real sources of these fears. To be sure, Danby—the leading figure among the ministers who supplanted the Cabal—favoured an anti-French line abroad and an Anglican stance at home. But though the king had allowed Danby to revive persecuting measures against the dissenters and had even encouraged talk of stricter enforcement of the penal acts against recusancy, he proved more reluctant to sever his ties to France and so Louis XIV was allowed to continue to recruit troops in Charles's kingdoms. Not until 1677 could Danby, supported by the elder Finch and other royal advisers, persuade the king of the advantage to him of a breach with France. By that time, it was too late. Suspicion of Charles's Francophilia had be-

[1] Ibid.
[2] Samuel Parker, Bp. Parker's history of his own time (London, 1728), p. 244.

come so widely entrenched that a determined opposition—stirred up by the Earl of Shaftesbury and encouraged by French subventions—was able, by refusing any substantial grant of supply until war was declared, to frustrate the Lord Treasurer's plans in 1677 and the spring of 1678 for a new 'triple alliance' of Spain, the United Provinces and England against Louis.

Thus, the appearance of Titus Oates in the summer of 1678 eager to testify to the existence of an international Catholic conspiracy supported by France against king, parliament and church was a spark sufficient to inflame the country. All the fears and grievances of a political generation now boiled over, with help from Shaftesbury, into the hysteria of the popish plot. Among the first and most important victims it claimed was Danby himself, impeached on evidence of his dalliance with France (on royal orders) provided by his ex-protegé, Ralph Montagu. The next victim was the Cavalier parliament, dissolved early in January 1679 by Charles who was fearful of the disclosures Danby might make if he had to defend himself against impeachment.

But the Court's position was not improved in the elections of the following month, and the opposition's increased strength was all too evident once the new parliament convened on 6 March 1679.[1] As Sir Robert Southwell wrote by way of explanation to the Duke of Ormonde in April,

There is now spread an universal demand for reformation, which the sober men limit to things moderate; but there are more who are unreasonable, and many, I fear, have no limits at all. Popery is the handle of this reformation, and the arguments deduced from it are becoming irresistible...Our real insecurity as to France is dreadful unto all...So that, while this insecurity governs, Popery must be prosecuted, which is thought a perfect limb thereof; and therefore in all probability we have many leagues to sail upon that tack.[2]

Among the supporters of the Court who failed to secure re-election in February 1679 was Daniel Finch, apparently because

---

[1] Browning, *Osborne*, I, 315–16; Feiling, *Tory party*, pp. 175–6.
[2] *HMC Ormonde*, n.s. IV, xviii.

Lord Bruce (now manager of the Seymour interest at Great Bedwyn) backed a rival candidate, Colonel John Dean. Lord Bruce's opposition and what Finch felt to be unfair practices were too strong a combination for him despite his previous benefaction to the borough.[1] But Finch's loss of his seat did not prevent his being named in April as one of the new commissioners of the Admiralty with a salary of £1,000 p.a.[2] This appointment seems to have come as a complete surprise to him; as he later recalled, he had 'never askt nor thought' of it, and he attributed his selection to his father's influence with the king.[3] But at this juncture, the Chancellor's own position at Court seems to have been too shaky for him to have been the prime mover of his son's preferment.[4] In any case, Daniel's appointment was only a part of a wholesale ministerial reshuffle whose centre-piece was the formation of a new Privy Council—a move which was announced on 20 April, the day before the selection of an entirely new set of Admiralty Commissioners was made public. Among the members of the reconstituted Privy Council were many of Danby's most prominent opponents including Shaftesbury, who was named Lord President.

This drastic shake-up, apparently undertaken on the advice of Temple, Essex and Sunderland, marked the adoption of a new royal strategy. Faced with widespread discontent and a growing

---

[1] HMC Finch, II, 54; Memoirs of Thomas, Earl of Ailesbury, written by himself, ed. W. E. Buckley (Roxburghe Club, London, 1890), I, 33–4. It is not clear whether Finch's failure owed anything to his parliamentary record as a moderate courtier; Dean was later to oppose the first Exclusion bill (A. Browning and D. Milne, 'An Exclusion bill division list', BIHR, XXIII (1950), 222).

[2] Luttrell, I, 13; CTB, VI, 81. Two months earlier, Daniel's younger brother Heneage, who had served previously as the Duke of York's Solicitor, had been named by the king to succeed Sir Francis Winnington as Solicitor-General.

[3] LRO, Finch MSS., Political papers 148, p. 4; HMC Finch, II, 53.

[4] Though Temple's account of the discussions leading up to the decision to reform the Privy Council suggests that the Lord Chancellor was informed of the scheme at an early stage, the Chancellor himself told Sir Robert Southwell that 'he was called in only at the conclusion of this work' (The works of Sir William Temple Bart. (London, 1770), II, 494–5; HMC Ormonde, n.s. IV, 505). In any case, rumours were circulating at this time that the elder Finch's ouster was imminent and Southwell reported on 3 May that he 'does prepare his mind not to be surprised at it' (HMC Ormonde, n.s. IV, 509).

clamour for the exclusion of the Duke of York from the succession to the throne within and without parliament, Charles seems to have resolved upon an outward show of conciliation, hoping thereby to hold the support of moderate elements in parliament while dividing the opposition.[1] Thus, the members of the new Admiralty Board—like those of the reformed Privy Council— were hardly a homogeneous group. On the one hand, Sir Henry Capel (named First Commissioner and also sworn a Privy Councillor), Sir Thomas Lee, Sir Thomas Meres, and Edward Vaughan of Trawsgoed were among those leading members of the opposition whom Charles hoped either to win over to the Court or to discredit by seemingly taking them into his confidence.[2] On the other, Sir Humphrey Winch was a courtier of the old stripe, while Edward Hales (later to figure as one of the principals in *Godden vs. Hales*) was the crypto-Catholic member for Canterbury.[3] It was with this motley array of shipmates, then, that Daniel Finch launched his official career—borne into office in the midst of the gravest political crisis between the Restoration and the Revolution on the strength of his father's standing at Court and his own record as a moderate courtier in the Cavalier parliament.

[1] J. R. Jones, *The first Whigs* (London, 1961), p. 62.

[2] All four were designated by Shaftesbury in a list he prepared just after the elections to the first Exclusion parliament as 'old worthy' members (J. R. Jones, 'Shaftesbury's "Worthy Men"': A whig view of the parliament of 1679', *BIHR*, xxx (1957), 232–41). Lee, Meres and Vaughan all voted for the first Exclusion bill, but in the third Exclusion parliament Meres supported 'limitations' instead. Capel sided with the Court on the first Exclusion bill, but in October 1680 it was he who moved its successor (Browning, 'An Exclusion Bill Division List', pp. 208, 213, 214, 224; Jones, *First Whigs*, pp. 65, 134, 178).

[3] For Winch (designated 'old vile' by Shaftesbury) and Hales (designated 'new Doubtful'), both of whom voted against the first Exclusion bill, see Browning, *Osborne*, iii, 55; Jones, 'Shaftesbury's "Worthy Men"', pp. 236, 238; Browning, 'An Exclusion bill division list', pp. 208, 214.

APPENDIX

Speeches (and their sources) of Daniel Finch as a member of the Commons of the Cavalier parliament

A. Session of 4 Feb.–28 March 1673

None.

B. Session of 27 Oct.–4 Nov. 1673

1. A defence of the conduct of Sir Edward Seymour as Speaker, probably delivered on 27 Oct. (see Grey, II, 186–8). Holograph draft in LRO, Finch MSS., Political papers 32.

C. Session of 7 Jan.–24 Feb. 1674

1. A defence of Secretary Arlington, 19 Jan. Briefly noted in Grey, II, 309–11; holograph version in LRO, Finch MSS., Political papers 34.

2. In favour of a modification of the Oath of Supremacy to satisfy those dissenters who 'scruple' it (see *CJ*, IX, 300). Holograph draft in LRO, Finch MSS., Political papers 28.

D. Session of 13 April–9 June 1675

1. A defence of Danby on 26 April. See Grey, III, 40–9; holograph version in LRO, Finch MSS., Political papers 37.

2. Against Sir William Coventry's Place bill, 29 April. Summary in Grey, III, 57–8; holograph version in LRO, Finch MSS., Political papers 37.

3. Against including the word 'all' in an address for the recall of British troops in French service, 11 May. Grey, III, 135–6.

4. Against a proposed resolution to accept no new bills during the remainder of the session and urging upon the House the wisdom of considering a relaxation of the penal laws against dissenters, 17 May. Summary in Grey, III, 163; holograph version in LRO, Finch MSS., Political papers 37.

E. Session of 13 Oct.–22 Nov. 1675

1. Against making high treason the penalty for contravention of the bill against illegal exactions, 21 Oct. Grey, III, 321–2.

2. Urging the increasing of the sum recommended by the committee on a bill of supply for the Navy, 6 Nov. Grey, III, 415.

F. Session of 15 Feb.–6 April, and 21–8 May 1677

1. In favour of supply, 21 Feb. Summary in Grey, IV, 124–5; holograph version in LRO, Finch MSS., Political papers 150.

2. In defence of his father against criticism of the Court of Chancery, 23 Feb. Summary in Grey, IV, 146; holograph summary in LRO, Finch MSS., Political papers 42.

3. In favour of raising supply by a land tax, 2 March. Holograph notes in LRO, Finch MSS., Political papers 43.

4. Against a bill to indemnify constituencies for non-payment of wages to their members of parliament, 3 March. Grey, IV, 179.

5. In favour of a generous supply, 5 March. Holograph notes in LRO, Finch MSS., Political papers 43.

6. In favour of a generally-worded address to the king on foreign affairs, 6 March. Summary in Grey, IV, 197; holograph notes in LRO, Finch MSS., Political papers 43.

7. In favour of the extension of the additional excises for another three years, 12 March. Holograph notes in LRO, Finch MSS., Political papers 43.

8. Against an address to the king about the Duke of Norfolk, 15 March. Grey, IV, 254.

9. In favour of the bill to secure the Protestant religion, 20 March. Summary in Grey, IV, 292; holograph notes in LRO, Finch MSS., Political papers 43.

G. Session of 28 Jan.–13 May, 23 May–15 July 1678

1. Against a proposal to manage the war by parliamentary commissioners, [31 Jan.?]. Holograph draft in LRO, Finch MSS., Political papers 150.

2. Concerning an abuse of privilege, 1 Feb. Grey, V, 53.

3. In favour of an immediate grant of supply, 4 Feb. Summary in Grey, V, 72–3; holograph version in LRO, Finch MSS., Political papers 48.

4. In defence of the Speaker's procedure at the last adjournment, 9 Feb. Summary in Grey, V, 137–8; holograph version in LRO, Finch MSS., Political papers 150.

5. Against a bill for the resumption of crown lands, 20 Feb. Grey, V, 191–2.

6. Against an address condemning the royal ministers, 10 May. Summary in Grey, V, 379; holograph notes in LRO, Finch MSS., Political papers 51.

7. In defence of his father, 1 June. Holograph notes in LRO, Finch MSS., Political papers 51.

8. On the expulsion of Sir Solomon Swale from the House, 19 June. Grey, VI, 107.

H. Session of 21 Oct.–30 Dec. 1678

1. Against the motion that the Duke of York remove himself from Court, 4 Nov. Summary in Grey, VI, 139–40; holograph version in LRO, Finch MSS., Political papers 57.

2. In defence of his father against charges of misconduct, 9 Nov. Grey, VI, 181.

3. Urging consideration of measures to hinder Catholics from holding military posts, 19 Nov. Holograph version in LRO, Finch MSS., Political papers 57.

4. In favour of the bill disabling all Catholics save the Duke of York from sitting in either House, 21 Nov. Grey, VI, 254.

5. In favour of calling Bedlow before the House immediately instead of adjourning, 26 Nov. Grey, VI, 276–7.

6. Lamenting the king's rejection of the Militia bill, 30 Nov. Grey, VI, 302.

7. Urging consideration of measures to secure the kingdom against the Catholic threat rather than attacks upon the royal ministers, 2 Dec. Grey, VI, 312.

8. Two speeches against making the articles of impeachment against Danby charges of treason, 21 Dec. Summaries in Grey, VI, 374–5 and 383–4; holograph version of the second in LRO, Finch MSS., Political papers 57.

CHAPTER 3

AT THE ADMIRALTY BOARD

1679–84

'No king ever did so unaccountable a thing to oblige his people by', lamented Samuel Pepys, 'as to dissolve a Commission of the Admiralty then in his own hand, who best understands the business of the sea of any prince the world ever had, and things never better done, and put it into hands which he knew were wholly ignorant thereof.'[1] If the Admiralty Commission of 1679 is to be judged solely on the criterion of administrative effectiveness, Pepys—though hardly a disinterested critic—was surely right. Handicapped by inexperience (none of the seven Commissioners appointed in April 1679 had ever previously served either at sea or in naval administration), hampered by lack of funds for much of its life, and distracted by factionalism among both its own members and the naval personnel, the Admiralty Commission had a woeful record.[2] When it was instituted in 1679, the navy had seventy-six ships in sea pay and a reserve of stores worth £60,000. At its supersession five years later, there were only twenty-four ships at sea, the value of the reserves had fallen to a scant £5,000 and the debt of the navy had risen by over one-quarter.[3] Even worse was the state of the thirty new men-of-

---

[1] *Samuel Pepys's naval minutes*, ed. J. R. Tanner (Navy Record Society, London, 1926), p. 71.

[2] A more detailed treatment of the Admiralty between 1679 and 1684 is provided by W. A. Aiken, 'The Admiralty in conflict and commission', in *Conflict in Stuart England*, ed. W. A. Aiken and B. D. Henning (London, 1960), pp. 205–25. My assessment of the Commission's record and Finch's part in its administrative work draws heavily on this study and also on J. Ehrman, *The navy in the war of William III 1689–1697* (Cambridge, 1953), ch. VIII. I have also had recourse to the principal manuscript sources for the Board's history, particularly BM Add. MSS. 36783; PRO, Adm. 13/550-3, 2/1749-52, 3/277-9; Bodl. Rawlinson MSS. A228.

[3] *Pepys' memoirs of the royal navy, 1679–1688*, ed. J. R. Tanner (Oxford, 1906), pp. 6–8.

war authorized by parliament in 1677 and completed under the Board's aegis which were rotting away in harbour without ever having put to sea.[1]

To try to apportion the blame for this administrative debacle would be a futile task; all who had a share in the management of naval affairs, from the king downward, were at fault. What is evident, however, is that Daniel Finch—as a member of the Board from its inception and as First Commissioner from February 1680—cannot be exempted from responsibility for its mismanagement. Although genuinely concerned to root out corruption in the sea service, to strengthen discipline and to encourage the promotion of capable seamen, all too often Finch was betrayed by his own inexperience.[2] At the same time, far too much of his energy was expended in pursuing quarrels with his colleagues, with the Board's Secretary and with Admiral Arthur Herbert. While Finch in later years was to regard his appointment to the Admiralty Commission of 1679 as 'an act of God's good providence' since it prepared him for the naval responsibilities he would have to shoulder under William III, at the time his service on the Board neither enhanced his stature nor advanced his political career.[3] Suffice it to conclude with John Ehrman that 'ignorance and faction in the Admiralty Commission...allowed the administrative and material obstacles to take charge, which always arose so easily in the conditions of the time, and the work of the previous six years [was] largely undone'.[4]

But to assess the significance of Finch's service at the Board solely on the basis of his and his colleagues' showing as naval administrators would be to ignore the broader implications of the Commission's history. Born, as Pepys himself acknowledged, as

[1] Ibid. pp. 9–12. Pepys's account is largely substantiated by Deane's report of 4 Nov. 1685, summarized by A. Bryant, Samuel Pepys, saviour of the navy (London, 1957), pp. 139–40; and by Bonrepaux's account of 8/18 Feb. 1686, cited by T. B. Macaulay, The history of England from the accession of James the Second (London, 1896), i, 300 and note.
[2] Aiken, 'The Admiralty', pp. 205–13.
[3] LRO, Finch MSS., Political papers 148, p. 7.
[4] Ehrman, The navy, p. 202.

an expedient to blunt political discontent, the Board's changing composition and internal differences during its life, as well as the time and manner of its death, were closely linked to the course of the Exclusion crisis and to the shifting political balance at Court during Charles's last years on the throne.[1] A word or two about Finch's own political position during the Exclusion controversy might, then, be in order before plunging into an account of his tenure at the Admiralty.

Identified with the Court by reason both of his father's post as Lord Chancellor and of his own stance in the Commons of the Cavalier parliament, Finch was to be a determined foe of Exclusion. But as his father and other Tory courtiers such as Sir Edward Seymour, as well as the Earl of Halifax and those Country moderates who followed his lead, Finch was to advocate proposals to limit the power of a Catholic successor.[2] As he later recalled,

I oppos'd the Bill of Exclusion...not that I thought...that the right of Succession was an indelible character, that even the legislative power could not abrogate, or that the oath to the King his heirs and Successors precluded a Parliament from doing it, (as Secretary Jenkins vehemently, but without any Colour of Law, argued) Nay I was as apprehensive as any the most zealous for the bill, of the dangers to which our religion would be expos'd under a Popish King...yet there might have been such restrictions of his power (and such were offerd from the throne) as would have rendred a King a very harmlesse Creature.[3]

Thus, among the initial opponents of Exclusion, Finch ranged himself with the Court Tories and those Country moderates headed by Halifax who favoured 'expedients'.

Nor was the question of the succession the only issue on which Finch and Halifax took a similar line during these years. Just as the elder man took the lead in the Lords in the first and second Exclusion parliaments in advocating legislative relief for the dis-

---

[1] LRO, Finch MSS., Political papers 148, p. 2.
[2] For his support in the Cavalier parliament of earlier proposals along these lines, see above p. 12.   [3] LRO, Finch MSS., Political papers 148, p. 2.

senters, so Daniel was to play a prominent part in the Commons' proceedings on this question during the 1680 parliament.[1] Indeed, it may well be that Halifax was as great an influence on Daniel during the Exclusion controversy as his father had been earlier. Certainly, the two were acquaintances of some years' standing by 1679. Not only did they have mutual cousins, the Thynnes of Longleat, but also Halifax had helped to negotiate Daniel's marriage to Lady Essex.[2] Even more suggestive is the fact that it was their mutual cousin Sir Thomas Thynne who secured Finch a seat at Lichfield, Staffordshire, for the second Exclusion parliament 'knowing', as Thynne explained to Halifax, 'how entirely he is devoted to your Lordship'.[3] Thus Daniel's spirited defence of Halifax, when the Earl came under fire in the Commons in November 1680, was a testimony to his friendship with and admiration for the 'Great Trimmer', though Finch did not stint himself during that turbulent session in rebutting attacks on other ministers, such as Seymour, who also were exposed to the House's wrath.[4]

If Finch's support of Limitations aligned him with the Court Tories and at least temporarily with Halifax as well, it separated him from the Duke of York and his personal following headed by Lord Hyde (since James and his adherents regarded Limitations as even more dangerous than Exclusion), while it also distinguished him from the Courtiers pure and simple of the stripe of the Earl of Sunderland.[5] Nor was the readiness of both Daniel and his father to back restrictions on the power of a Catholic successor the only source of difference between them and the duke. The moderate, even timorous counsels of the Lord Chancellor were anathema

[1] HMC House of Lords, 1678–88, pp. 105–8, 130–1, 159; Discourses concerning government by Algernon Sydney, ed. T. Hollis (London, 1763), section I, pp. 67, 69, 78, 101.
[2] HMC Finch, II, 16–17.
[3] Althorp Spencer MSS. 31/51 (26 July 1679), quoted by H. C. Foxcroft, The life and letters of George Savile, Bart., first Marquess of Halifax (London, 1898), I, 179.
[4] Finch's speech in defence of Halifax is summarized in Grey, VIII, 28–9; that in defence of Seymour in Grey, VIII, 91–4. A holograph version of the latter is in LRO, Finch MSS., Political papers 62. [5] See, for example, HMC Dartmouth, I, 34, 36.

to James, and he also appears to have disapproved on administrative grounds of Daniel's conduct at the Admiralty.[1] Indeed, the Commission itself was a symbol of James's seclusion from Court and Council during the years of the Exclusion crisis, for until its creation he had continued to act as *de facto* head of the Admiralty despite his formal disqualification under the first Test Act.[2] As for Sunderland, he was a man whom neither the Lord Chancellor nor Daniel seems ever to have been able to bring himself to respect or to trust.[3] Then, too, Sunderland was one of the principal supporters at Court of Daniel's chief foes at the Admiralty, Secretary John Brisbane and Vice-Admiral Arthur Herbert.[4]

During the first two years of the Admiralty Commission's life, then, the overriding political question that impinged upon its affairs was that of Exclusion—not least because the massive ministerial reshuffle of April 1679 that had brought the Board into being had a very limited effect on the parliamentary opposition to the Court and to James. To be sure, Charles was able in the spring of 1679 to detach Halifax and some lesser men from the opposition, but the Commons—'enraged to see all fresh-water men in the Admiralty'—flatly refused on 14 May 1679 to grant the supply requested for the navy.[5] Moreover, not even the bait of Limitations offered in the speeches of the king and the Lord Chancellor on 30 April deflected a considerable majority of the lower House from pressing forward with James's disablement from the succession. On 21 May the first Exclusion bill was committed by a vote of 207 to 128. Six days later, the king prorogued the parliament, and on 10 July he dissolved it and summoned another to meet in October.[6]

[1] *HMC Dartmouth*, I, 53. See also *The letters and the second diary of Samuel Pepys*, ed. R. G. Howarth (London, 1932), p. 140.   [2] Burnet, II, 204.
[3] *HMC Finch*, II, 78. See also the derogatory remarks made by Finch about Sunderland in his fragmentary memoirs, LRO, Finch MSS., Political papers 148, p. 9.
[4] Below, p. 35 and n. 1.
[5] *HMC Ormonde*, n.s. IV, 505. See also *ibid.* p. 509; All Souls College MSS. 242, newsletter of 25 April; Grey, VII, 265–78.
[6] J. P. Kenyon, *Robert Spencer Earl of Sunderland 1641–1702* (London, 1958), pp. 26–9.

However, the results of the ensuing general election held out little hope to the Court of a more compliant Commons. Though Finch managed to gain election at Lichfield on Thynne's interest and successfully reasserted his own interest at Great Bedwyn in favour of his brother William (recently made Solicitor to the Queen), the tide ran strongly against the Court in most constituencies.[1] Even at Lichfield victory was gained only after Finch's own hasty trip to Staffordshire to bring down the election writ which he had especially procured from his father and after Thynne had promised the electors that 'Mr Finch should not be a Courtier'.[2] The generally inauspicious election results prompted Charles to prorogue the Houses to 26 January 1680. Then in December, as a sharp riposte to the circulation of petitions for the speedy assembly of parliament by Shaftesbury and his followers, the king (despite objections from Essex, Halifax, Temple and the Lord Chancellor) publicly declared that he would not summon the Houses until the following December.[3]

The effects of the dissolution of the first Exclusion parliament and of the postponement of the meeting of the second were soon felt at the Admiralty. Not only did these developments leave the Board straitened for funds (the £300,000 promised for 1680 was now cut by one-third); they also greatly increased the uneasiness of those Commissioners who favoured Exclusion.[4] By January 1680 Vaughan 'upon pretence of his sicknesse' was refusing to attend the Board any longer, Lee was reported to be 'next Door' to relinquishing his post, while Capel's resignation had been rumoured ever since his brother Essex had retired from

---

[1] HMC Finch, II, 54–6; Jones, First Whigs, pp. 92–106.

[2] Bodl. Carte MSS. 243, fo. 383, unsigned account of the Lichfield election, 16 Aug. 1679. I am indebted for this reference to Dr J. R. Jones of the University of East Anglia. See also HMC Finch, III, 419–20.

[3] BM Add. MSS. 29572, fo. 175, Charles Hatton to Viscount Hatton, 18 Dec.; Kenyon, Sunderland, p. 34.

[4] BM Add. MSS. 36783, fo. 139, project for ships to be kept at sea when the charge of the navy is reduced to £300,000; Bodl. Carte MSS. 39, fo. 107 [Sir R. Reading to the Duke of Ormonde, 2 Feb. 1680]. But cf. W. A. Shaw's calculation at CTB, VII, pt. I, xxviii.

the Treasury the previous autumn.[1] The king's formal prorogation of parliament on 26 January 1680, this time to April, coupled
with the announcement that he had recalled James from his exile
in Brussels, was for them the final blow. The remaining Exclusionists on the Privy Council made a concerted withdrawal on 31
January, while Capel and Vaughan resigned from the Admiralty
Board at the same time, to be followed some weeks later by Lee.[2]

The new appointments to the Admiralty Commission that
followed reflected Charles's continuing determination to withstand demands for James's disablement. On the one hand, Finch
was gratified both by being designated as First Commissioner and
by being admitted on 4 February to the Privy Council in Capel's
stead, reportedly 'to make amends for the disgust' taken earlier
by the Finches 'that he being the eldest son of a Baron was not
before sworne before Sir Henry Capell'.[3] On the other hand, to
strengthen the Commission two former naval administrators,
Viscount Brouncker and Sir Thomas Littleton, were named to fill
the vacancies left by the departure of Vaughan and Capel, and
they took their places at the Board on 21 February.[4] These
appointments—coupled with the promotion of the Board's
Secretary, Thomas Hayter, to the Comptrollership of the navy
and his replacement by John Brisbane—seem to have been little to
Finch's liking.[5] Not merely had Hayter (who apparently owed his
post to Finch) been 'kicked upstairs' to make room for the inexperienced Brisbane, but also Finch's two new colleagues were
in his eyes 'creatures of the Duke [of York]' and their appoint-

---

[1] HMC Ormonde, n.s. IV, 578; BM Add. MSS. 29577, fo. 231, C. Lyttleton to Lord
Hatton, 31 Jan.; CSPD, 1679–80, p. 283.
[2] Sir Thomas Lee attended the Board for the last time on 7 Feb. (PRO, Adm. 3/277,
passim).
[3] Bodl. Carte MSS. 39, fo. 113, [Sir R. Reading to the Duke of Ormonde], 14 Feb.;
PRO, PC 2/68, fo. 3.
[4] PRO, Adm. 3/277, p. 17. Once appointed, Brouncker seems to have successfully asserted
precedence until Daniel succeeded his father as Earl of Nottingham (O. A. R. Murray,
'The Admiralty, part III', Mariner's Mirror, XXIII (1937), 329).
[5] Brisbane was appointed in mid-January much to the discontent of several other Board
members besides Finch (BM Add. MSS. 29577, fo. 223, C. Lyttleton to Lord Hatton,
10 Jan.; HMC Ormonde, n.s. IV, 578).

ments the first steps in the revival of James's influence at the Admiralty.[1] To compound matters, Brisbane was soon to show himself a firm friend to Vice-Admiral Herbert, who by this time had established himself as the Board's chief disciplinary problem within the navy.[2]

Even before Finch's promotion, Herbert had been embroiled with the Commissioners over a complaint from Lord Inchiquin (the Governor of Tangier), and by February 1680 they were pressing Charles for his recall.[3] The most serious of the charges now levelled against him was that of dispatching two ships under his command to Livorno with private shipments of bullion despite the Board's strict injunctions against the practice of the 'Good Voyage'.[4] But Herbert escaped with only a reprimand, for Charles had a high regard for him and he also had influential friends at Court, among them Sunderland and the Duke of York.[5] Indeed, the Commission was obliged to remind Sunderland before even so much as a letter was sent to Herbert to express royal displeasure at his flagrant breach of instructions.[6] Further, in recognition of his timely assistance during the siege of Tangier in the spring of 1680, Herbert was raised to the rank of Admiral the following July.[7] It was at this time that Finch, perhaps realizing the obstacles to dislodging Herbert, attempted a reconciliation with him, employing Henry Sheres (the new Surveyor-General of Tangier) as his go-between. But though relations between the Admiral and the First Commissioner were temporarily patched up in the summer of 1680, it was not long before the two were at odds again as further reports of Herbert's misdeeds were made to

---

[1] LRO, Finch MSS., Political papers 148, pp. 4, 6; HMC Ormonde, n.s. IV, 578; PRO, PRO 31/3/144, Barillon au Roi, 12/22 Feb. 1680.
[2] Their correspondence survives in Bodl. Rawlinson MSS. A 228.
[3] PRO, Adm. 2/1749, p. 105; PRO, Adm. 3/277, pt. I, pp. 170, 175, 179.
[4] PRO, Adm. 3/277, pt. II, p. 17.
[5] For Herbert's relations with the duke, see, for example, his reference to him as 'my Master' at BM Add. MSS. 41803, fos. 11–12, Herbert to Sir Thomas Lynch, 24 May 1680. [6] PRO, Adm. 3/277, pt. II, p. 31.
[7] Bodl. Rawlinson MSS. A 228, p. 140, Sir Leoline Jenkins to Herbert, 13 June; PRO, Adm. 2/1749, p. 337.

Finch during the following autumn and winter by Inchiquin's successor, Colonel Sackville, as well as by Sheres.[1]

By the spring of 1681, however, Daniel was better placed to deal with Herbert since the Finches were then at the height of their influence at Court, thanks to their showing—particularly Daniel's own—in the second and third Exclusion parliaments. In August 1680 the king had announced that the parliament elected the previous summer would at last be convened for business on 21 October. But despite Charles's propitiatory gesture of sending James to Scotland (a move, backed after no little wavering, by a majority of the Privy Council including the Lord Chancellor and Finch) and despite the willingness the king expressed in his opening speech to concur in any 'new Remedies' which did not alter the succession, the Commons were to show themselves adamant in their insistence upon Exclusion.[2] Indeed, as Sunderland discovered to his own dismay, the Exclusionist majority in the lower House was not even prepared to initiate measures for supply until the king had agreed to James's removal from the line of succession.[3] None the less, the opponents of Exclusion in the Commons made a stronger stand than expected when the disabling bill was proposed to the House on 2 November.[4] Among the leading spokesmen for the Court on this occasion was Daniel Finch, who dilated on the measure's injustice to James and the possibility that a civil war might ensue if it were passed. 'Consider,' he urged, 'what a miserable prospect of affairs we shall have before us, what unextinguishable flames we are kindling in this nation, what wretched confusion we are raising to ourselves and entailing upon our posterity.'[5] Instead of pressing on with so unprecedented and dangerous a proposal, the House—he argued—

[1] BM Lansdowne MSS. 193, fos. 30–1, 67–9, Henry Sheres to Finch, 30 July 1680, 31 Dec. 1680, 30 Jan. 1681; Bodl. Rawlinson MSS. A228, pp. 179–80, Brisbane to Herbert, 7 March 1681; HMC Finch, II, 103–4, 107, 110.
[2] Kenyon, Sunderland, pp. 49–61; Bodl. Carte MSS. 233, fo. 295, newsletter, 19 Oct. [1680]; FSL, Newdigate newsletters, no. 996, 19 Oct.; Grey, VIII, 94.
[3] Kenyon, Sunderland, pp. 60–1.   [4] HMC Ormonde, n.s. v, 475.
[5] LRO, Finch MSS., Political papers 63. See also Grey, VII, 410–11.

ought to explore more fully the alternatives to Exclusion and so should resolve itself into a Committee of the Whole to consider those expedients that the king had offered on several occasions.[1]

One of the expedients which Finch himself strongly favoured was the passage of measures to ease the dissenters of persecution under the Clarendon Code in order to unify the 'Protestant interest' of the kingdom. Though Finch preferred the way of comprehension, as did most conciliatory Anglicans since that held out the possibility of the re-creation of an all-inclusive national church, to toleration, which would make permanent the existing divisions among English Protestants, he was willing to allow 'a limited exercise of their Religion' to those dissenters who would accept no compromise with Anglicanism in the hope 'that we might be united, at least in interest and affection'.[2] And serving as the chairman of a committee appointed on 3 November to bring in a bill 'for Uniting his Majesty's Protestant Subjects', Finch was responsible for the drafting of bills both for comprehension and toleration as part of what was the most far-reaching parliamentary effort before 1689 to revise the Restoration religious settlement.[3]

But neither comprehension nor toleration was to be enacted in 1680 for the opposition majority in the Commons, balked of Exclusion by the Lords, would settle for nothing less.[4] Even the specific limitations on the power of a Catholic successor suggested by Finch and other speakers in the debate of 7 January 1681—the appointment of Privy Councillors by the Houses, the requirement

[1] Finch's suggestion that the House transform itself into a Committee of the Whole to consider limitations seems to have been part of a concerted Court strategy (BM Add. MSS. 32681, fo. 67, Sir Leoline Jenkins to Henry Sidney, 2 Nov.).
[2] LRO, Political papers 148, p. 3. Finch's account of his attitudes is confirmed by G. Whitehead, *The christian progress of George Whitehead* (London, 1725), p. 395; *A supplement to Burnet's history of my own time*, ed. H. C. Foxcroft (Oxford, 1902), p. 317.
[3] For a detailed account of these proposals, Finch's part in shaping them, and their fate, see H. Horwitz, 'Protestant reconciliation in the Exclusion crisis', *Journal of Ecclesiastical History*, xv (1964), 201–17.
[4] Although the Lord Chancellor was absent when the Exclusion bill was considered by the Lords on 15 Nov., it was not a politic illness but rather 'a very great fitt' of his old nemesis, the gout, that kept him home (*HMC Finch*, ii, 96; cf. Feiling, *Tory party*, p. 196 and n. 2).

that such Councillors should approve all acts of a Catholic king, and the banishment from England of 'the most considerable Papists'—were not sufficient to turn the tide.[1] Convinced, then, of the futility, perhaps even the danger, of keeping this parliament on foot any longer, Charles prorogued it on 10 January and dissolved it eight days later, summoning in its stead a new parliament to meet at Oxford late in March.

Though Finch was once more returned for Lichfield on Thynne's interest (as well for Newton, Isle of Wight, on the Court's interest), he was unable to attend when the Houses assembled at Oxford on 21 March.[2] Detained in London by the imminent birth of his sixth child, he was absent when the Commons again rejected Limitation proposals, this time couched in the form of a regency scheme supported by the Lord Chancellor by which the Prince and Princess of Orange would be empowered to rule in James's name.[3] When it became clear that nothing would satisfy the lower House but Exclusion, Charles—convinced that the intransigence of the opposition had swung political sentiment outside the Houses in his favour and bolstered by the renewal of cordial ties with France—promptly dissolved the parliament.

Despite Finch's absence from the Oxford parliament, the services of the Finches did not pass unrecognized by the royal brothers. Daniel, who had been one of the most frequent speakers for the Court in the 1680 parliament, received James's personal thanks for his resistance to Exclusion, conveyed to him in late November by the duke's follower and Finch's old friend, Colonel George Legge.[4] Moreover, the duke, anxious perhaps to have Finch removed from the Admiralty, suggested to Lord Hyde the following month that Daniel might be promoted to the Treasury

[1] Grey, VIII, 273–5.
[2] His election at Lichfield was petitioned against by George Bridges, but the session ended before the disputed election was settled (Longleat Thynne MSS., vol. XVII, fo. 111, Finch to Thynne, 26 March 1681; HMC Finch, II, 106; CJ, IX, 707).
[3] Burnet, II, 276–7; Diary of the times of Charles the second by the Honourable Henry Sidney, ed. R. W. Blencowe (London, 1843), II, 177.
[4] HMC Dartmouth, I, 53.

Board to fill the place vacated by the ouster of Godolphin after he had joined with Sunderland in supporting Exclusion.[1] But the king and his chief advisers had other plans for Finch, plans broached to the Lord Chancellor by Charles himself even before the prorogation of the 1680 parliament. The post the king was prepared to offer to Daniel was none other than Sunderland's Secretaryship.[2] This, indeed, would have been a great advancement; none the less, Finch eventually decided to decline it.

Finch's rejection of so flattering an offer was, in part, prompted by his assessment of the immediate political situation. As he later related,

I was very apprehensive of the Inclinations of the King and Duke to France and popery to which I could never be subservient, and. . . I also knew the tempers of the 3 ministers [Halifax, Hyde, and Seymour] and that it was impossible for them long to agree, or for me so to behave myselfe towards them but that they would suspect my partiality and consequently be my Enemies.[3]

But the decisive consideration was the Lord Chancellor's declining health and Finch's fear that the severe demands on his time which would be made by the Secretaryship would prevent him from assisting his father with both official and family affairs.[4] Thus in an interview with the king in mid-January, he refused the royal offer, excusing himself on the grounds that his acceptance might lead to criticism that Charles was unduly favouring his family since already his father was Lord Chancellor, he was head of the Admiralty Board, and his younger brother was Solicitor-General.[5] Even so, the Finches did not go altogether unrewarded. On the advice of Seymour and the Lord Chancellor, Sunderland was replaced with their mutual kinsman, Viscount Conway, while in May 1681 the elder Finch was created Earl of Nottingham.[6]

[1] Clarendon correspondence, I, 49.
[2] LRO, Finch MSS., Political papers 148, p. 8. See also FSL, Newdigate newsletters, no. 1031, 18 Jan. 1681; PRO, PRO 31/3/148, Barillon au Roi, 24 Jan./3 Feb.; HMC Ormonde, n.s. V, 559.
[3] LRO, Finch MSS., Political papers 148, p. 8.   [4] Ibid.
[5] Ibid. See also HMC Dartmouth, I, 56.
[6] BM Add. MSS. 28053, fo. 234, Conway to Lord Danby, 30 Jan. 1681.

For the moment, then, the Finches were high in the king's favour and this was reflected in Daniel's temporary ascendency at the Admiralty. His greatest success in the renewed conflict with Herbert came in the summer of 1681 when he managed to secure rejection of the Admiral's scheme for carrying on the war against the Algerine corsairs by putting all convoys of merchantmen to Spain and the Mediterranean under his command. Although this proposal was initially supported by the rest of the Admiralty Commissioners, Finch maintained that not only was this project unnecessary since Herbert's own force was perfectly adequate to extract a reasonable peace from Algiers, but also it was unwise since to put the convoys under the Admiral's command was merely to place him in a position to extort money from the merchants to ensure the protection of their cargoes. And his arguments, backed by those of the Lord Chancellor, finally carried the day in the Privy Council.[1] Disheartened by Finch's victory on this issue as well as by other rebuffs suffered at the First Commissioner's hands at this time, Herbert seems to have decided that it would be wise to trim his sails at least temporarily.[2] Late in 1681, then, he dispatched a letter of submission to Brisbane which appears to have been intended for Finch.[3]

By the time Brisbane received this letter, however, the balance was already beginning to shift at Court once more. The immediate issue was whether Charles, as Halifax and Tory courtiers such as Seymour urged, should summon a new parliament now that it was evident that sentiment had swung sharply to the king's side and that a number of leading Exclusionists were only too willing to come to terms with the Court.[4] Though neither the

[1] Aiken, 'The Admiralty', pp. 218–19.
[2] E.g. the dispute between Captains Booth and Wheler, the latter a favourite of Herbert, over the capture and disposition of an Algerine ship was, on the intercession of Sheres, Sackville and Finch, eventually decided in Booth's favour by the king (Bodl. Rawlinson MSS. A228, pp. 196–7, Admiralty Board to Herbert, 6 May 1681).
[3] Ibid. p. 268, Brisbane to Herbert, 30 Jan. 1682.
[4] Kenyon, Sunderland, pp. 78–9; Foxcroft, Halifax, I, 324–5, 351; Feiling, Tory party, p. 190; Jones, First Whigs, p. 196.

Lord Chancellor nor his sons seem to have taken an active part in the manoeuvring for position that was going on within the Court and appear to have acquiesced in the proscriptive measures now under way against the Exclusionists, there are grounds to believe that they were inclined to the course of conciliation unsuccessfully advocated by Halifax and Seymour.[1] Nor is it likely that they were pleased with the revival of French influence at Whitehall that the last year had brought.

As moderate counsels became increasingly unfashionable at Court, Finch's position at the Admiralty suffered. On 2 January 1682 Charles finally announced his choices to fill the vacancies left by Lee's resignation in 1680 and Littleton's death in 1681. The new Commissioners were Rear-Admiral Sir John Chicheley and Henry Savile, both cousins of Sir Thomas Thynne.[2] None the less, the First Commissioner was afraid that he could count upon the support of neither. Savile (though appointed on the instance of his brother Halifax) was a close friend of Brisbane, while Chicheley (another client of the Duke of York) was at odds with Finch's friend Legge, Herbert's rival for James's favour.[3] Indeed, Finch seems to have feared he would now meet with consistent

[1] In April 1681 Barillon reported that the Lord Chancellor was busy preparing with the Secretaries of State a manifesto justifying the dissolution of the Oxford parliament, in July the Lord Chancellor and Finch were among those who signed the Council's order for the arrest of Shaftesbury on a charge of high treason, in November Heneage Finch was among the counsel for the Crown in the *Quo Warranto* action against London (PRO, PRO 31/3/148, 4/14 April; PRO, PRO 30/24/6a, Privy Council order of 2 July; *The diary of John Evelyn*, ed. E. S. de Beer (Oxford, 1955), IV, 320, n. 1). None the less, the Chancellor at this stage still seems to have been opposed to James's return to England (*The life of James the second, king of England*, ed. J. S. Clarke (London, 1816), pp. 677–8). See also Sir John Lauder's suggestive eulogy of Lord Chancellor Nottingham in his *Historical observes of memorable occurents in church and state, from October 1680 to April 1686* (Bannatyne Club, Edinburgh, 1840), p. 85.

[2] Foxcroft, *Halifax*, I, 335. The new Commissioners did not take their place at the Board until 26 Jan. (PRO, Adm. 3/278, pt. II, p. 13).

[3] Longleat Thynne MSS., vol. XVII, fo. 117, Finch to Thynne, 19 Jan. 1682. Chicheley, who had been suggested as a possible member of the Board by James as early as December 1680, was reported later in 1682 to be very favourable to Herbert, while Savile was said in 1683 to have 'a very mean opinion' of Finch (*Clarendon correspondence*, I, 49; BM Add. MSS. 28053, fos. 291–2, Wheler to [Herbert], 13 Nov. 1682; *HMC Dartmouth*, I, 93).

opposition from a majority of the Board, since Brouncker and Hales had already shown themselves hostile to his efforts to leash Herbert. Nor was Finch alone in reading the new appointments in this light. Brisbane seems to have shared his view and he now decided, with Hales's concurrence, not to deliver the Admiral's conciliatory letter to the First Commissioner.[1] At the same time, Hayter was removed from the post of Comptroller and only Finch's intercession secured his retention as assistant to his successor, Sir Richard Haddock.[2] To these changes, Finch's reaction was despairing. 'Lett things be as they will', he wrote to Thynne, 'I shall have every day more and more satisfaction or rather quiet in this office than I have had heretofore, because I am resolv'd every day lesse and lesse to concerne myselfe in the management of it.'[3]

Despite this resolution, Finch could not refrain from speaking his mind at the Board. By May 1682 tempers among the Commissioners were so high that when he objected to the substance of the new orders to be sent to Herbert upon conclusion of a peace with Algiers on the grounds that they allowed the Admiral too great a latitude, he was warned by Meres that others of his colleagues 'were consulting to represent this to the king by way of complaint' against him.[4] Though this threat never materialized, further alterations at Court to his disadvantage were in train during the year following Savile's and Chicheley's appointments. In March 1682 James was at last allowed to return to England, and on the Duchess of Portsmouth's initiative Sunderland was readmitted to the royal brothers' favour in July. An even greater blow was the death on 18 December of his father, who was succeeded as Lord Keeper by Lord Chief Justice North—a Tory courtier, but no friend to the Finches.[5] A month later, Sunderland

---

[1] Bodl. Rawlinson MSS. A228, p. 268, Brisbane to [Herbert], 30 Jan. 1682.
[2] PRO, Adm. 3/278, pt.II, p. 5; LRO, Finch MSS., Political papers 148, p. 6; CSPD, 1682, p. 20.
[3] Longleat Thynne MSS., vol. XVII, fo. 117.   [4] HMC Finch, II, 175.
[5] Brisbane, on occasion, invoked North's assistance against Finch (Aiken, 'The Admiralty', pp. 221-2). See also Burnet, III, 89.

was restored to his secretaryship, and Sunderland, as Brisbane assured Herbert, 'was allwaies a fast friend to you and will be soe againe'.[1]

Even before Sunderland's return to office, Herbert had begun lobbying at Court to be made a member of the Admiralty Commission.[2] Not surprisingly, his pretensions seem to have been opposed by the new Earl of Nottingham and also by Legge (elevated to the peerage as Baron Dartmouth in December 1682) who was no longer on speaking terms with Brisbane.[3] The Duke of Grafton (now Vice-Admiral in the deceased Prince Rupert's place), whose hostility to Brisbane had been carefully cultivated by the First Commissioner, also appears to have raised his voice in protest.[4] But their opposition was of no avail. As early as January 1683, Charles's promise to appoint Herbert to the Board as soon as a vacancy occurred was already 'in many people's mouths'.[5] When plans began to be made in the spring of 1683 for England's withdrawal from Tangier, Herbert was recalled, and on 28 August he was seated as a supernumerary member of the Board until one of the seven established places should be vacated.[6]

While Herbert took his seat at the Board, Dartmouth set sail for the Mediterranean, saddled with the invidious task of supervising the demolition of the harbour works at Tangier and the evacuation of its inhabitants.[7] As the account of their voyage kept by Dartmouth's assistant, Samuel Pepys, reveals, the two were regaled during their stay in the Mediterranean with tales of Herbert's favouritism, indiscipline and corruption.[1] At the same

---

[1] Bodl. Rawlinson MSS. A228, p. 349, 9 April 1683.
[2] BM Add. MSS. 28053, fos. 291–2.
[3] BM Add. MSS. 28054, fo. 209, Brisbane to Herbert, 8 Jan. 1683.
[4] Bodl. Rawlinson MSS. A228, p. 356, Brisbane to Herbert, 1 May 1683.
[5] BM Add. MSS. 28054, fo. 209.   [6] PRO, Adm. 3/278, pt. III, p. 110.
[7] The decision to abandon Tangier seems to have been Charles's own, though Sunderland had long advocated just such a step, and it was only the determined opposition of Halifax, Dartmouth and Secretary Coventry that prevented the king from proceeding to sell the fortress to France (Kenyon, *Sunderland*, p. 53 n.; *The Tangier papers of Samuel Pepys*, ed. E. Chappell (Navy Record Society, London, 1935), pp. 34–5; All Souls College MSS. 317, autobiographical fragment of Sir William Trumbull, p. 8). Herbert and Brisbane also seem to have thought Tangier not worth the keeping (Bodl. Rawlinson MSS. A228, p. 268).

time, Dartmouth was having his own troubles with Brisbane and a majority of the Admiralty Commissioners who took umbrage at not being informed of the purpose of his mission and also at his private correspondence with Nottingham.[2] Thus by the time that Dartmouth and Pepys returned to England early in April 1684, both were thoroughly convinced of the necessity of a change in the management of the Admiralty.[3] Nor were Dartmouth's aims confined to the Admiralty. He had been party the previous spring to an abortive attempt to reunite the Court Tories and the Duke of York's following against Sunderland and Halifax, and he now seems to have thought of setting himself up (no doubt, with James's backing) at the head of a party 'in opposition to thos of Halifax on one side, Rochester, Sunderland and Portsmouth on the other'.[4]

Though Halifax was rightly sceptical of Dartmouth's grander pretensions, a reform of the Admiralty was by no means out of the question in the spring of 1684.[5] To begin with, Nottingham had at last gained the upper hand on Brisbane; both Charles and James had reluctantly consented earlier that year to the Secretary's displacement should he not behave himself with respect towards the First Commissioner.[6] Moreover, the death of Viscount Brouncker on 5 April, as Dartmouth remarked to Pepys three days later, gave the Duke of York the 'opportunety to bring you to the Admiralty, and if my Lord Nottinghame can help out Brisbane Mr Sheeres with your assistance, may againe put some life into the sea service'.[7]

But the duke, dependent as he was on the Duchess of Ports-

[1] *Tangier papers*, pp. 90, 101, 113, 117–18, 121–2, and *passim*.
[2] *HMC Finch*, II, 186–7; *HMC Dartmouth*, I, 20, and III, 121–3. There were also recriminations between the Board and Dartmouth once the expedition returned to England (PRO, Adm. 2/1751, p. 54; *HMC Dartmouth*, III, 48–9; *Letters and second diary of Pepys*, p. 169).
[3] *Tangier papers*, pp. 221–2, 244.
[4] Kenyon, *Sunderland*, p. 93; Foxcroft, *Halifax*, I, 415, n. 1, quoting Sir John Reresby's *Memoirs*.   [5] Foxcroft, *Halifax*, I, 415, n. 1.
[6] *HMC Finch*, II, 187.   [7] *Letters and second diary of Pepys*, p. 169.

mouth and Sunderland, was not prepared to take any action at this juncture, especially as the duchess and the Secretary had already begun to lay the groundwork for a much bolder stroke.[1] Their aim was nothing less than the dissolution of the Commission itself and the restoration of James to his place as Lord Admiral in all but name.[2] This scheme only ripened slowly, and on 17 April Herbert was allowed to take his seat as a full member of the Board in Brouncker's stead.[3] None the less, the Commission's days were numbered. On 11 May the king revoked its patent and declared that in future he would direct naval affairs himself with his brother's help.[4]

In five years, then, the wheel had come full circle. Born as an expedient to mute opposition, crippled by faction and inexperience during its life, the Board was dissolved now that Charles at last felt sufficiently secure to restore his brother to his former control of the Admiralty. As Barillon, anticipating the move by a fortnight, put it to Louis XIV,

C'est un coup decisif et qui achevera de confondre les esperances de ceux qu'se flattent toujours de l'opinion que le Roy d'Angleterre ne demeura pas ferme dans la conduit qu'il a tenue depuis quelques années.[5]

Nottingham, however, was not altogether dismayed by the king's decision. Indeed, he had not even bothered to attend the Board for most of its last weeks of life, bereaved as he was by the death of his wife Essex who had sickened after the birth of her eighth child on 19 March 1684 and succumbed eleven days later to 'a gangroen in her bowells, caused by the violent defluxion of some sharp humor not to be forseen...nor to be remedied'.[6] The

---

[1] Kenyon, *Sunderland*, pp. 96–7.
[2] Barillon was acquainted with the plan early in March 1684 (PRO, PRO 31/3/157, 9/19 March).
[3] *A Descriptive catalogue of the naval manuscripts in the Pepysian Library at Magdalene College, Cambridge*, ed. J. R. Tanner (Navy Record Society, London, 1903–23), I, 58.
[4] *The London Gazette*, no. 1929.   [5] PRO, PRO 31/3/158, 28 April/8 May.
[6] KAO, Dering MSS., U275, A4, diary of Sir Edward Dering; entry in Finch family prayer book in Nottingham's hand printed in Finch, *Burley*, I, 183.

loss of she whom Nottingham thought 'the best woman in the world' left him griefstricken,[1] but the Admiralty Commission's demise, as he later recalled, was

to my no little satisfaction, for I was very uneasy with such Company, and such a Secretary, and yet in decency and respect to the King could [not] quitt this station (as some had rudely and mutinously his Service) least I might have incurr'd the same Censure, especially in the King's opinion, who was very gracious to me.[2]

Thus, Nottingham's circumstances as Charles's reign drew to its sudden close were quite different than they had been when he took office in 1679. Though he had not excelled as a naval administrator, he had in the intervening years distinguished himself in parliament as an opponent of Exclusion and an advocate of Comprehension, and even after the dissolution of the Admiralty Board he continued to serve as a member of the Privy Council.[3] Even more important, Mr Finch was now the Earl of Nottingham —heir not only to his father's title and property, but also to his headship of the extensive Finch family and to his position as the patron of a distinguished group of younger Anglican clergy that included the Lord Chancellor's former chaplain John Sharp, and Sharp's friends, John Tillotson, Edward Stillingfleet and Thomas Tenison.[4] Firmly established in his own right by the time of Charles's death early in February 1685, Nottingham awaited— perhaps not without some uneasiness—what James's reign would bring.

[1] Nottingham to Reverend Thomas Woodroff, 30 April 1684, reprinted in C. F. Smith, *Mary Rich Countess of Warwick (1625–1678)* (London, 1901), pp. 302–3.
[2] LRO, Finch MSS., Political papers 148, p. 7.
[3] PRO, PC 2/70, *passim*.
[4] For a full discussion of the Finch family circle and the first and second Earls' relations with the clergy, see below, chapter 13.

CHAPTER 4

THE DEFENCE OF THE CHURCH

1685–8

Although James's reign opened auspiciously enough for even the staunchest adherent of the established order with the new monarch assuring his Privy Council that he would 'defend and support' the Church of England, the king's initial resolve to advance cautiously the cause of Catholicism in England was soon discarded.[1] Emboldened by the grant of a generous revenue by the parliament he summoned in the spring of 1685 and by the swift crushing of the Duke of Monmouth's uprising in succeeding months, James felt secure enough by autumn to contemplate asking the Houses when they reassembled in November both to repeal the Test and Habeas Corpus acts and to restore the Catholic peers to their seats in the Lords.[2]

Nottingham's reaction to this shift in royal policies was not long delayed. Though he was throughout James's reign to be reluctant to commit himself to all-out opposition to the king, he was to prove even more unwilling to countenance any move to upset the existing order for the benefit of the Catholic minority. Thus by the time that James dismissed Halifax from the Lord Presidency in late October 1685 after his refusal to pledge himself to support the new royal policies, Halifax and Nottingham were already concerting their moves together in conjunction with

---

[1] At Rochester's request, James agreed to make this promise public and the Solicitor, Heneage Finch, then drew up a copy of his statement which was issued as a proclamation. James later claimed that Finch's version was worded more strongly than his original statement (Barillon au Roi, 9/19 Feb. 1685, printed in C. J. Fox, *A history of the early part of the reign of James the second* (London, 1808), app. p. xvi; *Life of James the Second*, II, 4).

[2] Barillon au Roi, 19/29 Oct. and 26 Oct./5 Nov., printed in Fox, *James the second*, app. pp. cxxii–cxxvi; Browning, *Osborne*, I, 373; Foxcroft, *Halifax*, I, 454.

others of 'those who are called Court Lords' such as the Earl of Danby and Bishop Compton of London, amid rumours that the upper House at least would not fall in tamely behind the king.[1] In particular, Nottingham busied himself, in anticipation of Court proposals in the coming session, with the drafting of speeches defending the Habeas Corpus act and the exclusion of the Catholic peers from the Lords.[2]

It was not from the upper House, however, that the king received his first check, for his opening speech—calling for supply to keep on foot his enlarged army and declaring his intent to retain the Catholic officers he had appointed the previous summer—did not sit too well with the Commons. Although a vote of supply was carried on 12 November, Sir Thomas Clarges (a close friend of Halifax) and Sir Edmund Jennings (a creature of Danby), followed by Sir William Twysden (a kinsman and adherent of Nottingham) and other members of parliament, vehemently denounced the existence of a standing army staffed by Catholics.[3] Nor did their speeches go unheeded. With Solicitor-General Finch dividing against the Court and serving as chairman in Committee of the Whole, the House on the following day prepared and approved an address asking that the Catholic officers be dismissed, while promising to indemnify them for having served without taking the oaths.[4]

As the Commons' hostility to James's measures became increasingly evident, the anticipated opposition in the Lords also raised its head. Discontent among the peers found its most notable expression on 19 November when a motion to appoint a

[1] Halifax to Chesterfield, Oct. 1685, reprinted in Foxcroft, *Halifax*, I, 455, from *Letters of Philip, second Earl of Chesterfield*; PRO, PRO 31/3/162, Barillon au Roi, 29 Oct./8 Nov.

[2] These drafts are to be found in LRO, Finch MSS., Political papers 60, 75, 121.

[3] Morrice, I, 496; Barillon au Roi, 16/26 Nov. printed in Fox, *James the second*, app. p. cxiii; BM Lansdowne MSS. 253, 'The several debates of the House of Commons Pro et Contra', fos. 25–51; *PH*, IV, 1371–5. For Twysden's attachment to Nottingham, see below p. 262.

[4] *The autobiography of Sir John Bramston of Skreens*, ed. Lord Braybrooke (Camden Society, London, 1845), p. 213; *PH*, IV, 1377–9.

day to consider the king's speech was made in the royal presence by the Earl of Devonshire. He was seconded not only by Lords Mordaunt, Anglesey, Halifax and Nottingham, but also by the Bishop of London. Speaking, he said, for the whole episcopal bench, Compton warned that the civil and religious constitution of the realm was in danger. Clarendon and Jeffreys, the new Lord Chancellor, argued that the House's earlier address of thanks precluded further discussion, but eventually Devonshire's motion was carried without a division.[1]

This taste of what was in store for him was enough for James. Fearful that the combined hostility of the Houses might be too great to overcome, especially if a proposal of the Lords to consult the judges on the legality of his actions produced an unfavourable verdict, he prorogued parliament on 20 November without even waiting for the passage of the Supply bill agreed to by the Commons.[2] The prorogation was followed, moreover, by the dismissal of a number of office-holders who had spoken against the Court in the Commons and by the displacement of Bishop Compton from the Privy Council and his post as Dean of the Chapel Royal.[3]

While whispers about other royal measures continued to fly about Westminster, Nottingham's attention was taken up by domestic cares. Since Essex's death in March 1684, the problem of raising the 'little reliques' of their mother—a daughter Mary born in 1677 and a son John born in 1682—had been no little concern to him, and he had soon begun to think of remarriage.[4] Sometime in the autumn of 1685, he had initiated negotiations through Lady

---

[1] PRO, PRO 31/3/162, Barillon au Roi, 19/29 Nov. and 23 Nov./3 Dec.; BRO, Downshire MSS., vol. I, G. Dolben to Sir W. Trumbull, 19 Nov.; *Autobiography of Bramston*, pp. 216-17; *Memoirs of Sir John Reresby*, ed. A. Browning (Glasgow, 1936), p. 398; Foxcroft, *Halifax*, I, 458-9.

[2] Barillon au Roi, 20/30 Nov. printed in Fox, *James the second*, app. pp. cxl-cxli; *HMC Egmont*, II, 168.

[3] *Het Archief van den Raadpensionaris Antonie Heinsius*, ed. H. J. van der Heim (The Hague, 1867-80), I, xcvi.

[4] Lady Essex's dying request to Nottingham was that he 'breed' their children 'up in the fear of God' (Finch, *Burley*, I, 184).

Anne Grimstone (a distant relation) for the hand of her niece Anne, the daughter of Viscount Hatton of Kirby.[1] Among those consulted by her father about the proposed match was John Fell, then Bishop of Oxford, who gave it his hearty approval remarking,

The account which your lordship sends concerning my Lord of Notingham's proposal to you, is the best news which I have heard of late. It being not easy for your lordship to find out so honourable and so secure a settlement for your daughter, as with him. To be Son-burnt [a gentle pun on the suitor's colouring and the existence of a son surviving his first marriage][2] is I know a mighty disadvantage; but your daughters living happily, will be of more moment to hir than the being mother of an Earle.[3]

Lady Anne's consent was soon won, a dowry of £10,000 was agreed upon, and on 29 December 1685 Nottingham was wed for a second time, the office on this occasion being performed by his father's old chaplain, Dr John Sharp, in the church of St Giles in the Fields, London.[4]

The second Countess Nottingham, only eighteen at the time of her wedding, was to outlive Nottingham by some thirteen years. Despite the considerable disparity in their ages, it seems to have been not merely a fruitful match but also a most contented one. No more than a fragment of the correspondence between husband and wife survives, but it would appear that Lady Anne took to heart Bishop Fell's injunction to 'comport with the temper of a grave husband' and to 'render herself a meek helper' to him.[5]

With his remarriage and the birth early in 1687 of a son, christened Heneage (the first of Anne's twenty-two children), the problem of finding suitable quarters for his family became one of

[1] BM Add. MSS. 29569, fos. 177, 179, A. Grimstone to Lord Hatton, Dec. [1685].
[2] For other references to Finch's dark complexion, which led him to be known as 'the Jew', 'Dismal', and 'Don Diego', see BM Add. MSS. 7080, fo. 1, 'Timon' to R. Newport, 19 [Jan.] 1693; J. Macky, *Memoirs of the secret services of John Macky, Esq., during the reigns of king William, queen Anne, and king George I* (Roxburghe Club, London, 1895), p. 43.
[3] BM Add. MSS. 29582, fo. 5, 10 Dec.
[4] Finch, *Burley*, I, 98. For the terms of the marriage settlement, see LRO, Finch MSS., Miscellaneous papers; Habakkuk, 'Daniel Finch', p. 155.
[5] *Hatton correspondence*, II, 61.

Nottingham's major preoccupations. A London residence was, at least for the time being, no problem since the family house on the outskirts of the capital at Kensington (purchased by the first earl in 1661 from Sir John Finch who had inherited it from Daniel's grandfather) could still, if barely, accommodate Nottingham's growing establishment, which at this time already included nearly forty servants.[1] But Nottingham had long found the house on the country estate at Milton, Buckinghamshire, which he had bought in 1677 too cramped, and he now seems to have felt that with the addition to his estate of Lady Anne's dowry he could afford something better. What he began to look for, then, was a suitably sized country house, somewhere in the vicinity of his father-in-law's estate at Kirby (Northamptonshire), where he could indulge his own love for hunting and riding and also bring up his sons to a knowledge of estate administration as 'part of a gentleman's calling'.[2]

However, neither Nottingham's eventually unsuccessful quest for a suitable country house nor his disapproval of James's policies let him to withdraw completely from the Court and the capital. He even continued after James's prorogation of parliament to attend the Privy Council on occasion.[3] None the less, he must have been well aware that any hopes of office he may have cherished were unlikely to be realized in the new reign, particularly after his censure of Jeffreys' performance as Lord Steward in the abortive trial of Lord Delamere in January 1686.[4] Indeed, rumours of his brother's ouster from the solicitorship were already circulating early in 1686 though it was not until April, when Heneage refused to act for the crown in *Godden vs. Hales*, that he was

[1] Habakkuk, 'Daniel Finch', pp. 143–4, 171.
[2] *Ibid.* pp. 144, 172. For Nottingham's zeal for hunting and riding, see, for example, Longleat Thynne MSS., vol. XVIII, Sir R. Southwell to Viscount Weymouth, 6 Oct. 1696; *Clarendon correspondence*, II, 253.
[3] PRO, PC 2/71, *passim*.
[4] *A complete collection of state trials and proceedings for high treason and other crimes and misdemeanors from the earliest period to the present time*, ed. T. B. Howell (London, 1809–26), XI, 560–1; BM Add. MSS. 28569, fos. 58–9, Viscount Weymouth to [?], 30 Jan. 1686; Morrice, II, 415.

removed.[1] Despite the younger Finch's refusal to serve, James did secure judicial sanction to dispense with the provisions of the first Test Act in June, and four Catholic peers were promptly made Privy Councillors. A month later, the king announced the establishment of an ecclesiastical commission with far-reaching powers and a jurisdiction that embraced the Universities as well as the Church. And the Commission's first step was to summon before it one of the king's most prominent ecclesiastical opponents, Bishop Compton, to show cause why he had not suspended John Sharp for an allegedly offensive sermon against the pretensions of the Church of Rome. Furthermore, early in the autumn Jeffreys began a major purge of the commissions of the peace throughout England in an effort to displace those hostile to royal policy.[2]

With parliament kept in abeyance by repeated prorogations, there was little opportunity for Nottingham to give vent publicly to his sentiments. None the less, not only did he intervene on Sharp's behalf at Court, but also when Compton sought his opinion as to whether or not he should contest the legality of the Ecclesiastical Commission Nottingham apparently advised him to do so.[3] As a memorandum he drafted on this question indicates, he was convinced that 'the King had no power to erect this court'.[4] However, he also seems to have counselled caution in the framing of such a challenge. As he pointed out to Archibishop Sancroft some months later, since the Commissioners were also Privy Councillors, they had in that capacity the power to summon anyone to appear before them. It would be well, then, for anyone cited before them to answer the summons in person.[5] In the same vein, he also persuaded his new father-in-law, Viscount Hatton (the *Custos Rotulorum* for Northamptonshire), not to offer any

---

[1] Luttrell, I, 368, 375–6. See also *PH*, v, 326.
[2] F. C. Turner, *James II* (London, 1948), p. 328.
[3] *HMC Downshire*, I, 188; Braybrooke (ed.), *Autobiography of Bramston*, p. 233. See also Foxcroft, *Halifax*, I, 472–3.   [4] LRO, Finch MSS., Political papers 150.
[5] Bodl. Tanner MSS. 29, fos. 33–4, Bishop Turner to Archbishop Sancroft, 6 June 1687.

recommendations for the filling of the vacancies in the county's commission of the peace created by Jeffreys' alterations, 'for (besides many other reasons)...by doing so [you] become a kind of surety for their good behaviour, and in this age tis well if a man can so act himself as not to give offence'.[1]

But all too many found they could not avoid giving offence, for only complete adherence to the king's aims could secure or hold the royal favour by late 1686. Encouraged by Sunderland, James reluctantly dismissed Clarendon and Rochester at the turn of the year; despite their loyalty to him, they were unwilling to assist in pro-Catholic measures either in Ireland or in England. Their removal was followed by a series of royal interviews with members of parliament in which James pressed them to agree to the repeal of the penal statutes and the tests, with all who refused being deprived of whatever offices they held.[2] Nottingham was not among those 'closeted', perhaps, as he himself believed, because the king 'thought it would be to no purpose'.[3] Certainly, his views were well known, while the threat of removal was unlikely to influence him since he held no position save the merely honorary one of Privy Councillor.[4] In any case, it soon became clear that this sort of pressure was unlikely to cow the Houses. Thus, parliament was prorogued once more while the king and Sunderland, in a new effort to secure a favourable session, turned now to the heiress presumptive and her husband, the Princess and Prince of Orange. Offers of an alliance against France coupled with the promise to consult William and Mary on all official appointments if they would support Court policies were made in

[1] BM Add. MSS. 29594, fo. 6, 19 Nov. 1686.
[2] Kenyon, *Sunderland*, pp. 147–8.
[3] LRO, Finch MSS., Political papers 148, p. 9.
[4] Nottingham was described by both Barillon and Bonrepaux late in 1687 as opposed to the Court, though the latter thought his characteristic caution savoured of timidity ('*il a peu d'esprit*') (PRO, PRO 31/3/173, Barillon au Roi, 17/27 Oct.; PRO, PRO 31/3/174, Bonrepaux's report of Dec.). Nottingham is also included among those hostile to James's measures on two lists printed in Browning, *Osborne*, III, 152–63. See also K. D. H. Haley, 'A List of the English Peers, *c.* May, 1687', *EHR*, LXIX (1954), 304–6.

March 1687 to Dyckvelt, the Envoy-Extraordinary of the States-General and the prince's personal representative.[1]

While Dyckvelt dallied over these propositions, James had already begun to shift to another tack—an alliance with the dissenters against the established church and its adherents. In April 1687 he issued his first Declaration of Indulgence which suspended both the penal laws and the tests in an open bid for dissenting support. Moreover, after Dyckvelt at last rejected the royal offers, the king not only dissolved his first parliament but also opened a sapping operation against the citadels of vested Anglican privilege —the Universities and the other great endowed foundations. However, his efforts to intrude Catholics into Magdalen College were bitterly resisted by its Fellows, while the Trustees of the Charterhouse, who included Nottingham, Halifax, Danby, Ormonde and Sancroft, refused either to permit Sunderland to sit amongst them (on the grounds that he had not taken the oaths) or to honour a royal mandate on behalf of an aged Catholic.[2]

Meanwhile, Dyckvelt had not been idle. Acting on his secret instructions from William which authorized him, so Burnet relates, 'to try all sorts of people and to remove the ill impressions that had been given them of the prince', a series of meetings was arranged at the Earl of Shrewsbury's town house.[3] Besides Shrewsbury, those 'chiefly trusted' were Lords Halifax, Nottingham, Danby, Mordaunt and Lumley, along with Bishop Compton, Admiral Herbert and Edward Russell.[4] Since Dyckvelt does not seem to have committed any report of these gatherings to the mails, no detailed accounts of them survive. But they seem to have

[1] Kenyon, *Sunderland*, pp. 149–52.
[2] *A relation of the proceedings at the Charterhouse &c* reprinted in T. Burnet, *The sacred theory of the earth* (London, 1719), II, 1–12; Morrice, II, 159; Longleat Thynne MSS., vol. XVIII, fo. 190, Sir R. Southwell to Viscount Weymouth, 18 July 1687. For Nottingham's part in the Savoy episode and his aid to the deprived Fellows of Magdalen, see Foxcroft, *Halifax*, I, 483; Bodl. MSS. Top. Oxon. c325, fo. 71, Sir T. Clarges to Rev. Moore, 23 Nov. 1687.
[3] Burnet, III, 174.   [4] *Ibid.* pp. 180–1.

consisted, on the one hand, of assurances by William's emissary of the prince's concern for the preservation of the Church of England, and, on the other, of the expression by the English participants of their personal devotion to prince and princess as well as opinions of James's chances of success. That plans of concerted resistance were discussed in these meetings, not to speak of schemes entailing direct intervention by William, is extremely improbable. At this juncture, such suggestions were never broached to Nottingham nor was the prince ready to commit himself so far.[1] Nottingham's letter to William, one of several entrusted to Dyckvelt when he returned to the continent in June, merely commented that the bearer had been fully informed 'of affairs here at this time' and assured the prince of 'the universal concurrence of all Protestants in paying the utmost respect and duty to your Highness'.[2]

Nevertheless, it may have been at this time that James was informed that Nottingham was concerting in opposition against him, for these meetings had not wholly escaped the notice of the Court.[3] But Nottingham, informed by Dartmouth of the accusation against him, had no difficulty in denying to the king the charge that he had had meetings with Sir Edward Harley, Sir Thomas Lee, Woodley Charlton and others, for apart from Lee he barely knew those with whom he was supposed to be conspiring.[4] For the moment at least, Nottingham's conscience was clear, and the king fully accepted his disclaimers.[5]

Yet if the charge of plotting against the king were false, it is true that Nottingham was finding it more and more difficult to reconcile not merely his desire not to affront James but even his

---

[1] Ibid; Foxcroft, Halifax, I, 479–84; L. Pinkham, William III and the respectable revolution (Cambridge, Mass., 1954); S. B. Baxter, William III (London, 1966), pp. 223–34.
[2] PRO, SP 8/2, printed in Dalrymple, II, app. II, 193.
[3] Kenyon, Sunderland, p. 157. Barillon reported that Halifax, Devonshire, Danby and Nottingham 'ont leurs relations secrettes en Hollande et confèrent souvent avec ceux du mesme party qui sont les gens d'Eglise Anglicane dont la pluspart ont esté membres de la Chambre Basse dans les precédens Parlemens' (PRO, PRO 31/3/173, 17/27 Oct. 1687).
[4] LRO, Finch MSS., Political papers 148, p. 10.
[5] Ibid.

allegiance to the king with his concern for the preservation of the established order. Indeed, only the hope—which he was to voice repeatedly during the coming months—that James's tactics could not possibly succeed seems to have sustained him. His letter of September 1687 to William, which Count van Zuylestein carried back to Holland after a hasty round of consultations in England, makes this point clearly.

I think it is very probable [he wrote] that the present resolution is to have a parliament; the sudden and surprising declaration of indulgence to men, who a little before were hated, and laboured under great severities; the placing them in offices of trust in corporation towns; the encouragement of them to stand for members of the next parliament, and the particular reason that is given them for it, which is, to repeal the penal laws, in which the Protestants and the Papists seem to have a joint interest; and this, that it may appear the more specious without abrogating the test: all these are evidences of their intentions to advise the calling of a parliament, and together with the King's progress into the country, look preparatory to it.

Nevertheless, when I consider what little hopes they can justly have of any fruit of those endeavours when a parliament shall meet, I do conclude that they will change their councils, and that there will be no parliament this winter.[1]

A coalition of the dissenters and the Catholics would, so Nottingham maintained, inevitably founder on the rock of the Test Acts. On the one hand, it was unlikely that the dissenters would agree to their repeal because they would not willingly bear the odium or danger of being 'factors for popery'. Moreover, they might hope to secure, after James's death, a 'more firm and lasting security' than the present régime could offer. On the other hand, the Catholics would hardly consent to the passage of a statutory indulgence to the dissenters until agreement had been reached on repeal of the Tests. And even if this hurdle could be overcome, Nottingham contended that

there are so many other things that will be taken into consideration by a parliament, and of a nature so contrary to the present interest and humour of

---

[1] PRO, SP 8/2, printed in Dalrymple, ii, app. ii, 204.

the Papists, that it will be next to impossible that there should be time to bring such a bill to perfection, how zealously soever it may be prosecuted in the House of Commons, or otherwise encouraged.

All which difficulties the Papists cannot be so blind as not to foresee, or so vain as to contend against them, as yet, in a parliament.[1]

However, Nottingham's assessment of the situation, in which Halifax concurred, was in part based on the premise of a Protestant successor to James.[2] Thus, the rumours of the queen's pregnancy which began to be heard at Court late in October 1687 put a somewhat different face upon the royal projects. On 10 November a meeting of the Catholic secret council was held, evidently to discuss the political situation in the light of this new development. And the following day, Father Petre, James's rash Jesuit adviser, was sworn of the Privy Council.[3] This step seems to have taken most members of the Board by surprise, particularly Nottingham who arrived only after Father Petre had been introduced.[4] But for him, at least, James had gone too far. He had continued to attend the Council, if with increasing irregularity, even after several Catholic peers had been made members, but he was not prepared to sit with Father Petre. From that day, then, he absented himself from the Council for the rest of the reign, though he never formally sought leave to resign.[5]

While the prospect of a Catholic heir emboldened James and the Catholic extremists, it does not seem to have aided the work of the royal 'regulators'. After repeated purges of the county magistracies and corporation councils, Sunderland still felt the time was not ripe for the calling of a general election, and in March 1688 he persuaded James to postpone the summons of a new parliament until after the queen's delivery.[6] Instead, James early in May issued his second Declaration of Indulgence in an

[1] Ibid. pp. 205–6. [2] Ibid. pp. 202–3, 207–9.
[3] Kenyon, Sunderland, pp. 169–70; PRO, PC 2/72, p. 524.
[4] LRO, Finch MSS., Political papers 148, p. 10; Morrice, II, 199–200.
[5] LRO, Finch MSS., Political papers 148, p. 10; PRO, PC 2/72, passim. Cf. Burnet, III, 278.
[6] Kenyon, Sunderland, pp. 171–7, 187–92.

effort to firm up dissenting support, ordering at the same time that it be read in every church throughout the kingdom. However, the king and Sunderland, in attempting to compel the Anglican clergy to become accomplices to royal policy, had gravely miscalculated. Under this pressure, the church stood firm. The initiative in resisting the order to read the Declaration came from a small group of prominent London clerics, among them Sharp's friends Tillotson, Patrick and Stillingfleet. In their consultations, the advice of many including that of Clarendon, Rochester and Halifax was sought, but especially that of Nottingham 'who has most reputation and who they place most confidence in'.[1] While Clarendon urged that the Declaration should not be read and his brother Rochester counselled obedience, Nottingham (with Halifax) once again took a cautious line which, so one Williamite reported, 'almost ruined the business'.[2] Apparently Nottingham believed that a refusal to obey by only a part of the clergy would be even more disastrous than if all were to concur in reading it.[3] Above all, what he wanted to avoid was dissension among their number for he, like Sunderland, felt that only James could gain from such a split.[4]

However, encouraged by the assurance of a number of dissenter leaders that they would not willingly accept any toleration save one granted in parliament, a majority of the London clergy resolved to refuse and even the more hesitant finally conceded that they would not occasion internal division by following James's command.[5] Heartened by their support, Archbishop Sancroft and six other bishops then drafted a petition to the king avowing their loyalty but asserting that his use of the suspending power was illegal and declaring that they could not comply in it.

[1] Morrice, II, 255.
[2] BM Add. MSS. 34515, fo. 67, transcript of J. Johnstone's letter of 27 May. See also *Clarendon correspondence*, II, 171–2.
[3] Morrice, II, 255.
[4] Kenyon, *Sunderland*, p. 194.
[5] BM Add. MSS. 34515, fos. 65–6, transcript of Johnstone's report of 23 May; E. Calamy, *Memoirs of the life of the late Reverend Mr John Howe* (London, 1724), pp. 139–41.

A saving clause was added which explained that they acted not 'from any want of due tenderness to Dissenters' with whom they were ready to come to 'a temper' when parliament and convocation met.[1]

The drama of the confrontation of crown and church was speedily played out. James was astounded and dismayed when the bishops presented their petition to him on 18 May. But after wavering for more than a fortnight, he resolved to prosecute them for issuing a seditious libel, since a version of their address had been published (without their connivance) and widely dispersed almost immediately after its presentation.[2] Given the near unanimity among the Anglican clergy and the backing of many leading dissenters, Nottingham now believed the time was ripe for a clear-cut legal challenge to James, and he urged the prelates' counsel to contest the legality of the suspending power at their trial—a bold tactic which his brother Heneage (one of the bishops' lawyers) was at first reluctant to consider.[3] A move was also on foot among the nobility to petition James on the bishops' behalf. Shrewsbury and Lumley were active in organizing it and Nottingham indicated that he was ready to lend his support, although Halifax proved reluctant to commit himself in this fashion.[4] But such a step was rendered needless by the acquittal won by the bishops on 30 June, while the doubts cast by the judges on the legality of the royal declarations of indulgence amply justified Nottingham's advice to his brother.

Even before the trial, however, a small group of influential opponents of the Court was preparing the ground for a far greater check to the king. By the spring of 1688, William was at last pre-

[1] R. Thomas, 'The seven bishops and their petition, 18 May 1688', *Journal of Ecclesiastical History*, XII (1961), 56–65.

[2] *Ibid.* pp. 65–70.

[3] *Collectanea curiosa, or miscellaneous tracts relating to the history and antiquities of England and Ireland, the universities of Oxford and Cambridge, Etc.*, ed. J. Gutch (Oxford, 1781), I, 358–9.

[4] BM Add. MSS. 34515, fos. 77–8, transcript of Johnstone's letter of 13 June; BM Add. MSS. 34510, fos. 136–7, English transcript of van Citters' dispatch to the States-General, 23 June/2 July; Dalrymple, II, app. II, 227–8.

pared to intervene decisively in England in defence of his right of succession, and the birth early in June of a Catholic heir to the throne—widely held to be suppositious—could only have confirmed him and the more virulent of James's English foes in their readiness to resort to force.[1] Among those privy to the prince's plans in England, the most important were Mordaunt, Shrewsbury, Edward Russell and Henry Sidney. Halifax was discreetly sounded out, but he gave no encouragement to such a project. Devonshire and Danby, however, both 'went in heartily to it', as did Bishop Compton. And on the suggestion of Danby and Compton, William's design was also opened to Nottingham.[2]

Nottingham, as he penned an account of this episode many years later, recalled his own feelings vividly:

I was informd...that the Prince was ready to come to relieve England from its fears and to assert their civil and religious rights if...he could be assurd of the concurrence of any number of the Considerable Noblemen and gentlemen of England upon which it was propos'd that a letter should be prepared and wrote and signd by Us and such others as might be trusted to invite the Prince and to assure him of our utmost assistance. This was the greatest difficulty that ever I was plung'd into in my whole life; I was indeed satisfyd in my owne mind that the Prince of Orange had a just cause for such an attempt, the Princesse's right of Succession to the Crowne being likely to be defeated, not onely by the Birth of the Prince of Wales which at that time was suspected...but also by the proceedings of King James in putting all the offices and power in the Kingdom into the hands of Papists as fast as he could, etc. I was indeed asham'd to quitt the Company who had admitted me into their Secrets and on the other hand I did not dare to proceed in an affair of which the next step would be high treason, in violation of the Laws (which are the rules of our conduct) and that allegiance which I ow'd to the Soveraigne and which I had confirm'd by my solemn oath.[3]

Fearing to 'doe Evil that good may come of it' and yet apprehensive that 'our religion and liberties' would perish if this opportunity were not taken, Nottingham hastened in his 'great

[1] Baxter, *William III*, pp. 223–34.   [2] Burnet, III, 274–8.
[3] LRO, Finch MSS., Political papers 148, p. 10.

perplexity' to consult two of his closest friends among the clergy, Stillingfleet and Bishop Lloyd of St Asaph.[1] He posed his dilemma to them in the form of an hypothetical question. Could one 'in Conscience endeavour to oppose by Force a manifest designe of destroying our religious and civil rights and liberties, though such an attempt by Force to defend them could not be justifyd by the known standing Laws of the realm'?[2] When they both replied in the negative, Nottingham hesitated no longer

but went to Mr Russell, and told him I came with the utmost Shame and confusion of face to acquaint him that I could proceed no farther in the measures which had been discourst of at our meeting, I had endeavourd, with the most earnest desire of concurring with them, to perswade my-selfe that I might doe soe with a good Conscience. I had adviz'd with some persons who I thought could better judge of a Case of Conscience than my-selfe, I told him the question, which I propos'd to them and the manner in which I did it that they might have no suspition of any actual designe and much lesse of any persons engaged in it and I told him their answer, which, I protested to him, I did as much and as truely regrett, as it was possible for him and his noble friends to resent the resolution I must take pursuant to it; for which it became me to ask their pardon though I could not expect to obtaine it.[3]

Although Sidney thought Nottingham's withdrawal to be the product of cowardice, the persistence later in his career of conscientious scruples concerning the legality of the Revolution strongly suggests that he was not dissembling at this time. None the less, the plotters could not afford to disregard the possibility of betrayal. They even seem to have considered whether or not to silence him, but Danby dissuaded them from violent action.[4] Nottingham's reluctance to violate his oaths may also have been reinforced by his belief that direct intervention by William was unnecessary. Certainly, the bishops' acquittal could be interpreted as evidence for such optimism—optimism that the earl did express in a letter of late July sent to the prince after another round of de-

[1] *Ibid.*   [2] *Ibid.* p. 11.   [3] *Ibid.*
[4] Burnet, III, 279, and the notes of Dartmouth and Onslow; Devonshire House 'Notebook', *sub* 'Nottingham Ld'.

tailed discussions with Count van Zuylestein. While acknowledging that 'the birth of a Prince of Wales, and the designs of a further prosecution of the Bishops and of new modelling the army and calling of a parliament' did not inspire confidence, Nottingham maintained that he could not 'apprehend from them such ill consequences to our religion, or the just interests of your Highness, that a little time will not effectually remedy' nor could he 'imagine that the Papists are able to make any further considerable progress'.[1] He added, perhaps to excuse his last-minute refusal to sign the 'Invitation', 'I beseech you not to misconstruct my opinion as proceeding from any want of zeal to the service of your Highness...for I shall always discharge my duty to you with the utmost fidelity'.[2]

If Nottingham continued to comfort himself during the months after the bishops' acquittal with the thought that James's measures could not succeed, the king and his advisers were even more sanguine in the face of the extensive mobilization of the Dutch forces in July and August. Not until mid-September was either James or Sunderland brought to realize the grave danger in which the régime stood.[3] And even then, though military and naval preparations were hastened, the most urgent aspect of defence against the invasion—the conciliation of the discontented and estranged nobility, gentry and clergy—advanced only spasmodically.

For a few brief days, James allowed Sunderland's overwhelming panic to dictate his actions. A proclamation issued on 21 September promised the summons of a free parliament and the protection of the church's rights. Furthermore, the king agreed the following day to consult with the Anglican bishops and lords in London. But on the 25th, the writs were withdrawn while James considered instead, until dissuaded by Sunderland, the arrest of Halifax, Danby, Shrewsbury, Nottingham and other suspected

[1] PRO, SP 8/2, printed in Dalrymple, II, app. II, 236–7.
[2] Ibid. p. 237.
[3] Clarendon correspondence, II, 189; Turner, James II, pp. 411–15; Kenyon, Sunderland, pp. 205–15.

sympathizers of the prince.[1] Again, though James declared his readiness to restore the Fellows of Magdalen and to abolish the Ecclesiastical Commission in an audience with six of the bishops on the 28th, he also assured his Catholic courtiers a week later that he would concede nothing to their disadvantage.[2]

Under these circumstances, Nottingham's audience of 5 October—arranged by royal request—did not prove very satisfactory to the king. Though Nottingham kissed hands, he would neither resume his seat on the Privy Council nor commit himself by offering advice that he suspected James would not heed.[3] As he guardedly wrote to Lord Hatton (taking care to disguise his hand and writing in the third person): 'My Lord Nottingham has bin at Court and I heare the King is much dissatisfy'd with him for saying nothing to him relating to the present State of affairs.'[4] At the same time, he assured his father-in-law that though he could not discuss the grounds for his behaviour in a letter, 'I believe they would be satisfactory to your Lordship who knows he [Nottingham] will never engage in any action against the allegiance he owes in conscience to the King.'[5] Yet even after James on 22 October ordered Father Petre not to attend the Privy Council any longer, Nottingham (as well as Clarendon) refused to resume his seat at the Board, making it clear to the king in an audience that day 'there were others at that board, who were not qualified to sit there; and he could not join in council with them'.[6] In short, while he would not take up arms against the king, Nottingham was also unwilling to accept any responsibility for royal policy until he was sure James had really seen the errors of his ways.

None the less, the royal tactics of two steps forward and one backward continued throughout October, with the king's hopes

[1] F. A. J. Mazure, *Histoire de la révolution de 1688 en Angleterre* (Paris, 1825), III, 74; Kenyon, *Sunderland*, p. 218 and note.

[2] *Clarendon correspondence*, II, 191, 193; Kenyon, *Sunderland*, p. 219.

[3] Mazure, *Histoire de la révolution*, III, 131–2; BM Add. MSS. 17677 UUU, fo. 633, van Citters' secret report of 5/15 Oct.

[4] BM Add. MSS. 29569, fo. 374, 6 Oct.

[5] *Ibid.*   [6] *Clarendon correspondence*, II, 195–6.

buoyed by the news received on the 27th that the prince's fleet had been badly damaged by storms. But when William's declaration came into James's hands on the 31st, he was dismayed to read that the prince had been invited by many lords, both spiritual and temporal. During the next two days, he spoke to several of the bishops, among them Compton. While he accepted readily their protestations of innocence, he sought from them and their brethren a public repudiation of the invasion. Though they put him off temporarily by asking for an opportunity to consult their colleagues, James was not deterred from putting the leading temporal peers under similar pressure.[1] Thus on the evening of 4 November Nottingham, Halifax and their friend the Earl of Burlington were also interviewed by the king.[2] But James had even less success with them than he had had with the bishops. In a private audience lasting over an hour, all three denied involvement in the prince's expedition, and politely, yet resolutely, declined to sign an address 'abhorring' the invasion. Moreover, though Nottingham and Halifax apparently expressed their sorrow at the ill condition of the king's affairs, neither offered him his service or assistance.[3] Following their lead, the bishops declined two days later to sign any address of abhorrence, on the grounds that they had already been prosecuted for alleged illegal interference in matters of state and that they could only act in conjunction with the temporal peers.[4]

Nevertheless, the news of William's landing at Torbay on 5 November did move both the temporal and the spiritual peers then in London to action in an effort to avoid a bloody civil war. On the 8th, Rochester and Clarendon took the initiative by suggesting to Bishops White of Peterborough and Lloyd of St Asaph

[1] Turner, *James II*, pp. 422–3.
[2] BM Sloane MSS. 3929, fo. 105, official newsletter of 10 Nov.
[3] *Ibid*. BM Add. MSS. 17677HH, fos. 499, 504, van Citters' dispatches of 6/16 and 9/19 Nov. Van Citters, in the first of these two letters, reported that the king was so dissatisfied with the results of these conversations that he contemplated imprisoning all those who would refuse to 'abhor'.
[4] Turner, *James II*, pp. 423–4.

the preparation of an address calling upon the king to summon parliament.[1] But it was Halifax, Nottingham and Viscount Weymouth (the former Sir Thomas Thynne) who actually joined the two bishops in drafting a petition whose design, as Nottingham explained to his father-in-law, 'was to pray the King to call a Parliament forthwith free in all respects both of coming sitting and debate: it being better and easier to prevent a disease than to cure it'.[2] Moreover, it was the three peers who persuaded White and Lloyd that the address should be made 'only by such Lords and Bishops as had not made themselves obnoxious by any late miscarriages'.[3] Thus, when the two prelates began to solicit signatures to the draft on the 12th, they encountered some resistance, especially from Clarendon. Not only was he offended by their failure to consult him in drafting the address; he also took exception to the decision to exclude his brother Rochester and others who had in any way been involved in James's proceedings against the Anglican Church. As Nottingham observed, this 'was apprehended by the Earl of Clarendon and some of the Bishops as a pique of Lord Halifax to Lord Rochester'.[4] Nottingham recognized there was 'unkindness enough' between the old rivals, but he agreed with Halifax that to allow Rochester to sign the memorial would only lead William to suspect it as a 'trick of the Court'.[5] So considerable was the disagreement over this issue that the original framers of the petition, whose enthusiasm was also waning 'now that it has taken air and is blown upon, and perhaps in the present Circumstances is wisht for even by the Court', eventually decided to abandon the proposed address.[6]

Rochester and Clarendon, however, were not content to let the matter rest. No sooner had the first petition been dropped than they began, in concert with some of the bishops, to prepare a second. But Nottingham, Halifax and Weymouth, along with a number of other lay peers, decided to stand aloof from this effort.

[1] *Clarendon correspondence*, II, 201.   [2] BM Add. MSS. 29594, fo. 131.
[3] *Ibid.*   [4] *Ibid.* fos. 131–2; *Clarendon correspondence*, II, 202–3.
[5] BM Add. MSS. 29594, fos. 131–2.   [6] *Ibid.* fo. 132.

Apart from their reluctance to associate themselves with those implicated in James's illegalities, Halifax and Nottingham in particular were disturbed by the second memorial's failure to include any provision to allow those who had joined the prince to sit in any parliament now to be convened.[1] Indeed, Nottingham believed that 'to joyn with the other Lords might be construed an obstruction to that reformation which is necessary to establish the peace of the kingdome'.[2] Yet he would certainly have maintained, as did his friend Weymouth, that his reasons for refusing to join in the second petition 'were neither want of zeale for my countrey, nor service to his Majestie'.[3] But he could serve both king and kingdom only when James was ready to abandon entirely the policies that had brought him to the edge of the abyss.[4]

Even after William's landing, however, James was not ready to accept the counsel offered by those Protestant peers most attached to him. When the petition prepared by the Hydes and the bishops was presented to him on 17 November, shortly before he left to join his army at Salisbury, the king could not conceal his displeasure with its request for the immediate summoning of a 'Parliament Regular and free in all its Circumstances'.[5] All he would say was 'that he would call a Parliament as soon as it was convenient, but it could not be whilst the invasion and rebellion lasted'.[6] But it was a very chastened and crestfallen monarch who returned to London on the 26th. His army had been paralysed by

---

[1] BM Add. MSS. 17677 HH, fo. 511, van Citters' report of 20/30 Nov.; E. Campana di Cavelli, *Les dernier Stuarts et la château de Saint-Germain en Laye: documents inédits et authentiques* (Paris, 1871), II, 333–4; A. Boyer, *The history of King William the third* (London, 1702–3), I, pt. II, 244. There appear to be no grounds for the rumour reported to the Duke of Beaufort that Nottingham declined to sign the petition because he was misled 'by an untruth told him' by Halifax (Bodl. Carte MSS. 130, fo. 313, [17 Nov.]).

[2] BM Add. MSS. 29594, fo. 132; *Clarendon correspondence*, II, 205.

[3] Longleat Thynne MSS., vol. XVa, fo. 65, Weymouth to Sir R. Southwell, 20 Nov.

[4] Morrice, II, 319.

[5] BM Add. MSS. 47351, fo. 60, copy of the petition with list of signatories.

[6] *Clarendon correspondence*, II, 205. See also BM Add. MSS. 17677 HH, fos. 507–8, van Citters' report of 16/26 Nov.

indecision and demoralized by one defection after another; even James's son-in-law Prince George had deserted him while Princess Anne had fled to the insurgents at Nottingham. Shortly after his arrival, James sent to see Halifax and then summoned those Protestant peers still in town to meet with him the following day.[1]

With the Catholic peers absent and with the king at last prepared to hear his Protestant lords' advice as to 'what was best to be done in the present exigency', Nottingham and Halifax for the first time spoke their minds, tactfully but forcefully.[2] They agreed with Rochester, who had opened the discussion, that a parliament should be convoked and that negotiations should be opened with William, but at the same time they warned that further concessions would be necessary. James, they thought, should make them now of his own volition rather than appear to be compelled to do so later. In particular, they urged the removal of all Catholics from office and the grant of a general pardon. They also seem to have recommended the proclamation of a strict neutrality in European affairs.[3] 'Lord Nottingham spoak in a very soft language,' Morrice reported, 'but things smart enough.'[4] James, indeed, was taken aback by the extent of the retreat urged upon him; he agreed to dispatch the parliamentary writs, but said for the rest that he would 'take one night's time to consider of them'.[5]

After pondering these counsels, the king sent for Nottingham and Halifax on the 28th for the first of a series of private interviews the two peers had with him during the next three days.[6] In the privacy of the royal closet, they seem to have been even more outspoken than they had been in public, pressing their advice on James while refusing to be tempted by offers of high

[1] BM Add. MSS. 24487, fo. 40, newsletter of 28 Nov.
[2] *Clarendon correspondence*, II, 208–10.
[3] Foxcroft, *Halifax*, II, 16 and n. 4; Luttrell, I, 481; BM Egerton MSS. 2717, fo. 413, newsletter of 29 Nov.; BM Add. MSS. 25377, fo. 174, Terriesi's report of 3/13 Dec.
[4] Morrice, II, 329.   [5] *Clarendon correspondence*, II, 211.
[6] *Ibid.* p. 212; *The letters of Rachel Lady Russell*, ed. Lord John Russell (London, 1853), I, 264; BM Add. MSS. 28053, fo. 367, newsletter of 1 Dec.; D'Adda's report of 30 Nov./ 10 Dec. quoted in Foxcroft, *Halifax*, II, 17, n. 4.

office.[1] They did, however, agree to serve as emissaries to the prince, and by the 30th James was able to announce their appointment and that of Godolphin to act with them. At the same time, he published a general pardon.[2] On the following afternoon, the three commissioners were entrusted with their instructions by the king in a private audience.[3] They were to acquaint the prince that writs had been dispatched for a meeting of parliament at Westminster on 15 January and to adjust with him 'all such things as shall be necessary in order to the Freedome of Elections, and that the Parliament may sitt without feare of Disturbance'.[4] Further, they were to request William not to bring his army any closer than forty miles to London, but if he refused to agree, they were empowered to inquire what other safeguards for a free parliament he wished. Apparently after some representations from the Commissioners, James issued a supplementary instruction later that day allowing them to offer the withdrawal of the main body of the royal forces to an equal distance from the capital.[5]

Although some of the other peers envied their appointment, none of the king's representatives was overjoyed at so thankless a task. Their powers were all too circumscribed and they were well aware that their mission might be construed as merely an attempt to delay the prince's advance on London. As Nottingham confided to Hatton,

My Lord Clarendon...had a great mind to have bin one of the Commissioners a place which I doe not hear any of the 3 Lords desird but purely obeyd the King; for in all probability this will have no effect; the affairs of the Prince being such as will admitt little delay especially since the King of Frances troops have already advanced to Boisleduc.[6]

---

[1] *Clarendon correspondence*, II, 212; D'Adda's report of 30 Nov./10 Dec.
[2] *The London Gazette*, no. 2406.   [3] *HMC Second Report*, p. 14.
[4] The originals of both the initial and additional instructions, as well as copies of the Commissioners' official correspondence, are to be found among the papers of Owen Wynne, their secretary, in All Souls College MSS. 273 (unfoliated).
[5] All Souls College MSS. 273.
[6] BM Add. MSS. 29595, fo. 283, [1 Dec.]. See also Foxcroft, *Halifax*, II, 19–22; cf. *HMC Buckingham, Etc.*, p. 452.

Despite such forebodings, the Commissioners set out the morning of 2 December to meet William, to be received by him six days later at his temporary headquarters in Hungerford.[1]

However he regarded their mission, William was obliged to 'go through the motions of negotiating with the King'.[2] Yet even as he assured the worried Clarendon, who had joined him a few days earlier, that he was resolved to observe his declaration, he also remarked to him that while 'he had but little acquaintance with Lord Nottingham...he did a little wonder, the Lords Halifax and Godolphin came to him in this errand'.[3] To reassure his English adherents that he would not betray them, William refused the Commissioners' request for a private interview and ordered that they deliver their message in the presence of the English peers and gentlemen in his camp.[4] Acting as their spokesman, Halifax then set out the proposals they had been authorized to make by James. Immediately afterwards, they retired to an ante-room, and at William's desire drew up and signed a copy of what Halifax had said.[5]

Although William was anxious to prevent the Commissioners from conversing with the Englishmen in his camp, they do not seem to have had much difficulty in doing so. In a letter to Secretary Middleton dispatched the evening of the 8th from their lodgings at Ramsbury, they reported that they had found among their countrymen at Hungerford 'no kind of Disposition' to halt their army's march and a general insistence on the removal of Catholics from all posts, civil and military.[6] Furthermore, some had declared

that though they could be secure in coming to Parliament, yet if the King should bee perswaded to Dissolve it, before their Grievances bee redressed, and

---

[1] Dalrymple, II, app. II, 338; *A selection from the papers of the Earls of Marchmont*, ed. G. H. Rose (London, 1831), III, 100–1.
[2] Pinkham, *Respectable revolution*, p. 185.   [3] *Clarendon correspondence*, II, 214.
[4] Bodl. Rawlinson MSS. A 139 B, p. 278, printed in Foxcroft, *Halifax*, II, 24–6; *Clarendon correspondence*, II, 219–20; E. M. Thompson, 'Correspondence of Admiral Herbert during the Revolution', *EHR*, I (1886), 532.
[5] Bodl. Rawlinson MSS. A 139 B, p. 278.   [6] *Ibid.*

their Libertyes secured, it would be a certaine Delay, and very much hazzard their dessein for the Good of the Publick, which by the methods they are now in, they think, they shall quickly obtaine.[1]

The Commissioners' pessimistic prognosis may well have owed much to their conversation with Gilbert Burnet. After his confidence had been gained by Nottingham's and Halifax's undoubtedly sincere intimations that they were 'very little fond of the Imployment' they came upon and their disclaimer that 'it was put on them by their Enemies', Burnet probably was most forthright.[2] Certainly, he told Halifax that the prince would be delighted should James leave the kingdom.[3] In turn, his frankness was rewarded by some pointed remarks from Nottingham who, if we can trust Burnet's original account of these hurried talks, observed that 'if the prince did not take his measures right, he would find the hardest part of his work before him at London, when perhaps we might think he had all in his hands'.[4] The accuracy of this assessment would soon be brought home to William, not least by Nottingham's own conduct.

However, the Commissioners were agreeably surprised by the preliminaries put forward by the prince the morning of the 10th. Rejecting the demand of his more extreme followers that the writs issued by James be recalled, William's answer—delivered to them at Littlecote—was more moderate than they had anticipated.[5] Apart from stipulating the removal from office of all Catholics and any others who had not taken the oaths, he demanded assurances for the personal safety of his adherents, the stationing of both armies at least forty miles from London, and the garrisoning of the Tower of London, Tilbury Fort and Portsmouth on mutually acceptable terms to prevent the landing of any French forces. He also requested permission to come to London should James decide to stay there as well as the assignment

---

[1] Bodl. Rawlinson MSS. A 139 B, p. 278.
[2] Thompson, 'Correspondence of Admiral Herbert', p. 532.
[3] *Supplement to Burnet's History*, p. 300.
[4] *Ibid.*   [5] *Clarendon correspondence*, II, 221.

of a 'sufficient part of the publick Revenue' for the maintenance of his troops until the meeting of parliament.[1]

In reply to these preliminaries, the Commissioners informed the prince that they were empowered to agree to some but not all of them, and declared they would return to the capital as quickly as possible to lay them before James. In the meantime they desired him not to advance nearer than thirty miles to London before the 13th which, they concluded, 'by our Computation is the soonest an Answer can be returnd'.[2] Despite their lack of authority, the royal representatives 'seemed to be very well satisfied' with William's proposals.[3] And Nottingham, in particular, was reported to have expressed the hope that the king would agree to all William's requests.[4]

But the royal emissaries' hopes of an accommodation were quickly dashed. They reached London the afternoon of the 11th only to find that James—whose last doubts about the wisdom of flight could only have been erased by their pessimistic letter of the 8th—had stolen away that morning, leaving the capital threatened by anarchy. Needless to say, they 'were extremely concerned to find that the Prince's good inclinations and their good offices were rendered abortive'.[5] Now the issue facing the kingdom was no longer on what terms James was to continue to rule but who was to govern, while Nottingham could hardly avoid committing himself definitely to one camp or the other.

[1] Foxcroft, *Halifax*, II, 29–30.
[2] BM Add. MSS. 28103, fo. 72. [3] Burnet, III, 341–2.
[4] *Journaal van Constantijn Huygens, den zoon, van 21 October 1688 tot 2 Sept. 1696* (Historisch Genootschap, Utrecht, 1876–8), I, 40–1.
[5] *Original letters illustrative of English history*, ed. Sir H. Ellis (London, 1827), 2nd ser. IV, 173.

CHAPTER 5

COUNSEL FOR THE CONSTITUTION

1688-9

The two months that separated James's flight early on the morning of 11 December 1688 from the proclamation of William and Mary as king and queen on 13 February 1689 were as decisive for Nottingham's political career as they were for England's course. Hitherto, while dissociating himself from royal measures, Nottingham had adhered to his oaths to James (save for concealment of his knowledge of the invitation to William). But now Nottingham, and many others, were confronted in its most acute form with the dilemma of allegiance: which loyalty, to king or kingdom, should be foremost?

To be sure, James's flight had not been wholly unforeseen. Two or three days before he left London, Bishop Turner of Ely and the Earl of Rochester had persuaded the Archbishop of Canterbury to send out letters requesting the peers to assemble at the Guildhall to 'take uppon them the Government for the preservation of the Kingdome and this great Citty' should James withdraw from England.[1] Yet when the Lords did gather at the Guildhall on this summons a few hours after their sovereign's hasty departure, the 'contrivers' of the meeting quickly discovered that they could not dictate its proceedings. The declaration which Turner and Rochester had prepared—a request to the Prince of Orange to secure the calling of a free parliament to enact 'effectual Securitys for our Religion and Laws' that the king might be called home again 'with Honor and Safety'—was sharply criticized. A number of its more fervent expressions of loyalty were excepted

---

[1] Bodl. Rawlinson MSS. D 836, fos. 113–14, draft of a letter of 17 Feb. 1689 in Bishop Turner's hand. See also *Memoirs of Ailesbury*, I, 197–8.

against, and consequently omitted.[1] Then Lords Culpepper, Weymouth and Pembroke (the two latter close friends of Nottingham) were nominated to accompany the Bishop of Ely in carrying the amended declaration to William.[2]

On the 12th, both Nottingham and Halifax, who had returned to London late the previous day, joined the other peers who were now meeting at Whitehall.[3] The following morning, however, their discussions were interrupted by a messenger bearing the news that James's flight had ended in Kent and that he was now in the hands of a rabble near Sheerness. After some hesitation, they dispatched Lord Feversham at the head of a company of cavalry with orders to protect the king but to allow him to depart for France if he desired.[4] William was equally startled to learn of James's detention and disturbed even more by the possibility of his return to London. Nor were his apprehensions groundless, for the king's re-entry into his capital on the 16th prompted a spontaneous outburst of popular loyalty.[5] But James was allowed little time to re-establish himself. After conferring on the 17th with twelve of the peers present at Windsor, William sent Halifax (who had joined him a day earlier), Shrewsbury and Delamere to request him to leave London.[6] Within hours after James's departure for Rochester under Dutch guard, William arrived at St James's. Among the crowds that came to wait on him that evening was Nottingham, although he soon left in the company of a number of bishops and London clergy seemingly bent on a

---

[1] Bodl. Rawlinson MSS. D 836, fos. 113–14; Foxcroft, *Halifax*, II, 57–9.
[2] Bodl. Rawlinson MSS. A 77, 'The Interregnum or the Proceedings of the Lords of the Council and others from the withdrawing of King James the second to the meeting of the Convention', p. 7; Foxcroft, *Halifax*, II, 57.
[3] PRO, SP 31/4, fo. 207.
[4] Bodl. Rawlinson MSS. A 77, pp. 12–13; Foxcroft, *Halifax*, II, 58; *Hatton correspondence*, II, 123.
[5] Morrice, II, 379–80; Burnet, III, 353.
[6] Pinkham, *Respectable revolution*, pp. 198–9; *Clarendon correspondence*, II, 228–30; Burnet, III, 354–7. Notes of this meeting in Halifax's hand are among the Althorp Savile MSS., box 4, and are partially printed in D. H. Somerville, *The king of hearts* (London, 1962), p. 50 n.

private consultation.[1] The subject of their conclave was not disclosed, but the fears that beset many of the clergy and peers were no secret, and the talk of the prince's supporters that 'the King's going away is a cession of his right to the Crowne' only reinforced them.[2]

While hopes of some accommodation had not been altogether destroyed, the initiative—now that James was isolated at Rochester—lay with William. Late on the 20th, he finally sent out summons to all the lords in London to meet with him at St James's the next morning. Once they had assembled, he informed them that they had been called together 'to advise the best manner how to pursue the ends of my declaration in calling a free Parliament', and he then left them to consider of it.[3] After squabbling over the choice of lawyers to assist them in their deliberations, the peers settled down on the 22nd to try to resolve the vexed question of how to convene a parliament.[4] But at first they made little progress. There were some who seem to have urged that the prince should claim the crown by right of conquest and then issue the writs, but he had already let it be known that he would not violate his declaration so blatantly.[5] Others suggested that the procedures laid down in the Triennial Act of 1641 might be invoked, but the lawyers were dubious since the Triennial Act of 1664 had omitted all the provisions of its predecessor for bringing a parliament into being in default of royal action.[6] Still hopeful of some agreement with James, Nottingham apparently pressed the assembly to address the king to send out the writs.[7] He spoke for many who favoured, as one observer related, 'making the King

[1] Morrice, II, 366; *Clarendon correspondence*, II, 231.
[2] *Hatton correspondence*, II, 127.
[3] Tindal, XII, 167–8.
[4] Bodl. Rawlinson MSS. A 77, pp. 13–16; Foxcroft, *Halifax*, II, 59. Apparently, a number of lawyers in addition to those finally named were also suggested, among them Heneage Finch. But many objected to him as unfit because of his involvement in the crown's legal proceedings of the mid-1680s (Morrice, II, 385).
[5] Burnet, III, 361–2.
[6] Bodl. Ballard MSS. 45, fo. 22, [R. Sare to A. Charlett], 22 Dec.
[7] Burnet, III, 362.

all the offers in the world that are consistent with Safety and for settling upon the same Basis our Ancestors so long lived under'.[1] The divisions among the peers were only heightened when it was moved that they should all sign the Association agreed upon by William's followers at Exeter. Though he acknowledged the nation's great debt to the prince, Nottingham refused, explaining in a lengthy oration that he believed to do so would be inconsistent with his oath of allegiance to James.[2] Pembroke, Somerset, Maynard, Wharton and all the bishops save Compton also declined to subscribe.[3] A solution seemed as far away as ever, then, when the assembly finally adjourned late that evening.

But James, maladroit to the last, once again overcame the prince's difficulties for him while making the position of constitutionalists like Nottingham increasingly untenable. Early on the 23rd, he took advantage of the deliberately lax mounting of guard by his Dutch escorts to flee, and this time he was not halted. When the news reached London later that day, his supporters were aghast and Archbishop Sancroft, who had at last agreed to attend the consultations at St James's, now decided to continue his abstention.[4] Yet the king's flight finally spurred the lords to action, although unanimity was achieved only after a prolonged debate, fortunately recorded in part not only by Clarendon but also by their chairman Halifax.[5]

The proceedings on the 24th were opened by Lord Berkeley who moved to 'enquire what was become of the King' and suggested that a letter James had left for the Earl of Middleton should be considered. He was seconded by Clarendon and

[1] Bodl. Ballard MSS. 45, fo. 22. See also *Clarendon correspondence*, II, 232–3; Morrice, II, 382–3; HMC Dartmouth, III, 140–1.
[2] Morrice, II, 382–3; BM Add. MSS. 38496, fo. 3, French copy of van Citters' dispatch of 25 Dec./4 Jan.
[3] F. A. J. Mazure, *Histoire de la révolution de 1688 en Angleterre* (Paris, 1825), III, 277–9; HMC Dartmouth, III, 143. Wharton, so Morrice relates, finally agreed to sign the Association (Morrice, II, 385).
[4] *Clarendon correspondence*, II, 233–4.
[5] Althorp Savile MSS., box 4. Unless otherwise noted, the following summary of the debate is drawn from Halifax's notes.

Nottingham, but Mordaunt, Fauconberg and Culpepper spoke against such a step. Had not Godolphin intervened to inform the assembly that he had seen the letter and to assure them 'it would give...no satisfaction', Berkeley's proposal would (in Clarendon's opinion) probably have been carried, but it was now voted down.[1] Lord Paget then rose to propose that the Princess of Orange be declared queen. As soon as she was proclaimed, he pointed out, a parliament could be summoned. His motion was supported by Lord North who declared that the king's withdrawal constituted a 'demise in law', while Lord Montagu suggested, instead, that the procedure embodied in the Exclusion bill to convene the Houses should be adopted. Both these expedients were attacked by Bishop Turner and also by Pembroke, who recommended the convoking of a 'convention' on the precedent of 1660. Clarendon followed by urging that the 184 members who could be returned on those writs which James had issued should assemble and order, in conjunction with the peers, the issue of the remainder. But Mordaunt and Delamere replied by denouncing any who might be chosen in such a fashion. At last, Nottingham rose to address the assembly again. He began by opposing the motion to elevate Mary to the throne speaking, so Clarendon reported, 'with great moderation and tenderness towards the King'.[2] The kingdom, he argued, 'cannot come to have a parliament but by the King', and for this reason he avowed he still 'would treat with the King'. He then closed, as Halifax cryptically recorded, by calling for 'a Guardian or Regent'.

A document in Nottingham's hand found among his own papers provides a fuller insight into the proposals he advocated in his final speech. In this draft, which he had probably prepared the previous day, Nottingham set down under the following heads the terms of the political settlement he favoured at this juncture:

[1] *Clarendon correspondence*, II, 234–5; Foxcroft, *Halifax*, II, 59.
[2] *Clarendon correspondence*, II, 234–5.

1. That all laws civil or Ecclesiastical be ratified and established.

2. That all the late violations of the laws and the pretences of prerogative and power by which they have been effected shall be declared void.

3. That notorious offenders be brought to condign punishment by due course of law or as shall be adjudged by Parliament.

4. That the Prince of Orange shall have the sole disposal and ordering of all forces by sea and land.

5. The disposal and nomination of all officers civil and military, and all the preferments in the Church to which the King had a right.

6. That the determination of the legitimacy or illegitimacy of the Prince of Wales be left to the Parliament and He be brought back into England.

7. That such determination shall be confirmed by the King's assent to an act of Parliament.

8. That the Prince of Orange be garanty for the performance of all or so many of the precedent articles as shall be desired by a free parliament.

9. In case the King shall agree to these proposals, that for a full security for the performance of them, the Lords and Commons shall take the oath of allegiance at their entrance into parliament upon this express condition to be declared by the King in case of non-performance of his part the Lords and Commons shall be absolved from all the obligations of the oath.

10. And that the King will hearken to the advice of his parliament in such other matters as shall be reasonable for the security of the Protestant religion and the rights, laws, and liberties of the subject.

11. That the King will return to his people and forthwith call a free parliament.

12. That so much of the public revenue as shall be necessary for the Public service be appropriated thereunto and the Prince of Orange or such as he shall appoint to direct the issuing of it.

13. That parliament shall be assembled every year and sit for thirty days under the like limitations and methods as were directed by the Triennial Bill.[1]

However great the restriction of James's powers, Nottingham's plan would still recognize him as king. For this reason, it proved unpalatable to the majority of the peers. At length, a compromise of sorts was reached when it was decided that both the problem of James's status and that of the Prince of Wales's legitimacy should

---

[1] LRO, Finch MSS., Political papers 77. See also Boyer, *History of King William III*, I, pt. II, 319.

69

be left to the consideration of a convention to be summoned by circular letters issued by the prince. In the interim, William would be asked to assume direction of civil and military affairs.[1] From Nottingham's point of view, this solution had the great advantage of leaving open any decision on the crucial question of whether or not James's right to the crown had lapsed. Thus he consented to serve on a committee appointed to draw up the addresses embodying the resolutions of the peers.[2] Four days later, after an assembly composed of members of Charles II's parliaments as well as the Lord Mayor, Aldermen and fifty Common Councillors of London had seconded the address of the lords, William formally accepted the administration of the kingdom for the time being.[3]

The peers' deliberations had been marked by a wide diversity of opinion. But perhaps the most basic division which emerged from their debates was that separating those who wished to preserve a limited but hereditary monarchy (or at least its traditional forms) from those who were prepared to override precedent and custom either on the grounds of necessity or for more doctrinaire reasons. Yet this broad distinction between 'conservatives' and 'revolutionaries' should not cloak the substantial differences within each of these groups. Among the conservatives were numbered not only the advocates of James's recall but also the supporters of a regency.[4] Then, too, there were those who believed that James had disabled himself by flight and that his heir, the Princess of Orange, should be proclaimed in his stead. Dis-

---

[1] E. M. Thompson, 'Correspondence of Admiral Herbert', p. 535. In asserting that William had authorized his supporters to propose the calling of a convention, Miss Pinkham seems to have misconstrued the report of van Citters which she cites for this statement (Pinkham, *Respectable revolution*, p. 207 and n. 8; BM Add. MSS. 38496, fo. 4).

[2] Foxcroft, *Halifax*, II, 59. [3] Pinkham, *Respectable revolution*, pp. 208–10.

[4] BM Add. MSS. 38496, fo. 7, French copy of van Citters' report of 1/11 Jan. I am greatly indebted in the following discussion of political opinion on the eve of the Convention to Dr A. Simpson's treatment of this question in his Oxford D.Phil. dissertation of 1939, 'The Convention Parliament 1688–1689', ch. II. Above all, he has convincingly demonstrated that for a number of the bishops and some lay peers who eventually supported a regency, hopes of James's restoration were not—as Sir Keith Feiling had asserted—'dead and buried' (Feiling, *Tory party*, p. 248).

crepancies of opinion were also to develop among the revolutionaries, but in the weeks before the Convention and during its first meetings the conservatives' lack of unanimity was to prove decisive.

Relatively little is known in detail about the composition of the wing that favoured the king's recall. It included not only peers such as Ailesbury whose actions were motivated by a deep sense of personal loyalty, but also those foremost exponents of the doctrine of passive obedience—the bishops, along with nobles of Clarendon's stripe.[1] James's second flight had gravely weakened the position of this group, while Sancroft's refusal to 'declare himself' had deprived them of a valuable rallying point. But perhaps their worst handicap was the pervasive distrust of the king. It was probably for this reason that Bishop Turner, the most capable of the prelates loyal to James, had begun to toy with the proposal of a regency as early as 17 December, and by mid-January most of his brethren had been won round to his view that for the time being it would be futile to contend for a restoration.[2] Yet their decision to support the establishment of a regency should not be misconstrued as an abandonment of their hopes of a resumption. What Turner and some of the other bishops envisaged was only a 'Regency *pro tempore*' which would leave 'a door still open for Treating and Accomodating' with James.[3]

Promotion of plans for a regency was not, however, confined to those who favoured the king's reinstatement in power. To a body of influential peers headed by Nottingham, a scheme which, while recognizing the validity of James's title, would divest him of the exercise of the royal powers he had so greatly abused, appeared to be the most desirable solution of the constitutional havoc left in his wake. It is difficult to distinguish the members of

[1] *Memoirs of Ailesbury*, I, 218, 223, 229–30, and *passim*; Bodl. Clarendon MSS. 90, fos. 14–15, Clarendon to the Princess of Orange, [Jan. 1689].
[2] Dalrymple, II, app. II, 336; Bodl. Rawlinson MSS. D 836, fos. 114–15; Bodl. Tanner MSS. 28, fos. 318–19, Turner to Sancroft, 11 Jan.; Morrice, II, 400, 415, 424, 430–1, 433–4; *Diary of Evelyn*, IV, 614; *Clarendon correspondence*, II, 252; Burnet, III, 374–5.
[3] Bodl. Rawlinson MSS. D 836, fos. 104–5.

this group, apart from Nottingham and Pembroke, from the lords who viewed a regency only as a temporary expedient, save by their reactions to the decisions of the Convention. Yet both Turner's own testimony and the relatively small number of non-jurors among the proponents of a regency in the upper House strongly suggest that the majority of them did not share the secret reservations of the Bishop of Ely, Clarendon, and others.[1] It was for this band of peers that Nottingham would speak in opposing the elevation of either the princess or the prince to the throne.

Nottingham's own scruples stemmed neither from a belief in passive obedience nor from personal devotion to the king. His hostility to James's policies dated from the first year of the reign, and only the obligation which he felt his oath of allegiance imposed upon him had prevented his joining in the invitation to William. Moreover, unlike Clarendon and some of the bishops, he had never been convinced that parliament was incapable of modifying the succession or dissolving the oaths by which he, as a private person, was bound.[2] Rather, his objections were primarily legal and constitutional in character. Above all, what he wished to avoid was a formal denial of James's right to the crown for, as he was to emphasize during the Convention, he feared that such a step would shake the foundations of the monarchy itself. Thus, just as Montagu had harked back on 24 December to projects current during the Exclusion controversy, so Nottingham during the same debate had revived the plan for a regency that he and his father had favoured at that time. No doubt, he would have preferred that the king accept this proposal, but he was apparently prepared to support its imposition by parliament without his consent.

None the less, there were still others among the conservatives who, though firmly opposed to the unprecedented step of declaring the throne vacant, were also dubious about the virtues of a regency. Indeed, the debates of the 24th had revealed that a number of

<hr>

[1] Bodl. Rawlinson MSS. D 836, fos. 104–5, 115.   [2] Above, p. 22.

peers thought the most plausible resolution of the constitutional impasse was to declare Mary, as James's heir, queen. And under the capable leadership of the Earl of Danby, who arrived in London from the north on 26 December, this group was to play a vital role in the Convention.[1]

As the date fixed for the Convention's meeting approached, the conservatives may well have been apprehensive of defeat. Though William scrupulously refrained from any attempt to influence the course of the elections, it was commonly reported that he and Mary would be made king and queen.[2] But Nottingham was not prepared to concede the question without at least a trial of strength. On 16 January he asked Rochester to tell Clarendon that he 'was resolved to support the King's cause in the Convention, and was very desirous the Archbishop should come thither; and, therefore, desired [Clarendon] to endeavour to prevail with him'.[3] Although Clarendon was unable to move Sancroft to action, Nottingham still estimated that conservative sentiment would be stronger in the upper House.[4] Thus when the Convention opened on 22 January, Sir Thomas Clarges—'upon concert with lord Nottingham and Mr Finch'—moved the Commons to put off consideration of the state of the nation on the grounds that not all its members had yet arrived.[5] A postponement until the 28th was agreed to, but this move by Nottingham to enable the peers to exert their presumably more conservative influence upon the subsequent debates of the lower House was frustrated by William's adherents among the peers, chief of whom now was Halifax— the Speaker *pro tempore* of the Lords. When Halifax learned of the

[1] Bodl. Ballard MSS. 45, fo. 24, [R. Sare to A. Charlett], 21 Jan.; Bodl. Clarendon MSS. 90, fo. 12; Browning, *Osborne*, I, 420–3.
[2] *Clarendon correspondence*, II, 248; Pinkham, *Respectable revolution*, p. 221.
[3] *Clarendon correspondence*, II, 248. Nottingham was also pressing Hatton to come to London in time for the session (BM Add. MSS. 29594, fo. 141).
[4] Sancroft's position, as Dr Simpson has demonstrated, has been misconstrued by all those who relied on his biographer D'Oyly. For his reconstruction of Sancroft's views, see Simpson, 'The Convention parliament', pp. 67–72 and app. E.
[5] *Clarendon correspondence*, II, 252–3; *PH*, v, 34–5; Morrice, II, 437.

Common's decision, he bluntly told his old friend Clarges on the 23rd 'that it was very strange that he made such a motion; that it was just so much time lost; for the Lords should not proceed upon any public business, till they saw what the Commons did'.[1] Forewarned in this fashion by Halifax, Clarges hastened to urge Clarendon 'to move my lord Nottingham tomorrow, that the lords might enter with all speed upon the public business of the kingdom'.[2] But when Clarendon arrived at Westminster on the morning of the 24th, he found that Nottingham had gone hunting. So it was not until the 25th that the conservatives moved the House to proceed immediately to an examination of the state of the nation. Nottingham supported the motion at length, but it was strenuously opposed by Halifax, Devonshire and Winchester, with the result that the House was adjourned until the 29th.[3]

The belief alike of conservatives and revolutionaries that William's 'Interest in the house of Commons was better than in the house of Lords' was vindicated by the events of the 28th.[4] Only Finch (who proposed a regency), Clarges, Sir Christopher Musgrave and Lord Fanshawe spoke in opposition to the majority, and without dividing the Commons adopted the resolution

that king James the Second, having endeavoured to subvert the Constitution of the Kingdom, by breaking the original Contract between king and people, and by the advice of Jesuits and other wicked persons, having violated the fundamental Laws, and having withdrawn himself out of this Kingdom has abdicated the Government, and that the throne is thereby become vacant.[5]

---

[1] *Clarendon correspondence*, II, 253.
[2] *Ibid.*
[3] *Ibid.* p. 254; A. Simpson, 'Notes of a Noble Lord', *EHR*, LII (1937), 92.
[4] FSL, v.b. 150, fo. 13.
[5] A number of reports of this debate state that Finch spoke for James's recall (FSL, Newdigate newsletters, 1965, 19 Jan.; Bodl. Rawlinson MSS., D 1079, fo. 2). Indeed, a number of his fellow Commoners seem to have inferred that he favoured the king's return, but Finch explicitly disavowed any such intent in his third speech of the 28th (*PH*, v, 49; BM Add. MSS. 38496, fo. 13, French copy of van Citters' dispatch of 29 Jan./8 Feb.).

Once the Commons' vote was formally communicated to the Lords on the 29th, they went into Committee of the Whole, with Danby in the Chair, to consider of it.[1]

Clarendon was the first to speak to the Commons' resolution. His denunciation of the notion of abdication was followed by a scathing exposure from Bishop Turner of the inconsistencies of the lower House's vote which he compared to an 'accumulative' charge of treason. Delamere, Mordaunt and Montagu retorted by recalling the threat James's measures had posed to the nation's liberties. Then Nottingham rose for the first time to address the Lords.[2] Conceding for the sake of argument the 'king to have done all that is suggested', Nottingham contended—with copious citation of statute and precedent—that the Commons' resolution was contrary to the law of the land. That the king had in any way 'forfeited' his right to the crown he vigorously denied on the grounds that parliament was incapable of judging him. To assert that the Houses could do so, he pointed out, was tantamount to making them the supreme power—a revolutionary step. Neither, he argued, could there be said to have been a 'cession' of the crown, for James's first flight had failed and his second withdrawal had been prompted by fears for his own safety. 'Lett us not', he pleaded, 'justify his fears by after acts'. Even had there been a 'cession' of the English crown, Nottingham reminded his listeners that such an explanation might not extend to James's Scottish crown. He then went on to attack the theory that there had been a 'demise'. On the one hand, the king still lived. On the other, a 'demise' implied that the grant of the revenue for life to James had expired. If so, this was a serious matter since the Convention did not have the power to vote it anew, and this would be

---

[1] A hitherto unnoticed account of their proceedings in Danby's hand, in BM Egerton MSS. 3345, bundle 3, provides a far more detailed record of their deliberations than any other source. Unless otherwise indicated, the following summary is based on these notes.

[2] Nottingham's initial speech is the longest recorded by Danby whose summary is strikingly similar to the notes Nottingham prepared for his speech (LRO, Finch MSS., Political papers 78). The following account draws on both documents.

most inconvenient both for William and the kingdom. Finally, Nottingham observed that if the theory of a 'demise' were to be accepted, it would be necessary to investigate the Prince of Wales's legitimacy in order to ascertain who was James's rightful heir. And though he did not think that this question was 'a matter that will obstruct your final resolution', it was one 'which will and must in decency obstruct your methods to that final resolution. For should you not consider the pretences for him, you will furnish the world with a better and perhaps more probable arguement for his legitimacy than as yet they have produced.'

Nottingham's speech provoked several rejoinders, but the most pertinent came from Halifax who challenged Nottingham and others who disputed the Commons' resolution 'to shew either that there is no danger or to shew a Remedy'. To this, Rochester replied by suggesting that there was a solution to the constitutional problem which did not involve the extreme step of declaring the throne vacant. Since it was agreed that James was not fit to govern, he moved that a regency be established. But Halifax countered that such an arrangement, since it would only be temporary, would arouse 'Many Expectations of [the] King's return to Government'. His criticism hit home, for Turner's and his brethren's intent in supporting this proposal was not unsuspected.[1] However, either as a desperate expedient or because he was resigned to James's permanent exclusion from power, Rochester now amended his motion to a regency 'during the King's life'.[2] This proposal was then seconded by Pembroke who referred to the difficulty many would have to take the oaths to a new monarch as 'right and Lawfull'.

[1] *Clarendon correspondence*, II, 244; Morrice, II, 400, 424, 433–4.
[2] The MSS. minutes of the Lords confirm that the motion read 'during the life of the said King James' only after amendment (*HMC House of Lords*, 1689–90, p. 14). As Turner later related, 'the onely point of a Regency during the King's Life, a point urged by some on our side while the rest of us at last gave Our Consents to it, is hardly to be Defended; I mainly opposed it in private, as liable to as great objections as the Deposing, but it was propos'd only to amuse and gaine time and playd upp by us Uppon Assurance enough that it would not be Accepted' (Bodl. Rawlinson MSS. D836, fo. 114).

With the debate now centred on the proposal for a regency for life, Nottingham took the floor again to argue that such a scheme would be the best solution to the awkward constitutional and political situation.[1] On the one hand, a disjunction of power and title, he maintained, 'comes nearest to the formes of our law'. Similar measures, he observed, were resorted to during royal minorities or when an heir to an estate was a 'lunatick'. On the other hand, a regency would avoid the practical inconveniences of other courses; the oaths would remain in force, the question of the Prince of Wales's legitimacy need not be considered, and the revenue would not be lost. Nevertheless, the practicality of Nottingham's plan to make 'the Prince of Orange Custos Regni with the administration of royal powers uncontrollably by [James] during the said King's life' was sharply questioned by Halifax and Danby.[2] But their criticisms were touched upon only in passing by Nottingham in the last speech of the debate recorded by Danby. Rather, Nottingham once again concentrated on setting forth the dangerous consequences of acceptance of the Commons' resolution, stressing that his concern was 'not for the monarch but the Monarchy, not the persons but things'. However, a majority of the House was still not convinced that a regency would be 'the best and safest way to preserve the Protestant Religion and the laws of the kingdom'. When the question was put, the 'Not Contents' carried it by three voices.[3]

Though the proposal of a regency for life had been rejected, it had failed of approval only because Danby and others who favoured Mary's claims had joined with those who advocated the crowning of William in opposition against it.[4] None the less, the

---

[1] The following summaries of Nottingham's second and third speeches are based upon his own notes and drafts in LRO, Finch MSS., Political papers 78 and 150, and upon Danby's notes.

[2] LRO, Finch MSS., Political papers 150; Browning, *Osborne*, I, 426–7.

[3] *HMC House of Lords*, 1689–90, pp. 14–15.
   Feiling, *Tory party*, p. 252.

notion that the throne was, or could be, vacant was equally abhorrent to the 'Maryites'. Thus during the following days, they acted with the adherents of a regency in waging a desperate rearguard struggle against approval of the lower House's vote. On 30 and 31 January, the peers again debated its terms and finally agreed, without dividing, to replace 'abdicated' with 'deserted'— a term whose constitutional implications were somewhat more restricted. Further, with the votes of the 'Maryites' providing the margin of victory, an attempt to substitute an immediate declaration of William and Mary as king and queen for the assertion of a 'vacancy' was lost on the previous question by a vote of 52 to 47. Then the 'vacancy' clause itself was defeated by a majority of fourteen.[1]

However, the inability of the proponents of a regency to come to any agreement with the flying squadron led by Danby as to how the government should be reconstituted was to prove fatal. As Sir Richard Temple observed on 2 February when the Commons took up the upper House's amendments, 'the lords have left out the whole conclusion in the matter'.[2] Fearful of any possibility that James might be restored, the lower House refused, nemine contradicente, to accept any alterations.[3] But despite the Commons' insistence on their original wording, a majority in the Lords could still be mustered against it. Two days later, 'abdication' and 'vacancy' were rejected once more, and a committee headed by Nottingham was named to draw up the reasons of the Lords' disagreement for presentation to the Commons.[4] Despite this conservative victory, there had been a marked revulsion in the upper House when it appeared that a letter from James which Preston had brought to its attention on the 4th was countersigned by the detested Melfort.[5] Moreover, the committee's statement, which Nottingham reported to the House on the 5th, for the first time hinted that some supporters of a regency

[1] HMC House of Lords, 1689–90, pp. 15–17.   [2] PH, v, 61.
[3] Grey, IX, 46–9; CJ, x, 18.   [4] LJ, XIV, 116–17.
[5] Simpson, 'Notes of a Noble Lord', p. 93.

might be prepared to acquiesce in an assertion of Mary's right to the crown. No concessions were made concerning the objectionable phrases, but the influence of Danby and his ally Bishop Compton was evident in its final clause which stated that, even if the Commons' conclusions with regard to James were correct, 'Allegiance is due to such Person as the Right of Succession does belong to.'[1] In turn, the suggestion that the king's heir, presumably the Princess of Orange, might be crowned in his stead produced the first real division in the Commons. But even with the aid of the few supporters of a regency, Mary's adherents in the lower House were badly outnumbered, and so once again the 'vacancy' clause was sustained.[2]

Complete deadlock had now been reached between the Houses; external pressure, not oratory, was to break it. It was obvious to all both in and out of parliament that it was necessary to establish some form of government without delay.[3] And William was now ready to speak his own mind. At a private gathering on the evening of 3 February attended by Halifax, Shrewsbury, Danby and several other peers, William made it clear he would accept neither the office of regent nor the role of prince consort to Mary.[4] He would be content to be crowned jointly with his wife only if the administration of the government were placed in his hands for his lifetime. He was willing, however, to recognize Princess Anne's claims to the extent that her heirs might be preferred in the succession to any children he might have by a second wife.[5] When it became clear during the next few days that Anne would waive temporarily her rights should

---

[1] LJ, XIV, 117; Browning, Osborne, I, 428. To the 'Maryites', this allusion to the heir to the throne was unmistakable. Whether Nottingham accepted it merely as a constitutional truism—since he had argued previously that the Prince of Wales's claims could not be ignored if the Convention did take it upon itself to determine the issue of the succession—or as a recognition of Mary is not clear.

[2] CJ, X, 19–20; Grey, IX, 53–65; Browning, Osborne, I, 428–9, and III, 393–4; Feiling, Tory party, p. 253.

[3] Ibid. p. 254.

[4] Pinkham, Respectable revolution, pp. 233–4 and n. 57. See also Spencer House 'Journals' in Foxcroft, Halifax, II, 203.   [5] Burnet, III, 395–6.

Mary die before William, the final obstacle to such a disposition of the crown was removed.[1]

Although the peers' decision was foreclosed in this fashion by those taken outside parliament, they still adhered to the traditional forms of procedure. On the morning of the 6th, they proceeded to choose their representatives, among them Nottingham, to the 'free conference' arranged with the Commons.[2] But the confrontation of the delegates of the two Houses was curiously inconclusive. For the most part, the arguments of the Lords' debate of 29 January and of the conference of 5 February were merely rehearsed once more, though Nottingham did avow that he was now prepared to admit that a king could 'abdicate' by 'implicit acts, contrary to the kingly office'.[3] Full agreement was impossible since the Commons' managers were unwilling to answer the question posed by Nottingham (and reiterated by Rochester and Clarendon) as to whether the vacancy in the throne was meant to extend only to James or to his heirs as well, while the peers were almost as reticent when the Commoners demanded to know who did occupy the throne if it were not now vacant. None the less, Pembroke did strongly hint at Mary while Nottingham indicated that he, too, might be prepared to accept her accession.[4]

Agitated debate broke out in the Lords after their managers returned from the conference to report its failure. 'All was said by the Lords on one side that could be thought of against agreeing with the Commons and to support the succession.'[5] Nottingham,

---

[1] Anne does not seem to have publicly committed herself before the sixth when Lords Dorset and Churchill carried a message from her to the Houses *during* the free conference which indicated that she would waive her rights during William's life (FSL, Newdigate newsletters, 1971, 7 Feb.; Bodl. Rawlinson MSS. D 1079, fo. 13).

[2] *LJ*, xiv, 118.

[3] *PH*, v, 66–108, esp. p. 82; *HMC House of Lords*, 1689–90, pp. 17–18.

[4] *PH*, v, 90, 106. Nottingham's words were, 'If you mean by "Abdication and Vacancy" only that the King has left the government, and it is devolved upon the next successor, that may perhaps satisfy my lords, and we may agree upon some settlement.—I must confess any government is better than none; but I earnestly desire we may enjoy our ancient constitution.' [5] Simpson, 'Notes of a Noble Lord', p. 94.

in particular, strongly denounced Halifax's contention that 'necessity' demanded the abrogation of James's title, but his efforts availed little for tempers were running high. Finally, nothing could be heard but shouts for 'the Question, the Question'.[1] When the House at last divided, it was carried by at least fifteen votes to abandon their amendments.[2] Then, shortly after 4 p.m., the Marquess of Winchester rose to move that the prince and princess be declared king and queen. Nottingham, Clarendon and Rochester once again warned that to take this step would be to render the crown elective, but when the question was put they did not see fit to divide the House.[3]

The surprisingly large majority in the upper House on the 6th in favour of agreement with the Commons appears to have been the result of several developments. To begin with, there was William's statement of his wishes and Anne's acquiescence in them. Furthermore, the ranks of the revolutionaries had been enlarged, through threats and cajolery, by several peers who had not previously attended the Convention.[4] Finally, at least ten members who had heretofore supported the Lords' amendments either absented themselves altogether on the 6th or withdrew before the question was put.[5] The abstention of many of these peers was not accidental; indeed, it seems to have been advised by Nottingham himself. As early as the debate of 29 January, he had indicated that he would feel obliged to obey a king *de facto*, and in succeeding debates he had reiterated this point.[6] Now, as his close friend Weymouth later related, Nottingham 'prevailed with him and

---

[1] *Ibid.; Clarendon correspondence*, II, 261.
[2] *HMC House of Lords*, 1689–90, p. 18. Thirty-eight peers formally dissented from the upper House's vote (*LJ*, XIV, 119). Nottingham had also prepared a protest, but a number of those who met the morning of the 7th to enter their dissents in the Journal wished to amend his draft while others were for omitting it altogether. The latter course was eventually adopted, as Clarendon noted, in the hope 'thereby to gain the more of our companions to subscribe with us' (Simpson, 'Notes of a Noble Lord', pp. 95–6).
[3] *Clarendon correspondence*, II, 261; Morrice, II, 459–61.
[4] *Clarendon correspondence*, II, 261.
[5] *Ibid.*; Simpson, 'Notes of a Noble Lord', pp. 94–5.   [6] Burnet, III, 378.

some more to stay away, that the other side might carry the question; for fear of a civil war, if they had lost it'.[1]

Once the Lords has resolved to offer the crown to William and Mary, Nottingham lost little time in revealing his intention to comply with their vote. He declared to the House, so Danby told Reresby, 'that he had not consented in the least to this change, but had opposed the Prince his accession to the crown, not believing it legall, but that since he was ther, and that he must now owe and expect his protection from him as king *de facto*, he thought it just and lawfull to swear allegiance to him'.[2] He continued, however, by pointing out that the oaths sworn to a king who claimed the crown of right would be scrupled by many in the new reign, and for this reason he urged the Lords to draw up new ones. Halifax opposed this proposal because it would cast doubts on the titles of the new sovereigns, but Danby intervened to support Nottingham's suggestion with the result that it was approved without a division.[3] On the 7th, the new oaths, drafted by a committee headed by Nottingham, were carried and incorporated in the Declaration of Right which, with the crown, was presented to William and Mary on 13 February.[4]

In the coming months, Nottingham's loyalty to the settlement he had so vocally resisted was often to be aspersed, but there can be no doubt of the sincerity of the pledge that he made in the presence of his fellow peers on the 6th. Certainly, when Clarendon proposed a concerted withdrawal from the Lords to those who had opposed the grant of the crown, Nottingham as well as Pembroke strongly dissented. 'We must support the government as well as we can', he told Clarendon; 'the lords can never answer

---

[1] Dartmouth's note at *ibid.* pp. 404–5, and see also p. 398 n.; *The Letters of Rachel Lady Russell*, ed. Lord John Russell (London, 1853), I, 269.

[2] *Memoirs of Sir John Reresby*, ed. A. Browning (Glasgow, 1936), pp. 558–9.

[3] Bodl. Ballard MSS. 45, fo. 27a; *Clarendon correspondence*, II, 261; *Memoirs of Reresby*, 558–9.

[4] *LJ*, XIV, 119–20; *HMC House of Lords*, 1689–90, p. 29; *Memoirs of Ailesbury*, I, 234. The actual drafting of the new oaths, according to Ailesbury, was done by Bishop White of Peterborough.

it if they leave the House.'[1] In short, the tale later told by Burnet, that Nottingham confided in him sometime before the 6th that 'though he could not argue nor vote, but according to the scheme and principles he had concerning our laws and constitution, yet he should not be sorry to see his side out voted', bears the earmarks of authenticity.[2]

Nottingham's readiness to accept the new order did not pass unnoticed by William. The new king, a 'Trimmer' by preference, had no mind to be governed by anyone, least of all by the Whigs, many of whom he suspected of being 'commonwealthmen'.[3] This bias, as well as his awareness of the need to consolidate support for his rule, was reflected in the partisan balance he attempted to achieve in the new administration. While the claims of those who had favoured his elevation to the throne were acknowledged by the appointment of Shrewsbury as first Principal Secretary, of Halifax as Lord Privy Seal, and of Lord Mordaunt, Lord Delamere, Sir Henry Capel, Richard Hampden and William Sacheverell to the Treasury and Admiralty Commissions, Godolphin was also made a member of the Treasury Board and Danby reluctantly accepted the Lord Presidency. Moreover on 14 February Nottingham—whom William respected as an 'honest man' despite his advocacy of a regency—was named to the Privy Council.[4] Three weeks later, his acceptance of the second Principal Secretaryship of State was also announced.[5]

It has been conjectured that Nottingham's appointment as Secretary was the outcome of a 'bargain' struck between the earl and William before 6 February, but there is no evidence to

[1] Simpson, 'Notes of a Noble Lord', p. 97. See also BM Add. MSS. 19253, diary of Lord Chesterfield, for an account of Nottingham's refusal sometime after William's coronation in April to accept a commission from James which named him, Weymouth, Chesterfield and Sancroft as regents of the kingdom in his absence.

[2] Burnet, III, 378.

[3] Foxcroft, *Halifax*, II, 65 and n. 2, 203.

[4] *The London Gazette*, no. 2428; Foxcroft, *Halifax*, II, 202. Although Nottingham was not present at the Privy Council's first meeting, he took his place at the Board when next it assembled on the 16th (PRO, PC 2/73, pp. 1, 4).

[5] *The London Gazette*, no. 2433.

support such a hypothesis which can not be more plausibly related to Nottingham's concern to minimize the constitutional consequences of any parliamentary action while also providing for some practicable form of government.[1] Rather, it would seem that the offer made to him of a responsible post in the new régime was the product of Halifax's recommendation and the king's own desire to secure the support of so respected a leader of the 'Church party'.[2] In any event, the significance of Nottingham's appointment can hardly be overestimated.[3] Not merely were a number of prominent Whig contenders for the Secretaryship disappointed, but also William's readiness to employ him eased the deepseated fears of many that the king's Calvinist propensities and the advice of his more extreme partisans might result in the exclusion of the 'Church party' from power and an attack on the Anglican establishment.[4] Moreover, Nottingham's sponsorship of the new oaths and the willingness he demonstrated to take office under William was an example calculated to bring those who had joined in or sympathized with his opposition to the grant of the crown to accept and support the new government.[5] It was on

---

[1] Cf. Feiling, *Tory party*, pp. 260–1. Indeed, as late as 2 Feb. Nottingham had told Dyckvelt (then acting as one of the prince's advisers on strategy) that he could not accept the theory that the throne was vacant (*Journaal van Constantijn Huygens*, 1, 80).

[2] Halifax claimed the credit for Nottingham's appointment, but he also told Reresby that William himself had 'had a mind [he] should be in business' (*Memoirs of Reresby*, p. 564). Burnet also seems to have urged his employment, along with the selection of Heneage Finch as Lord Chancellor of Ireland (BM Add. MSS. 32681, fos. 317–18). The delay in Nottingham's selection seems to have stemmed from a conflict of intentions. Nottingham would have preferred a seat on the Treasury Board, William wanted to make him first Commissioner of the Great Seal or possibly even Lord Chancellor, Nottingham finally agreed to serve instead in the Secretaryship which Danby had earlier declined (Foxcroft, *Halifax*, II, 205; Burnet, IV, 4; Boyer, *History of King William III*, II, 2; Browning, *Osborne*, I, 439, 445).

[3] Terriesi, the Florentine envoy, believed his influence in the new government might well rival that of his colleagues Shrewsbury, Halifax and Danby (BM Add. MSS. 25377, fo. 381, 8/18 March).

[4] For the frustrated ambitions of Lord Montagu and Richard Hampden, see *HMC Buccleuch–Whitehall*, I, 349; Foxcroft, *Halifax*, II, 204 and n. 10; Devonshire House 'Notebook' *sub* 'Montague Lord'.

[5] For the invocation of Nottingham's name and views as a justification for taking the oaths, see *A vindication of those who have taken the new Oath of Allegiance to King William and Queen Mary* (London, 1689), pp. 9–10; Bodl. Ballard MSS. 3, fo. 55, W. Wake to

these grounds that Burnet observed, in the original draft of his *History*, 'I reckon I do not exceed the severe rules of history when I say that Nottingham's being in the ministry, together with the effects that it had, first preserved the church and then the crown.'[1]

A. Charlett, 22 May [1689]. See also G. M. Straka, *Anglican reaction to the Revolution of 1688* (Madison, Wisc., 1962), *passim*.

[1] *Supplement to Burnet's history*, pp. 314–15.

CHAPTER 6

THE CONTEST FOR THE
KING'S FAVOUR

1689–90

When Nottingham accepted the Seals on 5 March 1689, many of the issues attendant upon the Revolution remained to be resolved. Among the outstanding problems facing the new rulers, their ministers, and the Convention (which by its own act had now constituted itself a parliament) was what revenue was to be settled upon the crown, what penalties were to be meted out to those implicated in James's measures, and what form the religious settlement was to take. Still to be determined, too, was the question of whether William's 'balanced' ministry would work together and whether the most prominent of the English ministers—Shrewsbury, Halifax, Danby (made Marquess of Carmarthen in April), and Nottingham—could 'live well' with one another.[1] Whatever William's expectations on this score, Nottingham does not seem to have been very optimistic. Consequently, he was anxious to preserve his own freedom of action, at least in parliamentary proceedings. As he told William when he took the Secretaryship, 'he foresaw that there were many steps yet to be made in which he would oppose that which would be pretended to be his service; but he would follow his own sense of things in parliament though he would be guided by the king's sense out of it'.[2]

The first test of the new administration came over the terms of

---

[1] These four are referred to as the leading English members of the administration in BM Add. MSS. 25377, fo. 381, Terriesi's report of 8/18 March 1689; Luttrell, I, 568; HMC Roxburghe, Etc., p. 118.
[2] Supplement to Burnet's history, p. 315. See also Foxcroft, Halifax, II, 206.

86

the religious settlement. And here Nottingham, as a long-time advocate of Anglican-Dissenting reconciliation as well as a trusted spokesman of the Church party, had a key role to play. Indeed, even before he took office, he had become engrossed in the preparation of proposals for both comprehension and toleration, in conjunction with the leading London clergy (Sharp, Tillotson, Tenison, Patrick, Fowler and Stillingfleet) and some of the bishops.[1] The fruits of their labours were two separate bills, the first a measure for toleration which Nottingham introduced in the Lords on 28 February, the second a measure for comprehension which he laid before the upper House on 11 March.[2] The former was distinguished only by minor changes from its predecessor of 1680, but the latter looked back not only to the Comprehension bill of 1680 but also to the Wilkins proposals of 1668 and the Worcester House Declaration of 1660.[3] On 14 March both bills were read a second time and were then assigned to a select committee headed by Nottingham.[4]

To this point, Nottingham's measures had encountered little opposition, and support for them, despite some misgivings, had been forthcoming from most of the bishops still attending the House.[5] None the less, the prospects for a religious accommodation were hardly as auspicious as they had been the previous spring. It was not merely that James's ouster had removed the Catholic threat; it was also that the accession of the Calvinist William had divided the Anglican clergy over the issue of allegiance while encouraging the dissenters to seek greater concessions than they had formerly thought possible. This was

---

[1] S. Patrick, The auto-biography of Symon Patrick (Oxford, 1839), p. 141; LRO, Finch MSS., Political papers 84; HMC Finch, III, 194; Bodl. Ballard MSS. 45, fo. 48, undated newsletter to A. Charlett, c. 15 March.

[2] LJ, XIV, 134, 145.

[3] R. Thomas, 'Comprehension and Indulgence', in From uniformity to unity 1662–1962, ed. O. Chadwick and G. Nuttall (London, 1962), pp. 245–6.

[4] LJ, XIV, 147–8.

[5] BM Add. MSS. 36707, fo. 59, [A. M.] to James Harrington, 28 Feb.; Lancashire Record Office, Kenyon MSS., W. Banks to R. Kenyon, 28 Feb.; Morrice, II, 488.

evident in Nonconformist reaction to the Lords' Comprehension bill. Roger Morrice complained (not altogether justifiably) that it was less generous than the scheme Nottingham had sponsored in 1680, while one of Dr Smallridge's correspondents claimed that 'the dissenters dislike the whole'.[1] Moreover, as a memorandum drafted by Lord Wharton early in March makes clear, comprehension seemed to many dissenters to be secondary to securing the repeal of that section of the Test Act which obliged all prospective officeholders to receive the sacrament under Anglican auspices.[2] No sooner, then, had the Toleration and Comprehension bills been committed by the Lords than they were moved to appoint a committee to devise an alternative to the sacramental test. This proposal was carried on 15 March, but only over strong opposition.[3] It was at this juncture that William himself intervened. Without consulting any of his English advisers save the elder Hampden, the king summoned the Houses on 16 March to announce that he favoured the removal of the sacramental test and 'the Admission of all Protestants that are willing and able to serve'.[4]

However, the dilution of the Anglican monopoly on office and place was no part of any religious settlement that Nottingham had envisaged and not even royal endorsement of a revision of the Test Act could sway him. Exercising that freedom of action in parliament which he had reserved to himself upon taking office, Nottingham joined Danby, Devonshire and other Anglican peers in attacking a motion for the repeal of the sacramental test that was made in committee of the whole on the 21st. He maintained, so one observer reported,

---

[1] Morrice, II, 498; Bodl. Ballard MSS. 39, fo. 31, 14 March. See also the objections raised by [John Humfrey], *King William's Toleration* (London, 1689), p. 20.

[2] Bodl. Carte MSS. 81, fo. 752. See also Bodl. Ballard MSS. 45, fo. 36, newsletter to A. Charlett, 16 April.

[3] G. Every, *The high church party 1688–1718* (London, 1956), p. 33.

[4] *LJ*, XIV, 150; Burnet, IV, 12–13; Devonshire House 'Notebook' *sub* 'Hambden Senior'. Wharton's memo, cited above, n. 2, is endorsed 'to be discoursed with Mr Hampden'.

that since our Religion is the Established Religion he thinks it impracticable and Dangerous to admitt any kind of Dissenters in to any share of the Government and Desired leave to give two instances to Confirme what he said. The first was that of Holland where only the Synod of Dort men Injoy places of power and Authority. The second was that of Dantzick which Government or free town at first consisted of Calvinists but by permitting a *single* Lutheran to be put into an office he so improved the Interest of his party that a change of that Government soon followed and became Lutheran and is so now.[1]

Such appeals to interest and fear proved sufficient; on the 21st and again on the 23rd, the upper House rejected provisos which would have opened the way for dissenters to hold office.[2]

Yet, Nottingham's opposition to the repeal of the sacramental test did not mean that 'he was abandoning his own bill' of comprehension.[3] Although his stands on these two related, but for him distinct issues have often been confounded as a result of garbled reports of the debate of the 21st, his support for comprehension and his hostility to the admittance of dissenters to office were not contradictory.[4] Rather, they were consistent with his own conception of the purposes to be served by Anglican–Presbyterian reunion. Not only would such an accommodation put an end to that opposition of interest among the two chief English Protestant groups which Charles and James had tried to turn to the Catholics' account, but he also hoped that it would eventually lead to a reduction in the number of other dissenters if they were allowed only the limited type of 'indulgence' provided for by his Toleration bill.[5] Thus while he was prepared to contemplate the entry into governmental office of former Presbyterians once a comprehension had been effected, he was also intent upon insuring that any who remained outside this enlarged

[1] Bodl. Ballard MSS. 45, fo. 58, newsletter to A. Charlett, [23 March].
[2] *LJ*, XIV, 154, 159.
[3] Feiling, *Tory party*, p. 265, n. 2.
[4] The confusion arose in part because Sir Keith Feiling mistakenly implied, and later writers assumed, that the letter at Bodl. Ballard MSS. 45, fo. 58 (above, n. 1) referred to the debates of 25–26 March in the select committee sitting on the Comprehension and Toleration bills.
[5] LRO, Finch MSS., Political papers 148, p. 3. See also *The conduct*, p. 40, n. 1.

religious establishment should be barred from office. It was, indeed, at this time that he drafted a bill—the first ancestor of the Act against Occasional Conformity that eventually reached the statute book under quite different circumstances over two decades later—which penalized anyone who qualified for office by receiving the sacrament in Anglican fashion but then reverted to attendance at dissenting meetings.[1] This proposal was not introduced as a separate measure in 1689, but its main clause was to be added to the Lords' Comprehension bill just before it was sent down to the Commons.[2]

But though Nottingham could reconcile comprehension with the maintenance of the sacramental test for those who remained outside the establishment, Anglican fears of dissenting encroachment on their political supremacy were not without effect in the proceedings on the Lords' Comprehension bill. On the very day that the Lords first voted down a revision of the Test Act, the select committee sitting on the toleration and comprehension measures agreed to delete that section of the latter which provided for the supplementary ordination of those clergy not episcopally ordained.[3] Five days later, the committee also voted, 9 to 3, to withdraw the clause making kneeling at Communion optional.[4] At the same time, it was agreed that the royal commission for church reform to be established under the measure should be obliged to report to convocation as well as to parliament.[5] Nor were efforts to reverse the committee's alterations, once the bill was reported to the House on 4 April, wholly successful. The section concerning posture at Communion was restored, but that relating to non-episcopal ordinations was not.[6] If in this way the terms of the original bill were narrowed, they were eased in another vital respect on Burnet's initiative. Clergy, instead of

---

[1] LRO, Finch MSS., Political papers 83.
[2] Thomas, 'Comprehension and Indulgence', pp. 248–9.
[3] House of Lords' Record Office, Lords' Committee Book, 1689, p. 45.
[4] Ibid. p. 51.   [5] Ibid.
[6] HMC House of Lords, 1689–90, pp. 50–1.

being obliged to 'approve of the doctrine and worship and government' of the church, were only to be required under the amendment he successfully sponsored to promise to 'submit to the present constitution of the Church' and to 'conform' to its worship and government.[1] On 8 April the Lords also accepted Nottingham's proviso against the practice of occasional conformity when used to qualify for office, and then gave the bill its final reading.[2]

Meanwhile, the conflict over the shape of the religious settlement had become increasingly intense in the lower House. The Tories, who had been badly outnumbered in the debates over the disposal of the crown, now found that in alliance with a number of moderates and Whig churchmen they could fight on more favourable terms. Two days after the Churchmen in the Commons—led by Sir Robert Sawyer, Heneage Finch, Sir Thomas Clarges, Sir Christopher Musgrave and Sir Joseph Tredenham— has resolved at a meeting held at the Devil Tavern on 16 March to oppose the royal proposal for a revision of the Test Act, an attempt to circumvent the sacramental test was rejected by the House.[3] Furthermore, on the 28th a move to add a proviso to the Coronation Oath which would have committed the House to the proposed comprehension was defeated.[4] As one observer jubilantly commented on 21 March, 'The Church of England has a Majority in both Houses, however it happened, that they knew their strength no sooner.'[5] But the defenders of church tradition and privilege did not have it all their way. Although they managed on 1 April to shelve a bill to repeal the Corporation Act of 1661, they were not able to forestall the appointment that same day of a committee headed by the younger Hampden which was charged with the preparation of a bill of comprehension.[6]

---

[1] *Ibid.* p. 49 and n. 2; Burnet, IV, 18–19.　　[2] *HMC House of Lords,* 1689–90, p. 52.
[3] Morrice, II, 505; *CJ,* X, 52; Bodl. Ballard MSS. 45, fo. 57.　　[4] *PH,* V, 208–11.
[5] BM Add. MSS. 36707, fo. 62, A. M. to [J. Harrington], 21 March. See also *HMC Portland,* III, 435; Morrice, II, 534.
[6] *CJ,* X, 74–5; BM Loan 29/140, bundle 3, Sir E. Harley to R. Harley, 2 April.

The scheme that emerged from Hampden's committee was a measure both of dissenting disappointment in the Lords' bill and of Whig anger at the setbacks they had suffered during the past weeks. Like the Lords' plan it stemmed from the 1680 bill, but the deviations from its predecessor were far more radical in character.[1] Hampden, so one outraged churchman wrote, 'made the Church of England more Dissenters and not the Dissenters Church of Englandmen'.[2] Not surprisingly, Hampden's proposals had a stormy reception in the Commons on 8 April. An agitated debate was capped by a motion of Sir Edward Chisnall that consideration of the measure be adjourned 'till Doomsday'. Finally, the House ordered that its second reading be delayed until the 18th.[3]

On the 9th, then, the lower House turned to the Lords' bill, but instead of proceeding with it the Commons were moved by the Whig Privy Councillor William Harbord to draw up an address to the king thanking him for his promise to preserve the Church of England 'as by Law Established'. Harbord added that although he 'apprehended that very many had jealousies of the King in that point...he could assure them his Majesty was altogether of the judgement of the Church of England'. He also suggested that the proposed address should include both a request to the king to summon convocation and an assurance that it was not the House's intention in asking for convocation's assembly to delay or in any way hinder the proposed toleration.[4]

Harbord's motion was rapidly approved, *nemine contradicente*, and a committee composed of staunch Anglicans as well as of dissenting sympathizers was named to prepare the memorial.[5] After some alterations by the Lords, it was presented to the king by both Houses on the 19th.[6] William's reply, brought to

---

[1] For its provisions, see R. Thomas, 'Comprehension and Indulgence', pp. 249–50. A version even more favourable to the Presbyterians and endorsed 'An Act offered by the dissenters' is in Lancs. R.O., Kenyon MSS., box 6, no. 32.
[2] Bodl. Ballard MSS. 45, fo. 35, newsletter to A. Charlett, 9 April. See also *Hatton correspondence*, II, 128.
[3] *CJ*, x, 84; Morrice, II, 527–8; Bodl. Ballard MSS. 45, fo. 35.
[4] Morrice, II, 530–1.   [5] *Ibid.*; *CJ*, x, 84.   [6] *CJ*, x, 86, 91; *LJ*, xiv, 177.

parliament by Nottingham, was not long delayed. In it, he promised to summon convocation but he also urged the Houses to proceed with the indulgence designed for the Protestant Non-conformists.[1] No further action was taken by either House on comprehension, but they did not go back on their engagement to forward a measure for toleration. Even before the address had been submitted to the king, the Lords had passed Nottingham's Toleration bill, intact save for the loss of a clause exempting dissenting schoolmasters from prosecutions under the penal statutes.[2] And on 17 May this bill was approved with only minor alterations by the Commons, after an amendment moved by Clarges to limit the indulgence to a seven-year term was rejected.[3]

The sequence of events from Harbord's speech of 9 April to the passage of the Toleration bill six weeks later has given rise to the hypothesis that a political bargain of sorts was struck between the opposing factions in parliament on ecclesiastical issues.[4] This supposition would seem to be confirmed by a report of the outcome of a meeting of 160 'church of Englandmen' at the Devil Tavern the evening of 9 April. There it was agreed to go whole-heartedly into the address that Harbord had proposed which, so one reporter noted, 'is done with his own [William's] Consent I suppose at the motion of the Earl of Notingham'.[5] Yet if there is no difficulty in accepting the view that by mutual consent comprehension was relegated to convocation while toleration was carried by the Houses, there is little evidence to suggest that this bargain also included a surrender on the part of Nottingham and other Tory leaders on the last major ecclesiastical issue, the

[1] *LJ*, xiv, 183.
[2] *HMC House of Lords*, 1689–90, p. 35.
[3] *PH*, v, 263–6; Grey, ix, 252–4; *CJ*, x, 87, 133, 137; Morrice, ii, 558.
[4] Feiling, *Tory party*, p. 266.
[5] Bodl. Ballard MSS. 45, fo. 35. See also Knatchbull's comments, made after discussing the prospects for convocation with Nottingham in December 1689: 'I thought he had been a good deal the author of their meeting and I believe with very sober and good intentions' (BM Add. MSS. 33923, fo. 465).

question of whether or not the new oaths were to be imposed upon the beneficed Anglican clergy.[1] Actually, it was Nottingham and Carmarthen who took the lead in the upper House in mid-April in efforts to modify a Commons' proviso to the Lords' original Oaths bill which had the effect of obliging clerical incumbents to take the new oaths.[2] But despite the Lords' approval of a counter-amendment which allowed a discretionary power to the King in the imposition of the oaths upon the clergy and despite support for this revision by Heneage Finch and other Churchmen in the Commons, a majority of the lower House remained adamant.[3] In short, it was only when it became clear that the Commons could not be persuaded to recede from the position that no substantial distinction between clergy and laity should be made in the application of the new oaths that the Lords reluctantly yielded on 23 April by a vote of 45 to 42.[4]

All in all, then, the terms of the religious settlement were not altogether to Nottingham's liking. Although his Toleration bill had been passed, comprehension—which he had always regarded as a necessary concomitant to the grant of an indulgence to dissenters—had not. Moreover, though the challenge to the Anglican monopoly of office and place had been beaten back, the Churchmen had been compelled to accept the enforcement of the new oaths upon the beneficed Anglican clergy, including the bishops. None the less, it would seem that Nottingham—unlike Burnet or Halifax—still cherished hopes of favourable action by convocation on comprehension, while at the same time he did not hesitate to lend his authority to efforts to persuade hesitant clergy to take the new oaths that he himself had sponsored as a means of

[1] Sir Keith Feiling, for example, cites a debate of 20 April in which he claims that the leaders of the Church party in the Commons assented to the enforcement of the new oaths upon the beneficed clergy. As Dr A. Simpson, however, has pointed out, there is no report of such a debate either that day or any other (Feiling, *Tory party*, pp. 265–6; Simpson, 'The Convention Parliament', pp. 288–91).

[2] *LJ*, XIV, 183–4, 186; *HMC House of Lords*, 1689–90, pp. 54–5; *PH*, V, 227–31; Every, *High church party*, p. 36.

[3] Grey, IX, 214; *CJ*, X, 93, 95–6, 98, 102.   [4] *HMC House of Lords*, 1689–90, p. 55.

easing the scruples of those committed to the notion of an indefeasible hereditary succession.[1] If, then, this was not in his eyes the best possible settlement, it was at least a viable one which might yet be improved.

With this disposition of the chief ecclesiastical issues, parliament was now in a position to make more rapid headway on other fronts. Yet in the three months after the passage of the Toleration bill in mid-May, very little was accomplished. Instead, the Commons were diverted by a series of forays against the ministers which were accentuated by quarrels with the Lords. The focal point of the Commons' discontent was the dismal state of the Irish Protestants who, by late May, had been reduced to a few strongholds in Ulster, thanks first to the delay in sending an English force to Ireland and then to the miscarriage of the relief expedition to Londonderry commanded by Colonels Richards and Cunningham. Nor did the inconclusive naval engagement in Bantry Bay in early May between a French flotilla and Admiral Herbert's undermanned and undersized squadron improve the temper of the lower House.

Nevertheless, as the Commons' debate of 1 June revealed, there was more to the matter than simple distress at the state of Irish affairs. Many members with Whig sympathies had not reconciled themselves to William's appointment of men who had been associated with the obnoxious policies of the past two reigns or who had opposed the declaration of 'vacancy' in the early days of the Convention. Thus, after it was agreed on the 1st that Richard's and Cunningham's conduct should be investigated, John Howe urged the House not to halt there, alleging that 'it could not be doubted' but that their negligence had 'had encouragement from greater persons than themselves'.[2] Howe went on, then, to propose that the king be addressed to remove from his presence all those who had formerly been impeached by parliament. This barely concealed attack on Carmarthen and Halifax, the ministers

<hr>

[1] Above, p. 84, n. 5.   [2] Morrice, II, 564. See also *PH*, v, 281.

chiefly held responsible for Irish affairs, was seconded by other members who demanded the dismissal of those who had received French bribes to dissolve past parliaments as well as any who had served on James's Privy Council.[1] Moreover, while Howe's venom was mainly reserved for the Lord President and the Lord Privy Seal, he did not neglect to cast aspersions in other directions as well.[2] Indeed, his demand for an inquiry into why Admiral Herbert had had so small a force at Bantry Bay seems to have been directed mainly against Nottingham, who had played a prominent role in the English commission appointed in March to negotiate the terms of naval co-operation with the Dutch and at whose door common fame laid the responsibility for the Dutch contingent's late arrival.[3] This attack does not seem to have come as a complete surprise to the northern Secretary who had, so soon as the news of Bantry reached England, begun to draft a memorandum defending the proceedings of the English commissioners and laying the chief blame for delay upon the Dutch themselves.[4] But for the moment, Nottingham was not called upon to justify himself publicly, while little came of the Commons' murmurings save a resolution of 4 June (directed against Carmarthen) which asserted that a royal pardon could not be pleaded to an impeachment.

However, the Common's 'aking tooth' for Halifax, Carmarthen and Nottingham was not so easily assuaged.[5] Thus, when the northern Secretary issued at Carmarthen's request a warrant on 20 June for the arrest of the Lord President's son Danby on suspicion of treasonable practices in fitting out an armed vessel for privateering, he soon found himself in serious trouble with the lower House.[6] What was initially a family affair became a matter of concern to the Commons, for Danby was one of their mem-

[1] PH, v, 281–4; Morrice, II, 564.   [2] PH, v, 283; Luttrell, I, 541.
[3] Ehrman, The navy, pp. 251–2; HMC Portland, III, 437.
[4] HMC Finch, II, 208–9.
[5] The phrase is Charles Bertie's (HMC Rutland, II, 126).
[6] CSPD, 1689–90, p. 159; Browning, Osborne, I, 455.

bers. Always watchful of their privileges, they took prompt action—their appetite whetted by the prospect of an opportunity of calling Nottingham to account. As one reporter commented, 'since better occasions are wanting, they design to make use of this to have him turn'd out'.[1] Since Danby had been released by Nottingham on his promise to appear again if summoned, the Lord President's impetuous heir was inclined to make light of the whole episode when he testified before the House on 24 June. But the Commons were not so easily thrown off the scent and a committee was named to inquire of the Secretary the grounds of his warrant and the manner in which Danby had been treated. On the 28th, Clarges presented Nottingham's version of the incident, and after a confused and wandering debate in which both Harbord and Musgrave spoke on his behalf, the House eventually decided merely to vote the grant of the warrant a breach of privilege and to proceed no further.[2] Moreover, though Nottingham came in for a share of calumny during the next fortnight for his part in the Lords' stubborn resistance to the Commons' attempt to secure a full rehabilitation of the arch-informer Titus Oates, it was Halifax and, to a lesser extent, Carmarthen who bore the brunt of the lower House's criticism for the remainder of the session.[3]

But while the Commons persisted in attacking the leading ministers (save for Shrewsbury), they had little time or energy left to deal with more pressing questions, and finally William in disgust prorogued the Houses on 20 August. The king took this step only after considerable deliberation, for by mid-summer he was in a serious quandary. On the one hand, he was irritated with Carmarthen and, to a lesser degree, with Nottingham. Actually, in the king's eyes Nottingham's worst fault was his reversion—

[1] BM Add. MSS. 36707, fo. 67, newsletter to J. Harrington, 22 June.
[2] *PH*, v, 363–8; *CJ*, x, 193, 196–7, 199–200.
[3] For Nottingham's part in the debate over Oates's status and the reaction his stand provoked, see *LJ*, xiv, 292, 310; *PH*, v, 391–4; BM Add. MSS. 29573, fos. 268–9, C. Hatton to Viscount Hatton, 11 July.

after a period of coolness—to 'caballing' with the Lord President.[1] However, William also complained to Halifax in August that Nottingham, like Carmarthen, would not resign despite parliamentary criticism; if he wanted to rid himself of them to appease the Whigs he must dismiss them.[2] This he was not prepared to do, although for a time Halifax thought that he intended to revoke the Commission of the Great Seal and to offer the Lord Keepership to Nottingham.[3] On the other hand, the king's dissatisfaction with the Commons was very great. The attacks on his ministers, particularly Halifax, were most distasteful to him and he had done his best to quiet Howe.[4] Furthermore, he had been angered by the failure of his Whig officials to defend the administration in the Commons and by their readiness to join in assaults on some of his principal advisers.[5] Still another source of irritation was the lower House's resistance to an amendment to the Bill of Rights in favour of the Electress of Hanover's claim to the throne, despite the approval of this proviso by the Lords.[6] But what most distressed the king was the Commons' failure to settle the ordinary revenue, to grant adequate supplies to finance the war and to pass an Indemnity bill.[7]

Under these circumstances, William's thoughts began to turn towards the possibility of basing his government chiefly on the Church party, which he viewed as a middle group between the Jacobites and the more violent Whigs.[8] Nottingham seems to have done all he could to move the king in this direction, not least by encouraging royal suspicion of the Whigs as 'republicans' at heart. As Burnet relates, the Secretary

[1] Foxcroft, *Halifax*, II, 221, 232.   [2] Foxcroft, *Halifax*, II, 230.
[3] *Ibid.* pp. 221–2.
[4] Browning, *Osborne*, I, 453.
[5] Foxcroft, *Halifax*, II, 228–30.
[6] For Nottingham's support of this proviso and its fate, see Lords' R.O., Lords' MSS. minutes, 22 May and 12 July 1689; *LJ*, XIV, 279; Foxcroft, *Halifax*, II, 227; *CJ*, X, 187, 190.
[7] Foxcroft, *Halifax*, II, 224–7. See also William's speeches and messages to the Houses of 25 March, 26 April, 28 June and 12 July (*PH*, V, 198, 235, 368–9, 380–1).
[8] Foxcroft, *Halifax*, II, 227, 229, and *passim*.

spared no costs nor pains to have an account of all that passed in the city, and in other angry cabals: and he furnished the king very copiously that way; which made a deep impression on him, and had very bad effects.[1]

One result of William's own leanings and Nottingham's promptings was that by September it seemed there was a serious possibility of a dissolution, while in all likelihood it was the king's readiness to consider the convening of a new parliament that led to Shrewsbury's first offers of resignation late in August.[2] But William was not yet prepared to make so far-reaching a decision and he was also reluctant to part with Shrewsbury. For the time being, then, the southern Secretary was persuaded to stay on while the king resolved to try the parliament once more.

If William was not yet prepared to rely primarily on the Church party, he does seem to have leaned increasingly on Nottingham's advice in ecclesiastical affairs, and with the coming of autumn there was a renewed spurt of activity on this front. To begin with, William early in August and again in September dispatched Nottingham to Lambeth, ostensibly to assure Sancroft that he need not leave the archiepiscopal palace though he now stood suspended for his refusal to take the new oaths, but probably also to try to devise some formula to avert a schism in the church.[3] At the same time, the king acted to fill up several bishoprics and deaneries vacant by death or promotion. His nominations, announced early in September, were drawn from the circle of clerics associated with Nottingham and Tillotson, with Stillingfleet being named Bishop of Worcester, Patrick Bishop of Chichester, Sharp Dean of Canterbury, Kidder Dean of Peterborough, and Tillotson himself Dean of St Paul's.[4] The first week of September was also marked by the passage of a royal warrant authorizing the formation of a commission of ten bishops and

---

[1] Burnet, IV, 5.
[2] HMC Finch, II, 247; Private and original correspondence of Charles Talbot, duke of Shrewsbury, with king William, Etc., ed. W. Coxe (London, 1821), pp. 6–14.
[3] Luttrell, I, 567, 577–8. See also Foxcroft, Halifax, II, 232.
[4] Bennett, 'William III and the episcopate', p. 118.

twenty other clergy to consider alterations and reforms in the liturgy, ceremonial, canons and courts of the church.[1] Thus, planning for comprehension—the subject of summer-long discussions between the Bishops of St Asaph and Salisbury and 'the Cheife of the Dissenters'—was now taken up by an official church body which was to submit its work first to convocation and later to parliament.[2]

However, once the special commission assembled early in October, it became apparent that the continued failure to come to any sort of arrangement with the recalcitrant clergy, coupled with the abolition of episcopacy in Scotland, was having its effects even on many of those clerics who had taken the new oaths. Of the thirty commissioners appointed, only twenty responded to the royal summons, and some of them later withdrew from the commission as well.[3] None the less, the rest of the commissioners went on with the work of reform and revision only to discover when convocation met on 21 November that a majority of the lower House was in no mood to heed royal wishes.[4] Yet even after Tillotson was overcome in the contest for the Prolocutorship of the lower House by William Jane (one of the seceders from the commission), William and Nottingham did not give up hope. A defect in the original commission authorizing the convocation to act was fortuitously discovered, and the revised commission was carried to convocation on 4 December by Nottingham. With it came a letter from William desiring the members to consider the proposals to be laid before them with 'an impartial zeal for the peace and good of the Church'.[5] Nottingham himself then addressed the assembly in an eloquent plea against 'all partial Prepossessions and Animosities in their Proceedings'.[6] But it was of no avail, and convocation was adjourned on 13 December for five weeks.

[1] CSPD, 1689–90, pp. 242–3.
[2] Morrice, II, 574–5, 578; The diaries and letters of Philip Henry, ed. M. Lee (London, 1882), p. 364; FSL, Newdigate newsletters, 2057, 29 Aug.
[3] Bennett, 'William III and the episcopate', p. 119.   [4] Ibid. pp. 119–20.
[5] Burnet, IV, 58.
[6] Boyer, The History of King William III, II, 157.

During the recess, one last effort was made to alter its course. With the king's approval, negotiations were again opened with the suspended prelates at the instance of Compton and Lloyd of St Asaph, seconded by others of William's clerical advisers as well as a 'leading chiefe minister', no doubt Nottingham.[1] But Sancroft, Turner and Lloyd of Norwich rejected all their proposals, informing the emissaries that 'if the King thought it fit for his own sake, that they should not be deprived, he must make it his business'.[2] So withered the hope of any compromise over the oaths or any progress on internal reform and comprehension at this time, and the convocation was soon dissolved with the termination of the Convention parliament.[3]

Royal frustration on the ecclesiastical front was paralleled by a series of parliamentary setbacks. The Houses were reconvened on 18 October, almost six weeks earlier than had originally been anticipated, because of the pressing need for funds. William's opening speech, which had been carefully scrutinized by Nottingham, Carmarthen and other Privy Councillors, consisted mainly of a plea for the speedy grant of further supplies to carry on the war.[4] The king made only one further request; that was for the passage of a bill of indemnity.[5] But though the Commons quickly carried a general resolution in favour of supply, they soon abandoned the difficult task of devising means to raise the two million pounds they had promised for the more exhilarating pursuit of uncovering scapegoats for the miscarriages of the past campaign. Nor was the House satisfied with condemning the misdeeds of subordinates, whether it was the Irish Commissary Shales or the Navy Victualling Board. Time and again, the Whigs at least returned to the more serious point; the employment of

---

[1] Bodl. Rawlinson MSS. Letters 98, fos. 93–4, [Bishop Turner of Ely to T. Turner, 20 Dec.]. See also BM Lansdowne MSS. 1013, fo. 15, W. Kennett to Rev. Blackwell, 3 Jan. 1690.

[2] Clarendon correspondence, II, 299. See also Morrice, III, 87, 107; Every, High church party, pp. 62–3.

[3] For Nottingham's attempts to revive comprehension during the 1692–93 session, see Bodl. D. D. Ashurst MSS. C1, H. Ashurst to I. Mather, 18 Oct. 1692.

[4] Morrice, II, 616–17; PH, v, 403.   [5] PH, v, 404.

those who had been Charles's and James's servants, they claimed, was the cause of the misconduct of the war.[1] Thus by early December, the Commons still had made little progress either in providing supply or in agreeing upon the terms of an indemnity.[2] At the same time, the record of the Lords was hardly more distinguished. Not only was the vendetta against Halifax renewed, but also Carmarthen's enemies were active once again.[3] On 23 November a motion was made in a half-empty House to add a clause to the Bill of Rights declaring all pardons void in cases of impeachment, and only a lengthy harangue from Nottingham kept Carmarthen's foes at bay until enough ministerial supporters could be summoned to defeat this proposal.[4]

In the face of the continuing parliamentary stalemate, Nottingham and Carmarthen once again began in November to press William for a change of men and measures. The crux of their advice seems to have been that the Church party was the stronger both in parliament and in the country, and hence that Tory fears about dissenting influence at Court should be eased and Tory sensibilities catered to if William hoped to obtain an adequate supply.[5] At the same time, Nottingham was busy canvassing members of both Houses in an attempt to persuade them that the king would espouse the church interest.[6] He also appears to have intimated to Clarges—a 'bigott' to the church—and to Musgrave that places might be found for them on the Privy Council should they distinguish themselves in support of supply.[7]

[1] PH, v, 418–19, 425–33, 435–43, 446–61, 462–7.
[2] CJ, x, 283, 299, 305, 316.   [3] Foxcroft, Halifax, II, 91–107.
[4] Journaal van Constantijn Huygens, I, 210; Browning, Osborne, I, 459–60.
[5] Morrice, II, 644.
[6] For the best documented example of Nottingham's attempts to influence members of parliament, see the account in the transcript of Sir John Knatchbull's diary where he relates that on 1 Dec. Nottingham promised him 'his favour to the King if I would list my selfe in that [gap in MSS.] in the house which did now use its endeavours to make itt appear to the King the Church party was the strongest' (BM Add. MSS. 33923, fos. 464–5). Nottingham had a similar interview with Rochester the same day (Clarendon correspondence, II, 296–7).
[7] Foxcroft, Halifax, II, 242–3; Nottingham University Portland MSS. PWa 299, Lord Sydney and T. Coningsby to [Portland], 27 Sept. 1690. Nottingham had also been

By mid-December, the counsels of Nottingham and Carmarthen seemed to be having some effect on William. Though he was still not ready to dissolve the Houses, he was now seriously considering adjourning them for a month—a step which, as Shrewsbury protested to him, would be taken as a declaration in favour of the Tories.[1] Certainly, Nottingham strongly pressed for a long recess on the grounds that a short holiday adjournment would be likely to antagonize the Tory country gentlemen, who were already beginning to leave London to spend Christmas by their own firesides.[2] Distorted rumours of these counsels which did, however, accurately reflect William's growing readiness to hearken to the advice of his northern Secretary and the Lord President, spread rapidly in mid-December:

there was a very common discourse as Soon as ever they [the Commons] had sent up the Money bill [the two shilling land tax] to the lords...that the Parliament would be Adjourned that they might keep their Christmasse, and then not called to sitt again, but Dissolved, and that there would be a Lord Chancellor, and Lord Treasurer...to witt, Nottingham, [and] Danby [sic, Carmarthen].[3]

Although William eventually allowed himself to be dissuaded from a long adjournment by Shrewsbury, the fear that he might be contemplating entrusting himself to the Church party only served to provoke the Whig extremists. Taking advantage of the general dissatisfaction in the Commons with the management of the war and the House's inability to comprehend why the funds voted the previous spring had been insufficient, they proposed on 14 December that the House should represent to the king 'the ill Conduct and Success of our Affairs' and request him 'to find out the Authors of Miscarriages, and to appoint Affairs to be managed by persons...more to the...satisfaction of his subjects'.[4] John

dealing with Seymour in much the same fashion (Devonshire House 'Notebook' *sub* 'Nottingham Ld').
[1] *Correspondence of Shrewsbury*, pp. 14–16. [2] *Ibid.*
[3] Morrice, III, 44. See also Luttrell, I, 617; *HMC Downshire*, I, 324; BM Add. MSS. 29578, fo. 30, Sir C. Lyttleton to Viscount Hatton, 14 Dec. [4] *PH*, v, 481.

Hampden's speech spelled out what other Whigs only hinted at: he called for the dismissal of the 'three men who came to Hungerford from king James'. Trust in them, he maintained, was sadly misplaced, for they would have persuaded the Prince of Orange 'to go out of England'.[1] Though Clarges and Sir Edward Seymour came to the defence of Nottingham, Halifax and Godolphin, they concurred in the general criticism of the conduct of the war. The proposal for the address was approved, and Hampden was named chairman of the committee appointed to prepare it.[2] Equally if not more ominous in Nottingham's view was the committal five days later of the bill restoring corporations for, as he observed to Hatton, in its present form 'it restores the Corporations as they were in the year 1660 and consequently readmitts all sorts of dissenters'.[3] Even the Common's rejection on the 21st of the text of the proposed address against him was no great comfort, since it was recommitted to cries from Howe and others that it was not yet 'home enough'.[4]

Thus when parliament was adjourned on 23 December for a week, Nottingham was by no means at ease, though he resolutely informed the king that 'hee would not go, till hee put him away'.[5] He was also fearful that with many of the supporters of the church absent in the country, 'some things may be attempted by those that remain here'.[6] What particularly worried him was the report that a clause to remove the sacramental test as a qualification for municipal office might be added to the Corporation bill.[7] To meet this new threat, Nottingham began to solicit proxies in case the measure reached the Lords, and he also tried to persuade those

[1] *PH*, v, 478–9.   [2] *Ibid*. pp. 473–81.
[3] BM Add. MSS. 29594, fo. 185, 24 Dec.; *CJ*, x, 312–13. Cf. *A letter concerning the disabling clauses lately offered to the House of Commons, for regulating corporations* (London, 1690), pp. 3–4. I am indebted for this last reference to Dr D. R. Lacey of the U.S. Naval Academy.
[4] *PH*, v, 502–7; Boyer, *History of King William III*, II, 166; Morrice, III, 67. For William's hostile reaction to the proposed memorial, see Foxcroft, *Halifax*, II, 243.
[5] *Ibid*. p. 242.
[6] BM Add. MSS. 29594, fo. 185; BM Add. MSS. 17677KK, fo. 9, van Citters' report of 27 Dec./6 Jan. 1689/90.   [7] BM Add. MSS. 29594, fo. 185.

members whom he thought would oppose the bill to stay in town. 'You must not goe and leave the Church of England to be run downe', he told Sir John Knatchbull when that worthy came to pay his compliments before departing for the country: 'I doe not speake for myself (for the House of Commons was then addressing against him and others) but I beseech you Sir John do not goe away now.'[1]

Withal, the situation was not quite so bleak as it seemed to Nottingham. Though William had decided on a short recess on the advice of Shrewsbury and Sir John Trevor, he had also come to the conclusion that if the Commons would not lay aside partisan disputes after they reassembled and 'give money enough to make up the Two Millions...there was nothing to be done with them'.[2] In effect, then, the approval on 2 January by a half-empty House of the addition to the Corporation bill of a series of amendments which would have purged from borough councils all those involved in the surrender of charters during the past two reigns was a pyrrhic victory for the Whigs.[3] And the fact that the backers of the 'Sacheverell clause' had the temerity to let it be known that if the king 'interposed or medled in it, they would not finish the money bills' was merely a testimony to their desperation.[4] Certainly, this was not the tack to take with William, nor was he prepared to allow the amendments to stand. When the measure came up for its third reading on 10 January, the Churchmen—reinforced by many members of parliament hastily summoned from the country and encouraged by intimations of royal support from Heneage Finch—were able to remove the obnoxious clauses from the bill.[5] Moreover, on 23 January the Lords, led by Nottingham, deleted that section of the bill which

[1] Ibid.; BM Add. MSS. 33923, fo. 465.
[2] Dalrymple, II, app. III, 80–4; Correspondence of Shrewsbury, pp. 14–16; Foxcroft, Halifax, II, 241–2.
[3] CJ, x, 322–3; Morrice, III, 74.   [4] Foxcroft, Halifax, II, 243.
[5] J. Ralph, The history of England during the reigns of K. William, Q. Anne, and K. George I (London, 1744–6), II, 182–3; Feiling, Tory party, p. 270; CJ, x, 329. See also Clarendon correspondence, II, 301.

declared the surrender of the charters to be illegal by a vote of 51 to 43.[1] But despite these attacks, the Whigs in the lower House were still strong enough to block Tory efforts to speed the passage of the Indemnity bill.[2]

While the party struggle raged in parliament, Nottingham and other Tory leaders sought to take advantage of Whig intransigence with renewed importunities for a dissolution. They argued, so Burnet recounts, that 'the breaking upon this point [the "Sacheverell clause"], as it would make the new elections sure to the church party in many places, so it would oblige them to the king, since he preserved them from the fury of this bill'.[3] But despite William's dissatisfaction with the Commons, it took one last piece of obstructionism to move him to action. It came over his decision to take charge personally of the Irish campaign during the forthcoming year.[4] Once news of the king's intentions began to leak out, murmurings against this project began to be heard among many members of parliament, with some Whigs even alleging that only a traitor could have advised exposing William to such danger.[5] Addresses against his journey were mooted in both Houses, and on the 25th a motion was made in the Lords that the king be requested not to go. After a prolonged debate in which most of the Tory peers, save Rochester and Carmarthen, and all the bishops present opposed such a vote, the debate was adjourned until the 27th.[6] Fearful that a resolution against his

---

[1] LJ, xiv, 423–4; HMC House of Lords, 1689–90, p. 432. Notes for Nottingham's speech in this debate are in LRO, Finch MSS., Political papers 94. Carmarthen argued that the surrenders were illegal (Morrice, iii, 99).

[2] Grey, ix, 520–2; Macaulay, History of England, iii, 528, n. 2.

[3] Supplement to Burnet's history, p. 338.

[4] His decision was made no later than mid-January, and he had certainly been contemplating such a step for some time before then (Luttrell, ii, 3; Foxcroft, Halifax, ii, 244; Macaulay, History of England, iii, 530–1).

[5] Ibid. See also Hampden's and Delamere's letters advising against the Irish trip (Dalrymple, ii, app. iii, 97–100; CSPD, 1689–90, pp. 381–2).

[6] LJ, xiv, 425–6; Morrice, iii, 102. Morrice, in a confused entry, adds that Rochester spoke for the address, and that Carmarthen was 'against his going, because they had [no?] notice from the King of his resolution to take this journey'. See also Browning, Osborne, i, 462, n. 3.

Irish expedition might be carried, William came to the Lords on the morning of the 27th and announced, to the dismay of the Whigs and the jubilation of the Tories, the prorogation of parliament to 2 April.[1]

The prorogation of the Convention parliament marked a major turning point in William's relations with the leading English politicians, though at the outset he was reluctant to face up to its full implications. Apparently, he had hoped that once the Houses had been dismissed he could leave for Ireland, but he soon found that the insufficiency of the funds which had been voted and the delays in their collection would necessitate another session.[2] But if he still wished 'hee could trimme a little longer', he knew that it would be futile to reconvene the old parliament, many of whose Whig members were 'outragiously offended' by the prorogation.[3] Moreover, he had ample promises from Nottingham and Carmarthen that should he call a new parliament, it would rapidly provide supply.[4] Their undertakings were reaffirmed by 150 Churchmen led by Sir John Lowther and Heneage Finch in a meeting at the Devil Tavern on 29 January.[5] Finally, on 6 February William dissolved the Convention parliament and summoned a new one to assemble on 20 March.

Although the king's hesitations lingered even after this announcement, he acknowledged to Halifax two days later, in reluctantly accepting his resignation, that if he now adjourned the new parliament to a later date, 'the Church party would take it ill'.[6] While he still hoped to retain the support of the Whig officeholders who looked to Shrewsbury for leadership, he also

---

[1] Macaulay, History of England, III, 532–3.
[2] Foxcroft, Halifax, II, 247; BM Add. MSS. 25379, fo. 317, Terriesi's dispatch of 31 Jan./10 Feb.
[3] Foxcroft, Halifax, II, 246–7; BM Add. MSS. 29573, fo. 392, C. Hatton to Viscount Hatton, 1 Feb.
[4] Foxcroft, Halifax, II, 247.
[5] Diary of Evelyn, v, 5; Morrice, III, 306.
[6] Foxcroft, Halifax, II, 246, 249. A week later, Carmarthen was still complaining of the king's 'slow steps' in 'his good intentions to the Church party' (Shropshire Record Office, Attingham MSS. 112/3, Carmarthen to [Earl of Abingdon], 15 Feb. 1690).

took other steps at this time to consolidate Tory support for the forthcoming session.[1] Not only did he agree to an arrangement whereby the newly deprived non-juring prelates might continue to receive the income from their sees for the time being, he also publicly encouraged the choice in the coming general election of 'moderate Men of the Church-Party'.[2] Furthermore, he undertook a series of governmental changes designed to ensure more capable administration as well as to appeal to the Tories by replacing some of the more violent Whigs with men more acceptable to them.

The first of these reshuffles had actually been initiated in the wake of Admiral Herbert's (now Lord Torrington) resignation from the Admiralty Board in mid-December. On the advice of Portland and Nottingham, William had moved early in January to name Sir Richard Haddock in his stead, but strong protests from Shrewsbury, Thomas Wharton and Sir Robert Howard to the effect that Haddock was a man obnoxious to the Commons had dissuaded him.[3] On 20 January, then, a compromise candidate —Lord Pembroke—was named to succeed Torrington. At the same time, Sir Michael Wharton and Sir William Sacheverell, who had long since ceased to attend the Board and who had also been prominent in Whig efforts to amend the Corporation bill, were dropped from the Admiralty Commission.[4]

Although Nottingham's original candidate for the vacancy on the Board had been blackballed, Torrington's resignation and his replacement by the Secretary's friend Pembroke both reflected and enhanced his growing ascendency in naval affairs. Handicapped by inexperience in foreign affairs and confined to merely routine diplomatic business by William's determination to reserve

[1] That William still hoped to retain the support of moderate Whigs is evident by his retention in office of Shrewsbury, Somers and the elder Hampden, and also by his refusal to consider Heneage Finch for the Lord Keeper's place (Foxcroft, *Halifax*, II, 249). Ralph, *History of England*, II, 1000 and note. See also *Clarendon correspondence*, II, 304; BM Add. MSS. 33589, fo. 315, Lord Weymouth to J. Smyth, 24 Feb.
[3] Morrice, III, 71, 75; BM Add. MSS. 29573, fo. 377, C. Hatton to Viscount Hatton, 4 Jan.; *HMC Finch*, II, 378.   [4] Ehrman, *The navy*, pp. 297, 322.

all major policy-making in this field to himself,[1] Nottingham had turned his attention soon after his appointment as Secretary to a sphere in which, as a former member and one-time head of the Admiralty Commission, he could and did lay some claim to expert knowledge.[2] Less than a month after he accepted the Seals, he had begun, with the king's approval, to use his position as Secretary to act as intermediary between William, the Admiralty Board, and Torrington while he was with the fleet.[3] Torrington's loss of royal confidence in the autumn of 1689, thanks to an undistinguished summer campaign at sea and a quarrel over the winter disposition of the fleet, and his subsequent resignation from the Commission thus left the way open to Nottingham to extend his control over naval affairs. Indeed, William, long anxious to find a reliable administrator to whom he might delegate his naval responsibilities and feeling himself badly let down in that respect by Torrington, was only too delighted to let Nottingham shoulder this burden, particularly since Torrington's rival in the fleet—Edward Russell—was not yet prepared to take on this task himself.[4] Torrington was continued in command of the fleet for the forthcoming campaign, but henceforth Nottingham was to figure as William's 'chief confidant on naval policy and as the undisputed means of communicating it to Admirals and Admiralty alike'.[5]

The shake-up at the Admiralty and Nottingham's emergence as chief minister for naval affairs was soon followed by a revamping at the Treasury. Here the principal problem was, as William told

[1] For William's monopolization of this sphere at the expense of all his Secretaries, see D. B. Horn, 'The Diplomatic Experience of Secretaries of State, 1660–1852', *History*, XLI (1956), 93. There was, however, one area of foreign policy where William seems to have been careful to allow his Secretaries some voice—Anglo–Dutch relations (G. N. Clark, 'The Dutch Missions to England', *EHR*, xxxv, 1920, 529–57).

[2] Nottingham, in fact, prided himself no little on this point (Dartmouth's note in Burnet, IV, 170).

[3] For this and the remainder of the paragraph, see Ehrman, *The navy*, ch. IX.

[4] Just before he left for Ireland, William appointed Russell, Russell's henchman Henry Priestman, and Sir Richard Onslow to fill the vacancies on the Admiralty Board left by the departure of Wharton, Sacheverell, and Sir John Chicheley (*ibid*. p. 342).

[5] *Ibid*. p. 321.

Halifax early in February, that 'hee must imploy such as would advance money'.[1] Neither Lords Monmouth and Delamere nor Sir Henry Capel—three of the more troublesome Whig office-holders—met this qualification, and it was reported that many Churchmen refused to lend money while they remained at the Board not only for political reasons but also because they were not reputed to be men of means themselves.[2] Their successors in the new commission issued in mid-March, Sir John Lowther, Sir Stephen Fox and Sir Thomas Pelham, were far more acceptable to prospective creditors of the government as well as to Carmarthen and Nottingham. In addition to advancing sizable sums themselves, their appointment proved a great spur to the newest loan being floated in the City, and over £150,000 was subscribed within a fortnight.[3]

While the changes at the Admiralty and the Treasury went forward, a reconstitution of the Lieutenancy of London and Middlesex was also urged upon the king by Nottingham and Carmarthen on the grounds that Churchmen had been almost wholly excluded from its ranks during the previous year.[4] In mid-February, the nomination of a new commission was delegated by William to Nottingham, Shrewsbury, Carmarthen and the Bishop of London. But the list they brought in, for which Bishop Compton seems to have been mainly responsible, met with severe objections for its Tory bias from Shrewsbury and the London Whigs.[5] None the less, Compton's recommendations were finally approved by the Privy Council early in March.[6]

[1] Foxcroft, *Halifax*, II, 247. The Customs Commissioners had already been pressed to lend money to the government (BM Add. MSS. 29573, fos. 346–7, C. Hatton to Viscount Hatton, 12 Nov. 1689).
[2] *Journaal van Constantijn Huygens*, I, 248. See also *The conduct*, pp. 59–60.
[3] Morrice, III, 125; Luttrell, II, 25. See also *The conduct*, pp. 54–6 and n. 35; Ralph, *History of England*, II, 1000.
[4] *The conduct*, pp. 54–6 and n. 35; Burnet, IV, 72–3; *Supplement to Burnet's history*, p. 340.
[5] *The conduct*, pp. 54–5; Burnet, IV, 72–3; BM Add. MSS. 17677KK, fos. 58–9, van Citters' dispatch of 11/21 March. For differing opinions of the makeup of the new Lieutenancy, see Luttrell, II, 21; BM Add. MSS. 29573, fo. 406, C. Hatton to Viscount Hatton, 11 March.
[6] *Supplement to Burnet's history*, p. 340; *CSPD*, 1689–90, pp. 487–8, 501–2.

Armed with these signs of royal favour, it was not surprising that the elections resulted in a substantial addition to Tory parliamentary strength. While Nottingham's own efforts on behalf of Tory candidates in Northamptonshire, Essex and the Cinque Ports were unavailing, the House of Commons that met on 20 March was 'at least moderately Tory' in composition.[1] The change wrought by the alterations at Court and at the polls was evident in the House's choice of a Speaker. Sir John Trevor, a courtier of long standing and unsavoury repute, was proposed for the Chair by Lowther and Clarges.[2] An attempt to re-elect Powle, the Speaker of the Convention, was made by the more violent Whigs headed by Sir John Guise and Sir John Thompson, but it was discouraged by the elder Hampden. The result was that Trevor's nomination was carried without a division for, as Roger Morrice sorrowfully noted, 'the other side...were not united in Mr Powle, and besides they are dispirited'.[3]

Trevor's easy victory was a telling confirmation of the development of a broad-based, if loose, confederation in the Commons composed of Churchmen, Carmarthen's personal following and a sizable group of moderate Whigs (many of whom held office).[4] Carmarthen was mainly responsible for the management of this disparate coalition, but Nottingham also played an important part. Two of his brothers, Heneage and Edward, now sat in the lower House for Oxford and Cambridge Universities respectively. Their choice as representatives of the two centres of church strength and influence clearly reflected the Finches' high standing in such circles—a position which Nottingham's own role during the past year as the leading spokesman of the Church party within the ministry and in the Lords had only strengthened.

[1] Browning, Osborne, I, 466. For Nottingham's electoral activities, see his letters to Hatton in BM Add. MSS. 29594, fos. 194–8; Longleat Thynne MSS., vol. XIV, fo. 269, H. Thynne to Viscount Weymouth, 12 March; BM Add. MSS., 42586, fo. 85, J. Beaumont to the Corporation of Rye, 5 March.
[2] Foxcroft, Halifax, II, 228; PH, v, 547.
[3] Ibid.; Morrice, III, 125.
[4] For Carmarthen's activities, see Browning, Osborne, I, 466–8, and III, 173–8.

Supply and the passage of an Act of Grace were the chief items of business urged on the Houses in the king's opening speech, and the Commons took prompt and favourable action on both when they came to be considered.[1] By 28 March a compromise on the question of the king's ordinary revenue had been reached.[2] Moreover, though Lowther's motion on the 31st for an extra-ordinary supply of £1,500,000 to carry on the war was eventually reduced by a fifth, the recriminations of disappointed Whigs such as Guise and Thompson about maladministration and the dissolution of the Convention parliament were ignored by the Commons' majority which was, as Clarges, 'weary of finding fault'.[3]

However, if there was little enthusiasm for inquiries into alleged mismanagement, it was hardly to be expected that the more violent Whigs would acquiesce quietly in the growing Tory bias of the administration, and it was not long before both Houses were diverted by a series of partisan disputes. The first move came in the Lords when on 26 March the Duke of Bolton introduced a bill which would have 'declared and enacted' that the Convention was a 'good and lawful Parliament' and recognized William and Mary as 'lawfull and rightful' sovereigns.[4] The opposition Whigs had chosen their point of assault skilfully for Tory scruples concerning the legality of the new régime were notorious. Yet not only Nottingham and Carmarthen, but also Devonshire and Shrewsbury spoke against the proposal on its first reading, for it was clearly designed as a divisive tactic.[5]

Nottingham's speech was a lucid exposition of his objections to such an unprecedented step.[6] First of all, he made it clear that his opposition to Bolton's measure did not stem from any desire

---

[1] The Act of Grace was not submitted to the Houses by William until May, but it was then quickly approved.
[2] CJ, x, 358-9; PH, v, 549-61.   [3] PH, v, 562-74.
[4] The various drafts of the bill are noted in HMC House of Lords, 1690-1, pp. 1-7.
[5] Bodl. Ballard MSS. 48, fo. 78; BM Add. MSS. 17677KK, fo. 71, van Citters' report of 28 March/7 April.
[6] The following excerpts from Nottingham's speech are taken from a draft in LRO, Finch MSS., Political papers 95.

to invalidate the acts of the Convention. Indeed, he specifically stated that he particularly hoped to see the Statute of Right and the Act of Toleration confirmed. But the appropriate procedure was to act on the Restoration precedent: 'here was no declaration or supposition of the Legality of that Convention or of its being a Parliament...but there being good laws then past and the exigency of affairs at the time requiring it, they were confirm'd by an expresse law for that purpose'. In this suggestion of an alternative, Nottingham would seem to have been echoing William's own preference for Portland, too, favoured this method.[1] Secondly, Nottingham asserted that while he was 'as zealous as any man to establish the King and Queen upon the Throne', it was also necessary 'to preserve the constitution of the government'. The best guarantee of their titles, which he firmly believed to be *de facto* and not *de jure*, was to shun 'curious and dangerous enquiries'. 'Tis sufficient', he continued, 'for every man to be ascertaind to whom his allegiance is to be paid', and it was obvious that the new oaths did precisely this. For these reasons, Bolton's bill was 'needlesse, unseasonable and so far from adding any security to the King...that it directly tends to the diminution both of him and the government'.

Despite the Secretary's objections, the Lords did agree to take up the measure. For a week, furious debate raged over its initial clause with Nottingham and Carmarthen leading those who wished to have the acts of the previous parliament 'confirmed' as, rather than 'declared' to be, valid. When a modified Whig version of the first section of the bill was rejected on the 5th with Halifax, Pembroke, Carmarthen and Nottingham heading the majority, deadlock seemed imminent.[2] However, there was also considerable sentiment within the House that 'a matter of so great consequence ought to receive some determination', especially as it was 'beginning now to be blown about that the Lords were

---

[1] Morrice, III, 130–1.
[2] Bodl. Ballard MSS. 48, fo. 78; *HMC House of Lords*, 1690–1, pp. 2–3; *Hatton correspondence*, II, 146–7.

against Recognizeing the King and Queen though that matter had never yet been under any debate'.[1] With Nottingham's apparent concurrence, the Lord President now advanced a compromise formula. King and queen were to be recognized in the terms employed in the Statute of Right, while instead of either 'declaring' or 'confirming' the acts of the Convention they would simply be 'enacted' to be good in law.[2] All would have been well had not Carmarthen, at the last moment, agreed to the insertion of the phrase 'were and are' with reference to the acts of the Convention. This addition made the substitute clause, in Nottingham's eyes, tantamount to the original version. Hence, he joined with sixteen other peers in a scathing protest against the passage in this form of the bill which denounced it as 'neither good English nor good sense'.[3] But by this time, the House was in no temper to be questioned for its decisions. After a heated debate on the 10th, it was voted to expunge the protest, while Nottingham himself barely escaped being sent to the Tower after several peers, most notably Mulgrave, took umbrage at his assertion that William had 'seized' the crown. Only his apt explanation and citation of scripture—'In the Day of his Power the People submitted unto him'—saved him from so ignominious a fate.[4]

However, Nottingham's tribulations were not yet over, for on 25 April Comptroller Wharton, with the king's acquiescence and Shrewsbury's support, introduced a bill in the lower House which would have required all officials to abjure James II.[5] Fearful that this proposal would be carried in the Commons, Nottingham set to work to mobilize his fellow peers against it, but on the follow-

[1] Bodl. Ballard MSS. 48, fo. 78.
[2] *Hatton correspondence*, II, 146–7. Nottingham's concurrence is suggested by his participation on the subcommittee named to redraft the clause recognizing William and Mary (*HMC House of Lords*, 1690–1, p. 4).
[3] *PH*, V, 577.
[4] An account of the incident in Carmarthen's hand in National Maritime Museum Southwell MSS., vol. XIII. See also *HMC House of Lords*, 1690–1, p. 4, n. 2; *Journaal van Constantijn Huygens*, I, 258; *Het Archief van Heinsius*, I, 29.
[5] Devonshire House 'Notebook' *sub* 'Shrewsbury Ld'; *CJ*, X, 390.

ing day it was defeated by a vote of 192 to 165.[1] Its rejection, attributable in part to a sudden change of heart by William, also reflected the great distaste abjuration roused in the mouths of many Churchmen.[2] Nevertheless, Lowther—who upon royal intimation had spoken against the measure on the 26th after advocating it the day before—and many other members of parliament were seriously concerned about the possibility of a counter-revolt while William was in Ireland. With encouragement from Carmarthen, who was all too conscious that the rejection of abjuration might be used as an electoral weapon against the Tories, bills imposing upon all officials a declaration against assisting James or his adherents were initiated in both Houses.[3] In each, they met the same fate—not outright defeat, but abandonment. Whig enthusiasm for Carmarthen's watered-down substitute for abjuration was only half-hearted, while staunch Churchmen such as Heneage Finch and Nottingham opposed them as 'destructive of the Government' and denounced them as schemes to 'garble' parliament.[4]

The parliamentary furore generated by Bolton's bill and kept alive by abjuration had far-reaching, if unexpected, effects within the administration. The Whigs had hoped that Nottingham's opposition to Bolton's measure would induce the king to remove him from office. But dissatisfied as he was with Nottingham's public reiteration of his *de facto* views,[5] William showed no signs

[1] BM Add. MSS. 29594, fo. 205, Nottingham to Viscount Hatton, 26 April; Bodl. Rawlinson MSS. A 79, fos. 70–8, a detailed account of the debates of 25–26 April; Grey, x, 73–87.

[2] For William's sudden change of mind, see the Devonshire House 'Notebook' *sub* 'Shrewsbury Ld'; Foxcroft, *Halifax*, II, 250; Morrice, III, 178; Burnet, IV, 80–1.

[3] Browning, *Osborne*, I, 472.

[4] *PH*, v, 607–13; Bodl. Rawlinson MSS. A 79, fos. 79–81; BM Egerton MSS. 3345, bundle 3, account of the Lords' debate in Carmarthen's hand. Nottingham's speech, summarized there, survives in LRO, Finch MSS., Political papers 81, and it is from this source that the quotation above is drawn. See also *HMC House of Lords*, 1690–1, pp. 40–4; Burnet, IV, 78–9.

[5] Foxcroft, *Halifax*, II, 250. For rumours of Nottingham's dismissal over this issue, see *The Rawdon papers*, ed. E. Berwick (London, 1819), p. 322; BM Add. MSS. 29573, fo. 428, C. Hatton to Viscount Hatton, 24 April.

of dismissing him. Nor was Nottingham to be provoked into resignation by the bill's passage in amended form.[1] The only discernible effect of the measure's successful progress through parliament, so far as Nottingham was concerned, was to set him at odds once again with the Lord President.[2] However, the failure of abjuration did prompt Shrewsbury, who had been threatening resignation on and off since the previous August, to come to a decision. Disgusted by the king's change of mind over the bill and increasingly resentful of the influence of Carmarthen and Nottingham, he attempted to quit his wearisome post late in April.[3] And this time, despite William's earnest entreaties, the most that Shrewsbury could be prevailed upon to do was to postpone his departure temporarily. Finally, a day before the king was to set out for Ireland, the southern Secretary sent the Seals to him by Edward Russell.[4] Consequently, both Shrewsbury and Comptroller Wharton were omitted from the council of nine William named to advise the queen during his absence. Nottingham, a member of this body, was now left sole Secretary of State, while his kinsman Sir Robert Southwell was appointed to accompany William as Irish Secretary. At the same time, William particularly recommended Carmarthen to Mary.[5]

So ended after fifteen months the contest for the king's favour that had been waged ever since the ministerial appointments of the previous year. None the less, William's decision to leave Carmarthen and Nottingham at the helm can hardly be described as an unmitigated triumph either for them or for the Church party. On the one hand, it was Whig obstructiveness that had at first inclined the king towards the Churchmen. Further, William to the very last had tried to persuade Shrewsbury not to resign, warning

---

[1] For reports that he intended to resign, see *HMC Portland*, III, 447; BM Add. MSS. 17677 KK, fo. 93, van Citters' dispatch of 25 April/5 May.
[2] Hunterian Library, Clarendon MSS., fo. 83, cited in Browning, *Osborne*, I, 481, n. 2.
[3] Burnet, IV, 81–2; *Journaal van Constantijn Huygens*, I, 267; Morrice, III, 139; *Memoirs of Mary, queen of England (1689–1693)*, ed. R. Doebner (Leipzig, 1886), p. 28; *The conduct*, p. 63; Foxcroft, *Halifax*, II, 250.   [4] Somerville, *The king of hearts*, pp. 65–6.
[5] Luttrell, II, 47, 53; *Memoirs of Mary*, pp. 28–9.

him that to leave 'would force him to put himselfe into Ld.
Caermarthens hands' and promising that should he continue 'his
party should bee the major part'.[1] On the other hand, William
was ready to disparage Nottingham to Halifax as late as May,
while Mary's *Memoirs* reveal that even she was not convinced of
the Secretary's fidelity to the régime when William left for
Ireland.[2] At best, then, Carmarthen and Nottingham had won by
default, and Nottingham in particular still had to gain the royal
couple's full confidence and to show that he was capable of fulfilling the responsibilities of his post.

[1] Devonshire House 'Notebook' *sub* 'Shrewsbury Ld'. See also *Memoirs of Mary*, pp.
23–4.
[2] Foxcroft, *Halifax*, II, 252; *Memoirs of Mary*, pp. 29–30.

CHAPTER 7

DEFEAT AT SEA

1690–3

If the dominant theme of English politics during the first sixteen months of William's and Mary's rule was the contest for the royal favour and for domestic political advantage waged among the leading ministers and their adherents in parliament, it was the conduct of the war that was to emerge as the central issue of the succeeding three and a half years. And just as it was the refusal of many of the Whigs in parliament to subordinate the domestic political struggle to the exigencies of the war that led William to dissolve the Convention and to lean more and more on Carmarthen and Nottingham, so the course of the war was to be the principal determinant of the ministers' fate. This was particularly marked in Nottingham's case, not only because he was to act as sole Secretary of State for eighteen of the next forty-one months, but also because of his role as William's minister for naval affairs.

The war, indeed, surged very close to home during William's absence in Ireland in the summer of 1690. On 30 June the Anglo-Dutch fleet was badly mauled by the French off Beachy Head, and the queen and her council were confronted with the threat of invasion. This disaster had not been altogether unforeseen. Torrington, the commander of the allied fleet, had tried to avoid an engagement once he learned that the French force was much stronger than his own. But the accounts of enemy strength which reached Nottingham's office from other informants directly contradicted Torrington's reports.[1] Thus Mary, advised by Nottingham and Russell (who had replaced Shrewsbury on the queen's council of nine) that 'good success from the ships now together'

[1] Ehrman, The navy, pp. 344–6.

could be expected, had approved the issue of positive orders to Torrington to give battle.[1] With no alternative but to fight, Torrington obeyed, but he allowed the Dutch contingent to bear the burden of combat in the hope of maintaining 'a fleet in being'. However, his strategy and his motives were misconstrued and even his skilful conduct of the fleet's retreat up the Thames could not save him from virtually universal obloquy.[2]

For the moment, the situation seemed bleak and a French landing was expected at any time. The council took feverish action: 'all imaginable care' was employed to reinforce the fleet, the militia was raised, a number of prominent Jacobite suspects were detained and an urgent call went out to William to return to England.[3] The king, however, was more sanguine than the council, and in the event the threatened attack never materialized.[4] Sickness aboard the French fleet, lack of stores and a shortage of troops precluded any landing in force, and by 5 August Nottingham could report to William that the French were returning to Brest.[5]

Although the danger of an invasion had receded by early August, the council's, and especially Nottingham's, difficulties were far from over. From early June onwards, in fact, he had been undergoing severe harassment from within and without the council. His troubles seem to have begun when he attempted to follow up Lord Melville's report, which had reached London just before the king's departure, of a conspiracy to overthrow the Scottish government.[6] Acting upon Melville's information, Nottingham issued a warrant on 5 June for the arrest on suspicion of complicity in the plot of Sir John Cochrane and Robert Ferguson (the Duke of Monmouth's former chaplain who had

---

[1] HMC Finch, II, 312, 313, 318; Ehrman, The navy, pp. 348–9.
[2] Ibid. pp. 350, 353–4.
[3] The conduct, pp. 79–80; HMC Finch, II, 334–5, 347–8; CSPD, 1690–1, pp. 55–6, 65–7; Browning, Osborne, 175–8, 180–2; Dalrymple, II, app. III, 109–10.
[4] HMC Finch, II, 364; Browning, Osborne, II, 180.
[5] Ehrman, The navy, p. 353; HMC Finch, II, 398.   [6] Burnet, IV, 110–13.

accompanied William on his expedition in 1688).[1] But while Cochrane finally admitted his involvement, Ferguson remained silent, and on 21 June his attorneys moved that he be bailed while attacking Nottingham for issuing an 'illegal and fantastic' warrant.[2] The Secretary was able neither to rebut this charge nor to prevent Ferguson's release since, despite repeated requests, none of the informations taken against Ferguson in Scotland had as yet reached Whitehall.[3] The difficulty, both Nottingham and Carmarthen soon concluded, lay with Postmaster-General Wildman —a friend of Ferguson's as well as of the mercurial Earl of Monmouth, another member of the queen's council.[4]

Monmouth, as his later career was amply to demonstrate, had unrivalled talents for stirring up trouble, and at this juncture he was bent on discrediting Nottingham. Not only was he apparently encouraging Wildman to interfere with the mails from Scotland; he was also trying to convince Mary and the other members of the council that there was a traitor in their midst. A series of 'lemon letters', informing the queen that her councils were betrayed and containing detailed accounts of the proceedings of the council of nine, had been arriving throughout June.[5] Nottingham, Carmarthen and Marlborough told the queen that Wildman was their author and that he was probably receiving his information from Monmouth.[6] At first, Mary was inclined to attribute their opinions to partisan prejudices, but she soon found that Russell also thought Monmouth responsible.[7] In any case, Monmouth's intent was soon made crystal-clear: he told the queen in an interview early in July that though he had 'a great deal of reason to esteem Ld. Nott.', he thought 'some in his office' were

[1] HMC Finch, II, 288–90; Morrice, III, 115; CSPD, 1690–1, p. 28.
[2] BM Add. MSS. 29573, fo. 468, C. Hatton to Viscount Hatton, 24 June. See also HMC Finch, II, 292, 305; Luttrell, II, 61.
[3] HMC Finch, II, 305, 316–17; CSPD, 1690–1, p. 37.
[4] Dalrymple, II, app. III, 120; Browning, Osborne, II, 165–6, 169.
[5] Dalrymple, II, app. III, 124–5, 133.   [6] Ibid. p. 133.
[7] Ibid. Shrewsbury, too, suspected Monmouth (Devonshire House 'Notebook' sub 'Shrewsbury Ld').

dishonest.[1] But when he began to enlarge on his subject, he received a sharp rebuke from Mary. She told him, as she later related to William, that

I found it very strange you were not thought fitt to choose your own ministers; that they had already removed lord Halifax, the same endeavours were used for lord Carmarthen, and wou'd they now begin to have a bout at lord Nott. too; it wou'd show they wou'd pretend ever to controll the King in his choise, which, if I were he, I wou'd not sufferr.[2]

Despite this rebuff, Monmouth persisted in his efforts to sabotage the work of Nottingham and the council in the hope of reversing William's decision to cast the balance in favour of the Tories. On the one hand, he tried with the help of the Duke of Bolton to obstruct the raising of the £100,000 loan sought from the City by the council in mid-July.[3] On the other, he assured Mary that he could secure double that amount at low interest, but only on the condition that the existing parliament was dissolved and a new one called.[4] Nottingham, however, was confident that endeavours to hinder the raising of funds in the City would fail; as he wrote to Southwell on 19 July, should the Whig aldermen prove recalcitrant 'there is another sort of men' who believed they could lend most of the sum required.[5] Three days later, the Secretary was able to inform William that the loan had been agreed to by the City.[6]

Unabashed, Monmouth was meanwhile adding to the council's problems over the disposal of the command of the fleet. Torrington, who had resigned his post once he brought the battered fleet safely up the Thames, had been imprisoned in the Tower, but the question of his replacement was a vexed one. Haddock, whose appointment William had contemplated in the spring when it

---

[1] Dalrymple, II, app. III, 133–4.
[2] Ibid. p. 134.
[3] Devonshire House 'Notebook' sub 'Murray'. See also Dalrymple, II, app. III, 157; Morrice, III, 171–2, 175, 180–1.
[4] Dalrymple, II, app. III, 141, 157, 159. See also Het Archief van Heinsius, II, 25.
[5] National Maritime Museum, Southwell MSS., vol. XII. Cf. HMC Finch, II, 371.
[6] HMC Finch, II, 377.

seemed that Torrington might resign, and Russell were the obvious candidates. But Russell declined to serve pleading inexperience, while Haddock was unwilling to act save as one of a commission.[1] Monmouth told the queen that he had 'reason to expect the command' himself, but the council eventually declined both his and Shrewsbury's offers to undertake the post.[2] Finally, the king approved the proposal of a commission, and after canvassing the claims of the various senior naval officers Mary and the council decided to name Haddock and Ashby while leaving the choice of the third member to William.[3]

By this time, the Admiralty Board, which had been almost completely ignored in the council's proceedings, was becoming restive. Not only were the Commissioners fearful that they might be called to account in the next session for a choice in which they had had no voice, but also they were opposed to the appointment of Haddock whom they suspected as Nottingham's candidate.[4] These troubled waters were further agitated by Monmouth and Bolton who were busy denigrating Haddock to any who might listen, including the Dutch envoy, as anti-Dutch and a Jacobite.[5] Thus, it was only after two stormy interviews between the queen and the board, as well as a repetition of the king's orders for Haddock's inclusion, that the commission for the joint admirals was finally acquiesced in by four of the seven Admiralty Commissioners.[6]

In the face of such harassment, Nottingham must have been no little gratified to discern Mary's growing confidence in him. Although the queen had described him at the beginning of the

---

[1] Dalrymple, II, app. III, 127, 131; Browning, Osborne, II, 173, 176; Ehrman, The navy, pp. 356–7.   [2] Dalrymple, II, app. III, 127, 131, 144–5.
[3] Ibid. pp. 144–5; Ehrman, The navy, p. 357.
[4] Dalrymple, II, app. III, 148.
[5] Het Archief van Heinsius, II, 24–5; HMC Finch, II, 399; BM Add. MSS. 17677KK, fos. 481–4, van Citters' report of 8/18 August; Devonshire House 'Notebook' sub 'Dutch Ambassador'.
[6] Dalrymple, II, app. III, 145–50, 152; HMC Finch, II, 378, 382–3, 398–9; Bodl. Carte MSS. 79, fos. 315–16, 322, Sir T. Lee to T. Wharton, 22 and 25 July, and 1 Aug.; Morrice, III, 179; Ehrman, The navy, p. 358.

summer as a man 'suspected by most as not true to the government', by mid-July she informed William that 'lord Nott. seems to be very hearty in all affairs; and, to my thinking, appears to be sincere, tho' he does not take much pains to perswade me of it, upon all occasions, as others do'.[1] Then, too, the success of Marlborough's expedition to Ireland must have been some compensation for Torrington's defeat. Marlborough's venture, which had been concerted secretly with the Secretary, was approved by the king in mid-August.[2] Not until his reply was received was the plan revealed to the other members of the council, and then their response was very lukewarm. Irked perhaps at not being informed of the scheme earlier, Carmarthen in particular opposed it, arguing that it would leave England destitute of regular troops should the French attempt a landing in the absence of the fleet.[3] None the less, on 17 September the expeditionary force sailed, and within a month Cork and Kinsale had fallen to Marlborough.

Both Nottingham and Carmarthen must also have been pleased with the course of the autumn parliamentary session, for the coalition patched together by the Lord President with the aid of the Churchmen leaders, Clarges and Finch, proved most effective.[4] The royal request for funds was met with dispatch; nearly four million pounds was voted for the following year before the end of the abbreviated session in early January 1691.[5] Moreover, the caution against distractions from the business of supply voiced in the king's opening speech was, for the most part, heeded. Except for an abortive attempt to address against Carmarthen, the lower

[1] Memoirs of Mary, p. 30; Dalrymple, II, app. III, 134.
[2] The conduct, pp. 86–7, 125; Dalrymple, II, app. III, 157; HMC Finch, II, 414–15; Sir W. Churchill, Marlborough his life and times (London, 1947), I, 287–8. It was apparently on Mary's orders that the plan was not disclosed to the rest of the council before the king was consulted.
[3] Dalrymple, II, app. III, 165, 168.
[4] Browning, Osborne, I, 484, and III, 178–9. See also Nott. U. Portland MSS. PWa 299.
[5] See Burnet's letter of 14 October, printed in Tindal, XIII, 420–1, n. b; the reports of the Brandenburg resident Bonnet printed in L. von Ranke, A history of England principally in the seventeenth century (Oxford, 1875), VI, 148–57; Burnet, IV, 116. The price of the Commons' acquiescence was the king's assent to a measure establishing a Commission of Accounts (Burnet, IV, 116, 118–19; Supplement to Burnet's history, p. 351).

House wasted little time in attacks upon the ministers.[1] Even Torrington's bitter strictures against Nottingham when the Admiral appeared before the Commons to justify his conduct of the fleet evoked little response.[2]

For the moment, then, William did not feel the need to make sweeping ministerial changes. The only major alterations made before he set out with Nottingham for the conference of Allied heads of state at the Hague early in January 1691 were the appointment of Henry Sidney as second Secretary and the reinstatement of Godolphin at the Treasury Board as First Commissioner.[3] Moreover, the rumours current during the spring of 1691 that the penitent Sunderland would be made Lord President, with the consequent 'promotion' of Carmarthen to the Lord Treasurership and Nottingham to the Chancellorship, were not borne out.[4] The Cabinet Council that William named before returning to the continent in May was little changed from that of the previous summer, save for the inclusion of Godolphin and Prince George and the omission of Monmouth and the disgraced Earl of Marlborough.[5]

Nottingham's reaction to these changes is not altogether clear. But if Carmarthen was unhappy with them, it may be suggested that Nottingham was hardly likely to mourn Monmouth's departure, while he may well have felt that he would be able to work amicably with Sidney since the latter was literally the 'king's man'.[6] In any event, Carmarthen and, to an even greater extent, Nottingham were to consolidate their ascendency in royal councils during 1691. The king's willingness to stand godfather (with Princess Anne as godmother) to Nottingham's most recent offspring in February 1691 and the inclusion that spring of his wife among the queen's bedchamber ladies were merely the

[1] PH, v, 649–50; Browning, Osborne, 1, 484–5; Morrice, III, 226.
[2] BM Add. MSS. 17677KK, fos. 338–9, van Citters' report of 18/28 Nov.; Journaal van Constantijn Huygens, 1, 364; Tindal, XIII, 420–1, n. b.
[3] Morrice, III, 219.   [4] CSPD, 1690–1, pp. 349–50.
[5] Notes of their meetings taken by Nottingham are in HMC Finch, III, app. III.
[6] For the Lord President's reaction, see Devonshire House 'Notebook' sub 'Carmarthen Ld'; Supplement to Burnet's history, p. 353.

public tokens of William's and Mary's growing esteem for him.[1] With the king's departure for Flanders for the summer campaign, Nottingham once again 'reigned unchallenged as the minister for naval affairs' with Russell as Admiral, while Carmarthen made the reduction of Ireland his particular concern.[2]

Nottingham's influence was also evident in other spheres, especially the ecclesiastical. Convinced at last of the futility of further attempts at compromise with the non-juring bishops by the discovery of Turner's and perhaps others of his brethren's involvement in Jacobite intrigues, Nottingham and Tillotson took the lead in the replenishment of the episcopal bench after the Secretary's return from the Hague in mid-April 1691.[3] Tillotson, himself, accepted the archbishopric of Canterbury, and great care was taken to nominate other able and respected clerics to the remaining vacancies in the hopes of averting further defections from the establishment.[4] But these plans almost went awry when Sharp and several of the other prospective prelates showed personal scruples at displacing the non-jurors. Only quick action by Nottingham and Tillotson, including an agreement with Sharp that he should become Archbishop of York when the ailing incumbent died and a pre-emptory order to Kidder to accept Bath and Wells, averted a public reinforcement of the non-jurors' stand.[5] When the dust cleared early in May, there were two new archbishops and seven other new prelates, all but one of them drawn from the circle of Nottingham's and Tillotson's friends.[6] Thanks to their efforts, the only complaints to be heard were those of some Whigs who alleged that the new bishops had Jacobite leanings and were too rigid churchmen.[7]

[1] Luttrell, II, 174; CSPD, 1690–1, p. 245; BM Add. MSS. 29594, fo. 236, Nottingham to Viscount Hatton, 15 Aug.; HMC Eighth Report, pt. I, 565.
[2] Ehrman, The navy, p. 374; Browning, Osborne, I, 487–8.
[3] Bodl. Tanner MSS. 27, fo. 237, W[illiam Lloyd, Bishop of] N[orwich] to [Sancroft], 24 Jan. 1691; Burnet, IV, 128–9.
[4] Memoirs of Mary, pp. 37, 39; Supplement to Burnet's history, pp. 358–60; The autobiographies and letters of Thomas Comber, ed. C. E. Whiting (Surtees Society, London, 1945–6), I, 24.   [5] Bennett, 'William III and the episcopate', p. 121.
[6] Ibid. pp. 121–2.   [7] HMC Seventh Report, pp. 198–9.

Nottingham's influence can also be detected in William's decision to implement a more conciliatory policy both in church and state in Scotland. Disillusioned by the excesses of the leaders of the restored Presbyterian Church, the king seems to have been more sympathetic in 1691 than ever before to the repeated pleas made by Nottingham, Carmarthen and other of his advisers on behalf of the dispossessed Episcopal ministers of his northern kingdom.[1] Upon his return from the continent in the autumn of 1691, a commission was appointed, which included both the Secretary and the Lord President, with instructions to try to mediate between the Scottish Presbyterians and Episcopalians.[2] The terms of the compromise proposed by the commissioners— the reinstatement into their livings of those Episcopal clergy who were willing to take the oaths to the government and to accept the Westminster Confession—were first made public by Lord Lothian in his opening speech as royal commissioner to the Presbyterian General Assembly in January 1692. News of his address was received with 'panegyrics' by Nottingham and Carmarthen, as well as by the king himself, for at last it seemed possible that a viable arrangement might be worked out.[3] At the same time, William also decided, as Nottingham had been urging on Portland for months, to appoint a number of the Episcopalian politicians to major official posts, and new commissions of the Scottish Privy Council, Exchequer and Treasury were announced early in March 1692.[4]

Indeed, the king's confidence in Nottingham was never to be

[1] Macaulay, *History of England*, IV, 186–8; Burnet, IV, 132–4; *Supplement to Burnet's history*, p. 357; *HMC Johnstone*, pp. 149, 150, 161; 'Letters to John Mackenzie of Delvine Advocate, one of the principal clerks of session, From the Revd. Alexander Monro, D.D. Sometime principal of the University of Edinburgh 1690 to 1698', ed. W. K. Dickson, *Scottish Historical Society*, 3rd ser., XXI, 217–18.

[2] Ranke, *History of England*, VI, 174; 'Letters to John Mackenzie', p. 222.

[3] J. M. Graham, *Annals and correspondence of the Viscount and the first and second Earls of Stair* (London, 1875), I, 172. See also *CSPD*, 1691–2, pp. 86–8, 92–4.

[4] For Nottingham's advocacy of these changes see, for example, his letter to Portland in *HMC Finch*, III, 172–3. For the ministerial alterations, see *CSPD*, 1691–2, pp. 166–7; Luttrell, II, 379; Graham, *Annals of Stair*, I, 180; Burnet, IV, 155.

greater than in the early months of 1692. Not only did William decide to leave him as sole Secretary of State again rather than to give in to pressure for a Whig candidate for the second secretary-ship after Sidney had been named Irish Lord Lieutenant, but he also seems to have been following Nottingham's advice in electing to try to reconcile the most prominent of the Tory malcontents, the Earl of Rochester, Sir Edward Seymour, and Sir Christopher Musgrave.[1] Despite the counsel of Sunderland, both Rochester and Seymour were sworn of the Privy Council on 1 March 1692, though Musgrave could not be tempted to take office.[2] More-over, on his departure for Holland five days later, William particularly commended Seymour to Mary. Sir Edward was also gratified by being included in the Cabinet Council and by being chosen to succeed Lowther on the Treasury Commission.[3]

However, the certainty of Nottingham's favour with king and queen should not obscure the difficulties with which he was faced at this juncture. For one thing, his relations with Carmarthen had taken a turn for the worse again. On the one hand, the Lord President was reported to be unhappy with Nottingham's alliance with Rochester and Seymour. On the other, Nottingham ap-parently resented Carmarthen's efforts to keep on good terms with a number of his personal enemies, among them Sir Robert Howard.[4] Nottingham may also have suspected the Lord Presi-dent of prompting his son Danby's disclosures of the previous autumn—disclosures which had led to charges of treachery being levelled against him by a number of the more violent Whigs in the confused Delavall affair.[5] For another, Nottingham's friend-ship with Admiral Russell, which dated back to the days of Charles II's Admiralty Commission, was also showing signs of

---

[1] BM Add. MSS. 52279 (unpaginated), Sir William Trumbull's diary, 26 Feb. and 5 March 1692; Burnet, IV, 153–4; Browning, *Osborne*, I, 498.
[2] BM Loan 29/79 (unpaginated), R. Harley to Sir E. Harley, 2 Feb.; Kenyon, *Sunderland*, pp. 248–52.
[3] Luttrell, II, 372, 375; BM Add. MSS. 17677 MM, fo. 139, Baden's report of 8/18 March.
[4] HMC *Seventh Report*, p. 207; *Journaal van Constantijn Huygens*, I, 510.
[5] For this affair, see Browning, *Osborne*, I, 493–5.

wear.[1] Russell, never the easiest of men to keep in good temper, had become more and more aggrieved by criticism of his conduct at sea the previous summer. For months, Nottingham had done his best to soothe the Admiral's injured feelings, and his patience did not go altogether unrewarded.[2] When Russell's outburst finally came in the autumn of 1691, in retort to parliamentary complaints of his failure to prevent French reinforcements reaching Kinsale the previous spring, it was directed chiefly against his old foe Carmarthen.[3] The king himself had to intervene between 'les Carmarthens et les Russells' to prevent disruption of the session.[4] Nevertheless, Russell's passing aspersions on Nottingham's capabilities did not fail to offend the Secretary.[5] Indeed, the prospect of devoting himself to another summer of vainly trying to placate the temperamental Admiral led Nottingham to ask the king to relieve him of his naval responsibilities.[6] But William, though he toyed with the notion of making Sir William Trumbull second Secretary, did not feel that he could politically afford two Tory secretaries, so Nottingham was once again saddled with the now unwelcome role of intermediary between Russell and the Cabinet Council.[7]

While Nottingham's relations with key colleagues were deteriorating, parliamentary dissatisfaction with the administration was growing. The absence of any striking successes at sea or on the continent during the summer of 1691 did not fail to provoke mounting complaints of mismanagement. At the same time, even those Whig ministerialists prepared to support the government's requests for supplies were becoming increasingly disgruntled by

[1] HMC Finch, II, 104 and passim.
[2] Ehrman, The navy, pp. 376–7.
[3] Het Archief van Heinsius, I, 36; Grey, X, 162–7; All Souls College MSS. 158, parliamentary diary of N. Luttrell, I, 4. For Russell's previous enmity to Carmarthen, see HMC Finch, III, 79; CSPD, 1690–1, p. 440.
[4] Ranke, History of England, VI, 164; Het Archief van Heinsius, I, 36.
[5] See a draft in Nottingham's hand of a reply to Russell's allegations (LRO, Finch MSS., Naval and Military papers 28).
[6] Ibid. Naval and Military papers 29.
[7] BM Add. MSS. 52279, 26 Feb. and 5 March 1692.

Nottingham's enhanced influence with the king.[1] But the roots of the administration's difficulties with parliament went still deeper. On the one hand, the Revolution had eased some of the traditional party differences between Whig and Tory, while William's preference for mixed ministries and a trimming domestic policy had further eroded old party ties. On the other hand, the heaviest taxes on land since Cromwellian times were now being levied to finance a massive military effort whose strategy, many members of parliament suspected, was dictated more by William's continental, than by English national interests. Thus by the session of 1691-2, the uneasy governmental coalition over which William presided, ranging in composition from ministerial Whigs of the stripe of Somers to staunch Churchmen such as Nottingham, found itself being challenged by a formidable 'country' opposition.[2] Realizing that 'recriminating has not often been successful', the 'New Country Party' headed by 'old courtiers' such as Musgrave and Clarges and 'old Whigs' such as Paul Foley, Sir John Thompson and the young Robert Harley concentrated on trying to ensure more efficient management of the war effort.[3] And their demands for the careful examination of every item in the estimates submitted to the Commons hindered no little the progress of the supply bills during the early weeks of the session.[4] It was only late in November, after the king had instructed his Privy Councillors in the Commons to inform the House he intended a descent against France in the coming year, that opposition began to slacken.[5]

All too conscious of the increasing restiveness of the ministerial

[1] For the Whig ministerialists' state of mind at this juncture, see A. K. Powis, 'The Whigs and Their Relations with William III in the period 1689-98' (M.A. thesis, University of London, 1940), ch. v; E. L. Ellis, 'The Whig junto in relation to the development of party politics and party organization from its inception to 1714' (D.Phil. dissertation, Oxford University, 1961), ch. III.
[2] Feiling, Tory party, pp. 286-93.
[3] HMC Portland, III, 481.
[4] See, for example, the debates of 6, 9, 14, 18 and 19 Nov. reported in All Souls MSS. 158, I, 1-3, 9-10, 28-31, 42-4, 48-56; PH, v, 656-7, 660-70.
[5] All Souls MSS. 158, I, 82-7; Ranke, History of England, vi, 170.

Whigs and the weakening of the administration's parliamentary position, Nottingham had encouraged the king to bring Rochester and Seymour into the government. But he pinned his chief hopes for the coming year on the implementation of the seaborne attack on France which he had been advocating for the past year and to which William had committed himself during the previous session.[1] Not only did Nottingham believe that the successful execution of this project would be a severe blow to France, but he also felt confident that it would go far to stabilize William's régime.[2] Indeed, he maintained that the success of the descent held out the promise of 'the establishment of their Majesties' throne, the perpetual security of this island, and the peace of Europe'.[3]

Planning for the descent probably did not begin in earnest until February when William held a series of secret meetings with Nottingham, Russell, and the proposed commanders of the land forces, the Duke of Leinster and Lord Galway.[4] However, when the first proposals were laid before the Cabinet Council early in March after William's departure for the Low Countries, it became evident that Nottingham's enthusiasm for the project was by no means shared by all his colleagues. In fact, a majority of Mary's advisers, headed by Godolphin, refused to proceed until further authorization was received from William late in March.[5] Preparations for the descent were then further delayed by the emergency mobilization measures ordered late in April against the threatened French invasion.[6] Yet the defeat inflicted by the Allied forces commanded by Russell on the French fleet off Barfleur not only removed any danger of an enemy landing; it also seemed to assure the success of the descent itself.

Actually, Nottingham's problems with the descent were just

[1] HMC Finch, III, 17, 26, 72, 99, 183–4.
[2] BM Add. MSS. 37991, fos. 5–6, Nottingham to William, 11 March.
[3] HMC Finch, IV, 232.
[4] The conduct, p. 92; LRO, Finch MSS., Naval and Military papers 21, resumé of Nottingham's correspondence concerning the descent. See also HMC Finch, IV, 18–19.
[5] BM Add. MSS. 27991, fos. 5–6.　　　　　　　　　　[6] HMC Finch, IV, 80–1.

beginning in late May. On the one hand, neither the infantry being sent from Ireland nor the transport ships being sent from the Thames had as yet arrived at Portsmouth, thanks to the delays imposed by the Cabinet Council's initial hesitations, the threatened French landing and a shortage of funds.[1] On the other, Russell was adamant that little, if anything, could be done either at St Malo or Brest without infantry.[2] And while the fleet waited upon the Irish regiments and the transports, William—under heavy French pressure in Flanders—was considering reinforcing his army with the five cavalry regiments that had been held behind in England for the descent.[3] Only Nottingham's vigorous protests, seconded by Carmarthen, finally decided him not to order the cavalry's embarkation for the continent.[4] Thus June slipped quickly away, and it was not until mid-July that the long-awaited transport vessels finally reached Portsmouth.[5]

By this time, Russell's waning enthusiasm for the project had reached the vanishing point. As early as 30 June the Admiral had informed Nottingham that the waters off St Malo were far too dangerous for anything to be attempted there.[6] And from this opinion, he could be moved neither by Mary's and Nottingham's pleas for reconsideration nor by the opinion of the generals that St Malo was the most feasible place to attack.[7] Furthermore, when Nottingham, in a private letter of 7 July, entreated Russell 'not to leave it possible to be objected to you that you have omitted anything', the Admiral took umbrage.[8] Interpreting the Secretary's caution to him as criticism of his conduct, he replied in biting terms that much of the difficulty in attacking St Malo now was due to the tardiness of the military preparations.[9]

Russell's readiness to read the worst into Nottingham's exhortations that everything possible be done to follow up the

---

[1] *Ibid.* pp. 151, 181.　　[2] *Ibid.* pp. 153, 190, 194, 228.　　[3] *Ibid.* pp. 240-1.
[4] *Ibid.* pp. 231-3, 243, 250, 254, 265; Browning, *Osborne,* II, 208-9.
[5] *HMC Finch,* IV, 315, 331.　　　　　　[6] *Ibid.* p. 270. See also pp. 252, 256.
[7] *Ibid.* pp. 287, 299, 318; Ehrman, *The navy,* p. 406.
[8] *HMC Finch,* IV, 299.　　　　　　　　　　[9] *CJ,* x, 718.

victory at sea can, no doubt, be accounted for in part by his usual sensitivity to criticism. Nor had his choleric disposition been improved by the dismissal of his friend Marlborough earlier in the year.[1] But the Admiral's anger with Nottingham had other roots as well, among them his belief that the Secretary was supporting a number of flag officers, particularly Killigrew and Delavall, whom he regarded as his enemies.[2] His suspicions were not altogether unfounded, even though his interpretation of Nottingham's reasons for favouring those officers was probably unjustified.[3]

Whatever its origins, Russell's mounting resentment against Nottingham was symptomatic of the frustration both felt in the face of the diminishing possibility of taking advantage of the allied naval victory. Finally, with August upon them, one last effort was made by the Cabinet to salvage something from the campaign. Nottingham, Carmarthen, Devonshire, Dorset, Rochester, Cornwallis and Sidney journeyed on 1 August to Portsmouth to hold a council of war with the land and sea officers. But neither in public nor in private could any of the flag officers be prevailed upon to undertake to cover an assault on St Malo.[4] There was nothing left now to do but to follow the orders sent by William in case all else should prove impossible. The troops were dispatched to Ostend for a projected attack on Dunkirk, while the fleet sailed for the French coast in the vain hope either of meeting the enemy or of preventing the French ships that had taken refuge at St Malo from getting to Brest.[5]

By this time, Nottingham's relations with Russell were at the

---

[1] Nott. U. Portland MSS. PWa 1348, Lord Sidney to Earl Portland, 31 July; Burnet, IV, 164–5. [2] *Ibid.* p. 165.

[3] While Killigrew, who spent the 1692 campaign on shore (with full sea pay), was pressing Nottingham to be promoted to Rear Admiral, Delavall was bombarding the Secretary with complaints of Russell's partiality. Meanwhile, Nottingham was seconding Delavall's candidacy as successor to Richard Beach on the Navy Board (Luttrell, II, 337; *CSPD*, 1691–2, p. 163; BM Egerton MSS. 2618, fo. 176; *HMC Finch*, IV, 142, 182, 192, 235–6, 328, 372).

[4] *Ibid.* p. 369; Nott. U. Portland MSS. PWa 1349, Lord Sidney to Earl Portland, 5 Aug. [5] *HMC Finch*, IV, 363, 373.

breaking point. As it became increasingly apparent during July that the Admiral was mainly bent on extricating himself from the danger of falling victim to the parliamentary onslaught that seemed certain to follow the summer's debacle, the remnants of Nottingham's fund of patience were rapidly dissipated.[1] Russell's efforts, particularly his letter of 29 July, to cast the blame for the failure of the descent upon the Cabinet generally and Nottingham specifically received short shrift from the latter in the lengthy justifications meant for the king's eyes which he penned to Portland.[2] To be sure, he conceded to Portland, neither the troops nor the transports promised for the project were ready at the end of May as had originally been intended, but this, he maintained, was primarily due to the disruption caused by the threat of invasion.[3] To the Admiral's contention that by mid-July it was too late in the summer to attempt anything against the French, Nottingham confessed his inability to answer 'as a seaman', but he pointed out that it seemed a very strange position since Russell had already indicated that the first and second rates could be kept at sea until the end of August and the remainder of the fleet until October.[4] 'Tis yet stranger', he continued, 'that if it be an objection, that either that or the attempt was not made sooner; at St Malo before the preparations there made land men necessary to attack the town...or else at Brest where land men are not so necessary.'[5] 'Upon the whole', Nottingham concluded, 'I can't but think this letter, tho' writt to me was designed for another place'—a comment borne out by the Admiral's public disclosure of its contents a few days later.[6]

But if Russell hoped to persuade the king that the responsibility for failure was not his, he had badly miscalculated. William had

[1] Their correspondence, once so cordial, became increasingly formal as Russell's recriminations multiplied and Nottingham's anger mounted.
[2] Sidney also took up the cudgels on behalf of the Cabinet Council (Nott. U. Portland MSS. PWa 1348–9, 1351, to Portland, 31 July, 5 and 9 Aug.).
[3] *HMC Finch*, IV, 355.   [4] *Ibid.* p. 369.
[5] *Ibid.*   [6] *Ibid.* pp. 356, 373–4.

been angered by the Admiral's obstinate refusal to consider an attempt either at St Malo or anywhere else and offended by the tone of his letter.[1] As Blathwayt assured Nottingham in a private note of 8 August,

the King is resolved...to support the committee and the reputation of their proceedings, though the Preparations must be acknowledged to have been very late, which is plainly a consequence of our want of money and other disabilities at home.[2]

While the principals in the summer's events busied themselves with mutual recrimination, the ministers began to reckon the parliamentary consequences. Seymour and Rochester were particularly pessimistic; the latter even advised in a memorandum to the king of mid-August that it might be necessary to reduce drastically the size of the English forces in Flanders during the coming year. Such a withdrawal, Rochester suggested, might be offset by increasing England's naval contribution to the war effort.[3] The views of the Cabinet Council, when it met to discuss the situation, tended to confirm Rochester's gloomy prognosis. All those present agreed that it would be very difficult, if not impossible, to induce the Commons to grant as large a supply for the coming year as they had done in the past. And even should they do so, it was unlikely that they 'would be of opinion that so great a share of the expence should or could be spent in Flanders'.[4] However, Nottingham, as well as Carmarthen, Lowther, Pembroke and Trevor, did hold out some hope to the king.[5] In a detailed letter to Portland commenting upon the opinions expressed by the Cabinet Council, Nottingham outlined his own assessment of the situation. The proposal to excuse the Dutch of their naval quota in return for the withdrawal of English troops from Flanders would have great appeal, he warned, particularly because there was much concern that the supply and payment of the forces on

---

[1] HMC Finch, IV, 373-4, 384.   [2] Ibid. p. 374.
[3] Dalrymple, II, app. III, 240-3.   [4] HMC Finch, IV, 423. See also p. 418.
[5] See Carmarthen's comments on Rochester's memorandum (Dalrymple, II, app. III, 240-3).

the continent was gravely depleting the English coinage. Yet acceptance of this proposal, he felt, would not only endanger the alliance but would also be impractical since England had neither ships enough nor sailors to man them without crippling her trade. Assuming, then, that an adequate supply could be obtained from the Commons, the only plan which would be of military value and also acceptable to parliament would be a massive invasion of France. Nottingham conceded that this was not necessarily the most advantageous method of carrying on the war, but he argued that it might well be the only feasible one given the probable reaction of the Houses to the events of the past summer.[1]

William was dismayed at the gloomy picture drawn by his ministers, especially 'as it differs very much from what the state of Europe certainly requires', and he enjoined them to keep their advice secret lest it prejudice further the grant of supply.[2] As he told the Houses in his opening speech of 4 November, the war effort could not be stinted. But taking his cue from his ministers' forecasts of parliamentary opinion and their recommendations on tactics, the king requested from the Houses not only their assistance but also their advice. Further, he informed them that despite the failure of the past summer, a descent 'with a much more considerable force' would be attempted the following year.[3] Not surprisingly, the Commons chose to proceed by considering first what advice they should offer, despite pleas of a severe shortage of funds from government spokesmen.[4] And not the least of their proposed recommendations involved the controversial issue of mismanagement of naval affairs.

Once the House began to inquire into the conduct of the previous campaign, Russell hastened to make prophets out of

[1] HMC Finch, IV, 425–8. For a similar assessment of the prospects for the coming session see BM Loan 29/135, bundle 7, P. Foley to R. Harley, 17 Sept.
[2] HMC Finch, IV, 440.
[3] PH, V, 707–9.
[4] All Souls MSS. 158, II, 9–10, 30–4; CJ, X, 697, 700.

those who had predicted that he would 'complain justify himself and accuse others'.[1] When he was questioned on 12 November about the failure to follow up the victory at sea, he denied all responsibility and claimed that it rested with those on shore.[2] Initially, the Commons confined their criticism to the Admiralty Commissioners (almost all of them Whigs), but it was obvious that their inquiries would not be allowed to rest there. Indeed, the Whig response to attacks on members of the Admiralty Board was to excuse them, as Smith did in the debate of 21 November, by arguing that 'they must receive their orders from above', and the House signified its acceptance of this contention in passing a resolution that henceforth all orders to the fleet should be transmitted by the Admiralty.[3] The speech of Comptroller Wharton's brother Goodwin that same day was an even clearer gauge of the way the wind was blowing. Not only did he assert (as did Paul Foley) that the burden of the Secretary's office was too great for one man to bear; he also impugned Nottingham's courage and condemned his failure to procure accurate intelligence.[4]

Meanwhile, a select committee of the Commons, named on the 16th, was busy trying to allot the blame for the miscarriage of the descent, and on the 27th Speaker Trevor privately warned Nottingham that its report would be 'levelled' against him.[5] Thus forewarned, Nottingham's friends were prepared when the House took up the committee's report three days later. After several speakers had descanted on the failure of the expedition against France and an address to request the removal of those Cabinet Councillors responsible for its mismanagement had been suggested, Sir Edward Seymour rose to defend Nottingham and

---

[1] BM Loan 29/135, bundle 7, P. Foley to R. Harley, 17 Sept. See also *HMC Portland* III, 502.

[2] All Souls MSS. 158, II, 21-2; Grey, V, 244-8.

[3] Accounts of the debate are in All Souls MSS. 158, II, 54-65; Bodl. Carte MSS. 130, fos. 339-40; Nott. U. Portland MSS. PWa 2389; Ranke, *History of England*, VI, 184-5; *PH*, V, 722-9.

[4] *PH*, V, 724; Nott. U. Portland MSS. PWa 2389. For a detailed refutation of the charge that Nottingham was negligent in obtaining intelligence, see *The conduct*, pp. 126-7; *HMC Finch*, III, vi-vii, and IV, xviii-xix.   [5] *CJ*, X, 701; *HMC Finch*, IV, 512.

himself from the charge of being 'either fools or Knaves'.[1] Russell and Leinster, he pointed out, had been consulted on the plans for the summer campaign. And in any case, the committee's report was both incomplete and partial since its members did not have before them all the relevant letters and papers, especially Nottingham's. Once they had been considered, Seymour maintained, 'I believe you will find the fault in another place.'[2]

Seymour's counter-attack did not pass unchallenged, especially by the ministerial Whigs led by the Comptroller. None the less, at this stage, the debate—save for a slip by one of the more violent Whig backbenchers, John Arnold, who denounced Nottingham by name—was still being carried on without specific reference to individuals. Rather, the Whigs attempted to capitalize on Tory scruples of conscience; John Smith, the Whartons, Sir Charles Sedley and Sir Edward Hussey all spoke against men of 'de facto principles'. They then moved an address which would have requested William to employ 'only those whose principles obliged them to stand by him and his right against the late King James'.[3] But after opposition from Lowther, Sir Henry Goodrick and Sir Richard Temple, the wording of the motion was greatly watered-down and then carried nemine contradicente.[4] However, a resolution calling for the consideration of all the papers relevant to the descent put forward 'by the friends of the Lord Nottingham... was opposed by his Enemies the Whiggs, so carried in the Negative'.[5]

The attack against Nottingham reached its climax on 5 December when the Commons again went into Committee of the Whole

[1] All Souls MSS. 158, II, 106–10.
[2] Ibid. p. 110.
[3] Ibid. pp. 110–17; BM Add. MSS. 34096, fo. 228, R. Yard to Sir W. Colt, 2/12 Dec.; PRO, SP 8/12, no. 146; Ranke, History of England, VI, 191; HMC Portland, III, 508.
[4] All Souls MSS. 158, II, 110–17; The conduct, pp. 105–7. The attack on de facto men did not die on the 2nd. It was followed by a salvo against Edmund Bohun—the Licenser of the Press, appointed by Nottingham on Bishop John Moore's recommendation—which produced his dismissal (Macaulay, History of England, IV, 353–61; Bodl. Tanner MSS. 25, fo. 360, E. Bohun to Bishop Moore, 22 Aug. 1692).
[5] All Souls MSS. 158, II, 117; BM Add. MSS. 34096, fo. 228.

to discuss their advice to the king. In spite of a determined rear-guard effort by his defenders, notably Seymour, Lowther, Musgrave and Sir Joseph Tredenham, it was carried by a single vote that those responsible for the miscarriages of the past summer 'were the council that had the management thereof'—a resolution which, Robert Harley explained, 'was expressly levelled at the Earl of Nottingham'.[1] Yet as Seymour took care to remind the House, 'if you will goe on to judge persons without hearing... assure yourself they will be heard in another place'.[2]

Sir Edward knew well of what he spoke, for a week earlier the Lords had begun their own investigation of the abortive descent.[3] Nottingham, if not the prime mover of this inquiry, certainly supported it, avowing in a lengthy oration that he was ready to justify himself to his peers.[4] On 6 December the Secretary laid an abstract of all his papers before the Lords, and three days later he openly took the offensive. Speaking in committee, he added to the materials he had already submitted considerable detail 'which more nearly touch'd Mr Russell, as if he had been wanting in several things that were incumbent upon him'.[5] As one observer remarked, 'there is a kind of warr declared between my Lord Nottingham and Mr Russell; and if you reflect upon...the votes in the House of Commons which were pushed on by Mr Russell and his friends, you will easily perceive by whom it was begun'.[6] Had not the king himself intervened in early January by asking Nottingham not to press the issue further, the 'war' between the Secretary and the Admiral in which the two Houses found themselves pitted against one another in defence of their own members

---

[1] All Souls MSS. 158, II, 148–51; *HMC Portland*, III, 509; BM Add. MSS. 34096, fos. 230–1, R. Yard to Sir W. Colt, 6/16 Dec.

[2] All Souls MSS. 158, II, 150.

[3] *LJ*, xv, 127; *HMC House of Lords*, 1692–3, p. 179.

[4] *The conduct*, p. 108; Luttrell, II, 630.

[5] BM Add. MSS. 34096, fo. 236, R. Yard to Sir W. Colt, 13/23 Dec.; *The conduct*, p. 108; Luttrell, II, 638; *HMC House of Lords*, 1692–3, pp. 179–80; *LJ*, xv, 135. A draft of Nottingham's speech is in LRO, Finch MSS., Naval and Military papers 29.

[6] BM Add. MSS. 34096, fo. 236. See also Bodl. Carte MSS. 130, fo. 343, R. Price to Duke of Beaufort, 15 Dec.

would have completely disrupted the session.[1] As it was, however, Nottingham—'having had before. . .the satisfaction of His Majesty's approbation of his service that summer, with thanks for his great labor and diligence in it'—complied with the royal request, and the Lords then abandoned their contest with the Commons.[2]

Although the parliamentary struggle ended inconclusively, it was not without effect at Whitehall. Royal support for Nottingham had not wavered since William's first angry reaction to Russell's behaviour in August. Whatever efforts were made to conciliate the Whigs on his return from the continent, the king had also taken care to reiterate his approval of the earl's conduct.[3] Moreover, when a petition was moved against Nottingham in the London Common Council in November complaining of his interference in City elections, the Court took 'all possible paines' to quash it.[4] Thus it was not surprising that when Russell objected to serving at sea the following campaign if he had to continue to receive his orders from Nottingham, William chose to retain his Secretary rather than the temperamental Admiral.[5] A tentative decision to replace Russell seems to have been made sometime in December, and on 22 January the names of the new Admirals— Killigrew, Delavall and Shovell—were announced, 'to the declared satisfaction of the Lord Nottingham and his friends and the discontent of the other'.[6]

---

[1] BM Add. MSS. 34096, fos. 239, 242, R. Yard to Sir W. Colt, 16/26 and 20/30 Dec.; HMC House of Lords, 1692–3, pp. 184 and 185, n. 2; HMC Seventh Report, p. 211; LJ, xv, 167, 173; Ranke, History of England, vi, 201; HMC Kenyon, p. 269. See also BM Loan 29/186, fo. 234, R. Harley to Sir E. Harley, 24 Dec. 1692, for a suggestion that Carmarthen, in his usual fashion, was doing his best to keep the pot upon the boil.

[2] The conduct, p. 109. If Nottingham's memoirs can be trusted on this point, the rumours reported by Bonnet of his impending resignation never had any substance. Cf. Ranke, History of England, vi, 192, 202, 206.

[3] The conduct, p. 109; HMC Seventh Report, p. 211.

[4] BM Loan 29/185, fo. 139, P. Foley to R. Harley, 1 Oct. 1692; Bodl. Locke MSS. C16, fo. 113, Lord Monmouth to J. Locke, 19 Nov. See also Luttrell, ii, 616.

[5] For Russell's attitude, see Luttrell, iii, 18; HMC Seventh Report, p. 211; Ranke, History of England, vi, 203; Ehrman, The navy, p. 412.

[6] Samuel Pepys' naval minutes, p. 290. See also Luttrell, iii, 18. The Whigs complained of Killigrew's and Delavall's supposed Jacobite sympathies (Burnet, iv, 186; Supplement to Burnet's history, p. 380).

However, the failure of Russell and the Whigs to secure Nottingham's ouster could not conceal the fact that William's administration could hardly muster a majority in parliament save on questions of supply. The progress of those two 'country' favourites, the Place and Triennial bills, graphically illustrated the government's weakness. The first of these measures, introduced by Sir Edward Hussey and supported by most of the Whigs as well as by the New Country party, had been approved by the Commons on 22 December with only Tory ministerialists such as Lowther and Seymour dissenting.[1] Nottingham, Carmarthen, Rochester, most of the bishops and a few court Whigs attacked the bill as an unseasonable encroachment on the royal prerogative and finally succeeded in defeating it by two votes on its third reading in the Lords, but their success was really a tribute to their assiduity in collecting proxies and the effects of William's own intervention against the measure.[2] Neither oratory nor royal lobbying could secure the rejection of Shrewsbury's Triennial bill, and it took a royal veto to prevent the measure from reaching the statute book this session.[3] To add to the government's woes was the Commons' angry investigation of, and address against, miscarriages in Irish administration.[4]

The source of the government's difficulties was by now unmistakable—the dissatisfaction of many 'country' members of parliament with the handling of the war effort coupled with the defection of the ministerial Whigs resentful of Nottingham's and Carmarthen's dominance at Whitehall.[5] The remedy was equally obvious, at least to Sunderland, who was once again pressing William to put himself in the hands of the Whigs.[6] But the king

[1] Ranke, *History of England*, VI, 198; All Souls MSS. 158, II, 217–19; *PH*, V, 745–7.
[2] *HMC Seventh Report*, p. 212; Ranke, *History of England*, VI, 199–200; Luttrell, III, 5; *HMC House of Lords*, 1692–3, pp. xii–xiii, xxxix, 279–81.
[3] *Ibid.* pp. 299–301; Ranke, *History of England*, VI, 206, 212; All Souls MSS. 158, II, 342–7; *PH*, V, 763–8. Fragmentary notes of Nottingham's speech against the bill are in LRO, Finch MSS., Political papers 104.
[4] All Souls MSS. 158, II, 381–8, 394–5, 425–88; *PH*, V, 768–9.
[5] For the Whigs at this juncture, see Powis, 'The Whigs 1689–98', ch. VI; Ellis, 'The Whig junto', ch. III.   [6] Kenyon, *Sunderland*, pp. 254–5.

still jibbed at becoming dependent on a party which he thought he could not trust.[1] Moreover, Nottingham remained *persona grata* to both William and Mary despite his *rapprochement* under parliamentary pressure with rabid Churchmen such as Seymour, Musgrave and Rochester.[2] None the less, some concessions to the Whigs could not be avoided. In the first reshuffle that William contemplated, Nottingham was apparently to have been promoted to the Lord Chancellorship.[3] But the earl refused this opportunity of a 'seasonable retreat'.[4] He did, however, once more ask the king to name a second Secretary to ease his burden of work and '*pour partager la moitié de la haine publique avec luy*'.[5] Yet he could hardly have been pleased either by William's choice of the old Exclusionist Sir John Trenchard to be his colleague or by Somers' elevation to the Lord Keepership. The Tory leaders did not trouble to conceal their dismay at the new appointments announced in March 1693; even Monmouth, angered by the royal veto of the Triennial bill, found some consolation in their 'so apparent and so great...ill humour'.[6]

William had only just left London to take ship at Harwich for the continent when the first ministerial quarrel erupted. Somers and the Whigs believed that they had secured a firm commitment from the king to name Sir Thomas Trevor to the now vacant Attorney-General's post, and the new Lord Keeper had already approached Edward Ward to take the subordinate position of Solicitor-General.[7] But at the last moment, William's resolution

---

[1] *Ibid.* pp. 254–6; *Memoirs of Mary*, p. 61.

[2] In April 1693 Mary stood as godmother to Nottingham's fourteenth child (Bodl. Carte MSS. 233, fo. 95, newsletter to T. Wharton, 20 April 1693). For Nottingham's relations with Rochester and Musgrave, see *CSPD*, 1691–2, pp. 332–3; BM Add. MSS. 29594, fo. 264, Nottingham to Viscount Hatton, 8 Dec.; LRO, uncalendared Finch MSS., 1693, Nottingham to Blathwayt, 4 July.

[3] Reports of his appointment began circulating as early as mid-January, e.g. BM Add. MSS. 29574, fos. 137, 154, C. Hatton to Viscount Hatton, 14 Jan. and 2 March.

[4] Ranke, *History of England*, VI, 215; Viscount Weymouth to Lord Eland, 25 July 1693, quoted in Foxcroft, *Halifax*, II, 173, n. 2.

[5] Ranke, *History of England*, VI, 215.

[6] Bodl. Locke MSS. C 16, fo. 115, 25 March. See also Kenyon, *Sunderland*, p. 256.

[7] *Miscellaneous State Papers, from 1501 to 1726*, ed. Earl of Hardwicke (London, 1778),

had been altered by representations in Ward's favour from Nottingham and the other Tory ministers.[1] Nottingham's reasons for preferring Ward to Trevor are not altogether clear. He professed to have no personal interest in the matter, but it may be that he had been offended by Trevor's imputations of misconduct against him made during the previous parliamentary session.[2] Somers was outraged at the king's change of mind and offered his resignation but his protests were of no avail.[3] Ward kissed the king's hand as Attorney-General on the 30th, while the disgruntled Trevor was continued as Solicitor.[4]

Another source of disagreement among the ministers was the plan for the descent that William had announced to the Houses at the beginning of the 1692–3 session. By April, Godolphin was again complaining both to the king and to his colleagues of the great expense and limited chances of success of such a venture.[5] But a number of the ministers including Nottingham, who had lost none of his enthusiasm for such schemes, received Godolphin's estimates with scepticism, and preparations were allowed to continue.[6] Nothing, however, eventually came of the proposed attack on Brest for late in May the main fleet was diverted to another service.

By this time, intelligence had reached England that the enemy's Brest and Toulon squadrons had probably joined, though their precise whereabouts was not known until mid-June. On 19 May,

II, 426–8; Luttrell, III, 59, 60; Bodl. Tanner MSS. 25, fos. 22, 26, H. North to Archbishop Sancroft, 21 March and 2 April.
[1] FSL, Newdigate newsletters, 2188, 30 March.
[2] All Souls MSS. 158, II, 210; Bodl. Tanner MSS. 25, fo. 26. At the same time, Nottingham seems to have been urging the appointment of the Churchmen's pet general, Trelawney, as Governor of Plymouth. As he wrote to the king on 25 March (in a draft later discarded), 'the late disposal of very many offices makes it at this time the more expedient for your Majesty's interests to bestow some mark of favour upon a man of his principles' (LRO, uncalendared Finch MSS., 1693).
[3] *Miscellaneous State Papers*, II, 426–8.
[4] Bad weather had brought the king back to London briefly (Luttrell, III, 62, 67).
[5] *CSPD*, 1693, pp. 102–3.
[6] *Ibid.* pp. 102–3, 111–12; Ehrman, *The navy*, p. 491; Luttrell, III, 53 and *passim*; National Maritime Museum, Southwell MSS., vol. XIV, Nottingham to Blathwayt, 3 May.

then, the allied fleet was ordered to escort the long-delayed Turkey convoy out of danger. But the joint admirals only accompanied the four hundred richly laden merchantmen and their escort under Rooke to fifty leagues south-west of Ushant, leaving them an easy prey for the combined French fleet cruising off the eastern coast of Spain. Furthermore, the main Anglo-Dutch fleet was forced to put in to Torbay early in July to revictual so that even the hope of revenging the imminent loss of the convoy evaporated.[1]

The outcry when news of the disaster reached England was enormous, and much of it was directed against Nottingham and 'his' three Admirals.[2] That he bore no direct responsibility for the disaster was made abundantly clear by the subsequent parliamentary inquiry. To begin with, when Trenchard had accepted the second Secretaryship, all the naval duties that had been engrossed by Nottingham were transferred to him.[3] When Blathwayt persisted in writing to the earl on sea affairs, Nottingham repeatedly reminded him they were no longer in his province, though the Secretary at War continued to complain that Trenchard did not keep the king fully informed.[4] Nor could the delay in the Turkey fleet's sailing, which had originally been scheduled for the autumn of 1692, be attributed to Nottingham. More than once he had urged its dispatch, and the initial postponement of its sailing until the early spring of 1693 had been caused by Dutch tardiness in readying their merchantmen.[5] Even the Levant merchants, whose first despairing reaction had been to clamour against Nottingham, were brought to admit the justice of his defence.[6] Finally,

[1] Ehrman, *The navy*, pp. 492–3, 500–1.
[2] A bit of doggerel survives to attest to popular sentiment: 'That the Turkey fleet was sold is true and not a sham; / You may find it out by searching as far as Nottingham', quoted in *The conduct*, p. 106, n. 49. See also BM Add. MSS. 29574, fos. 201, 206–7, C. Hatton to Viscount Hatton, 22 July and 1 Aug.; Nott. U. Portland MSS. PWa 1172, Sir J. Somers to Earl Portland, 25 July; Foxcroft, *Halifax*, II, 173, n. 2.
[3] *The conduct*, pp. 116–17. See also Ehrman, *The navy*, II, 412.
[4] LRO, uncalendared Finch MSS., 1693, Nottingham to Blathwayt, 21 April, 3 and 4 May, Blathwayt to Nottingham, 25 May/4 June, 3/13 July.
[5] HMC *Finch*, IV, 469; *The conduct*, pp. 121–3; Ehrman, *The navy*, pp. 491–2.
[6] *The conduct*, pp. 121–3, 128. The original petition was toned down considerably before presentation (Bodl. Carte MSS. 233, fo. 214, J. Vernon to T. Wharton, 26 July).

the charge levelled against him of failing to obtain adequate intelligence of the French fleet's movements was also demonstrated to be unfounded.[1] As he later informed the House of Lords, on the day the Turkey ships had sailed he had received a report of the French preparations at Brest which had been read at the Cabinet Council and then ordered to be sent to the Admirals.[2]

But whatever his actual responsibility, Nottingham was still regarded as the patron of the joint Admirals, and 'right or wrong the Whiggs lay all miscarriages at my Lord Nottingham's doore'.[3] Furthermore, despite his assertion to Blathwayt that he was not concerned to defend the Admirals, Nottingham realized that his fate might well be bound up with theirs.[4] Thus on 13 July Nottingham wrote Delavall asking to be furnished with a justification of their conduct for his own use. In addition, he helped to prepare their defence during the Privy Council's investigation of the affair the following autumn.[5]

Meanwhile, the pressure was building up on William to remove Nottingham on the grounds that his retention would only intensify parliamentary anger over the loss of the Turkey ships. Sunderland harped on this tune, and on the general need for a ministerial reconstruction, all summer long to Portland. And by early August, rumours of the earl's impending ouster, which Sunderland's ostentatious preparations for the coming session did nothing to dispel, were already making the rounds in London.[6]

---

[1] BM Add. MSS. 17677NN, fos. 337-8, L'Hermitage's report of 7/17 Nov.; Ranke, *History of England*, VI, 219.

[2] The intelligence from Brest, however, never reached the Admirals because of a misunderstanding between the Secretaries (*The conduct*, p. 117; *HMC House of Lords*, n.s. I, 101; *LJ*, XV, 343; *CSPD*, 1693, p. 162; Ralph, *History of England*, II, 470-1; BM Add. MSS. 29574, fos. 264-5, C. Hatton to Viscount Hatton, 18 Jan. 1694).

[3] BM Add. MSS. 29574, fos. 206-7, C. Hatton to Viscount Hatton, 1 Aug.

[4] LRO, uncalendared Finch MSS., 1693, Nottingham to Blathwayt, 14 July.

[5] *Ibid.* Nottingham to Delavall, 13 July; *ibid.* Naval and Military papers 30. See also Nott. U. Portland MSS. PWa 417, Nottingham to Earl Portland, 8 Aug.

[6] Kenyon, *Sunderland*, pp. 258-61; BM Add. MSS. 29574, fo. 206; NRO, Isham MSS. 1484, J. Isham to Sir J. Isham, 8 Aug.; LRO, uncalendared Finch MSS., 1693, G. Dolben to Nottingham, 3 Sept.; BM Add. MSS. 17677NN, fos. 226, 259, L'Hermitage's reports of 1/11 and 19/29 Sept.

Nottingham tried to put the best face possible on the situation, consoling himself with the thought that 'as I came into my post by his Majesty's command so I shall readily quitt it when it is for his service...and in the meantime [I] shall discharge my duty as becomes a faithful servant'.[1] Nevertheless, he was hastening to conclude negotiations for the purchase of a country estate on which he had had his eye since 1689, Burley in Rutland, formerly the property of the second Duke of Buckingham. 'I am very uneasy till it be perfected', he confided to Hatton late in July, 'that I may have the satisfaction of having some place to retire to.'[2] Unfortunately, his plans soon became public, and he now found himself accused of peculation as well as incompetence, if not treachery, since it was exaggeratedly reported that he was laying out £80,000 on his new purchase and planning to spend £50,000 more on building.[3]

When William returned to London late in October, Nottingham's worst forebodings were soon realized. Though the king was still reluctant to dispense with his services, he now felt he had no other choice.[4] William hoped that Nottingham would spare him the unpleasantness of a dismissal, but at the last moment Nottingham decided that to resign would constitute an admission of culpability on his part.[5] Indeed, it was reported that he was 'desirous to have justified himselfe in Parliament before he parted with his employment'.[6] But a scapegoat would be of little use at

[1] LRO, uncalendared Finch MSS., 1693, Nottingham to Delavall, 1 Sept. See also BM Add. MSS. 17677NN, fo. 226.

[2] BM Add. MSS., 29595, fo. 23, 27 July.

[3] Ibid. 29574, fos. 226-7, C. Hatton to Viscount Hatton, 5 Sept.; ibid. 17677NN, fo. 226. Actually, the estate only cost him £50,000 though he did lay out another £30,000 on building in the years after 1694—expenditures financed out of his wife's dowry, the profits of the Secretaryship, the sale of his house in Kensington to William in 1689 and the disposal of some of his Essex properties, and current income (Habakkuk, 'Daniel Finch', pp. 146, 151–70).

[4] Memoirs of Mary, p. 61. See also BM Add. MSS. 34594, fo. 130, William to A. Heinsius, 3/13 Nov., French transcript.

[5] Hatton correspondence, II, 198; BM Add. MSS. 17677NN, fos. 337–8, L'Hermitage's dispatch of 7/17 Nov.; Ranke, History of England, VI, 217, 219.

[6] BRO, Trumbull Add. MSS. I, A. Stanyan to Sir W. Trumbull, 6 Nov.

the end of the session, and on 6 November Trenchard was sent to Nottingham to demand the Seals. Nottingham, however, was determined to return the Seals himself to William for, as he told Trenchard, 'he received em from his hands and so would render em'.[1] That afternoon—with the comfort of the king's assurance, given in a private audience, that he was 'entirely satisfied of his. . . fidelity and zeal to his service'—Nottingham began to remove his possessions from the Secretary's office.[2]

[1] *Hatton correspondence*, II, 198. See also Ranke, *History of England*, VI, 219.
[2] LRO, uncalendared Finch MSS., 1693, a fragmentary account in Nottingham's hand of his interview with the king. See also BM Add. MSS. 17677NN, fos. 337–8; Luttrell, III, 221; *The conduct*, p. 123; Ranke, *History of England*, VI, 219.

CHAPTER 8

IN THE WILDERNESS

1693–1702

Nottingham's enforced retirement in November 1693—after having served for almost five years as a minister with important departmental responsibilities and as one of William's most trusted English advisers—greatly reduced his political influence. Instead of helping to formulate as well as executing policy, he found himself now in a position where frequently he could do little more than react to ministerial measures. Indeed, waiting upon events, instead of attempting to shape them, was to be the dominant characteristic of Nottingham's political career for the remainder of William's reign, since for the most part he did not choose to play the part of an active opposition leader.

In the months immediately after his ouster, Nottingham's chief concern was to fend off the parliamentary censure of his conduct sought by the Whigs. In the heated Commons' debates of November and December 1693 on the naval miscarriages of the previous summer, the former Secretary found himself accused not only of incompetence, but also of corruption and treachery, while Admirals Killigrew and Delavall were treated no more gently.[1] But despite the House's passage on 17 November of a resolution asserting that there had been 'notorious and treacherous mismanagement' in the loss of the Turkey convoy, the Admirals and, by implication, Nottingham were at least partially exonerated, if only by paper-thin majorities, by the Commons' votes of 29 November and 6 December.[2]

A similar investigation in the Lords provided Nottingham with

---

[1] *PH*, v, 775–87, 789–93, 797–800. The speech Nottingham prepared in reply to these charges is printed in *The conduct*, pp. 124–32.
[2] *PH*, v, 789–93, 797–800; *CJ*, xi, 5, 14, 21.

a forum to defend himself. The peers' interrogation of the Admirals revealed that they had not been notified before they separated from Rooke that the French fleet was at sea, and a motion in their justification was then approved by the upper House over bitter Whig protests on 10 January.[1] An explanation of the failure to inform the Admirals of the intelligence from Brest which Nottingham had received on 30 May was the next object of the Lords' inquiry, and the beginnings of one were provided as soon as the king was induced to permit disclosure of the Cabinet Council's deliberations on naval affairs. On the 15th Nottingham himself explained that he had brought the account of French movements to a Cabinet meeting on 31 May, while Godolphin and others testified that they had assumed it had then been passed on to Trenchard to be forwarded to the fleet.[2] Their testimony thus shifted the burden of explanation onto the Whig Secretary Trenchard, and the upper House agreed to refer the matter back to the Commons to inquire of their member. But the lower House, or at least its Whig members, were in no haste to interrogate Trenchard. Despite Seymour's taunt 'that he wase amazed that those very personns who were soe warme in pursuing the miscarriage in the Fleet should now be so cool', Trenchard was not questioned until 10 February, and then only because the Lords had once again raised the issue in conference with the Commons.[3] Nor did Trenchard's answers fully explain why the Admirals had not received the intelligence of French naval movements in time, but by this juncture neither the Whigs nor Nottingham were eager to pursue the matter further.

Although Nottingham was exonerated in this fashion by the parliamentary inquiries, he could hardly have avoided all bitter-

[1] *LJ*, xv, 339; *HMC House of Lords*, n.s. 1, 95, 100–1; BM Add. MSS. 29574, fo. 264, C. Hatton to Viscount Hatton, 18 Jan.
[2] *LJ*, xv, 342–3; *HMC House of Lords*, n.s. 1, 101; BM Add. MSS. 29574, fo. 264.
[3] *Ibid.* fo. 265, C. Hatton to Viscount Hatton, 23 Jan. See also *LJ*, xv, 361–2; *HMC House of Lords*, n.s. 1, 103; *CJ*, xi, 91; Ralph, *History of England*, ii, 470–2.

ness at his recompense for almost five years of devoted and laborious service to the government. As he remarked to Archbishop Sharp some months later, 'the King and people too have given me my quietus, and (if you will not think me arrogant and peevish) I will say too, *Sat patria Priamoque datum*'.[1] Then, too, his removal from the centre of government almost inevitably lessened his preoccupation with the immediate exigencies of the war effort and left him free to adopt a more critical attitude towards particular aspects of governmental policy. Thus, while his support for the war against France was never to waver, he was to be increasingly critical of William's strategic emphasis on the Low Countries, which he felt worked to the detriment of English national interests.[2] Moreover, he did not hesitate to advocate the passage of the Treason Trials bill in December 1693, despite the contention of ministerial spokesmen that its enactment would give impunity to traitors.[3] Again in April 1694, he joined Halifax, Rochester and Monmouth in opposing that section of the Commons' Tonnage bill which authorized the establishment of the Bank of England on the grounds that such an institution would monopolize the money market to the detriment of land owners seeking mortgages.[4]

None the less, Nottingham's removal from office did not at first seem to augur his alienation from William and the Court. Retirement did not alter his attitude towards the triennial legislation, which was still distasteful to the king. When the measure was introduced for the second time in two years in the Lords on 1 December 1693, Nottingham not only spoke against the proviso which enjoined annual sessions but was also one of only three peers who opposed it on the third reading.[5] Furthermore, after

---

[1] Gloucestershire Record Office, Lloyd-Baker MSS., box IV, bundle L, 13 Oct. 1694.
[2] See, for example, Nottingham's letters to Heneage Finch in December 1695 among the Finch MSS. at Chatsworth.
[3] BM Add. MSS. 17677OO, fo. 192, L'Hermitage's report of 27 Feb./9 March; Macaulay, *History of England*, IV, 478–9.
[4] BM Add. MSS. 17677OO, fos. 243–4, L'Hermitage's report of 24 April/4 May; Ranke, *History of England*, VI, 247; Luttrell, III, 298–9.
[5] *HMC Seventh Report*, pp. 217, 219; *HMC Hastings*, II, 233.

his dismissal, he continued to appear in the royal drawing-room and his wife remained in attendance upon the queen. Indeed, the countess's continued service as one of the ladies of Mary's bedchamber even seems to have allowed Nottingham to retain some voice in ecclesiastical appointments.[1] Thus, when Nottingham's younger brother Henry was offered the Bishopric of Man by the Earl of Derby, he turned it down after Mary induced the king to promise him the post he really wanted, the Deanery of York when next it fell vacant.[2]

Nottingham's hopes of remaining on good terms with king and queen must also have been complemented by the prospect of retirement which, at least at the outset, he found most appealing. Five years of virtually unbroken attendance at Whitehall had only confirmed his penchant for the pleasures of country life. By May 1694 he was so anxious to leave London for his new estate in Rutland that he told Hatton, 'I am resolved to go into the country though I live in the Stables at Burleigh.'[3] Once he reached Rutland in August and took up residence at Exton, a house of Lord Gainsborough he was to rent until the new mansion at Burley was built, he showed little desire to leave. In September he began the demolition of the ruins of the old house at Burley, and at the same time he informed his brother Heneage that, despite the urgings of friends, he did not intend to come up to Westminster 'till there be some particular occasion, which I will not believe, but from you'.[4]

To this resolve, Nottingham adhered until mid-December when the revival of the triennial legislation and also private concerns brought him up to London.[5] His return to the capital came at a

---

[1] BM Add. MSS. 29578, fo. 444, C. Lyttleton to Viscount Hatton, 15 Nov. 1693; *HMC Seventh Report*, p. 214; BM Add. MSS. 29565, fo. 501, Trumalier to Viscount Hatton, 22 Dec. 1694.

[2] Glos. R.O., Lloyd-Baker MSS. box III, bundle B, H. Finch to Archbishop Sharp, 3 Nov. 1694; Nott. U. Portland MSS. PWa 1150, Archbishop Sharp to [Earl Portland], 28 April 1697.

[3] BM Add. MSS. 29595, fo. 44, 1 May.   [4] Chatsworth Finch MSS., 10 and 27 Sept.

[5] Ranke, *History of England*, VI, 260; BM Add. MSS. 29595, fo. 66, Nottingham to Viscount Hatton, 7 Dec.

critical juncture. The day after he took his seat in the Lords, the Triennial bill, which seems to have been agreed to by William to induce Shrewsbury to return to office, was finally approved by the upper House in spite of Halifax's and his own speeches denouncing it as an indefensible invasion of the prerogative.[1] Moreover, on the 19th, the Treason Trials bill, sponsored by Heneage Finch in the Commons, was brought before the Lords for the third time in four sessions.[2] Not only did Nottingham support it himself, but he also urged Hatton to allow him to cast his proxy in its favour. 'All the parts of it', he advised his father-in-law, 'are extremely usefull to the Subject, and I protest I see nothing [that] can prejudice the Crowne though some great men will oppose it under colour of their Majesties Service.'[3]

Even more important than the legislation pending was the death of the queen on 28 December 1694. Lady Nottingham, who had been greatly devoted to Mary, was griefstricken, while Nottingham lamented the loss of one 'who on earth had not her equall'.[4] Her death, which severed the strongest of Nottingham's remaining ties with the Court, prompted in him on the one hand grave fears 'that some about the King may presse things...which the Queene might in some measure have prevented or restrained'.[5] On the other, it freed him to take a stronger stand against the increasingly Whig-dominated ministry than he had hitherto allowed himself. As he remarked to Hatton on 3 January, 'certainly some things are more expedient to be done than have bin formerly thought fitt or necessary'.[6] Not only, then, did Nottingham continue to press for the speedy implementation of the treason trials measure; he also spoke out on 22 January in favour of Lord Abingdon's motion that the state of the nation be taken under consideration.[7]

[1] *LJ*, xv, 444–6; Ranke, *History of England*, vi, 260; LRO, Finch MSS., Political papers 92.
[2] Burnet, iv, 253–4. [3] BM Add. MSS. 29595, fo. 68, 22 Dec.
[4] *HMC Lonsdale*, p. 105. See also BM Add. MSS. 29595, fo. 74.
[5] *Ibid.* fo. 72. [6] *Ibid.* fo. 74.
[7] *Ibid.* 29574, fos. 369, 376, C. Hatton to Viscount Hatton, 10 and 22 Jan.; *LJ*, xv, 468.

Friday, 25 January, was appointed by the Lords on the request of Abingdon and Nottingham, and when the peers assembled that day Nottingham delivered a long, carefully prepared address which—though '*fort respectueux pour le Roy*'—constituted a sweeping indictment of governmental policy since his dismissal.[1] He raised, first of all, the question of the propriety of the trials of the alleged Jacobite plotters in Lancashire and demanded a thorough examination of the proceedings there.[2] Secondly, he suggested that the queen's demise made it imperative that should the king go to Flanders the next summer (and he hoped he would not), '*des personnes de bon sens et qui ne fussent pas odieuses à la nation*' ought to be chosen to administer the kingdom in William's absence.[3] Thirdly, he drew attention to the deterioration of the coinage which, he argued, was not merely due to clipping but also to its export abroad to maintain both England's and her allies' troops. In addition, Nottingham strongly condemned the conduct at sea of the past year. Tollemache's fatal attempt on Brest he lamented as foolhardy, and he went on to deplore the dispatch of the fleet to the Mediterranean on the grounds that it left England's coasts unguarded. Finally, he again denounced the Bank whose operations, he claimed, would lower the price of land and injure trade.

Nottingham's full-scale attack on the ministers was seconded and expanded upon by Rochester, Halifax and Torrington, but Leeds (formerly Marquess of Carmarthen), Devonshire and Normanby disputed his contentions while Godolphin unkindly suggested that an investigation of naval affairs during Notting-

---

[1] BM Add. MSS. 17677PP, fo. 136, L'Hermitage's report of 29 Jan./8 Feb. For other accounts of the speech, see Ranke, *History of England*, VI, 268–9; Luttrell, III, 431–2.

[2] Peter Legh of Lyme, a close friend of Nottingham's younger brothers Henry and Edward, was one of the accused, and both brothers were industrious in their attempts to discredit the plot. Leeds, Halifax, Nottingham and Devonshire, according to Taff, were also to have been implicated (*HMC Kenyon*, pp. 329, 338, 371–2; *HMC House of Lords*, n.s. I, 445; Glos. R. O., Lloyd-Baker MSS. box III, bundle B, H. Finch to Archbishop Sharp, 3 Nov. 1694).

[3] BM Add. MSS. 17677PP, fo. 136. For Rochester's and Seymour's abortive attempts to press for the summoning of a new parliament on Mary's death, see *ibid.* fo. 137; Burnet, IV, 251–2; BM Add. MSS. 29574, fo. 379, C. Hatton to Viscount Hatton, 12 Feb.

ham's secretaryship might be equally in order.[1] Nor was the up-shot of his broadside much to his liking. On the one hand, when Nottingham went to Court a few days later, he received a public rebuff when William, on his way to church, declined to speak to him.[2] On the other, when the earl attempted to press his charges home in the Lords, he met with little success. By a vote of 33 to 23, the upper House refused to appoint a day to consider further his objections to the Bank.[3] Moreover, the examination of naval affairs and of the Lancashire plot which the Lords did agree to undertake proved most unsatisfactory from his point of view. On 22 February, after a detailed inquiry into the conduct of the Lancashire trials, a motion to declare that there 'hath been an evil and dangerous plot against the government' was barely defeated on the previous question, and Rochester and Nottingham then dropped the matter.[4] Five days later, a resolution approving the shift of the fleet to the Mediterranean was carried without a division.[5] Only over the issue of the coinage, increasingly a prob-lem of general concern, did Nottingham's eloquence have any effect. On 22 February the judges brought in a bill against clip-ping which was passed by parliament and assented to by William on 3 May—a first, though halting, step to cope with the situation.[6]

Chagrin at the failure of his attack upon the new ministers must have intensified Nottingham's desire to return to Rutland.[7]

[1] BM Add. MSS. 17677PP, fo. 138; Ranke, *History of England*, VI, 271.
[2] Algemeen Rijksarchief Heinsius MSS. 402, fo. 42, L'Hermitage to A. Heinsius, 29 Jan./8 Feb. However, Nottingham was named, along with a host of other Privy Councillors, as a Commissioner of Appeal for Prizes in June 1695 (*CSPD*, 1694–5, p. 204; *CSPD*, 1695, p. 112).
[3] *HMC House of Lords*, n.s. I, 459.
[4] *Ibid.* pp. 435–52; *LJ*, XV, 498, 503; Burnet, IV, 258; Ralph, *History of England*, II, 560–1; LRO, Finch MSS., Political papers 110, notes in Nottingham's hand for a speech condemning the trials.
[5] *HMC House of Lords*, n.s. I, 497; BM Add. MSS. 17677PP, fos. 141, 174–5, L'Hermitage's reports of 1/11 Feb. and 1/11 March; LRO, Finch MSS., Naval and Military papers 32, notes by Nottingham for a detailed review of the conduct of the fleet.
[6] *HMC House of Lords*, n.s. I, 510–11, 516–19; Burnet, IV, 253.
[7] L'Hermitage reported on 1 March that '*On dit que ce Comte* [Nottingham] *apres cette session de parlement a dessein d'aller demeurer à la campagne et de ne se plus mêler de rien*' (BM Add. MSS. 17677PP, fo. 175). See also *ibid.* fo. 213.

In addition, Halifax had been urging him, ever since a marriage between his heir Lord Eland and Nottingham's eldest daughter Mary had been arranged in January, 'to be gone' for Exton where the ceremony was to be held.[1] Only the long-delayed state funeral of the queen kept Nottingham in London until late March, and he then hastened to Exton even though he had not settled all his legal business in town.[2] So he was absent when the sensational tale of the East India Company's corruption of officials and politicians was uncovered by the Houses in the spring of 1695. The new scandal virtually ushered Leeds from the political scene, but it redounded to Nottingham's credit. Both he and Portland, it was revealed, had spurned large bribes offered by the old company.[3] This belated testimony to his honesty may have been some consolation to Nottingham if past accusations still stung. However, he seems to have been too busy with his plans for building to take much note of London gossip.[4] He does not even seem to have involved himself actively in the electioneering of the following autumn when the new parliament was chosen, although he must have been well informed of its progress by his son-in-law Halifax who kept in close touch with other Tory notables such as Frank Gwyn and Lord Weymouth.[5] Furthermore, despite the importunities of Lord Thanet and other political friends, Nottingham did not come up to London until early February 1696. Even then, his main object was to arrange for the sale of some of his Essex properties to help finance his building.[6]

None the less, his arrival in London and subsequent call with

[1] BM Add. MSS. 29595, fos. 78, 84, 88, Nottingham to Viscount Hatton, 22 Jan., 7 and 12 March. For details of the settlement, see Foxcroft, *Halifax*, II, 188, n. 4. The marriage was celebrated on 1 April, but the festivities were cut short by the sudden death in London on the 5th of the first Marquess of Halifax.
[2] BM Add. MSS. 29595, fo. 90, Nottingham to Viscount Hatton, 19 March.
[3] BM Add. MSS. 17677PP, fo. 246, L'Hermitage's report of 26 April/6 May.
[4] See, for example, his letter to Sharp of 29 May 1695 in Glos. R.O., Lloyd-Baker MSS., box IV, bundle A.   [5] See Halifax's correspondence in Althorp Savile MSS., box 7.
[6] BM Add. MSS. 29566, fo. 118, Earl Thanet to Viscount Hatton, 5 Dec.; *ibid.* 29595, fo. 92, Nottingham to Viscount Hatton, 10 Feb. See also Chatsworth Finch MSS., Nottingham to H. Finch, 9 Dec. 1695.

Halifax upon William at Kensington on 20 February did not fail to stir speculation, for the political situation was unusually fluid.[1] Despite some notable Whig successes in the elections of the previous autumn, the Court had not thought it wise to risk contesting Foley's bid for the Speakership. And while there was little opposition to supply for the war and Montague was able to push through his recoinage scheme, the working alliance that had developed between the Churchmen and the country members of parliament who looked to Foley and Harley for leadership was giving no little trouble to the Court's managers in the Commons on other important questions.[2] Not only did the lower House finally accept the peers' amendments to their resuscitated Treason Trials bill (thereby defeating Court hopes of disagreement), but they also passed a stiff electoral qualifications measure over Whig opposition.[3] Further, the proposal for the establishment of a parliamentary Council of Trade, which was sponsored by the Tories and the New Country party, found many supporters.[4] Nottingham, who had been acquainted with the plan by his brother Heneage early in December, wholeheartedly favoured it, provided the members of the Council were also named in the parliamentary act establishing it. As he wrote to Heneage,

I suppose the House does not intend such a Constitution shall depend on the pleasure of some ministers, nor shall they use it onely to gratify their friends, and to amuse people with a seeming care of trade, which has bin so shamefully neglected and prostituted to our neighbours.[5]

Much as William might grumble about being made a Doge of Venice, by late January the trade measure seemed destined for approval despite strong ministerial opposition. Even Sunderland, cannily gauging the way the tide was running, came out in its

---

[1] BM Add. MSS. 17677 QQ, fos. 285–6, L'Hermitage's report of 20 Feb./2 March.
[2] Feiling, Tory party, pp. 309–10; Kenyon, Sunderland, pp. 275–7.
[3] Feiling, Tory party, p. 317.
[4] See R. M. Lees, 'Parliament and the Proposal for a Council of Trade, 1695–1696', EHR, LIV (1939), 38–66.
[5] Chatsworth Finch MSS., 14 Dec.

favour.[1] Indeed, it seemed by early February that the Whigs were
losing their grip in the Commons, and Nottingham's arrival in
London coupled with his appearance at Court, ostensibly to
present his son-in-law Halifax to William, set off reports that he
would be made Lord Chancellor, Shrewsbury would be replaced
by Heneage Finch, and Russell would be succeeded by Torrington.[2] But if these rumours had any substance, the disclosure on
24 February of the assassination plot against William rapidly
dissolved it. The Junto Whigs, presented with this unexpected
opportunity, lost no time in turning it to their advantage. An
association terming William 'rightful and lawful' king and bind-
ing its signatories to revenge his death should he die by violence
was moved in both Houses, as once more the Whigs sought to
brand all those who had scruples about the legality of William's
title as Jacobites.

Junto tactics did not, however, inhibit either Nottingham or
his brother from airing their belief that William was only king *de
facto*.[3] And Tory sentiment in the upper House was strong enough
so that the peers finally agreed, on Leeds' initiative, to amend the
association to read that William 'hath a right by law to the crown
of this realm'. But this modification was as unacceptable to
Nottingham and other Churchmen as it was to the more violent
Whigs such as Monmouth and Tankerville.[4] Even after being
allowed several days by the House to consider his decision, Nottingham declined to sign the association in its revised form, and a
similar stand was taken by eighteen other peers and nearly one
hundred Commoners.[5] Furthermore, when the Whig proposal to

[1] Burnet, IV, 294-5; Kenyon, *Sunderland*, p. 277. For the progress of the bill, see *CJ*,
xv, 423-4; *HMC Hastings*, II, 253-4; Bodl. Carte MSS. 130, fo. 357, R. Price to the
Duke of Beaufort, 1 Feb.

[2] BM Add. MSS. 29578, fo. 543, C. Lyttleton to Viscount Hatton, 12 Feb.; *ibid.* 17677 QQ,
fos. 285-6; Bodl. Carte MSS. 130, fo. 359, R. Price to the Duke of Beaufort, 11 Feb.

[3] BM Add. MSS. 17677 QQ, fo. 308, L'Hermitage's report of 3/13 March; Burnet, IV,
306-7.

[4] Browning, *Osborne*, I, 533; BM Add. MSS. 29566, fo. 156, J. Verney to Viscount
Hatton, 5 March; *ibid.* 30000 A, fos. 19-20, Bonnet's dispatch of 28 Feb./9 March.

[5] *HMC House of Lords*, n.s. II, 206-12.

make the association compulsory on all officials and members of parliament was brought up to the Lords in April, Nottingham led the futile struggle to reject it.[1]

Royal reaction to Nottingham's stand against the association was swift and unmistakable, for William had always been sensitive to doubts cast upon his title. At a meeting of the Privy Council on 12 March 1696, the king 'call'd for the Councill Book and struck out with his own hand the Marquess of Normanby, Earle of Nottingham, and Sir Edward Seymour'.[2] So abrupt a severing of Nottingham's last official connection to the Court could only have confirmed his professed intention '*qu'il ne pretendoit plus ce mesler d'aucune affaire*'.[3] Certainly, he must have realized that with the Whigs riding the crest of public revulsion to the assassination plot, there was little hope of ousting them. Eighteen months later when Halifax pressed him to come up to parliament, his views had not changed. 'If I had no other business in town', he replied, 'I think I should not come for the parliament.'[4] Merely to oppose the 'designes of others' would be futile, particularly while there seemed little possibility of agreement among the disparate opposition on 'measures more suitable to the interest of England'. Without a positive programme and a full union, he feared that 'all struling in Parliament will not only be vain but leave some particular men exposed to resentment while others make their court by a compromise as has bin done heretofore'.[5] Thus, during the two years following his refusal of the voluntary association, Nottingham was able to indulge his preference for country life and to watch over his building work at Burley with little interruption.[6]

[1] *Ibid.* pp. 245–6; BM Add. MSS. 30000 A, fos. 110–11, Bonnet's report of 14/24 April; *ibid.* 17677 QQ, fos. 382–3, L'Hermitage's report of 14/24 April; *ibid.* 29595, fos. 106, 108, 110, Nottingham to Viscount Hatton, 7, 9, 14 April.
[2] *Ibid.* 35107, fo. 35, Privy Council memorandum.   [3] *Ibid.* 17677 QQ, fo. 308.
[4] Althorp Savile MSS., box 2, Nottingham to Marquess of Halifax, 22 Nov. 1697.   [5] *Ibid.*
[6] He came up to London twice when Parliament was sitting during these two years, but it was primarily his private affairs that prompted these trips. However, when he was in town he was prominent in the opposition to Fenwick's attainder in 1697 and to the bill of pains and penalties against Duncomb in 1698.

However, the conclusion of the Treaty of Ryswick in the autumn of 1697 brought many changes in its wake, not least the development of divisions among the Whigs (particularly over the issue of a standing army) and growing friction between them and Sunderland which, in turn, increasingly alienated William from the Junto.[1] Encouraged, perhaps, by these symptoms of Whig decline and the general reaction against the Court that followed the conclusion of the peace, Nottingham took an active part in the elections of the summer of 1698. In his own shire he was the first to vote against the Whig incumbent Sherard, who lost his seat.[2] In addition, he exerted his influence in Christ's College, Cambridge, on behalf of Anthony Hammond's candidacy for the University, while mobilizing his own and the Savile tenants in Northamptonshire for Sir Justinian Isham.[3]

The outcome of the 1698 election was a marked check to the Junto and the Court.[4] Although Nottingham was not completely satisfied, he thought the new House of Commons 'much better than the last'.[5] However, the opposition's hopes of electing a Speaker were disappointed. Despite the efforts of Nottingham and other prominent Tories, neither Seymour nor Colonel John Granville could be persuaded to withdraw from the contest, with the result that the ministers' choice, Sir Thomas Littleton, had an easy victory.[6] Yet even before the setback over the Speakership, Nottingham had resolved not to come up for the session 'till I see

---

[1] Feiling, *Tory party*, pp. 322–9; Kenyon, *Sunderland*, pp. 293–307. In late 1698 there were even rumours that Sunderland was cultivating Rochester and Nottingham (Longleat Thynne MSS., vol. xxiv, fo. 382, [Sir Henry Sheres] to Viscount Weymouth).

[2] *Letters illustrative of the reign of William III from 1696 to 1708...by J. Vernon*, ed. G. P. R. James (London, 1841), ii, 151.

[3] BM Add. MSS. 29595, fo. 150, Nottingham to Viscount Hatton, 20 July; Althorp Savile MSS., box 2, Nottingham to Marquess of Halifax, 15 April and 13 Aug.; NRO, Isham MSS., Nottingham to Sir J. Isham, 19 July.

[4] See the list of the old and new Commons printed in H. Horwitz, 'Parties, Connections, and Parliamentary Politics, 1689–1714: Review and Revision', *Journal of British Studies*, vi (1966), 55–69.

[5] Althorp Savile MSS., box 2, Nottingham to Marquess of Halifax, 27 Aug.

[6] Feiling, *Tory party*, pp. 330–1; BM Add. MSS. 17677 SS, fo. 386, L'Hermitage's report of 18/28 Oct.; Althorp Savile MSS., box 2, Nottingham to Marquess of Halifax, 12 and 19 Nov.

whether the House of Commons will find any other businesse for us [the Lords] than consenting to their money bills'.[1] Eventually, he did journey to London early in January 1699, but apart from opposing William's plea for the retention of his Dutch guards, he does not seem to have distinguished himself in the Lords during his three-month stay in town.[2] Nor did he play any more conspicuous a role in the following session. After finally moving his family into the still only partially-completed house at Burley in December 1699, he remained in residence there all winter save for a brief trip to London.[3]

However, the ebbing tide of Junto fortunes was eventually to carry Nottingham back from semi-retirement to the forefront of politics. The losses of the 1698 election had been followed by growing disruption within the ministry with Shrewsbury begging to be unburdened of office and Wharton, Orford and Montague at odds with the king and Sunderland. In an attempt to bolster the administration, William in the spring of 1699 had appointed Lords Lonsdale and Pembroke (both good personal friends of Nottingham) as Lord Privy Seal and Lord President, while the Earl of Jersey had been named Secretary of State. But the session of 1699–1700 had shown that 'patching' of this kind was futile.

With the Junto out of temper, the Commons' majority led by Harley pushed through a bill confiscating the forfeited Irish lands and addressed against the admittance of foreigners to the royal councils. The lower House was almost completely out of hand; as Vernon observed, 'there are none that I see who take upon them any management'.[4] Montague took refuge in a profitable sinecure, Orford huffily resigned, and William com-

[1] *Ibid.* 19 Sept.
[2] BM Add. MSS. 17677 TT, fo. 84, L'Hermitage's report of 31 Jan./10 Feb.; *ibid.* 29575, fo. 266, C. Hatton to Viscount Hatton, 8 Feb.; *LJ*, XVI, 377. Notes for his speech are in BM Add. MSS. 29587, fo. 76.
[3] His sole contribution to the Lord's debates was a speech attacking a Court-sponsored resolution condemning the Scottish Darien venture.
[4] NRO, Buccleuch MSS. 55, J. Vernon to Duke of Shrewsbury, 5 March 1700.

pleted the rout of the Junto when he finally took the Great Seal from Somers in April 1700.

Somers' dismissal seemed to indicate that the king was ready to turn to the Tories and to Country leaders like Harley. And once Attorney-General Trevor refused the Great Seal, it was rumoured that Nottingham was in line for the post.[1] William himself was in a quandary, and it was only after renewed negotiations with the Junto broke down that he reluctantly turned to the opposition. Before he left for the continent in July, Nathan Wright (a Tory lawyer of little distinction) was made Lord Keeper, and the following December the long-anticipated appointments of Rochester as Irish Lord Lieutenant and Godolphin as First Commissioner of the Treasury were announced.[2] At the same time, the old parliament was dissolved and a new one summoned to meet on 6 February 1701.

Nottingham's part in the formation of the new ministry is not at all clear. He spent the summer of 1700 at Burley celebrating the birth of his twentieth child (a girl), and came to London only briefly in August when his son-in-law Halifax died.[3] Moreover, no evidence survives to indicate that he was consulted by the new 'kingmakers'—Harley, Godolphin, Marlborough and Rochester —though he must have been kept well informed by his friends Weymouth, Musgrave and Seymour who were in close touch with them.[4] Yet as a respected Tory leader, he could not be ignored by the architects of the ministerial reshuffle, and it is possible that once Godolphin and Rochester took office he was offered the Chancellorship.[5] But whatever part he played in the

[1] Bodl. Ballard MSS. 10, no. 18, Bishop Moore to A. Charlett, 30 April; BM Add. MSS. 30000 D, fo. 165, Bonnet's report of 3/14 May.

[2] A month earlier, Sir Charles Hedges had been named Secretary of State in place of Jersey.

[3] BM Add. MSS. 47025, p. 53, P. Percival to Sir J. Percival, 4 June; NRO, Buccleuch MSS. 55, J. Vernon to Duke of Shrewsbury, 22 Aug.

[4] The most important evidence for the manoeuvres of the summer and autumn of 1700 is Harley's correspondence, particularly his letters to Guy. However, so far as they can be deciphered, they make no reference to Nottingham (HMC Portland, III, 625–42).

[5] For rumours of his appointment, see Bodl. Carte MSS. 228, fos. 343, 352, newsletters of 21 Dec. and 11 Jan. to Lord Huntingdon. His failure to assume a more public role

construction of the new ministry, there can be no doubt that he worked closely with Rochester and Godolphin in the parliament which assembled in February 1701.

Now that the Duke of Gloucester had died and Louis XIV had repudiated the second Partition Treaty, William hoped that his new ministers and Harley (who would accept nothing but the Speakership) could induce the Houses to provide for the Succession and to take firm measures against the extension of French power.[1] But while Harley was successful in guiding through the Commons the Act of Settlement establishing the Hanoverians as Anne's successors, it was only with the greatest reluctance that the Houses were brought to deal with the foreign crisis. When the king's opening speech was considered by the Lords, Nottingham, Normanby (the former Earl of Mulgrave), Rochester and Godolphin all spoke in favour of voting merely a general resolution of thanks to the king, although it was finally agreed under Whig pressure to urge him also to make such treaties as he thought necessary to preserve the balance of power in Europe.[2] However, it was not until June that the Commons could be brought to commit themselves to any more than the assistance to the States-General to which England was obliged by the Anglo-Dutch treaties of 1677.[3] It was Godolphin, seconded by Nottingham, who finally took matters in hand. All too conscious of the damage the new ministry and its adherents were incurring in the eyes both of William and the electorate by their failure to make better provision against France, Godolphin wrote to Nottingham on

in the ministerial changes may also have been due to the fall from favour the Finches seem to have suffered in the mid-1690s, the product of their attempts to discredit the Lancashire trials and to prevent the imposition of the association of 1696. Certainly, when Sharp put forward Henry Finch for the vacant Deanery of York in the spring of 1697, William—despite previous promises—flatly refused to consider him (Glos. R.O. Lloyd-Baker MSS., box IV, bundle Q, Archbishop Tenison to Archbishop Sharp, 14 May 1697).

[1] PH, v, 1232–3; Kenyon, Sunderland, p. 320.
[2] LJ, XVI, 596–7; BM Add. MSS. 30000 E, fo. 40, Bonnet's report of 14/25 Feb.; ibid. 17677 WW, fos. 156–7, L'Hermitage's report of 14/25 Feb.
[3] PH, v, 1235, 1243, 1250; Original letters of John Locke, Alg. Sidney, and Lord Shaftesbury ed. T. Forster (London, 1847), pp. 98–9.

8 June asking—if he approved the notion—to concert with 'our friends of the House of Commons' a vote in support of the king's foreign policy.[1] Nottingham did his job well for at the next 'general meeting' of the ministry's chief supporters, held at his lodgings early the following week, Godolphin's proposal was accepted.[2] And only a day or two later, on 12 June, Seymour and Sir Bartholomew Shower—taking their cue from a royal speech delivered to the Houses earlier that day—moved and won speedy agreement for an address promising to support 'such Alliances' as William thought fit to conclude in conjunction with the Dutch and the Imperialists 'for the preservation of the Liberties of Europe ...and for reducing the exorbitant power of France'.[3]

However, most of the 1701 session was devoted by the Tories in both Houses to pursuing the ousted Whig leaders. The heaviest fire came first from the Lords, with Nottingham and Rochester in the van of an attempt to condemn Somers, Orford and Halifax for their share in the making of the Partition Treaties.[4] After a move to submit to the Commons an address denouncing the treaties was rejected on 20 March, Nottingham (who headed the Lords' committee which had prepared the address) and Rochester were joined by nineteen other peers in a heated protest.[5] The Commons followed the upper House's lead by impeaching the three Whig lords, but realizing they lacked sufficient evidence for conviction they also presented an address calling for their permanent exclusion from the king's councils. But this attempt by the lower House to foreclose the impeachment proceedings was opposed by the Lords despite warnings from Rochester, Godolphin, Normanby and Nottingham of the dangers of a dispute

---

[1] NRO, Finch–Hatton MSS. 4053.
[2] BM Add. MSS. 30000 E, fos. 259–62, 283–4, Bonnet's reports of 13/24 June, 20 June/ 1 July; PRO, PRO 31/3/188, Poussin au Roi, 13/24 and 16/27 June.
[3] CJ, XIII, 626; BM Add. MSS. 30000 E, fos. 283–4; PRO, PRO 31/3/188, 13/24 June.
[4] PRO, PRO 31/3/187, Tallard au Roi, 15/26 March; BM Add. MSS. 7059, fo. 100, J. Tucker to G. Stepney, 17/28 March; HMC House of Lords, n.s. IV, 222.
[5] Ibid. p. 223; LJ, XVI, 628–9.

between the Houses.[1] As they had predicted, the session ended
with violent quarrels when a majority of the peers, after repeated
messages pressing the lower House to present its cases against the
Junto lords, proceeded to acquit them in the Commons' absence
over the protests of Nottingham and twenty-nine others.[2]

While Nottingham retired to Burley for the summer, negotiations between William and the party leaders, as well as those
between the king and the member states of the proposed alliance
against France, continued unabated.[3] Although Rochester finally
obtained the changes desired by the Tories in the commissions of
the peace in the north and in the London Lieutenancy, the king was
no little dissatisfied with his new ministers.[4] Apart from their
unrelenting pursuit of the Junto lords and the objectionable
constitutional clauses inserted in the Act of Settlement, he could
get no assurance from them that the feuding between the two
Houses over the impeachments would not be revived to the
detriment of supply once parliament reassembled.[5] Finally, despite Godolphin's pledge that the Commons would provide the
necessary funds, William—upon the representations of Sunderland and Somers—decided upon a dissolution when he returned
from the continent in November.[6] Godolphin immediately resigned while Nottingham, who had been planning to come up to
London to consult on measures for the coming session, altered his
plans and remained at Burley until shortly before the new parliament met on 30 December.[7]

---

[1] CJ, XIII, 492; BM Add. MSS. 30000 E, fos. 146–7, Bonnet's report of 18/29 April. See
also Nottingham's notes in BM Add. MSS. 29587, fo. 145.
[2] LJ, XVI, 718 and passim; HMC House of Lords, n.s. IV, 300; PH, V, 1310–15, 1320–1.
[3] In October, Marlborough sent copies of the treaties then concluded to Nottingham 'as
to a friend, whose judgment I much depend upon' (BM Add. MSS. 29594, fo. 95,
8/19 Oct.).
[4] Ibid. 30000 E, fo. 313, Bonnet's report of 25 July/5 Aug.; HMC Cowper, II, 434; LRO,
Finch MSS. Correspondence, box VI, bundle 22, Marquess of Normanby to Nottingham, 4 and 16 Sept.
[5] Feiling, Tory party, pp. 351–3.
[6] Ibid. p. 352; Miscellaneous State Papers, II, 443–61.
[7] LRO, Finch MSS. Correspondence, box VI, bundle 22, Nottingham to Marquess of
Normanby, 8 and 29 Sept.

Though the Whigs were disappointed in their hopes of gaining a clear predominance in the general election, the king's requests for supply met with little opposition in the Commons. Indeed, the Tories, outraged by Louis's recognition of the Pretender on James II's death and aware of the country's readiness to go to war, took the lead, and as Nottingham observed twelve years later, 'engaged us in this present war'.[1] It was Normanby who proposed and Nottingham who seconded the Lords' address of thanks to the king which expressed the House's resentment of French support of James III, while it was the recently-ousted Secretary Hedges who moved the initial resolution of the Commons which promised 'to make good all those Alliances your majesty has made, or shall make…for the preserving the Liberties of Europe and reducing the exorbitant power of France'.[2] Parliamentary indignation at Louis's step also prompted the introduction of Abjuration bills in both Houses. The lower House's bill, which was moved and drafted by Hedges, made the new oath obligatory for all office-holders and members of parliament. The Lords' measure, sponsored by the Whigs, called only for a voluntary oath, as a better means of distinguishing the truly 'honest'.[3] However, Nottingham's objections to the recognition of William as 'lawful and rightful' king were as strong as ever, and he opposed abjuration vigorously as did his brother Heneage. Despite efforts in both Houses by the Finches to substitute the oath in the 1696 association for the proposed abjuration and to clog the bills with other provisos, the Commons' measure for a compulsory oath was finally approved by the Lords on 24 February 1702.[4]

Once the Abjuration bill had been carried, Nottingham—to

[1] *The conduct*, p. 138.
[2] *PH*, v, 1332–3; BM Add. MSS. 17677XX, fos. 157–8, 160, L'Hermitage's reports of 2/13 and 6/17 Jan.
[3] *Ibid*. pp. 110–11, 114, 122; Burnet, IV, 549; BM Add. MSS. 17677XX, fo. 175, L'Hermitage's dispatch of 13/24 Jan.
[4] Burnet, IV, 549–54, 556–7; BM Add. MSS. 7074, fos. 168, 182–3, 188, J. Ellis to G. Stepney, 10, 20, 24 Feb.; *ibid.* 17677XX, fo. 231, L'Hermitage's report of 24 Feb./7 March; *LJ*, XVII, 45; LRO, Finch MSS., Political papers 97.

demonstrate his good faith and loyalty to the Hanoverian Succession—suggested that a union with Scotland would be a much more important security for the Protestant succession. He then moved an address for the dissolution of the existing Scottish parliament and the summoning of a new one on the grounds that 'the present parliament was at first a convention, and then turned to a parliament...so that the legality of it might be called in question'.[1] While a number of peers opposed the suggestion of a dissolution, few dissented from Nottingham's reminder of the need for a closer union between the two kingdoms. On the 28th, William (now seriously ill) took advantage of this stirring of interest in the question of Anglo-Scottish union to recommend the project to the Houses.[2] But for the moment no further steps were taken, for on 8 March the king died after the Abjuration bill had been given his approval by commission.

Nottingham was not a witness to London's rejoicings at Anne's accession, for troubled by the implication of the abjuration oath which he feared might compel him to swear 'against God's providence and Government of the World', he and Weymouth had taken refuge in the country a few days earlier to consider whether or not they could accept it.[3] However, the queen's surprise that 'he wou'd go out of town just now', and Normanby's and Lady Nottingham's urgings 'to come agen among us as soon as possible' prompted his hasty return to London.[4] Yet after paying his duty to the queen, Nottingham left for Burley on 24 March still uncertain whether he could take the new oath.[5]

[1] Burnet, IV, 558; HMC Roxburghe, Etc., p. 154.   [2] Ibid. pp. 154–5; PH, V, 1340–1.
[3] The phrase is Sharp's from his letter of 31 March to Nottingham in LRO, Finch MSS. Correspondence, box VI, bundle 22, but it goes to the heart of Nottingham's crisis of conscience. See Nottingham to Sharp, 10 Jan., printed in A. T. Hart, The life and times of John Sharp, archbishop of York (London, 1949), p. 332; Burnet, V, 11; BM Add. MSS. 29595, fo. 270, Nottingham to Viscount Hatton, 9 March.
[4] Ibid. 29588, fos. 16–17, [Lady Nottingham] to Nottingham, 10 March; LRO, Finch MSS. Correspondence, box VI, bundle 22, Marquess of Normanby to Nottingham, 10 March; BM Add. MSS. 29579, fo. 365, C. Lyttleton to Viscount Hatton, 16 March.
[5] Glos. R.O., Lloyd-Baker MSS., box IV, bundle K, Nottingham to Archbishop Sharp, 24 March; same to same, 7 April, printed in Hart, Sharp, p. 333.

Eventually Archbishop Sharp managed to ease his doubts, and on 20 April Nottingham, Weymouth and the archbishop attended the Lords to swear with due formality their allegiance to the new sovereign and to abjure the Pretender.[1]

Meanwhile, Anne had not been slow to reverse the direction of William's ministerial changes of the past winter. On 10 March Marlborough was named commander of the English forces in the Netherlands while Rochester, whose commission as Lord Lieutenant had never formally been revoked, was given an intimation to resume the duties of his post.[2] Moreover, once Nottingham took the oaths, the reports that he would 'come into business again', which had flown about immediately after Anne's accession, began to circulate once more.[3] For once, the political gossips were right. Even so, Nottingham's return to the Secretaryship was to be delayed for still another fortnight, for he was not willing to accept until he received assurances that he would be empowered to purge the London Lieutenancy and that Hedges would succeed Vernon in the other Secretaryship.[4] But at last all was settled to his satisfaction, and on 2 May Nottingham had the pleasure of being restored, with a colleague to his own taste, to the office from which the Whigs had driven him almost nine years earlier.[5]

[1] *LJ*, xvii, 104–5.
[2] *CSPD*, 1702–3, p. 361; BM Add. MSS. 29588, fos. 16–17; *ibid.* 7074, fo. 143, J. Ellis to G. Stepney, 17 March.
[3] For the earlier spate of rumours, see for example, *ibid.* 17677 XX, fo. 255, L'Hermitage's report of 17/28 March. For the later crop, see BM Add. MSS. 29573, fo. 130, A. Hatton to Viscount Hatton, [21 April].
[4] Algemeen Rijksarchief Heinsius MSS. 792, fo. 217, L'Hermitage to A. Heinsius, 24 April/5 May; BM Add. MSS. 7078, fos. 92–3, J. Ellis to G. Stepney, 24 April; *ibid.* 7074, fo. 119, same to same, 21 April; Burnet, v, 10. See also Dartmouth's note in Burnet, iii, 156, which suggests that Nottingham espoused Hedges's candidacy largely as a means of getting rid of Vernon.
[5] *The London Gazette*, no. 3806.

CHAPTER 9

THE PROMISED LAND

1702-4

When Nottingham accepted the Seals at a meeting of the Privy Council on 2 May 1702, England was on the very brink of war. Already Marlborough, with the full approval of the queen, had secretly committed the country to a joint declaration of war with the Emperor and the States General against France to be announced on the 4th.[1] But when the matter was opened to his fellow privy councillors early in May, there were dissenting voices. Rochester, with the support of several colleagues (most probably Normanby, now Lord Privy Seal, and Jersey, the Lord Chamberlain), maintained that it would be in England's interest to act only as an auxiliary in the coming struggle.[2] However, Nottingham, as well as Seymour (Wharton's successor as Comptroller) and Speaker Harley, seem to have sided with Marlborough, Pembroke, Devonshire and Somerset, and the Council eventually agreed to concur in full-scale English intervention.[3] Yet if Nottingham did not share Rochester's penchant for confining English efforts strictly to naval warfare, his views concerning the conduct of the war did not altogether conform to those of Marlborough. As he had commented to Normanby the previous autumn;

methinks tis very reasonable to hope that since we are entring a war of which the Successe under the best Conduct is much to be feard we shall not have it manag'd as the last was and be twice in danger of ruine by the same methods:

[1] Churchill, *Marlborough*, I, 541–2.
[2] Boyer, *History of Queen Anne*, p. 14; O. Klopp, *Der Fall des Hauses Stuart und die Succession des Hauses Hannover* (Vienna, 1875–88), X, 39–40, 43; Ranke, *History of England*, V, 311. For Jersey's opposition to continental war, see his letter to Nottingham in BM Add. MSS. 29589, fos. 121–2.
[3] Boyer, *History of Queen Anne*, p. 14; A. Cunningham, *The history of Great Britain: From the revolution in 1688, to the accession of George the First* (London, 1787), I, 267.

good gamesters will change their cards at least if they can't their fortune especially when they are master.[1]

The implications of this remark are not difficult to trace nor was Nottingham at pains to conceal them.

To concentrate the main allied strength in Flanders once more —as the Dutch desired and Marlborough favoured—would, Nottingham believed, prove futile. 'Considering that a good issue of this Warr does not depend on any Conquests in the Spanish Netherlands, nor are the States likely to make any', he observed to Marlborough in August 1702, 'then surely the Troops should be there employed, where they may most annoy France.'[2] The maritime powers, he contended, should exert their major pressure against France in those areas where they could use their overwhelming naval supremacy in conjunction with their land forces.

I have long been of opinion [he stressed to the Dutch Pensionary Heinsius] that no Warr can be of great Dammage to France, but that which is prosecuted...by a Fleet, and an Army accompanying it...I think the reasons for this assertion are so plain, that I need not mention them, and the last Warr is an unhappy instance of the truth of it.[3]

Thus Nottingham repeatedly urged upon both his colleagues and the ministers of the allies the importance of, as well as the opportunities offered by, attention to the war in Italy, the West Indies and on the Iberian peninsula. Of course, he was not alone in recognizing the significance of these theatres; to some extent, Godolphin and even Marlborough agreed with his emphasis.[4] None the less, his insistence that the allies should subordinate the struggle in Flanders to the demands made upon their resources by acting offensively elsewhere was bound, eventually, to provoke

[1] LRO, Finch MSS. Correspondence, box VI, bundle 22, draft of Nottingham's letter of 29 Sept. 1701 to Normanby.
[2] NRO, Finch–Hatton MSS. 275, pp. 75–6, 14 Aug.
[3] Ibid. 277, p. 1, 30 April 1703.
[4] For Marlborough's and Godolphin's recognition of the importance of Italy and Portugal see, for example, BM Add. MSS. 29588, fos. 155–8, 279–80, Godolphin to Nottingham, 31 Aug. and 29 Sept. 1702; Blenheim MSS. A/1/14, Marlborough to Godolphin, 26 July 1703.

the Dutch and to bring him in conflict with Marlborough. But undismayed by the prospect of disagreement which he, with characteristic self-assurance, did not perhaps foresee, Nottingham energetically began his tenure as Secretary of State for the Southern Province.[1]

Nottingham's first concern was to ensure that the Imperial troops under Prince Eugene in Italy were reinforced. As he wrote Marlborough shortly after the duke returned to the Netherlands in June 1702,

I can't forbear mentioning Italy which has bin too much neglected even by the Imperial Court and for which the Pensioner has not that regard as it deserves; and should Prince Eugene and his army be ruind or driven out of Italy we should quickly be convinced that the weight of the war on this Side would be almost insupportable.[2]

The expedient he initially proposed to Marlborough to be communicated to the Dutch for their concurrence was the recruitment of Swiss troops, but the Pensionary seems to have jibbed at so expensive a project.[3] Heinsius responded more favourably when Nottingham, on Count Wratislaw's suggestion, requested Marlborough to discover whether the Dutch were prepared to join England in furnishing subsidies to the Elector of Bavaria and the Duke of Savoy.[4] While both the English Secretary and the

[1] It should be noted that Nottingham in the day-to-day conduct of foreign affairs was, to a large extent, directed by the Cabinet Council. Important letters to envoys abroad, for example, seem to have been considered and approved by the Cabinet or the Lords of the Committee before their dispatch by the Secretaries of State. Several copies of Nottingham's letters to Methuen and Hill have notations on them similar to that on one of 3 Nov. 1703—'read in last councill' (BM Add. MSS. 29595, fo. 254; ibid. 29589, fos. 374–5, 378, 390; ibid. 29591, fo. 131). It was in the process of establishing and laying down general policy objectives that the divergent ideas of the ministers came to the fore.
[2] NRO, Finch–Hatton MSS. 275, p. 37, 30 June. See also his letters to Marlborough of 5 and 26 June in ibid. pp. 7–9, 33–4. (The originals of many of Nottingham's letters to Marlborough are at Blenheim, but except in cases where Nottingham's copy is not extant, only references to his letterbooks in the Finch–Hatton MSS. are cited.)
[3] Ibid. pp. 4, 7, Nottingham to Marlborough, 16 May and 5 June; PRO, SPF 87/2, fo. 5, Marlborough to Nottingham, 29 May.
[4] NRO, Finch–Hatton MSS. 275, pp. 7–9; Sir G. Murray, Letters and despatches of John Churchill, Duke of Marlborough (London, 1845), I, 4.

Pensionary recognized that neither of those shrewd bargainers was likely to commit himself before seeing the results of the 1702 campaign, Nottingham was most optimistic about the eventual outcome of the Imperial negotiations with Bavaria.[1] But allied hopes of Bavarian support were rudely shattered in September when the Elector seized Ulm and declared for France, while as yet the Duke of Savoy displayed little interest in extricating himself from Louis XIV's grip.

Spurned by both Bavaria and Savoy, all for the moment that remained for England was to revert to pressing the Emperor to reinforce Eugene with Imperial troops. The inducement that Nottingham offered on behalf of the English government to Wratislaw in a series of interviews which began in September 1702 was the dispatch to the Mediterranean of that sizable naval contingent which the Austrian ambassador had been requesting throughout the summer.[2] An allied fleet in the Mediterranean would, so Nottingham believed, be of great advantage. As he observed to Marlborough late in October,

I earnestly wish they [the Dutch] would concurre with us in sending a squadron to the Mediterranean...The reasons for it are not onely what I think I have formerly mentioned, the Securing our trade, probability of prevailing with Algiers to break with France, Securing provisions to Prince Eugene's Army, encouraging a revolution in Naples and Sicily, but I believe there may be an opportunity of destroying all the French Magazins of provisions for their Army in Italy.[3]

When Wratislaw was finally able to inform Nottingham early in December that the Emperor would considerably strengthen his

---

[1] NRO, Finch–Hatton MSS. 275, pp. 33–4; *ibid.* pp. 83–6, Nottingham to Hedges, 27 Aug.; PRO, SPF 87/2, fos. 15–16, Marlborough to Nottingham, 9 July; Murray, *Letters and despatches*, I, 4.

[2] NRO, Finch–Hatton MSS. 275, pp. 74–6, Nottingham to Marlborough, 14 Aug.; *ibid.* pp. 111–13, 145–9, Nottingham to Godolphin, 10 and 30 Sept.; *ibid.* pp. 156–9, Nottingham to Stepney, 2 Oct.; BM Add. MSS. 29588, fo. 217, Hedges to Nottingham, 13 Sept.; G. Trevelyan, *England under Queen Anne* (London, 1930–4), I, 262.

[3] NRO, Finch–Hatton MSS. 275, pp. 194–6, 27 Oct.

army in Italy, the project for a Mediterranean squadron to be sent by 1 February was approved by the Cabinet.[1]

Nottingham's ambitious plans for the naval expedition, which early in 1703 were expanded to include the provision of arms and funds for the Protestant rebels in the Cevennes, were, however, never fulfilled.[2] Instead, delay followed upon delay. Rooke, who had been designated to command the contingent, declined on the grounds that its numbers (thirty-two ships of the line) were not commensurate with his rank.[3] Sir Cloudesly Shovell was appointed in his stead, but still the squadron did not sail, for the Dutch ships—despite Nottingham's repeated reminders—failed to arrive. In fact, though the Dutch had initially agreed to the project, they were now having second thoughts.[4] Even Nottingham's warning to Marlborough early in April of the 'clamor' Dutch withdrawal from the scheme would provoke in England failed to produce action.[5] Not until May did the Dutch quota of ships finally sail to join Shovell, and by the time the allied fleet reached the Mediterranean it was too late for a rendezvous with the Cevennois and it could do little more than show the flag.[6]

None the less, the arrival of a strong allied naval contingent in

[1] *Ibid.* p. 231, Nottingham to Stepney, 8 Dec.; BM Add. MSS. 29591, fo. 130, notes of a meeting of 8 Dec. attended by Godolphin, Marlborough, Rochester, Nottingham and Rooke.

[2] For the proposed aid to the Cevennois, see Shovell's instructions in *CSPD*, 1702–3, pp. 705–6. There were never any grounds for the malicious reports spread in the spring of 1703 that Nottingham was averse to aiding the French Protestant opponents of Louis XIV because of 'the dangerous Consequence of assisting Rebels against their Natural Prince' (Boyer, *History of Queen Anne*, p. 84). In fact, Nottingham wholeheartedly supported a succession of schemes aimed at encouraging rebellion in France. See, for example, *The diplomatic correspondence of the Right Hon. Richard Hill*, ed. W. Blackley (London, 1845), I, 34, 54.

[3] BM Add. MSS. 29591, fo. 193, Rooke to Nottingham, 3 March.

[4] NRO, Finch–Hatton MSS. 277, pp. 22–3, 26–7, Nottingham to Marlborough, 16 March and 2 April; Blenheim MSS. A/1/14, Marlborough to Godolphin, 27 March and 4 April.

[5] NRO, Finch–Hatton MSS. 277, pp. 26–7. See also *ibid.* p. 9, Nottingham to Stanhope, 24 May; *The correspondence 1701–1711 of John Churchill first Duke of Marlborough and Anthonie Heinsius Grand Pensionary of Holland*, ed. B. Van't Hoff (The Hague, 1951). letter 118.

[6] Cf. *LJ*, XVII, 537; *HMC House of Lords*, n.s. v, 468–9.

the Mediterranean during the summer of 1703 may have helped to precipitate the Duke of Savoy's break with France.[1] England's chief contribution to the negotiations with Savoy, conducted in quasi-secrecy in Turin by the Imperial diplomat D'Aversperg, was firm promises of financial support.[2] Richard Hill, appointed English Envoy Extraordinary to Savoy in July 1703, did not even leave for Turin until a treaty was signed in November, for he was deliberately, though unsuccessfully, kept at the Hague to avoid arousing French suspicions. Once the Duke of Savoy had finally come to terms, Nottingham and his colleagues busied themselves with plans for employing his troops in a descent upon Toulon.[3] And though the attempt on Toulon was not to be made until 1707, the conclusion of the alliance with Savoy seemed to augur the fulfilment of English, and particularly Nottingham's, aims in Italy and the Mediterranean.

However, Nottingham did not confine his attention to the Italian theatre. Equally vital in his eyes, as well as to Marlborough, was the establishment of a base on the Iberian peninsula for English naval operations in the Mediterranean.[4] This strategy was William's originally, as were the means employed to advance it during the first year of the war.[5] While Sir George Rooke and the Duke of Ormonde jointly led an expedition which sailed in July 1702 with the object of seizing either Gibraltar or Cadiz, John Methuen was hastened back to his post in Lisbon to renew his efforts to secure Portugal's entry into the war.[6] Though the attempt on Cadiz ended in a debacle which reflected little credit on either Rooke or Ormonde, a treaty with Portugal was eventu-

---

[1] CSPD, 1703–4, p. 16; Trevelyan, England under Queen Anne, I, 306.

[2] Hill correspondence, I, 10–15, 23–5, and passim.

[3] With Hill's instructions to leave for Turin in November came a letter from Nottingham ordering him to propose the plan to the duke (ibid. pp. 56–7).

[4] For Marlborough's Mediterranean strategy, see above p. 168, n. 4, and Churchill, Marlborough, I, 572, 648. For an example of Nottingham's views, see NRO, Finch–Hatton MSS. 275, p. 111, Nottingham to Godolphin, 10 Sept. 1702.

[5] The journal of Sir George Rooke Admiral of the Fleet 1700–02, ed. O. Browning (Navy Record Society, London, 1897), pp. 144–5; Tindal, xv, 253.

[6] NRO, Finch–Hatton MSS. 275, pp. 33–4, Nottingham to Marlborough, 26 June.

ally concluded, much to Nottingham's satisfaction, in May 1703. Thus, he was no little angered to find himself, virtually on the eve of the signing of the agreement, being accused in Whig coffee-house circles of obstructing the negotiations. Late in April 1703, he was informed that John Pulteney, an officer of the Ordnance, had publicly charged him with hindering the proposed alliance as well as opposing the extension of aid to the rebels in the Cevennes.[1] But when Pulteney was summoned, on the Secretary's demand, before the Privy Council to substantiate his allegations, the best he could muster was 'a lame excuse'.[2] Nottingham was fully and publicly vindicated by the queen who announced that if Pulteney had not resigned immediately, she would have dismissed him.[3]

That Pulteney's accusations were groundless is evident not merely by his own inability to prove them but also by, as Dr Davenant remarked, 'it being notorious that no Minister can take a thing more to heart and labour it more industriously than my Lord Nottingham has done the Treaty with Portugal'.[4] To be sure, there was no love lost between the elder Methuen (a former henchman of Sunderland) and his superior in London.[5] Moreover, Nottingham was uneasy about certain concessions Methuen had made in the treaty, particularly his acquiescence in Pedro II's demand that English ships should strike the flag in his harbours.[6] None the less, it was not the Secretary's hostility towards the alliance with Portugal but his enthusiasm for it that perturbed the Dutch and Marlborough. Heinsius, in particular, was distressed by an article of the agreement which stipulated that peace should not be made until Philip V was dislodged from Spain, and the

[1] BM Lansdowne MSS. 773, fos. 6–7, Dr Davenant to H. Davenant, 4 May; Luttrell, v, 292; Original Letters of Locke, Sidney, and Shaftesbury, pp. 149–50.

[2] BM Lansdowne MSS. 773, fos. 6–7.

[3] Ibid.

[4] Ibid. fo. 7.

[5] BM Add. MSS. 19253, fo. 184, Nottingham to Lord Chesterfield, Aug. 1703; ibid. 29587, fo. 100; NRO, Finch–Hatton MSS. 276, p. 2, Nottingham to Hedges, 3 Sept. 1703.

[6] Ibid. 277, pp. 4–7, Nottingham to P. Methuen, 1 and 8 May; ibid. pp. 8–12, 33–4, Nottingham to Stanhope and Stepney, 24 May and 9 June. See also Burnet, v, 80–1.

Pensionary only approved it after considerable delay.[1] Nottingham, however, seems to have had no misgivings on this score.
Apart from the need to reassure the Imperialists that the maritime
powers had abandoned completely William III's partition plans,
he himself was sure that it would be disastrous for England should
Spain and the West Indies be left under French control.[2]

For the moment, it was Nottingham's eagerness to have hostilities initiated by Portugal in conjunction with the allies, even if
that meant denuding the army in Flanders, which was the major
source of friction between the English Secretary and the Pensionary of Holland. The problem was that Pedro II refused to declare
war against Spain until the twelve thousand soldiers the maritime
powers and the Empire were obliged to furnish him actually
arrived in Lisbon. In this situation, Nottingham left Marlborough
in no doubt about his own feelings; 'some way or other troops
must be had', he told him, 'that this favourable conjuncture be
not lost'.[3] Even before the news of the conclusion of the Portu-
guese treaty had reached London, Nottingham had begun to press
the Dutch through Marlborough to ready their proportion of
troops, as well as the men-of-war that would be needed to convoy
the transport ships.[4] At first, Heinsius refused to commit the
United Provinces until the full details of the agreement were
known.[5] When this excuse would no longer serve, the Dutch,
increasingly burdened by their military expenditures, were still
markedly slow to respond to Nottingham's repeated importunities.[6] Unable to pay the subsidies necessary to raise new levies in
Germany (as Nottingham had proposed) and unwilling to reduce

[1] Stanhope's report of 11 Sept. 1703, cited in Churchill, *Marlborough*, 1, 646.
[2] Later events were to justify Dutch apprehensions, but Nottingham even out of office
persisted in supporting the policy of 'No Peace without Spain'. See below, pp. 211–12,
229 ff.   [3] NRO, Finch–Hatton MSS. 277, p. 13, 24 May.
[4] *Ibid.* pp. 22–3, Nottingham to Marlborough, 16 March.
[5] Murray, *Letters and despatches*, 1, 73–4.
[6] In addition, they quibbled over the number of ships they were to supply for the expedition (NRO, Finch–Hatton MSS. 277, pp. 1, 3, 37–8, Nottingham to Heinsius, 30
April, 8 May, and 29 June; *ibid.* pp. 8–9, 42–3, Nottingham to Stanhope, 24 May,
13 July; BM Add. MSS. 29595, fos. 230–1, Nottingham to Heinsius, 24 May).

their forces in Flanders to furnish the contingent for Portugal, they pleaded that nothing need be done until the Archduke Charles arrived since Portugal's execution of the treaty was also dependent on his presence in Lisbon.[1] Furthermore, neither the Dutch nor Marlborough displayed great interest in the projects Nottingham persisted in urging upon them for employing the forces bound for Portugal for the seizure of Dieppe or Bordeaux on their way, since these schemes would necessitate the departure of the troops from the Low Countries at an even earlier time.[2]

As the date (1 September) for the dispatch of the allied contingent to Lisbon neared with no prospect of its departure, Nottingham finally gave vent to his frustration. Writing of the Dutch refusal to promise any more than twelve ships for this convoy, he remarked bitingly to Hill; 'The Pensioner's answer to you... will be much more useful than it is satisfactory; for it will be remembered in settling the quota next year, and will teach us how to fix the agreement.'[3] Imperial inability to provide their share of the men and subsidies promised to Portugal was an added cause of ill feeling between the English and the Dutch since Heinsius stubbornly declined to make any contribution towards fulfilling the Emperor's deficit.[4] Though Nottingham continued to insist that England should provide no more than one-half of the Imperial deficiency whatever the States General did on the grounds that to yield on this issue would only encourage the Dutch and England's

[1] NRO, Finch–Hatton MSS. 277, pp. 84–6, Nottingham to Hedges, 1 Sept. Meanwhile Stepney, on Nottingham's instructions, was pressing the archduke's departure in Vienna (*ibid.* pp. 10–12, 34, 44–6, Nottingham to Stepney, 24 May, 9 June, 16 July; Murray, *Letters and despatches*, I, 154–5).
[2] NRO, Finch–Hatton MSS. 277, pp. 1, 50, Nottingham to Heinsius, 30 April and 23 July; *ibid.* pp. 2, 51–2, 59–60, Nottingham to Marlborough, 30 April, 23 July, 6 and 10 Aug.; PRO, SPF 84/225, nos. 59–60, 75, Heinsius to Nottingham, 11/22 May, 25 May/ 5 June, 3/14 Aug.; Murray, *Letters and despatches*, I, 101, 156, 168.
[3] *Hill correspondence*, I, 16.
[4] G. van den Haute, *Les Relations Anglo-Hollandaises au début du xviiie siècle d'après la correspondence d'Alexandre Stanhope 1700–1706* (Louvain, 1932), pp. 181–5; *Correspondence of Churchill and Heinsius*, letters 125, 130, 133.

other allies to default further on their commitments, he was eventually overruled by Godolphin, seconded by Hedges.[1]

Marlborough, pressed on one side by Nottingham and on the other by Heinsius, did all he could to ease the situation. While leaving little doubt in the Pensionary's mind that he was distressed at the prospect of being reduced to the defensive in the Low Countries, he none the less urged the Dutch to accept their share of the Imperial quota and to arrange the dispatch of their own troops to Portugal.[2] Everything possible must be done to satisfy the English ministry, he repeatedly advised Heinsius, lest 'an ill use' of Dutch deficiencies be made during the next session of parliament.[3] At the same time, he succeeded in arranging that only half the English soldiers to be sent to Portugal should be drawn from his command.[4] Hence he was both surprised and dismayed by Nottingham's riposte to the Dutch refusal to assist in meeting the Austrians' quota. On 8 October Nottingham informed him that a further draft of two thousand men from the English forces in Flanders had been agreed upon by the ministers (without consulting the Dutch) and that the ships to transport them to the staging-point were on their way.[5] The duke had no alternative save to comply, but he sympathized with the vigorous representations made by the States General at this breach of treaty obligations.[6] Yet Nottingham at least was unrepentant. Indeed, he told Hill that the Pensionary should have expected this step since he had been warned that if England had to supply the whole Imperial quota further withdrawals would have to be made from its forces in Flanders. Moreover, he added,

[1] D. Coombs, *The conduct of the Dutch; British opinion and the Dutch alliance during the war of the Spanish Succession* (The Hague, 1958), pp. 58–9; NRO, Finch–Hatton MSS. 276, pp. 1–2, Nottingham to Hedges, 3 Sept.
[2] *Correspondence of Churchill and Heinsius*, letters 112, 114, 125, 130, 133, 142.
[3] *Ibid.* letters 119, 144.
[4] *Ibid.* letter 133; Blenheim MSS. A/1/14, Marlborough to Godolphin, 5 July.
[5] NRO, Finch–Hatton MSS. 277, 113–14, Nottingham to Marlborough, 8 Oct.
[6] Murray, *Letters and despatches*, I, 203. To add to the confusion, Nottingham's letter of 8 Oct. was lost when the packetboat carrying it was captured.

I am troubled to find he [Heinsius] is still of opinion...that our great effort must still be there, where we so fruitlessly spent our blood and treasure in the last war; and where this method must, in our present circumstances, be still more useless and ruinous than it was even in the last war.[1]

Though Nottingham's objective of opening the war in Spain seemed finally to be realized when the long-delayed expedition set sail for Lisbon early in 1704, his success left a wash of bitterness and distrust between the Dutch and himself in its wake.

The lack of Dutch co-operation and their recurrent delays in furnishing even those forces which they had promised were sorely felt by Nottingham in another sphere as well. Shortly after he had taken office in May 1702, an Anglo-Dutch expedition to the West Indies of some eight thousand troops and forty men-of-war had been proposed and approved by the English Cabinet. Preparations began in secret under the direction of a Cabinet subcommittee on which Rochester (the arch-exponent of a 'blue-water' strategy) and Nottingham (whose province included the West Indies) played prominent parts.[2] A detachment from the flotilla under Rooke and Ormonde was to be made once Cadiz had been taken and additional forces were to be sent directly from England under the command of the mercurial Earl of Peterborough.[3] English plans for the expedition seem to have advanced rapidly, and on 26 June 1702 Nottingham wrote to Marlborough to acquaint him with the project and to instruct him to obtain Dutch concurrence in it on the basis of the usual three to two ratio.[4] Urging the importance of the scheme upon Marlborough, Nottingham contended that 'Nothing can be more for our interest and to the

[1] *Hill correspondence*, I, 45–6.
[2] Notes of the meetings of the 'Secret Committee', as Nottingham referred to it, are in BM Add. MSS. 29591; the earliest meeting recorded is that of 26 May.
[3] BM Add. MSS. 29591, fo. 11; *CSPD*, 1702–3, pp. 109–10. The selection of Peterborough (the former Earl of Monmouth) was attributed by Macky to Nottingham, but, given the Secretary's gingerly treatment of that volatile nobleman, some doubt must be attached to his testimony (J. Macky, *Memoirs of the secret services of John Macky* (Roxburghe Club, London, 1895), p. 60; NRO, Finch–Hatton MSS. 275, pp. 120–1, Nottingham to Godolphin, 24 Sept. 1702).
[4] *Ibid.* 275, pp. 33–4.

prejudice of France than...to prevent France from the fruits he expects from the West Indies'.[1] But Nottingham's hopes were not to be realized. Although Sir David Mitchell was sent to the Hague a fortnight later to secure Dutch agreement, they at first temporized and then completely turned down the English request.[2] Yet Nottingham was able to find some consolation in this setback. 'We shall not have a ship or man from the Dutch,' he told Godolphin on 2 September, 'so the expectation of their coming will not delay this service.'[3]

In fact, it was Dutch tardiness that was partially responsible for the eventual abandonment of the project, for ten days after their initial refusal they agreed to contribute to the expedition.[4] Nevertheless, by the time their very tardy forces arrived in Portsmouth in mid-January 1703, both Marlborough and Heinsius agreed that it would be futile to attempt to carry through the original plans.[5] Instead, a small contingent under Admiral Graydon was finally sent in March with ignominious results.[6] Graydon's failure, a growing realization of the difficulties of waging war in West Indian conditions, Rochester's resignation in February 1703, and Godolphin's fear that England had 'too many irons in the fire' all seem to have militated against any major effort in the Caribbean during the remainder of Nottingham's tenure as Secretary.[7]

In addition to the difficulties Nottingham repeatedly met with from the Dutch in military and naval matters, their reluctance to prohibit commerce by mail with France deeply disturbed him. This traffic, he felt, gave their merchants a great advantage over their English competitors, while the trade in bills of exchange

[1] NRO, Finch–Hatton MSS. 275, pp. 33–4.
[2] PRO, SPF 84/225, nos. 27, 33, 36, 45, 48, 49, Sir D. Mitchell to Nottingham, 18, 23, and 28 July, 14, 25 and 28 Aug.
[3] NRO, Finch–Hatton MSS. 275, pp. 104–5.
[4] PRO, SPF 84/225, no. 52, Sir D. Mitchell to Nottingham, 8 Sept.
[5] *Correspondence of Churchill and Heinsius*, letters 76–8, 84; van den Haute, *Relations Anglo–Hollandaises*, pp. 310–11.
[6] *HMC House of Lords*, n.s. v, 465–8; *LJ*, XVII, 510; Burnet, v, 92–3.
[7] *HMC Portland*, IV, 59. See also R. Bourne, *Queen Anne's navy in the West Indies* (New Haven, 1939), esp. pp. 25–58.

enabled France to finance her military efforts in Italy to the detriment of the whole alliance.[1] To overcome the States General's objection to a ban on such activity, he and Hedges seem to have proposed early in the summer of 1702 that the English mails to France should be re-opened by allowing the resumption of the Dover–Calais packetboat service.[2] But Marlborough's remonstrances against this move and his warning that it might hinder rather than encourage the proposed ban on Dutch commerce with France resulted in Nottingham's abandonment of this tactic.[3] Nevertheless, he did not desist from efforts to bring the Dutch to agreement. During the autumn he advocated delaying the renewal of England's treaties with the United Provinces until some decision was reached on this troublesome issue.[4] But it was the Dutch request in November for an augmentation of English troops in Flanders which finally provided Nottingham with the means to press his point home. By persuading his brother Heneage and Sir Edward Seymour not to oppose the raising of the additional ten thousand troops but rather to insist upon the commercial prohibition as England's *quid pro quo*, he engineered the passage by the Commons of a proviso to that effect on 5 January and a similar resolution was then passed on the 9th by the Lords.[5] The Dutch had now no option save to acquiesce, but their resentment was considerable.[6]

[1] NRO, Finch–Hatton MSS. 275, pp. 14–15, 57–8, Nottingham to Marlborough, 16 June and 21 July. See also van den Haute, *Relations Anglo-Hollandaises*, pp. 255–64.

[2] NRO, Finch–Hatton MSS. 275, pp. 14–15; Blenheim MSS. A/1/14, Marlborough to Godolphin, 2 June; BM Add. MSS. 17677XX, fo. 339, L'Hermitage's report of 12/23 June.

[3] BM Add. MSS. 29549, fo. 96, Marlborough to Nottingham, 10 June; NRO, Finch–Hatton MSS. 275, pp. 57–8. Marlborough did agree, however, that this trade should be halted as quickly as possible (Blenheim MSS. E/12, Marlborough to Godolphin, 19 July).

[4] BM Add. MSS. 29588, fos. 193, 240, Hedges to Nottingham, 9 and 18 Sept.

[5] *HMC Portland*, IV, 55–6; Klopp, *Der Fall*, x, 227, citing Hoffman's reports of 5/16 and 8/19 Jan. Marlborough deplored the imposition of this condition, but explained to Heinsius that 'the whole bent of the nation is soe possest of the necessity of forbidding all commerce with France and Spain' that the demand could not be stifled (*Correspondence of Churchill and Heinsius*, letter 78).

[6] *Hill correspondence*, I, 248, 263.

These repeated skirmishes between Nottingham and the Dutch alarmed and angered Marlborough. When the Secretary warned him in May 1703 of the 'clamor' Dutch failure to send the ships promised for the Mediterranean squadron would occasion in England, Marlborough had remarked to his Duchess:

I can't say a word for the excusing the dutch for the backwardness of their sea preparations this year; but if that, or anything else should produce a coldness between England and Holland, France would then gain their point.[1]

When the Secretary had notified him of the withdrawal from Flanders of the two thousand additional troops for Portugal in October 1703, without consulting the Dutch, the duke—no little chagrined—had observed to the Lord Treasurer;

I cannot but say that the dutch argue very justly. If the queen can without their consent take these men, she may by the same reason recall the rest; and by the same reasoning they are at liberty to reduce as many as they please of their army.[2]

Most disturbing to Marlborough was Nottingham's opposition to taking the offensive in Flanders—a view which seems to have found some support among the Whigs as well.[3] As he confided to his wife,

If both parties agree that the war must not be offensive in this country [Holland], I am very much afraid the dutch will not think themselves very safe in our friendship...I cannot but be much concerned; for if this country is ruined, we are undone.[4]

None the less, it was neither Nottingham's military strategy nor his conduct of foreign affairs, but rather his stand on questions of domestic policy that was to produce his most serious differences with Marlborough and Godolphin.

From the day of her accession, the queen had been the focus of

---

[1] W. Coxe, *Memoirs of John duke of Marlborough; with his original correspondence* (London, 1818), I, 204–5.
[2] *Ibid.* p. 216.　　　　　　　　　　　[3] Churchill, *Marlborough*, I, 706.
[4] Coxe, *Marlborough*, I, 206. See also Blenheim MSS. C/1/1, Marlborough to Sunderland, 20 Oct. 1703.

a struggle for influence and power. On the one side were ranged Marlborough and Godolphin, seconded by Harley, anxious above all to ensure by whatever means necessary the successful conduct of the war which England was about to enter. Though nominally Tory in allegiance, both these 'Queen's Friends' were prepared to subordinate domestic issues to the demands of the task of subduing France. 'In comparison with that...what (asked Marlborough) were "the detested names of Whig and Tory?".'[1] On the other side were the Tory leaders in the ministry, most notably the queen's uncle Rochester and Nottingham, whose most vital concern was to reassert Tory supremacy after the frustrations and setbacks of the previous reign and to safeguard the position of the Anglican church threatened, they believed, by the encroachment of dissent. Confident of Anne's favour for and sympathy with their ambitions, they and their followers glimpsed the prospect of the promised land.[2] To be sure, there were differences even among Tory leaders; if he dissented from Marlborough's strategic emphasis on the Low Countries, Nottingham shared neither Rochester's preference for a 'blue-water' policy nor his primarily political approach to ecclesiastical questions.[3] But their divergences were overshadowed by their acceptance in action of a set of priorities substantially different from those of Marlborough and Godolphin—a set of priorities which placed domestic objectives at least on a par with the prosecution of the war.

The queen's first speech to parliament after her accession reflected this diversity of purpose among her closest advisers. 'Too much', she asserted, 'cannot be done for the encouragement of our allies, to reduce the exorbitant power of France', but she also declared her 'own heart to be entirely English'—a phrase inserted

---

[1] Feiling, Tory party, p. 367. See also Churchill, Marlborough, I, 500–3, 529.
[2] See, for example, a letter of Dr Smith to Pepys, 28 March 1702, in Private correspondence and miscellaneous papers of Samuel Pepys 1679–1703, ed. J. R. Tanner (London, 1926), II, 259.
[3] Unlike Rochester, Nottingham had wholeheartedly favoured comprehension in 1689 and had lent small encouragement to the Convocation 'high flyers' in their disputes with the bishops.

in her oration on Rochester's instance.[1] Again, though Marlborough was able to insist upon England's entrance in the war as a
principal despite Rochester's opposition and also to frustrate his
ambition of being made Lord Treasurer by inducing Godolphin
to accept this key post, he did not succeed in maintaining more
than the semblance of a coalition in Anne's appointments to high
office.[2] Only the Dukes of Somerset and Devonshire and the
Archbishop of Canterbury survived as members of the Cabinet to
counterbalance Nottingham and Hedges as Secretaries of State,
Normanby as Lord Privy Seal, Jersey as Chamberlain, Seymour
as Comptroller, and Rochester as Irish Lord Lieutenant.

Once Marlborough left for the continent again at the end of
May, Tory pressure for 'a more entire change, to be carried quite
through all subaltern employments' produced significant results.[3]
Archbishop Sharp of York, in whom Anne had great confidence,
had been pressingly summoned to London by Nottingham on the
queen's accession, and the Secretary and archbishop made their
influence felt in a number of the new ecclesiastical appointments, among them Henry Finch's long-delayed promotion to
the Deanery of York, Humphrey Prideaux's nomination to
the Deanery of Norwich, and Francis Nicolson's elevation to the
bishopric of Carlisle.[4] Nottingham, so William Grahme (one of
the queen's chaplains) complained a year later, 'lays his hands on
all church preferment. His brother, his chaplains, and his favourites are all taken care of, and her Majesty's chaplains and clerks of
the closet are put by.'[5] In addition, Nottingham's old friend
Weymouth was named to the Board of Trade (despite the Duchess

---

[1] PH, VI, 5; W. T. Morgan, English political parties and leaders in the reign of Queen Anne
1702-1710 (New Haven, 1920), p. 63.
[2] Churchill, Marlborough, I, 532-7.   [3] Burnet, V, 12.
[4] Glos. R.O., Lloyd-Baker MSS. box IV, bundle K, Nottingham to Sharp, 24 March;
ibid. box IV, bundle R, Sharp to Nottingham, 16 May; Luttrell, V, 164; Bishop of
Barrow-in-Furness, 'Bishop Nicolson's Diaries', pt. II, in Transactions of the Cumberland
and Westmorland Antiquarian and Archaeological Society, n.s. II, 160-2. With reluctance,
Sharp accepted the Almoner's post in Nov. 1702 when Bishop Lloyd was dismissed
after complaints from the Commons.
[5] HMC Westmorland, Etc., p. 337.

of Marlborough's disparagement of him as a man of faction) as was Heneage Finch's son-in-law Lord Dartmouth, while Lady Nottingham was honoured by being made one of the queen's bedchamber ladies.[1] Still, there was dissatisfaction among the extremists. Rochester was reported to be angered by his relegation to the Irish Lord Lieutenancy, St John lamented 'trimming' at Court (which he attributed to Sunderland's influence), and Atterbury bitterly observed that Nottingham was 'as deep as any body in all the new methods of moderation' when he was mistakenly informed that the Secretary had ignored 'Robin' Price's claims upon a judgeship.[2]

With the dissolution of William's last parliament on 25 May, the signal for the outbreak of partisan hostilities throughout the country was given by the queen herself in the closing speech to the Houses. Though she promised to maintain the Toleration Act, her final peroration—which Nottingham and Rochester had had added over Godolphin's objections—left little doubt of her preferences.[3] 'My own principles,' she declared, 'must always keep me entirely firm to the interests and religion of the church of England, and will incline me to countenance those who have the truest zeal to support it.'[4] In the hard-fought electoral campaign which followed the dissolution, Nottingham as Secretary of State was looked to by Tory candidates and patrons from every part of England to assist their efforts with the crown's influence. From Gloucester John Howe pressed him to obtain his reappointment as Lieutenant Colonel of the shire militia, from the seaport constitu-

[1] Luttrell, v, 175; Coxe, *Marlborough*, I, 118; R. Walcott, *English politics in the early eighteenth century* (Oxford, 1956), p. 98.
[2] *Correspondence of George Baillie of Jerviswood, 1702–1708*, ed. G. Eliot (Bannatyne Club, Edinburgh, 1842), p. 3; *The epistolary correspondence of Francis Atterbury, D.D. Lord Bishop of Rochester*, ed. J. Nichols (London, 1799), I, 131; BRO, Downshire MSS., vol. CXXXIII, H. St John to Sir W. Trumbull, 20 June and 3 July. See also BM Add. MSS. 29588, fo. 47, Weymouth to Nottingham, 5 June.
[3] Algemeen Rijksarchief Heinsius MSS. 792, fo. 270, L'Hermitage to Heinsius, 2/13 June. See also the drafts of this speech in Godolphin's and Nottingham's hands in NRO, Finch–Hatton MSS. 2559. Nottingham, it would seem, also favoured the inclusion of an exhortation for the enforcement of the laws against 'profaneness and immorality'.
[4] *PH*, VI, 25.

ency of Shoreham Dr Davenant urged him to secure the withdrawal of Samuel Atkins (a Commissioner of the Navy) whose
candidacy was prejudicing his own, and from Wigan his brother
Edward asked for the removal of troops quartered in the borough
in order to avoid their interference in the polling.[1] All these and
other requests Nottingham did his best to satisfy, while at the same
time he worked to secure the election of Tory candidates in
Norwich (through Prideaux, the new Dean), in Kent (with the
help of his kinsman Winchilsea), and in London by carrying out a
thorough purge of the Lieutenancy.[2]

By early August reports of Tory success from all quarters were
flooding Nottingham's mail. Cornwall, Colonel Granville assured
him, 'never sent up an honester set of Gentlemen than now, for
out of the forr and forty there are but two exceptionable persons'.[3] Weymouth jubilantly commented, 'Wee could not wish
better Elections than those in the North.'[4] From Goodwood, the
Duke of Richmond wrote to announce, 'Wee have had very good
luck in ower Parliament men here abouts'.[5] Yet the Tory electoral
victory, whose extent was certain to be enhanced when the many
disputed elections were settled in their usual partisan fashion, may
not have seemed the unmitigated blessing to all Anne's advisers
that it did to Nottingham and Rochester. Marlborough, Godolphin and Harley seem to have apprehended that the activities of
those who, like Nottingham's correspondent Lord Denbigh,
hoped 'a Church of England Parliament' would 'settle the affairs
of England a little better, than they have been of late' might
threaten the national unity and parliamentary calm they were so
anxious to preserve.[6] As early as 9 August Harley was warning the
Lord Treasurer that it would be necessary 'to prevent, by supply-

---

[1] BM Add. MSS. 29588, fos. 26–7, 47, 68–9, 70, 74, 79–80, 81, 83, 86–7.
[2] *CSPD*, 1702–3, pp. 104–5, 114–15; NRO, Finch–Hatton MSS. 275, pp. 35–6; BM Add.
MSS. 29588, fos. 89–90, 93–4, 102–3, 104, 115; Luttrell, v, 193; Blenheim MSS. E/36,
Lord Halifax to the Duchess of Marlborough, 5 May 1705.
[3] BM Add. MSS. 29588, fos. 113–14.
[4] *Ibid.* fo. 129.
[5] *Ibid.* fo. 98.   [6] *Ibid.* fo. 117.

ing proper antidotes...the artifice of some hot men'.[1] That there were, indeed, grounds for their fears was amply to be borne out by the progress of the bill against Occasional Conformity.

The session opened harmoniously enough on 20 October for the Whigs chose not to reveal their numerical weakness by contesting Harley's candidacy for the Speakership, and he was called to the Chair without opposition after being nominated by Heneage Finch.[2] A vote and an address of thanks for the queen's speech, concerted by Harley with Seymour and Musgrave, was carried without division save one moved by the Whigs to indicate their objections to the resolution's partisan phraseology.[3] Moreover, Godolphin's instances with Ormonde and Nottingham's representations to Wratislaw proved sufficient to stifle the complaints of the duke and the Prince of Hesse-Darmstadt against Rooke's alleged misconduct on the Cadiz expedition.[4]

However, the attempts early in December by the Whig majority in the Lords to sabotage the Occasional Conformity bill provided the spark to inflame the Tory majority in the Commons. The measure, which had been overwhelmingly approved by the lower House, was aimed at inhibiting the practice of some dissenters who were prepared to receive the Sacrament once yearly in order to qualify for office and who then reverted to attendance at their own congregations.[5] This circumvention of the Corporation and Test Acts was deplored by many Tories and churchmen, some for primarily political reasons while others were genuinely shocked by this profanation of the Sacrament. Not-

[1] Ibid. 28055, fo. 3.
[2] Ibid. 7078, fo. 165, newsletter, 20 Oct.
[3] Longleat MSS., Portland Miscellaneous, Godolphin to Harley, 22 Oct.; Blenheim MSS. A/1/11, Hedges to Marlborough, 27 Oct.; PH, VI, 48–50. Drafts of the queen's speech in Godolphin's hand with amendments by Nottingham (not by Harley as Sir Tresham Lever in Godolphin his life and times (London, 1952), inset opposite to p. 140, would have it) are in BM Loan 29/64, bundle 1.
[4] HMC Portland, IV, 51; Klopp, Der Fall, X, 216–17; Tindal, XV, 437–8.
[5] Occasional Conformity as a gesture of ecumenical unity was encouraged by such eminent Nonconformist divines as Baxter, Howe, and John Humfrey. It was also approved, under certain circumstances, by several bishops, most notably Sharp and Burnet.

tingham, himself, would seem to have been the author of the bill. He had first conceived of such a measure in 1689 and its main provisions had been added to the abortive Lords' Comprehension bill.[1] The proposal had been revived during the last years of William's reign as the use of occasional conformity to qualify for municipal office became more frequent and notorious.[2] At Nottingham's instigation and with the approval of no less a personage than the queen (who had been assured by Sharp that it would in no way 'interfere' with or 'undermine' the Toleration Act), the bill against Occasional Conformity had been introduced in the Commons in November 1702 by William Bromley and Henry St John.[3]

From the outset, Godolphin and Marlborough do not seem to have evinced any great enthusiasm for the bill, but the queen's fervent support compelled them (and Prince George) to appear in its behalf.[4] They hoped for its quick passage without dispute, but when deadlock threatened between the two Houses as a result of Somers' cleverly engineered amendments to it in the Lords and the upper House's passage of a resolution against tacking despite theirs, Nottingham's and Rochester's exertions to brand it as 'unseasonable', they grew seriously alarmed.[5] Already there were signs of revolt in the lower House. Not only was the land tax

---

[1] Above, pp. 89–90.

[2] Sir John Packington's bill of March 1701 'for the Better Preservation of the Protestant Religion' had included such a clause, and a similar proviso was put forward by Heneage Finch as an amendment to the Lords' Abjuration bill in February 1702 (*A letter from a clergyman in the country to a dignified clergyman in London vindicating the bill for the better preservation of the protestant religion* (London, 1702), p. 8; *CJ*, XIII, 750; Feiling, *Tory party*, p. 358).

[3] Dartmouth's note in Burnet, v, 49; *Letters of eminent men, addressed to Ralph Thoresby F.R.S.*, ed. J. Hunter (London, 1832), I, 436–7; T. Sharp, *The life of John Sharp, D.D., lord archbishop of York*, ed. T. Newcome (London, 1825), I, 304–6. The bill of 1702 differed in one important particular from that prepared by Nottingham in 1689 for it also covered municipal offices (LRO, Finch MSS., Political papers 83; *PH*, VI, 62–7).

[4] Churchill, *Marlborough*, I, 625–7.

[5] For the debates in the Lords, see Tullie House, Bishop Nicolson's diary, 2, 3, 4, and 9 Dec.; *HMC House of Lords*, n.s. v, 157–9. It was for this reason that Harley, so Feiling speculates, was so eager for Nottingham to apprehend the author of *The shortest way with the dissenters* (*Tory party*, p. 369).

being delayed, but also on 23 December Seymour moved for leave to bring in a bill for the resumption of grants made by William III.[1] In vain did Godolphin lament to Harley: 'do they [the Tory hotheads] forget that not only the fate of England but of all Europe depends upon the appearance of our concord in the despatch of our supplies?'[2]

As the dispute between the Houses over Occasional Conformity continued into January without sign of concession from the Lords, the Commons' fervour rose. Seymour, Musgrave and Granville even attempted to delay the sending of the measure for a malt tax to the upper House until satisfaction was received on the bill.[3] Furthermore, attacks against Lords Halifax and Ranelagh for alleged malversation in the previous reign were now mounted by the zealot-dominated Commission of Accounts and countenanced by Nottingham in the Lords.[4] But if the Secretary supported Seymour's efforts to compel the Lords to retreat on their amendments to the Occasional Conformity bill, he did co-operate with Harley's and Godolphin's attempts to mediate the troublesome disputes between the Houses of Convocation.[5] Moreover, he did not associate himself with Rochester's personal vendetta against Marlborough which flared up in December over the queen's endeavours to secure parliamentary confirmation of a £5,000 *per annum* grant to Marlborough and his heirs. Indeed, while Seymour and Musgrave—prompted by Rochester—led the opposition, Nottingham's brother Heneage made 'a very excellent discourse setting forth the great services of the Noble Duke'.[6]

Though the dispute between the Houses over Occasional Conformity eventually subsided and Seymour's scheme for the

---

[1] *CJ*, xiv, 76, 95. At the same time, a Place bill seems to have been quashed only by skilful ministerial intervention.   [2] *HMC Portland*, iv, 53.

[3] Tullie House, Nicolson diary, 15 Jan.; Klopp, *Der Fall*, x, 224; *The Norris papers*, ed. T. Heywood (Chetham Society, London, 1846), p. 123.

[4] *CJ*, xiv, 127 and *passim*; Tullie House, Nicolson diary, 2 and 5 Feb.

[5] *HMC Portland*, iv, 50; BM Add. MSS. 29584, fos. 101–2, Archbishop of Canterbury to Nottingham, 21 Jan. [1703]. Cf. however Burnet, v, 68.

[6] *The Norris papers*, pp. 102–3, 106–7; *HMC Portland*, iv, 53–4; Klopp, *Der Fall*, x, 232–3.

resumption of grants made little progress, by early February
Marlborough and Godolphin felt they could no longer tolerate
Rochester's presence in the ministry. They prevailed upon Anne
to request him either to prepare to leave for Ireland to preside over
the parliamentary session there or to resign.[1] Confronted with
this choice on 2 February, Rochester resigned and retired to sulk at
his country seat, though offers of partial satisfaction from the
queen conveyed to him by Prince George as well as the urgings of
his own followers temporarily brought him back to Court later
that month.[2] Other dismissals were also rumoured in early
February including that of Nottingham, but, for the moment, the
duke and the Lord Treasurer had no intention of taking any such
step since they were not ready to contemplate coming to terms
with the Junto Whigs.[3] As Marlborough explained to his wife in
June 1703,

I...do agree with you that the seven persons you mention [among them
Nottingham] do not do the queen that service they ought to do; but I can't
but be of the opinion, that if they were out of their places, they would be more
capable of doing her hurt. Some of them might, in my opinion, be removed as
15 [Jersey] and 42 [Buckingham]; but who is there fit for their places?[4]

No doubt, both he and Godolphin hoped Rochester's fate would
be an object lesson to those remaining in office.[5]

But if this was their purpose in ousting Rochester, they certainly
did not succeed in intimidating Nottingham (or, for that matter,
Seymour). The Secretary continued to press for the ouster of
those Whigs still in office, although he was forced to content
himself with only partial success.[6] As he commented wryly to

[1] Churchill, *Marlborough*, I, 628–9; *Correspondence of Atterbury*, I, 164.
[2] BM Add. MSS. 29588, fo. 392, Rochester to Nottingham, 2 Feb. 1703; *Correspondence
of Atterbury*, I, 164, 167; PRO, PRO 31/3/191, report of Vaudoncourt, 23 Feb./6 March.
[3] *Correspondence of Atterbury*, I, 160.
[4] Coxe, *Marlborough*, I, 204. See also pp. 200, 202.
[5] It was, perhaps, for this reason that Nottingham was given the duty of informing
Rochester of the queen's wishes (Klopp, *Der Fall*, x, 236; BM Add. MSS. 29588,
fo. 392).
[6] For his attempts to secure a change of the Flintshire commission of the peace on behalf
of Sir R. Mostyn and Sir T. Hanmer, see *CSPD*, 1702–3, p. 536; NRO, Finch–Hatton

Colonel Grahme, 'if my skill in cookery were improved your fare should be mended, in the mean time remember the house of commons proverb that half a loaf is better than no bread'.[1] By the time the Houses reassembled on 9 November 1703, Seymour was reportedly 'quite out' with Marlborough and Godolphin, while the duke ruefully predicted to his duchess that 'this Winter you shall find 42 [Buckingham] a more violent if possible party man than 10 [Nottingham]'.[2] Most important, neither Nottingham nor the Tory zealots in the Commons had any intention of renouncing their support for measures against occasional conformity. But though another bill against this 'scandalous' practice was carried in the lower House by a majority of nearly one hundred, the Whig peers were now joined in opposition to it by Marlborough and Godolphin who, while voting for the measure themselves, encouraged their dependents and those in place either to absent themselves or to vote against it.[3] Moreover, the 'duumvirs' even succeeded in persuading the queen that its revival was unwise. However, once the bill had been approved by the Commons, Anne confided to the Duchess of Marlborough that she thought it would be 'better for the service to have it pass the house of lords too', although she denied that this was 'a notion lord Nottingham has put into my head'.[4] In the event, the duke's and Lord Treasurer's intervention was enough to cast the balance, and this session the Lords rejected the measure without even giving it the benefit of a second reading.

The reaction in the lower House was less disastrous than Godolphin and Marlborough may have feared. A proposal to tack the measure to a money bill was canvassed, but without

MSS. 277, p. 61; BM Add. MSS. 29589, fo. 96. See also *ibid.* 29588, fos. 480–1; *HMC Westmorland, Etc.*, p. 337; *HMC Portland*, IV, 58–9.
[1] Levens Bagot MSS., file N, 7 Aug. 1703.
[2] BM Add. MSS. 7063, A. Cardonnel to G. Stepney, 19 Nov.; Blenheim MSS. E/2, 27 Sept. See also Longleat MSS., Portland Misc., Godolphin to Harley, [1 Nov. 1703].
[3] Churchill, *Marlborough*, I, 703–4; E. Calamy, *An historical account of my own life with some reflections on the times I have lived in (1671–1731)*, ed. J. T. Rutt (London, 1829), II, 15–16.
[4] Churchill, *Marlborough*, I, 704.

attracting much support.[1] Moreover, when an attempt was made late in January to delay the passage of a money bill, the Tory extremists found themselves deserted even by such stalwarts as Musgrave, Howe and St John, and when they forced a division they were routed by a vote of 185 to 71.[2] In addition, a recruitment bill which Marlborough and Godolphin hoped would provide the means to keep English forces abroad up to strength was passed despite strong opposition from Nottingham and other Tory peers to compelling men to serve.[3] Though the session ended with violent altercations between the Tory majority in the Commons and the Whigs in the Lords over the proceedings on the Scotch plot, the duke and Lord Treasurer had ample grounds for satisfaction. Working in close conjunction with Harley, they had managed to isolate the Tory hotheads of the lower House. It was now possible to consider the dismissal of some of their leaders in the ministry without having to turn to the Junto, for their successors could be chosen from the ranks of Harley's adherents. As Tucker (Hedges's undersecretary) observed on 4 April, the day following the prorogation of the 1703–4 session, 'the sober party seem to be well pleased and in humour, the others not so, being under apprehensions of alterations'.[4]

But while Godolphin was secretly preparing the ouster of Jersey and Seymour, Nottingham was also drawing the conclusion that ministerial alterations were needed. Yet the changes he contemplated were hardly those planned by the Lord Treasurer. Ever since he had taken office, Nottingham had pressed for the removal of those Whigs who had been continued in place. Until this time, however, he had been content to make progress gradually, consoling himself that 'half a loaf' was 'better than no bread'. However, the events of the previous session had convinced him

---

[1] BM Lansdowne MSS. 773, fo. 12, Dr Davenant to H. Davenant, 4 Jan. 1704; *HMC Downshire*, I, 818.
[2] BM Lansdowne MSS. 773, fo. 6, Dr Davenant to H. Davenant, 1 Feb.; *CJ*, XIV, 312.
[3] Churchill, *Marlborough*, I, 709; *LJ*, XVII, 503–4.
[4] *Hill correspondence*, I, 94.

that the dismissal of the remaining Whig ministers could no longer be postponed.

What had most angered Nottingham was the Whigs' virulent attack against him in connection with the so-called 'Scotch plot'. It was during the summer of 1703 that the English government had first learned that preparations to raise the Highlands were under way. In July Stanhope had reported to Hedges that unusually large sums of money were being transmitted from Holland to suspected persons in Scotland, and Nottingham had then set to work to uncover 'the practices in Scotland'.[1] Letters in code from France to David Lindsay (the Jacobite Earl of Middleton's former secretary) had also been intercepted. Though the crown's cryptographer Dr Wallis had been unable to decipher them in full, Nottingham wrote to the Duke of Queensberry (the royal commissioner in Scotland) warning him that they seemed to refer to an insurrection in Scotland being planned with French aid and requesting him to arrest Lindsay.[2] At the same time, Queensberry was dealing (with the queen's approval) with a mysterious informer who promised to disclose details of the plot on condition that his name was not revealed.[3] When the duke reached London in October, he acquainted Nottingham with the affair and told him he proposed to send this double agent back to France in the hope of obtaining further intelligence of Jacobite schemes.[4]

Unfortunately for Queensberry and Nottingham, the duke's informant was none other than Simon Fraser, Lord Lovat, who was duping both the Court of St Germains and the Scottish Commissioner for his own ends. Suffice it to say of his complicated intrigues that his disclosures to the duke seem to have been aimed at securing his immunity from arrest while in the British Isles and also at revenging himself on his old enemy (and Queensberry's

[1] BM Add. MSS. 29591, fo. 241, Nottingham to Godolphin, 23 July; LJ, XVII, 448; HMC Westmorland, Etc., p. 337.
[2] BM Add. MSS. 29591, fos. 241, 243–4; NRO, Finch–Hatton MSS. 277, pp. 59–60.
[3] Queensberry's letters to Anne in this affair are printed in part in LJ, XVII, 450–1.
[4] Nottingham's narrative account of the plot in LJ, XVII, 401.

political rival), the Duke of Atholl.[1] With the aid of a pass secured
for him under a false name from Nottingham (who did not know
for whom it was intended) by Queensberry, Fraser left England in
mid-November just before the earl became aware of his treachery.[2]

The revelation of Fraser's double-dealing came from two
sources. First of all, Sir John Maclean, a Jacobite of long standing
who was seized when he returned to England in November 1703
on the pretence of taking advantage of the indemnity recently
offered in Scotland, disclosed under questioning by Nottingham
that a revolt was being planned in Scotland which Fraser was to
lead.[3] When the Secretary informed Queensberry of this report,
the duke—no little taken aback—confessed that Fraser had been
his informant and that he had now returned to France.[4] Further
evidence of Fraser's machinations was not long in coming to light.
While in London, he had been in touch with Robert Ferguson
'the plotter', who was now deeply involved in Jacobite activities.
Ferguson, who claimed to have been suspicious of Fraser from the
outset, had wormed out of him enough to fear that he was being
used by Queensberry in a plot against Atholl.[5] Ferguson then
warned Atholl of Fraser's schemes and when Atholl, late in
November, learned from Nottingham that he had issued a pass at
Queensberry's request under the false name Fraser was known to
travel under, the duke laid this evidence and the confession of
Fraser's accomplices in London (who were now under arrest)
before the queen with an accusation against Queensberry.[6]

By this juncture, it was becoming evident that the information
Fraser had supplied to Queensberry of Atholl's alleged involve-

[1] For Fraser, see W. C. Mackenzie, *Simon Fraser, Lord Lovat his life and times* (London, 1908), esp. pp. 93–152.
[2] *LJ*, XVII, 401.
[3] *Ibid.* pp. 400–1.   [4] *Ibid.*
[5] Ferguson's narrative of 27 Dec. in *LJ*, XVII, 409–11. See also J. Ferguson, *Robert Ferguson the plotter* (Edinburgh, 1887), pp. 336–64.
[6] Boyer, *History of Queen Anne*, pp. 106–7. Atholl later presented a formal memorial to the queen vindicating himself and accusing Queensberry which is summarized in *ibid.* pp. 109–11.

ment with St Germains was likely to have been concocted for his own purposes. Yet Maclean's disclosures gave ample grounds to believe that a rising in Scotland had been designed. Other suspected persons, particularly one Boucher, were also seized coming from France. All this, however, amounted to no more than the usual complications of Jacobite intriguing. What made the Scotch plot a *cause célèbre* were the House of Lords' proceedings in the matter.

Exactly how the conspiracy was originally brought to the Lords' attention is somewhat of a mystery for their initial step— an order of 14 December that Boucher and his travelling companions be safely secured—was occasioned, so their *Journal* reports, by their 'being informed' by some undisclosed source about a letter from Boucher.[1] Their great interest in the plot was, no doubt, prompted by the widespread uneasiness in England aroused by the proceedings of the Scottish parliament, especially the passage the previous summer of the Act of Security which enjoined that the Scottish crown should not pass on Anne's death to the successor to the English throne unless Scotland's commercial and political grievances had been satisfied. Furthermore, the Whigs suspected the English ministry of secretly conniving at its passage because of its supposed Jacobite sympathies, although the queen—on the advice of her English ministers, especially Nottingham—had for some time delayed approval of the measure despite great pressure from Scotland.[2] More particularly, it is likely that the initial 'leak' concerning the official investigation of the Scotch plot came from one of the Whig members of the Cabinet, either Somerset or Devonshire, both of whom had grave doubts that Nottingham was really trying to get to the bottom of the affair. They also seem to have feared that Atholl, and Ferguson with the

[1] *LJ*, XVII, 348.
[2] For Nottingham's views, see his note of a conference he and Godolphin had with the queen on 15 July 1703 in BM Loan 29/64, bundle 1. See also NRO, Finch–Hatton MSS. 277, p. 72, Nottingham to Godolphin, 25 Aug.; BM Add. MSS. 29595, fos. 245–6, Nottingham to Atholl, 14 Aug.

duke's connivance, were bent on demonstrating it all to be a sham.[1]

The Lords' efforts to investigate the plot themselves were cut short on 16 December when they were informed, after it had been proposed in the House that they should question Maclean, that the queen thought it 'inconvenient to take it out of the Method of Examination it is now in'.[2] None the less, the stir caused by their proceedings prompted the queen the following day to acquaint the Houses of the conspiracy and to promise to provide full details 'as soon as the several Examinations...can be fully perfected, and made public without Prejudice'.[3] But the upper House, not content with this assurance, resolved to elect a select committee to interrogate Boucher and his fellow prisoners. In the ballot that followed seven Whigs—Devonshire, Somerset, Somers, Sunderland, Wharton, Scarborough and Townshend— headed the list, while Nottingham polled only ten votes, Marlborough twenty-five and Godolphin twenty-seven.[4]

However, the Tory-dominated Commons were not slow to take umbrage at what they regarded not merely as an usurpation of both their own privilege and the royal prerogative, but also as an unjustified gesture of 'no confidence' in the ministry, and particularly in Nottingham.[5] On 20 December an address to the queen was proposed in the lower House which denounced the Lords' actions, especially their taking Boucher and others from the queen's custody into their own.[6] The Whig reply was that the upper House had taken the affair into its own hands because 'the ministry could not be trusted with examining the evidence'.[7] Indeed, Sir William Strickland went so far as to condemn Nottingham by name, charging that he had ordered the release of an

---

[1] The hypothesis that it was Somerset or Devonshire who was responsible is supported not only by the leading roles both took in the Lords' investigations, but also by Nottingham's acknowledgment in subsequent debates 'that some things had been ordered in the cabinet council, which the dukes of Somerset and Devonshire...did not agree with him in' (Burnet, V, 134).   [2] LJ, XVII, 351.   [3] Ibid. p. 352.
[4] Klopp, Der Fall, XI, 16.   [5] HMC Frankland–Russell–Astley, pp. 153–4.
[6] CJ, XIV, 256–7.   [7] Correspondence of Atterbury, I, 276.

important suspect who had been seized at Hull.[1] His allegations provoked a heated debate which was finally adjourned until the following day.[2]

Godolphin was no little concerned at this threatened outbreak of hostilities between the Houses on still another issue, and it was probably he who encouraged the queen to ask Nottingham 'to use his interest in the House towards dropping this debate'.[3] But Nottingham refused, no doubt because he was now intent on securing a public exoneration.[4] Thus the debate was resumed on the 21st, and as John Verney reported to Lord Hatton,

after a solemn chalenge to those that told the story [of the Hull incident] and everybody else to say what they had to say against the Lord Nottingham... Secretary Hedges...fully vindicated my Lords honour by giving a full and very satisfactory account of that story.[5]

Then the House without dividing resolved,

That the Earl of Nottingham...for his great Abilities and Diligence in the Execution of his Office, for his unquestionable Fidelity to the Queen, and her Government, and for his steady adhering to the Church of England...hath highly merited the Trust her Majesty hath reposed in him.[6]

Furthermore, the Commons approved a strongly-worded address to the queen which voiced their 'great and just Concern...to see any Violation of your royal Prerogative' and condemned the Lords' proceedings, after first rejecting attempts to moderate its terms.[7]

Nottingham now had his vindication, but so far as Harley and

[1] *Ibid.*; Luttrell, v, 372; BM Add. MSS. 29568, fos. 153–4, J. Verney to Viscount Hatton 21 Dec.; John Rylands Library, Legh of Lyme MSS., box 57, T. L[egh] to [P. Legh], [21 Dec.].

[2] *CJ*, xiv, 257. For details of the incident Strickland was misrepresenting, see *CSPD*, 1703–4, pp. 58, 66–7, 88.   [3] *Correspondence of Atterbury*, i, 276.

[4] *Ibid.*; John Rylands Library, Legh of Lyme MSS., *loc. cit.*; BRO, Downshire MSS., C/15, [Sir C. Cottrell to Sir W. Trumbull], 22 Feb. 1704.

[5] BM Add. MSS. 29568, fos. 153–4.   [6] *CJ*, xiv, 260.

[7] *Ibid.* pp. 259–60. Godolphin and Harley evidently favoured the amendment, and Hedges, Howe and Harcourt joined the Whigs in supporting it (*Correspondence of Atterbury*, i, 277).

Godolphin were concerned the damage was done, since it was all too likely that the Lords would be affronted by the Commons' address. Nottingham's reluctance to have the question dropped was all the more unfortunate since even the Whig peers seem to have realized that they had made a false step, and had resolved to postpone their examination of the plot until the queen laid the full details before parliament.[1] Godolphin's worst fears were borne out by the subsequent transactions of the Houses. Not only did the two Houses continue throughout the session to address against one another's proceedings, but moreover when the Lords formally took cognizance of the plot in February, the Whigs left no stone unturned in their onslaught against Nottingham.[2] A secret committee, once again composed solely of Whigs, was appointed on 23 February.[3] After examining the prisoners (particularly Maclean), a vote of censure was moved on 24 March against the Secretary on the grounds that his narrative account of the plot and the papers he had submitted to the House by the queen's order were 'imperfect' and incomplete.[4] Though this motion was defeated on a previous question by a vote of 41 to 30, the Whigs did succeed the following day in carrying over the opposition of all the Tory ministers, as well as Godolphin and Marlborough, a resolution which condemned the government's failure to prosecute Ferguson for his attempt to discredit the whole plot.[5] As Somerset, after reviewing the proceedings of the Whig lords, commented to Stepney, 'wee have finish'd this sessions mighty well, notwithstanding all have been fought inch by inch'.[6]

[1] *Correspondence of Atterbury*, I, 277; HMC *House of Lords*, n.s. V, 301, n. 1.
[2] *LJ*, XVII, 371-4, 538-49; *CJ*, XIV, 343-5.
[3] *LJ*, XVII, 453. In turn, the Commons' majority, egged on by Nottingham, carried a vote on 29 February to address the queen against the establishment of the Lords' committee as 'of dangerous Consequence' and tending 'to the subversion of the Government' (BM Add. MSS. 29587, fo. 133; *CJ*, XIV, 362).
[4] *LJ*, XVII, 489-502, 523-4; Burnet, v, 131-4; Blenheim MSS. C/1/1, Sunderland's notes of the committee's proceedings.
[5] HMC *House of Lords*, n.s. V, 303-4; *LJ*, XVII, 523-5.
[6] *Epistolary curiosities; consisting of unpublished letters of the seventeenth century illustrative of the Herbert family*, ed. R. Warner (Bath, 1818), 2nd ser. p. 207.

By the end of the session, then, Nottingham was hardly in a mood to tolerate Somerset's continued presence in the Cabinet. On other issues, too, he thought the time had come for a showdown with Marlborough and Godolphin. They had not, he believed, given him their full support in his struggle with the Whigs over the Scotch plot. Not only did he feel that he had deserved a 'better answer from the Queen' in her reply to the Commons' resolution in his favour, but he had also been disappointed by the sudden prorogation on 3 April which had prevented the Commons' presentation of a further protest against the Lords' proceedings.[1] Furthermore, he had strongly resented their underhanded efforts to block the passage of the bill against Occasional Conformity, and he was now resolved, if necessary, to support the proposal to tack it to a money bill the following session.[2] Unaware that the dismissals of Jersey and Seymour were already planned, he had decided to resign if he did not receive satisfaction from the Lord Treasurer.[3]

His intentions were no secret to Marlborough and Godolphin. Though they were not prepared to importune the queen—with whom Nottingham still had considerable influence—to dismiss him, they certainly had no desire to prevent his resignation. Thus, when Nottingham made his position clear to Godolphin in mid-April, the Lord Treasurer was unyielding. His account of that decisive interview (misleadingly summarized in its printed version) is preserved in a letter to the Duchess of Marlborough:

By these safe hands I may tell you I have had a very long Conversation with Lord Nottingham...there was very plain dealing on both sides, and of his side many threatenings from the Tory's intermingled with professions to mee, his

[1] BM Add. MSS. 29595, fo. 258, Nottingham to Viscount Hatton, 11 Jan.; *Hill correspondence*, 1, 94; C. von Noorden, *Europaische Geschichte im achtzehnten Jahrhundert* (Dusseldorf, 1870–82), 1, 500; Bodl. Ballard MSS. 6, fos. 93–4, E. Gibson to A. Charlett, 25 April.
[2] Blenheim MSS. A/1/14, Marlborough to [Godolphin], 8 April. See also Blenheim MSS, E/20, Godolphin to the Duchess of Marlborough, [27 March]; *The London Gazette*, no. 4004.
[3] *Ibid.; Hill correspondence*, 1, 94.

Aim seem'd to bee to gett the Duke of Somersett and the Archbishop out of the Cabinet Councill, and Lord Carlisle out of the Lieutenancy, he was very positive that the Queen could not govern but by one party or the other, and that keeping the Duke of Somersett in the Cabinett Councill after what had past would render her Government contemptible; I found afterwards he had given Mrs Morley [the queen] a good deal of these sort of notions, and she seem'd to think it was not equall to displace some that had misbehaved, and keep in others, but after a little talk she resolved to send her messages thursday morning.

I could not bee certain by Lord Nottinghams discourse whether he would quitt or not, it lookd all that way but when it comes to the poynt, I question if he will doe it.[1]

But Godolphin, in doubting Nottingham's threat to resign, underestimated the depth of his feelings. On the evening of the 20th, he obtained another private audience with the queen. He then informed her, as Harley reported to his brother, 'he could not serve with that Cabinet'.[2] The queen warmly pressed him to reconsider, and finally she persuaded him to keep the Seals at least a few days longer.[3] But the announcement on the following morning of the long-designed removal of Jersey and Seymour could only have hardened his resolve.[4] On the 22nd at one o'clock in the afternoon, he delivered the Seals to the queen.[5]

Though his nephew St John and other observers questioned the wisdom of his decision, particularly in the light of the queen's willingness to continue him in office, Nottingham was fully convinced of the rightness of his break with the ministry.[6] As he explained to Richard Hill, he had resigned not from 'fear of my

[1] Blenheim MSS. E/20, 18 April. Cf. Coxe, *Marlborough*, I, 229.
[2] BM Loan 29/70, 22 April. See also HMC *Cowper*, III, 35.
[3] *Ibid.*
[4] There had been rumours of Seymour's dismissal, but Jersey's came as a complete surprise to all, including Jersey himself (BM Loan 29/70, R. Harley to E. Harley, 22 April; Middlesex R.O., Jersey MSS., Jersey to R. Hill, 5 May; BRO, Downshire MSS., vol. CXXXIII, H. St John to Sir W. Trumbull, 9 May).
[5] Luttrell, v, 416; BM Loan 29/70, R. Harley to E. Harley, 22 April. For a report that the queen was 'not at all uneasy' about Nottingham's resignation, see Blenheim MSS. E/20, Godolphin to the Duchess of Marlborough, [24 April].
[6] BRO, Downshire MSS., vol. CXXXIII, H. St John to Sir W. Trumbull, 2 May.

enemies' nor even because of 'the labours, and anxious cares, of a very troublesome office'.[1] Rather, it was that

the proceedings of those, who called themselves, and should have been too, my friends, in reference to myself, my country, and the Queen herself, were intolerable. And how sweet soever the quiet of a retreat is in itself, these have made it more so, and it is the only obligation I have to them.[2]

In two brief years, all his hopes had been soured. During the next seven years, he was to labour to fulfill them in an increasingly isolated opposition.

[1] *Hill correspondence*, I, 136–7.   [2] *Ibid.* p. 137.

CHAPTER 10

THE HIGH CHURCHMAN AT BAY

1704-11

Could Nottingham have foreseen the seven bitter and futile parliamentary campaigns he was to wage after he left office in April 1704, he might well have reconsidered his ultimatum to the Lord Treasurer and the queen. Yet at this time, Nottingham—though he extolled the pleasures of retirement to Hill—had no intention of giving up his efforts to further the cause of the church and to impose his own war strategy upon the ministry. His resignation stemmed not from a decision to withdraw from politics, but rather from a belief that he could continue this struggle more effectively in parliament than in the Cabinet. Thus, he spent much of the summer of 1704 at his house 'near the Privy Garden' in Whitehall preparing pamphlets against the Lords' proceedings on the Scotch plot and against the dissolution he feared the revamped ministry was contemplating.[1] His manifesto against a possible dissolution makes it clear that he was counting on the widespread resentment of the Churchills' 'engrossment' of the queen's favour, the growing apprehension produced by the political upheavals in Scotland, bitterness at the failure of England's allies to make their full contribution to the war effort, and anger at Marlborough's and Godolphin's obstruction of the bill against Occasional Conformity, to rouse the Commons against the ministry.[2]

As the opening of the 1704-5 session neared, every effort was made by the Church party's 'whips' to bring their adherents up

[1] Drafts of these pamphlets, which do not seem to have been published, are in BM Add. MSS. 29587, fos. 143-4; LRO, Finch MSS., Scottish papers 5, Political papers 129.
[2] LRO, Finch MSS., Political papers 129.

from the country as early as possible.[1] There was talk, too, of removing Harley from the Speaker's chair on the grounds that he was ineligible to preside after his appointment as Secretary of State.[2] At the same time, the ministry, reinforced by Harley and a number of his followers, was bent on getting 'as many as possible off'.[3] Depicting the alterations of the previous spring as ones of 'persons' not 'things', they laboured to reassure the country gentlemen 'that we are far from being in a whig interest'.[4] But if the attack on Harley's continuance as Speaker never materialized and supplies were quickly agreed upon, the ministers did not succeed in allaying the pressure for an Occasional Conformity bill.[5] In mid-November, Bromley—supported by many Tory office-holders—brought in the measure for a third time.[6] Fearful that it would be rejected once more by the Lords and confident of a majority in the lower House, the Tory zealots then took the fatal decision to 'tack' it to the land tax bill. Feelings were running high and at least some of the ministers, among them Solicitor-General Harcourt, feared defeat. As he warned Harley,

Universal madness reigns, the more enquiry I make concerning the Occasional Bill, the more I am confirm'd in my opinion, that if much more care, than has been, be not taken, that Bill will be consolidated. I find the utmost endeavours have been us'd on one side, and little or none on the other.[7]

[1] *HMC Westmorland, Etc.*, p. 338. Nottingham was also active in urging allies like Weymouth to be sure to attend (Longleat Thynne MSS., vol. XVII, fo. 296). For a detailed account of the proceedings of this session, see W. A. Speck, 'The House of Commons 1702–1714: A Study in Political Organization' (D.Phil. dissertation, Oxford, 1965), pp. 110–39.

[2] BM Lansdowne MSS. 1013, fo. 71, W. Kennett to Rev. S. Blackwell, 21 Oct.; *Vernon correspondence*, III, 270.

[3] BRO, Downshire MSS., vol. CXXXIII, H. St John to Sir W. Trumbull, endorsed '16 May' [1704].

[4] *Ibid.* See also *HMC Cowper*, III, 49–50.

[5] A division among the high Churchmen as to whom to support to replace Harley seems to have impeded the project of unseating him (BM Add. MSS. 7078, fo. 223, newsletter of 24 Oct.; *State papers and letters addressed to William Carstares during the reigns of K. William and Q. Anne*, ed. J. M'Cormick (Edinburgh, 1774), p. 730).

[6] Feiling, *Tory party*, pp. 376–7; *CJ*, XIV, 419, 433.

[7] BM Loan 29/138, bundle 5.

Harcourt's caution prompted Harley and his colleagues to re-double their exertions against the Tack.[1] All the prestige of the government and the influence of place and pension was brought to bear, and with no little success. On 28 November the motion to incorporate the bill into the land tax measure was over-whelmingly defeated by a vote of 251 to 134.[2] The zealots were routed; as Dr Smallridge lamented to Charlett a month later,

I find our Friends very much surpris'd and disturb'd, the Party which some weeks ago found it Self so strong, doth now upon all Divisions in the House appear so weak, as to be able to carry nothing they contend for.[3]

The Tory opposition in the Lords, headed by Nottingham, Rochester and Haversham, fared no better. Not only was the Occasional Conformity bill rejected in mid-December, but Haversham's assault of 23 November on the ministry made little headway. Only Nottingham and Rochester supported his call for an inquiry into Admiralty mismanagement, while their complaints of the export of bullion and coin could not move the House to order an investigation of the problem.[4] There was, however, widespread agreement with Haversham's declamations on the danger of the Scottish situation, but Tory attempts to censure the ministry for advising the passage of the Act of Security were virtually ignored during the Lords' debates on Scotland of 29 November and 6 December.[5] With Somers taking the lead, it was agreed instead to bring pressure on the Scots by limiting their trade with England, though Nottingham warned that this might

[1] P. M. Ansell, 'Harley's Parliamentary Management', BIHR, xxxiv (1961), 92–7; Tullie House, Nicolson diary, 28 Nov. Archbishop Sharp, at the queen's request, used his influence with Yorkshire members of parliament against the Tack (Sharp, Life of John Sharp, i, 304–6).

[2] CJ, xiv, 437.

[3] Bodl. Ballard MSS. 7, fo. 5, 23 Dec.

[4] Tullie House, Nicolson diary, 23 Nov.; Longleat MSS., Portland Misc., Godolphin to Harley, [23 Nov.]; Boyer, History of Queen Anne, pp. 163–5.

[5] Tullie House, Nicolson diary, 29 Nov. and 6 Dec.; Baillie correspondence, p. 14; Boyer, History of Queen Anne, p. 165. Notes for Nottingham's speeches are in NRO, Finch–Hatton MSS. 792 and 4055.

only further inflame relations between the two kingdoms.[1] Similarly, Tory protests against continuing Dutch trade with France were rebuffed later in the session.[2]

The failure of the Tory opposition in the 1704–5 session did not, however, deter Nottingham. Even before the writs for the election in the spring of 1705 were issued, he was hard at work preparing an election manifesto chiefly directed against the ministry.[3] All the grievances of the past three years were once again aired, accompanied by a forthright defence of the Tack and complaints of the crown's interference in elections.[4] Moreover, Nottingham—as did Rochester's protégé Dr Drake in his *Memorial of the Church of England* of July 1705—now declared that the church was endangered by the secret practices of the ministers who were deceiving the queen and the nation by employing occasional conformists and giving free rein to the Presbyterians in Scotland.[5]

The elections themselves were vigorously contested, particularly because the ministry was determined upon a purge of the supporters of the Tack.[6] Yet, while substantial gains were made by the Whigs, ninety Tackers—among them Richard Halford representing Nottingham's own shire, Rutland—were once again returned.[7] Thus Godolphin, who had to reckon with a badly divided Tory party, had little choice save to make some advances to the Whigs, especially since rumours of a *rapprochement* between the high Churchmen and a group of country Whigs under

[1] Tullie House, Nicolson diary, 11 Dec.; *Vernon correspondence*, ii, 279–80.
[2] BM Add. MSS. 17677 AAA, fos. 75–6, L'Hermitage's report of 23 Jan./3 Feb. 1706.
[3] Reports at this time that Nottingham and Rochester had had private audiences with the queen suggest that they may, once again, have attempted to set Anne against her ministers (*HMC Portland*, iv, 189–90; *Remarks and collections of Thomas Hearne*, ed. C. E. Doble (Oxford Historical Society, Oxford, 1885), i, 1).
[4] Again, Nottingham does not seem to have published this pamphlet which is preserved in LRO, Finch MSS., Political papers 121. [5] *Ibid.*
[6] Speck, 'House of Commons 1702–1714', pp. 314–22, 415.
[7] This figure, arrived at by both G. E. Cunnington, 'The General Election of 1705' (M.A. thesis, London, 1938), *BIHR*, xvii (1939–40), 145–6, and Speck, 'House of Commons 1702–1714', p. 320, is strikingly confirmed by a contemporary computation in Bodl. Carte MSS. 180, no. 144.

Peter King's leadership were in the air.[1] Indeed, Marlborough, upon learning that 'so great a number of Tackers and their adherents' had been returned to the new parliament pressed the queen to give 'incoragement' to the Whigs 'that they might look upon it as their own Concern, to beat down and oppose all such proposals as may prove uneasy to her Majesty's government'.[2] At the same time, however, he urged Godolphin to take 'all the Care imaginable...that the Queen be not in the hands of any Party'.[3] Already Newcastle had succeeded Buckingham (the former Marquess of Normanby) as Lord Privy Seal, and late in July the Lord Treasurer announced that the ministry would support John Smith, a Whig, for the Speakership.[4]

Ministerial dealings with the Whigs only served to confirm Nottingham's belief in Marlborough's and Godolphin's treachery, and the opposition Tories now united behind William Bromley's candidacy for the Speakership. The efforts of both sides ensured an attendance of no less than 457 members of parliament when parliament met on 25 October 1705. But the united forces of the Whigs, the followers of the ministers, and the placemen (only seventeen of whom defected) were sufficient to secure a majority of forty-three for Smith.[5] Undismayed by this initial setback in the Commons, the Tory peers took the offensive in the Lords. On 12 November Nottingham proposed an address which would have requested the queen to lay before the House all the proceedings in Scotland since the Lords had last met. After objections were made to the tendentious wording of his motion, it was amended on Godolphin's suggestion and then agreed to without a division.[6] Three days later, Haversham, seconded by Nottingham,

---

[1] *HMC Frankland-Russell-Astley*, p. 176; Nott. U. Portland MSS. PWa 410, J. Eyles to Duke of Portland, 27 July.
[2] Blenheim MSS. A/1/37, Marlborough to Godolphin, 6 July, quoted in Churchill, *Marlborough*, II, 28–9.   [3] *Ibid*.
[4] Nott. U. Portland MSS. PWa 410.
[5] W. A. Speck, 'The Choice of a Speaker in 1705', *BIHR*, XXXVII (1964), 20–46.
[6] Tullie House, Nicolson diary, 12 Nov.; *The private diary of William, first Earl Cowper, lord chancellor of England (1705–1714)*, ed. E. C. Hawtrey (Roxburghe Club, London,

Rochester, Buckingham, Anglesey and Winchilsea, brought forward the Tory peers' most important project. After dilating on allied military failures and Dutch trade with the enemy, he urged the necessity of inviting the presumptive heir to the crown, the Electress Sophia, to reside in England 'for the safety of the queen, for the preservation of our constitution, for the security of the church, and for the advantage of us all'.[1]

By raising the issue of the Hanoverian succession in this particularly embarrassing form, the opposition Tories—who had been in correspondence with Hanover and had received some encouragement from the Electress—hoped to shake the developing alliance between the Whigs and the ministry.[2] The queen's known distaste for such a proposal combined with Whig fears about Marlborough's and Godolphin's loyalty to the protestant succession would, they calculated, place the ministry in a very awkward position. Had this scheme been pressed when Rochester first mooted it in the previous session, it might have succeeded by surprise, but now the ministers, after failing to persuade the opposition peers to abandon it, had concerted counter measures with the Whigs.[3] Thus, Haversham's motion was opposed by Somers, Devonshire and Halifax, and was so overwhelmingly rejected on the previous question that its supporters abandoned it without further ado. Instead, at Godolphin's suggestion the House agreed to consider other means to secure the succession.[4] The joint plan of the ministers and the Junto—a Regency bill designed to

1833), pp. 13–14; BM Add. MSS. 17677 AAA, fos. 513–14, L'Hermitage's report of 13/24 Nov.

[1] PH, vi, 457–61. See also Tullie House, Nicolson diary, 15 Nov.; BM Add. MSS. 4291, fo. 38, Dr Davenant to H. Davenant, 16 Nov.

[2] Diary of Earl Cowper, p. 13; HMC Athole and Home, pp. 62–3; A. W. Ward, The Electress Sophia and the Hanoverian succession (London, 1909), pp. 382–4.

[3] Burnet, v, 190–1; BM Add. MSS. 17677 ZZ, fo. 514, L'Hermitage's report of 28 Nov./ 9 Dec. 1704; HMC Portland, iv, 154; Sharp, Life of John Sharp, i, 308–9. See also HMC Portland, ii, 191.

[4] BM Add. MSS. 17677 AAA, fos. 521–2, L'Hermitage's report of 16/27 Nov.; HMC House of Lords, n.s. vi, 322; LJ, xviii, 19. Three weeks later, the Commons also rejected a motion for an invitation (BM Add. MSS. 9094 (Coxe transcripts), fos. 221–2, J. Brydges to Marlborough, 4 Dec.).

ensure the maintenance of public order at the queen's death—
was introduced by Wharton on the 19th. Nottingham and his
associates, after vainly putting forward a series of amendments to
the bill, finally voted to reject it, but won little support for their
stand since the measure clearly answered their proclaimed fears
of the dangers of an interregnum.[1] Nottingham's and Rochester's
lamentations that the church was in danger received equally
short shrift. On 6 December the Lords resolved by a vote of 61
to 30 that 'the Church...is now...in a most safe and flourishing
Condition, and whoever goes about to suggest and insinuate, that
the Church is in Danger under Her Majesty's Administration, is an
Enemy to the Queen, the Church, and the Kingdom'.[2] The only
achievement of the Tory opposition during the session of 1705–6
was the partial setback they administered, with the aid of a
squadron of country Whigs, to the Court's attempts to repeal that
section of the Act of Succession which excluded placemen from
the Commons after Anne's death.[3]

By the spring of 1706, then, it must have been evident even to
Nottingham that the course of active opposition he had embarked
on two years earlier was leading nowhere. Not only had he failed
to secure the passage of the bill against Occasional Conformity,
but also his repeated denunciations of the ministry's mismanagement of the war had succeeded neither in shifting the major
military emphasis to Spain nor in ending allied defalcations on
their quotas. Furthermore, by forgetting, as George Granville
sagely remarked, that 'Ladies are to be courted, and not ravished',
he had forfeited completely the good will of the queen.[4] Even
before the proposal to invite the Electress had been advanced in

[1] *LJ*, XVIII, 36–7, 39–41; Burnet, V, 234–8; *Diary of Earl Cowper*, pp. 16, 22; Tullie House,
Nicolson diary, 19, 29, and 30 Nov. Drafts of the amendments proposed by Nottingham
are in LRO, Finch MSS., Political papers 124.
[2] *LJ*, XVIII, 43–4. The fullest accounts of the debate are in Tullie House, Nicolson diary,
6 Dec.; and BM Lansdowne MSS. 1034, fos. 4–5. Notes for Nottingham's speech are
in LRO, Finch MSS., Political papers 126.
[3] G. S. Holmes, 'The Attack on "The Influence of the Crown", 1702–1716', *BIHR*,
XXXIX (1966), 54–9.
[4] Levens Bagot MSS., file G, G. Granville to Col. Grahme, 21 Sept. 1706.

the autumn of 1705, Anne seemingly was convinced that Nottingham's and Rochester's conduct made it impossible for her to think of bringing them back into office.[1] Nottingham's insistence during the 1705-6 session that the church was in danger and, above all, his part in pressing for the invitation, had further incensed Anne, not least because the earl while Secretary had 'possessed her with deep prejudices' against just such a proposal.[2] Indeed, Dartmouth later commented that his advocacy of the invitation had 'made an impression upon the queen...that could never be overcome'.[3]

In addition to arousing Anne's resentment, the violence of the Tory opposition had compelled Marlborough and Godolphin to look increasingly to the Whigs for parliamentary backing.[4] Buckingham and Wright had been replaced by Newcastle and Cowper respectively in 1705. Then, with the queen's reluctant consent, Sunderland had been appointed Secretary in Hedges's stead in December 1706, while Halifax was dispatched on a mission of compliment to Hanover.[5] Nottingham's and Rochester's assaults upon the ministry had achieved the very result they so greatly feared—the conclusion of a working arrangement between the Junto and the ministers. Yet whatever the Tory peers might believe, Marlborough, Godolphin, and especially Harley still hoped they could maintain the administration on a quasi-coalition basis without succumbing to party tyranny, whether it was that of the high Churchmen or the Junto.[6] During the next two and a half years, it was the ministry's and the queen's struggle

[1] *Diary of Earl Cowper*, pp. 1-2.
[2] Burnet, v, 233, 238; J. Swift, *The history of the four last years of queen Anne's reign*, ed. H. Davis (Oxford, 1951), pp. 15-16.
[3] Dartmouth's note in Burnet, v, 233.
[4] See, for example, Godolphin's calculations in *HMC Portland*, IV, 291.
[5] At the time of Sunderland's appointment, the names of Rochester, Nottingham, Jersey and Buckingham were stricken from the list of Privy Councillors (Feiling, *Tory party*, p. 395).
[6] *Ibid.* pp. 379-90. For ministerial efforts to woo a number of high Church leaders back into the fold in 1706, see *HMC Bath*, I, 121; Morgan Library Autograph Collection, William III, misc. box XI, Marlborough to [Sir T. Hanmer], 21 June 1706.

to escape the gradually tightening grip of the Junto that was to dictate the often confused course of English politics. It was this contest of strength, which flared up spasmodically and often subsided quickly, that was also to offer to Nottingham and his friends their most promising opportunities to attack the administration during this period.

The session of 1706-7 was, save for the disputes over the proposed union with Scotland, a relatively quiet one. Despite Nottingham's complaints to Dartmouth of the gross neglect of the war in the West Indies, Marlborough's victorious campaign temporarily silenced his critics, while the Junto's success in securing Sunderland's appointment and Somers's involvement in the negotiations with Scotland kept them on good behaviour.[1] Then, too, Nottingham—who had long been an advocate of union—was reluctant to oppose in toto the treaty submitted to parliament in February 1707, and as early as the summer of 1706 he and Rochester seem to have decided against outright opposition.[2] They were, however, prepared to insist that the treaty should not be approved until the Anglican Church was accorded safeguards equivalent to those conceded to the Scottish Presbyterians. Thus on 14 January 1707, even before the Articles of Union had been laid before the English parliament, Nottingham— seconded by Rochester, Buckingham and Haversham—urged the Lords to 'provide betimes against the dangers, with which the church, by law established, was threatened, in case the Union was accomplished'.[3] The ministerial response to his initiative was not long delayed. Two weeks later, the Archbishop of Canterbury introduced a bill for the further security of the Church of England in the Lords. And despite Nottingham's criticism of Tenison's

[1] HMC Dartmouth, I, 294; WSL, Dartmouth MSS. D 1778, I, ii, 74, Nottingham to Dartmouth, 6 July 1706.
[2] Baillie correspondence, p. 157. For Nottingham's record of support for union, see above, p. 165; Tullie House, Nicolson diary, 30 Nov. 1702 and 11 Dec. 1704; LRO, Finch MSS., Political papers 148. However, he had hoped that union would result in some amelioration of the lot of the Scottish Episcopalians (Baillie correspondence, p. 11).
[3] PH, VI, 554. See also Luttrell, VI, 126-7; Tullie House, Nicolson diary, 14 Jan.

failure to consult Convocation before bringing it forward, as well as Tory efforts to entrench the Test Act, the Archbishop's measure was quickly approved by both Houses without substantial amendment.[1] Deprived of their main argument against the Union, Nottingham and the other Tory peers fell back on criticism of its terms when the treaty was considered by the upper House in February. It was, he claimed, the responsibility of those of the queen's English ministers who had advised her in 1703 to pass the Scottish Act of Security that the Scots were now able to extort so high a price for union.[2] Not only did he object to the payment of the large monetary equivalent to Scotland, but he also condemned the proposal to elect sixteen Scottish peers to sit in the Lords as a danger to the Anglican Church.[3] Though he protested that 'no man in all Brittaine has bin or can be more zealous for an Union than myselfe...[as] I have shewn upon all occasions, here and in Every Station and even [in] private Conversation', he concluded his denunciation of the terms of the treaty with a stern warning of the 'dire effects' they would produce in England.[4] But the rhetorical fireworks of Nottingham and Haversham were of no avail, and the treaty was quickly approved by both houses. Soon afterwards, Nottingham left Westminster for Burley.

The futility of his exertions in previous sessions seem, initially, to have prompted Nottingham to absent himself from the Lords the following year. As he wrote to Dartmouth from Burley early in October 1707,

if I were never so idle and had nothing to doe, I have a great deal to say against London, where I can do no good to any, but may [do] much harm to myselfe, at least I shall expose myselfe to great and unavoydable but yet fruitlesse vexation, instead of quiett and satisfaction which I enjoy here, more, I can truely say, than ever I had in my life.[5]

[1] HMC House of Lords, n.s. VII, 22–3; LJ, XVIII, 225; PH, VI, 559; Tullie House, Nicolson diary, 3 Feb.; Luttrell, VI, 134; Sharp, Life of John Sharp, I, 390–2. Nottingham's draft of the protest of 4 Feb. is in LRO, Finch MSS., Political papers 127.
[2] Notes for his speech are in ibid. Political papers 128.
[3] Ibid.; PH, VI, 566–9.   [4] Ibid. pp. 568–9; LRO, Finch MSS., Political papers 128.
[5] WSL, Dartmouth MSS. D 1778, I, ii, 87.

None the less, his resolution was not sufficiently strong for him to withstand the temptation offered by the extraordinarily chaotic political situation and the importunities of his friends which doubtless accompanied it. No sooner had he arrived in London early in December 1707 than he was plunged into a maelstrom of conflicting factions.[1] At its centre was the increasingly bitter struggle within the ministry for the queen's favour which was now being waged between Godolphin and Harley. This division among the 'triumvirate' had been precipitated by new Whig demands for the rewards of place and office for their support of the ministry, demands which the Lord Treasurer reluctantly and the Duchess of Marlborough enthusiastically had been pressing the queen to satisfy. But Harley, who had for the past two years been growing increasingly uneasy at the repeated concessions extorted from Anne by Godolphin in favour of the ever-insatiable Junto, was now actively working with the queen's connivance to form a new ministry with a moderate Tory bias from which the Lord Treasurer was to be excluded if he did not break with the Junto.[2] Encouraged by Poulet's assurance that 'enemies' actions have made in general all of the character of Churchmen more reasonable than any words of friends could do', Harley even approached the Commons' leaders of the opposition Tories, Bromley and Sir Thomas Hanmer, with promises of the royal favour if they would co-operate with him.[3] At the same time, the Junto lords and their following in the Commons—frustrated of their hope of church preferments for their clerical allies—were planning to bring the ministry to heel by launching assaults in both Houses on a number of very sensitive administrative prob-

[1] For the most recent analyses of the background to and events of the 1707–8 session, see G. S. Holmes and W. A. Speck, 'The Fall of Harley in 1708 Reconsidered', *EHR*, LXXX (1965), 673–98; Speck, 'House of Commons 1702–1714', pp. 157–227; H. L. Snyder, 'Godolphin and Harley: A Study of their partnership in politics', *Huntington Library Quarterly*, XXX (1967), 241–71.

[2] Holmes and Speck, 'The Fall of Harley', pp. 685–7.

[3] *HMC Portland*, IV, 426; Burnet, V, 340; *Vernon correspondence*, III, 345; Sharp, *Life of John Sharp*, I, 323.

lems. In turn, the opposition Tories, too wary of Harley at first to come to terms with him, chose rather to try to defeat the administration by expanding the Junto's attacks upon the ministry into a full-scale condemnation of its management.[1]

How closely aligned the leaders of the disparate opposition were to one another is not altogether clear, though there was talk that Wharton had been visiting Nottingham, but it is evident that the coalition of 'high Whigh and high Torie' functioned effectively only spasmodically.[2] On the one hand, the Junto peers shelved their complaints of naval mismanagement when they realized that the Tory lords who seconded them, Haversham, Guernsey and Rochester, were intent upon proving that the ministry, rather than Prince George's Tory-dominated Admiralty Council, was at fault.[3] In retaliation, the Tories sat silent in the Commons when the Whigs pressed a similar inquiry two weeks later.[4] On the other hand, a group of Whigs in the Commons led by Solicitor-General Montague, Sir Richard Onslow and Peter King, and the Tory Churchmen co-operated to frustrate the Court's hopes of maintaining the Scottish Privy Council and to alter substantially the government's Recruitment bill.[5]

It was, however, on the question of the conduct of the war, particularly in Spain, that the opposition Tories came closest to toppling the government. In the Lords, an investigation of the military disasters of the previous summer in the Peninsula (which had been capped by the rout of the allied forces under Lord Galway at Almanza) was launched on 16 December with Nottingham, Rochester and Haversham vigorously defending the

[1] Burnet, v, 340.
[2] PRO, PRO 31/3/194, Tallard au Roi, 17/28 Dec. 1707; J. Brydges to W. Cadogan, 24 Dec., printed in *Huntington Library Quarterly*, xv (1951–2), 38–9.
[3] Tory intentions were made clear by Haversham's speech (*PH*, vi, 598–600).
[4] BRO, Downshire MSS., vol. LIII, J. Bridges to Sir W. Trumbull, 21 Nov.; PRO, PRO 31/15/6, pt. 2, vol. XI, J. Addison to Lord Manchester, 16 Dec.; *Vernon correspondence*, III, 287.
[5] Duke of Manchester, *Court and society from Elizabeth to Anne* (London, 1864), II, 266, 273–4; *Vernon correspondence*, III, 291–2, 310–11, 318, 321–2; *HMC Lonsdale*, p. 117; *CJ*, xv, 461, 512.

now-disgraced Earl of Peterborough and imputing English set-backs to Galway, the Junto's favourite.[1] Three days later, Nottingham opened a frontal attack against the ministry, complaining of the deplorable state of the nation's coin, the decay of trade and the futility of the war in Flanders. He concluded his tirade with a motion for the replacement of Galway and the dispatch of twenty thousand men to Spain from the Low Countries.[2] Rochester and Peterborough repeated his call for reinforcements, and the Whig lords Wharton, Townshend and Sunderland joined in stressing the importance of the war in Spain. Marlborough, in reply, conceded the argument and informed the House that measures were already in train for the dispatch of a sizable contingent to the Peninsula for the following campaign. Somers, quick to take advantage of this change in policy, then proposed a resolution 'that no peace could be honourable or safe...if Spain and the Spanish West Indies were suffered to continue in the power of the House of Bourbon'.[3] Once this motion was carried virtually unanimously, the Lords' proceedings subsided into a detailed examination of Peterborough's conduct, with Nottingham and Rochester vainly striving throughout January to secure his vindication.[4]

In the Commons, Hanmer, Bromley and Freeman, 'treating that matter in conformity to their friends in the House of Lords', had greater success.[5] It soon became evident from the statements of St John (the Secretary at War) that only a small number of the troops provided for the Spanish theatre had actually been present at the battle of Almanza. Taxed with this discrepancy on 29 January by Hanmer, St John was unable to provide a satisfactory

[1] PRO, PRO 30/15/6, pt. 2, vol. XI, J. Addison to Lord Manchester, 16 Dec.; *Vernon correspondence*, III, 297.
[2] *HMC Egmont*, II, 220–1; *Vernon correspondence*, III, 300–1; PRO, PRO 31/15/6, pt. 2, vol. XI, J. Addison to Lord Manchester, 23 Dec.; J. Brydges to W. Cadogan, 24 Dec., in *Huntington Library Quarterly*, XV (1951–2), 38–9. Notes for Nottingham's speech are in LRO, Finch MSS., Political papers 132.
[3] Churchill, *Marlborough*, II, 303–5.
[4] *Vernon correspondence*, II, 303, 307; Duke of Manchester, *Court and society*, II, 269; *Original letters of Locke, Sidney, and Shaftesbury*, pp. 189–91.
[5] *Vernon correspondence*, III, 298.

explanation. Hanmer's motion that a representation of this 'great neglect' be drawn up (which he hinted would be followed up by a vote of censure for the misapplication of funds) was supported by Peter King and other disaffected Whigs. It was not until the Junto's following finally came to the government's aid late in the debate of the 29th that an adjournment was carried, and then only by a vote of 187 to 172.[1]

The parliamentary crisis confronting the ministry was not, however, to be resolved at Westminster but at Whitehall, for the real source of Godolphin's difficulties was the queen's refusal to satisfy the Junto's demands which, in turn, had produced their temporary conjunction with the Tories against the government. Moreover, knowledge of Harley's continuing efforts to win over the opposition Tories combined with the Secretary's apparent condemnation to the queen of his colleagues' mismanagement in Spain had convinced Godolphin by late January of his perfidy, and Marlborough—after no little wavering—finally came down on the Lord Treasurer's side a week later on 6 February. Even so, it did not prove easy for Marlborough and Godolphin to secure Harley's ouster. Indeed, it was only the unwillingness of Somerset and the other ministers to work with Harley and to accept the Lord Treasurer's and the duke's resignations, combined with parliamentary threats mounted by the Junto to impeach Harley, that finally brought the Secretary to surrender on 10 February.[2]

While this bitter struggle raged within the ministry, Nottingham suddenly left London not to return for the remainder of the session.[3] His departure at this critical juncture would seem to have been a measure of his disgust with Rochester's and Haversham's failure to join with him in bringing 'matters of more weight' than Peterborough's conduct 'upon the stage' and also his dis-

---

[1] Duke of Manchester, *Court and society*, II, 272; *Vernon correspondence*, III, 328–30.
[2] Holmes and Speck, 'Fall of Harley', pp. 689–98. But cf. Snyder, 'Godolphin and Harley', pp. 267–70 and n. 93.
[3] His last recorded day of attendance in the Lords was 31 Jan. though Bishop Nicolson mentions that he was present on 5 Feb. (*LJ*, XVIII, 440 and *passim*; Tullie House, Nicolson diary, 5 Feb.).

trust both of Harley (whose assurances that the queen was prepared to countenance the Tories he declined to believe) and of
Marlborough and Godolphin.[1] Certainly, his suspicion of Harley
and his reluctance to consider a reconciliation with the Lord
Treasurer not only characterized his conduct during the 1707–8
session, but also during the following one.

With Harley at last out of office (along with St John, Harcourt
and Mansell), the split between the Court and the Junto was
temporarily patched up. Nevertheless, the bulk of the promotions
that followed the February purge of Harleyites was distributed
among those Whigs who had remained loyal to the ministry
during the preceding months, rather than to the Junto and its
adherents. But the elections in the spring of 1708 left Godolphin
increasingly little room for manoeuvre. The Whig tide was running strongly; even in his own shire, only one of Nottingham's
candidates was elected.[2] Yet the Lord Treasurer, all too cognizant
of the queen's aversion to the Junto, did not yield without a
struggle. By mid-summer, it was common gossip in London that
the Court 'will not go into the Whigs', and that the ministry was
still hoping to build a parliamentary majority from the moderates
of both parties.[3] Godolphin even seems to have gone so far as to
open negotiations with the opposition Tories, but without success. As the Duke of Roxburghe (Nottingham's new son-in-law)
informed one of his Scottish correspondents, 'to my knowledge
287 [Nottingham] is more averse to them [the ministers] than
ever'.[4] Indeed, the distance between the ministry and the high

[1] HMC Portland, VIII, 280; LRO, Finch MSS. Correspondence, box VII, bundle 25, copy
   of letter from Nottingham to Bromley, [late Oct. or early Nov. 1708]; ibid. box VI,
   bundle 22, draft of letter from same to same, 20 Dec. 1708.
[2] For his efforts on behalf of the Tory nominees, Halford and Horseman, see NRO,
   Isham MSS. 2965, Nottingham to Sir. J. Isham, 5 May. For a calculation of the overall
   results, see Speck, 'House of Commons 1702–1714', p. 418.
[3] Duke of Manchester, Court and society, II, 381. See also Baillie correspondence, pp. 193–4;
   Marchmont papers, III, 335–6.
[4] Baillie correspondence, p. 194. Nottingham had only consented to the marriage of his
   daughter, the widowed Marchioness of Halifax, to the Duke of Roxburghe after
   considerable hesitation, but once the couple were wed in January 1708 he seems to

Tories was so great that when rumours reached them at this time that an invitation to a member of the Hanoverian family was being considered by the Whigs and the Lord Treasurer, Haversham was dispatched to Windsor to inform Anne that she could now count on their opposition to this proposal.[1]

As the opening of the new parliament neared, the Churchmen once again nourished high hopes of capitalizing on the discord between the Junto and the Court which, by October 1708, had resulted in the former's sponsorship of Peter King's candidacy for the Chair against the government's nominee, Sir Richard Onslow.[2] In a series of meetings late in September, the opposition Tories under Bromley's leadership agreed to press their adherents as secretly as possible 'to get a good appearance' at the opening of the session on 16 November 'to push for a Speaker and hope for Success from the Divisions they say are of the other side'.[3] In addition, Bromley cautiously approached Harley and Harcourt through a mutual friend, Dr Stratford of Christ Church, with a proposal that they unite behind a jointly acceptable candidate for the Chair.[4]

Nottingham was kept fully informed of these manoeuvres by Bromley, and seems to have approved his tactics.[5] But despite Bromley's promptings, Nottingham was 'determined' to remain at Burley, a resolution which was only reinforced by the Court's

have warmed to his new son-in-law. He even persuaded the Duke of Leeds to order his son Carmarthen to vote for Roxburghe in the 1708 election of the representative Scottish peers (*HMC Dartmouth*, I, 294; WSL, Dartmouth MSS. D 1778, I, ii, 87–8; *Letters relating to Scotland in the reign of Queen Anne*, ed. P. Hume Brown (Scottish History Society, Edinburgh, 1915), p. 185).

[1] Levens Bagot MSS., file B, W. Bromley to Col. Grahme, 25 May; Coxe, *Marlborough*, II, 511.

[2] Letters of Sunderland to Newcastle printed in Trevelyan, *England under Queen Anne*, II, 414–16; *HMC Portland*, II, 205; *Vernon correspondence*, III, 366.

[3] NRO, Isham MSS. 1705, W. Bromley to Sir J. Isham, 15 Oct. See also Levens Bagot MSS., file W, J. Ward to Col. Grahme, 2 Oct.

[4] *HMC Bath*, I, 193; *HMC Portland*, IV, 504–5; Tindal, XVII, 103; BM Loan 29/158, bundle 7, letters of Stratford to Harley, esp. that of 8 Oct.; BM Loan 29/128, bundle 3, letters of Bromley to Harley; BM Loan 29/310, letters of Bromley to Harley.

[5] LRO, Finch MSS. Correspondence, box VI, bundle 23, Bromley to Nottingham, 2 and 23 Oct.

final capitulation to the Junto late in October and Harley's failure ('notwithstanding his professions') to make his appearance in London.[1] Moreover, as he informed Bromley, he would much prefer if possible a renewal of the alliance with King and his squadron of country Whigs 'with whom I again wish we might enter into measures for carrying [on] the common interests of our countrey and exposing those who are building upon the ruine of it' to an arrangement with Harley.[2] As he confided to Bromley,

As much as I wish an increase of our number by any just ways and would not therefore refuse the concurrence of Mr Harley yet to deal freely I do not expect any assistance from him...tis very probable he will desire to meet with you and he should not be refused but I think you should rather hear his proposals not make any to him or if once you should try him and acquaint him with any matter you designe to bring into Parliament, if he does not readily concurre nay if he will not even lead, for a new convert or rather penitent ought to be forward especially he knowing that he could depend on you to support him, I should conclude he came rather to baffle than promote your measures.[3]

Only if a resolution was taken to 'lay open our grievances and boldly to remedy [them] effectually', Nottingham concluded, would he be willing to come up to London.[4]

However, Bromley's reports in early December that the Whigs, in conjunction with the Court, intended to bring in a bill to repeal the sacramental test and also a general naturalization measure thoroughly alarmed Nottingham.[5] The first, he lamented, 'delivers us up to our enemies at home', the latter to 'our friends abroad'.[6] To forestall such pernicious measures, he saw no alternative but to open a full-scale assault upon the ministry, even though there was now little prospect of attracting any Whig support.[7] The government's most vulnerable point, he

[1] LRO, Finch MSS. Correspondence, box VI, bundle 23, Bromley to Nottingham, 11 Nov.   [2] Ibid. draft of Nottingham's letter to Bromley, 15 Nov.
[3] Ibid.   [4] Ibid.
[5] Ibid. Bromley to Nottingham, 7 Dec.
[6] Ibid. draft of Nottingham's letter to Bromley, 20 Dec.   [7] Ibid.

suspected, was the defenceless state of Scotland at the time of the abortive French invasion the previous spring as well as its subsequent failure to take any measures against Jacobite plotters in the northern kingdom.[1] He also suggested to Bromley that Rochester, seconded by the Archbishop of York, the Bishop of Lichfield and Coventry, and the Bishop of Ely, might try to persuade the queen to do 'what she can to prevent' the introduction of the obnoxious bills, 'and at last of denying them if ever they be presented to her'.[2] Finally, when he learned early in January that Rochester had already seen the queen and failed to move her, he left Burley for London to press the inquiry on the Scottish invasion which had already been begun by Haversham and to lend his support to the opposition to the General Naturalization bill.[3]

Nottingham's two-month stay in London must have proved most frustrating. The combined forces of the Court and the Junto were able to stifle investigations of the invasion in both Houses and to overcome with little difficulty Nottingham's efforts to defeat, or at least to amend, the Naturalization bill.[4] As the prorogation neared, Godolphin was able to inform Marlborough that 'our session is like to conclude...much better in all respects than Wee had reason to hope for'.[5] Certainly, at this juncture, the Tories had little hope of defeating the ministry despite the persistence of friction between the Junto and the Lord Treasurer. Even the breakdown of the peace negotiations with France in June 1709 seemed to presage little parliamentary trouble for the government. In despair, the Tories resolved during the 1709–10 session

[1] *Ibid.* a memorandum in Nottingham's hand dated 29 Dec. in which he suggests a series of questions designed to demonstrate the ministry's mishandling of counter-invasion measures.
[2] *Ibid.* draft of Nottingham's letter to Bromley, 20 Dec.
[3] *Ibid.* Bromley to Nottingham, 31 Dec.; *ibid.* Lord Guernsey (the former Heneage Finch) to Nottingham, 27 Dec. Haversham's speech of 12 Jan. shows many similarities of detail to Nottingham's memorandum of 29 Dec. (*PH*, VI, 762–6).
[4] *LJ*, XVIII, 667–8; Tindal, XVII, 113–21; BM Add. MSS. 22202, fos. 24, 48, French newsletters of 8 Feb. and 15 March; *ibid.* 31143, fo. 313, P. Wentworth to Lord Raby, 18 March; Tullie House, Nicolson diary, 25 Feb.
[5] BM Add. MSS. 9104 (Coxe transcripts), fo. 191, 19 April.

'to sit quite [*sic*]' in the hope that the ministers 'will soon run themselves a ground'; Haversham omitted his annual harangue against the ministry on the plea of illness and Nottingham remained at Burley.[1]

If on the surface all seemed clear sailing for the ministry and the Junto, Tory confidence that they would ruin themselves was not wholly groundless. Though Anne had been forced to concede defeat in February 1708, and compelled to submit to the Junto's repeated demands for office during the following months, the Treasurer and the Churchills—by their efforts to win and hold the support of the Whigs—had almost completely alienated the queen.[2] Meanwhile, behind the scenes Harley was maturing his plans to free Anne from the Junto's clutches. Keeping in touch with the queen through the new royal favourite Abigail Masham, he was rallying the discontented of all stripes, most notably Somerset and Shrewsbury, to his standard.[3] By January 1710 Harley was at last ready to take the offensive. With characteristic subterfuge, his ally Lord Rivers was made Lieutenant of the Tower by the queen. At the same time, Anne demanded the appointment of Abigail's brother, Colonel Hill, to the command of a regiment. Marlborough was prepared to resist these unwelcome impositions and even offered his own resignation in protest, but Godolphin and the Whig lords, save for Sunderland, were not. Finally, an uneasy compromise was worked out. The queen agreed to abandon her request for Hill, Marlborough returned to London, and all efforts to force Anne to dismiss Abigail were dropped. But the damage was done; the queen's plea for Abigail, whom she believed to be threatened by a parliamentary address, had brought promises of support not only from the likes of Leeds, Ormonde and Rochester, but also from Somerset, Cowper and even Somers. Whig unity had been shattered, while the

[1] BM Add. MSS. 31143, fo. 435, P. Wentworth to Lord Raby, 3 Jan. 1710; BRO, Downshire MSS., vol. LIII, J. Bridges to Sir W. Trumbull, 10 Jan. 1710.
[2] Churchill, *Marlborough*, II, 407–23, 474–80, 640–2, 647–8.
[3] *Ibid.* pp. 480–4, 643–7.

differences between the ministers and Anne were now public knowledge.[1]

The ministry also contributed substantially to its own downfall by deciding to bring an impeachment against one of its most notorious high-flying clerical opponents, Dr Henry Sacheverell. What began as a propaganda display designed to silence criticism from the high Churchmen and to vindicate the legitimacy of 'Revolution principles' ended in public humiliation. While Nottingham hastened to London to denounce the impeachment as illegal and to assert that the cornerstone of the Revolution settlement was not the resort to arms but rather the Convention parliament's vote that James had abdicated (a resolution he had then staunchly opposed), the London mob and the countryside were once again roused by the cry of the 'Church in Danger'.[2] Furthermore, the ministry was hit by a wave of desertions; Shrewsbury, Pembroke and Lexington even voted for Sacheverell's acquittal, while Somerset and Argyll laboured successfully to defeat all but token punishment of the doctor.[3]

Heartened by Sacheverell's escape and the promise held out by the ferment in his favour, Nottingham returned to Burley in April 1710.[4] He was met there 'by most of the Gentry and Clergy of the County on horseback, besides a great number of persons on foot, who welcomed his lordship...giving him thanks for the great and good services he had done the Queen, the church and Dr Sacheverell'. Furthermore, they pledged their votes to Nottingham's heir, Daniel Lord Finch, whom he intended to put

---

[1] *Ibid.* pp. 662–9; *The Wentworth papers, 1705–1739*, ed. J. Cartwright (London, 1883), pp. 102–5; *HMC Portland*, IV, 531; LRO, Finch MSS. Correspondence, box VI, bundle 23, newsletter of 29 Jan. 1710.

[2] Feiling, *Tory party*, pp. 416–17; *LJ*, XIX, 105–18; *HMC Portland*, IV, 534–5; NRO, Finch–Hatton MSS. 281, Nottingham to his wife, 7 and 14 March. Notes for Nottingham's speeches, as well as drafts of the numerous protests presented during the course of the trial and a draft refutation of the Whig bishops' assertions of the legitimacy of resistance, are in LRO, Finch MSS., Ecclesiastical papers 5.

[3] Coxe, *Marlborough*, III, 166; Churchill, *Marlborough*, II, 673–4.

[4] See his comments to Wotton (his son's former tutor) retailed in Christ Church College, Wake MSS., vol. I, W. Wotton to W. Wake, 22 April.

forward for one of the Rutland seats at the next election.[1] At the same time, the queen—confiding only in Harley—suddenly named Shrewsbury to succeed the Marquess of Kent as Lord Chamberlain. Tories like Guernsey and Rochester hurried to pay their compliments to him, while advising Nottingham to extend his congratulations to his erstwhile opponent.[2] As for Godolphin, he could do little but accept Shrewsbury's professions of good will and the queen's assurances that the changes would be carried no further. Playing skilfully upon the divisions within the ministry and upon Whig hopes that something could be salvaged from the wreckage, Harley then secured the dismissal of Sunderland in June and Godolphin in August. Somers, flattered by the queen's confidences, and Halifax, tantalized by the prospect of agreement with Harley, did not lift a finger to save Harley's new victims until it was too late, while Wharton—absent in Ireland—could do nothing.[3] As Swift later recalled, 'the Removal of the last Ministry was brought about by several Degrees; through which means it happened, That they and their Friends were hardly recovered out of One Astonishment, before they fell into Another'.[4]

The overthrow of Godolphin and the Junto must be attributed chiefly to Harley and his allies backed by the queen. Not surprisingly, the majority of the new appointments at first went to his own followers. It was not long, however, before the high Churchmen began to clamour for their share of preferments, the alteration of the lieutenancies and commissions of the peace, and the dissolution of parliament.[5] The names of Nottingham and his friend Lord Anglesey had been put forward as possible replacements of Sunderland though the appointment eventually went to

---

[1] Christ Church College, Wake MSS., vol. I, W. Wotton to W. Wake, 22 April; BM Loan 29/320, Dyer's newsletter of 13 April.

[2] LRO, Finch MSS. Correspondence, box VI, bundle 23, Guernsey to Nottingham, 18 April. There is no evidence, however, that Nottingham acted on this suggestion.

[3] Feiling, Tory party, pp. 417–18.   [4] Swift, Four last years of the queen, p. 4.

[5] Chatsworth Finch MSS., Nottingham to Guernsey, 17 June; WSL, Dartmouth MSS. D 1778, V, 79, H. Finch to Dartmouth, [Aug.]; BM Loan 29/159, bundle 4, Weymouth to R. Harley, 18 Aug.; HMC Portland, IV, 545–6, 563, 570, and passim.

Guernsey's son-in-law Dartmouth, and London rumourmongers had ample material for speculation throughout the summer, particularly about the relations between Harley and the more extreme Tories.[1]

But whatever Rochester's role in the complex intrigues that brought down the ministry may have been, it is clear that Nottingham's part was negligible. He was content to spend the rest of the spring and the summer at Burley despite the advice of his daughter, the Duchess of Roxburghe, that he should come up to London to urge his claims to office.[2] Indeed, with the possible exception of Anglesey, it would seem that none of the high Churchmen were in Harley's confidence at the outset. The new Chancellor of the Exchequer had not abandoned his old preference for an administration of moderates, and he did all he could to preserve the good will of the great Court dukes Somerset and Newcastle, while imploring Boyle and Cowper not to resign.[3] Not until late summer did Harley, despairing of the moderate Whigs and convinced of the necessity of dissolution, turn to the Tories. On 1 September Bromley was finally able to provide some good news to his now anxious friends in the country:

The scene being opened [he informed Colonel Grahme], I have had repeated assurances that no interest will be considered but the churche's. They are willing to make their Bottom as wide as they can, and to receive those who are of Distinction, and have no Blemish, provided they will come in on the same Interest...a Dissolution [is] soon promised...I hope your Expectations and merits will be fully answered, and that all Throughers shall be taken care of, as they now promise.[4]

Three weeks later, the dissolution was announced, Rochester (who in his last year was to display unwonted moderation) was named

[1] Dartmouth's note in Burnet, VI, 9; HMC Fifth Report, p. 190; F. Salomon, Geschichte des letzen Ministeriums Königin Annas von England (1710–1714) und der englischen Thronfolgefrage (Gotha, 1894), p. 27; BM Add. MSS. 31143, fo. 505, P. Wentworth to Lord Raby, 30 June; BRO, Downshire MSS., vol. CXXXVI, newsletter of 22 May.
[2] LRO, Finch MSS. Correspondence, box VI, bundle 23, Lady Roxburghe to Nottingham, 31 Aug.
[3] Feiling, Tory party, pp. 418–20. See also Harley's scheme of administration in Miscellaneous State Papers, II, 485–8.   [4] Levens Bagot MSS., file B.

Lord President, and the Duke of Buckingham was appointed Lord Privy Seal.

For Nottingham, however, the outlook was hardly so bright. Despite the rumours that awarded him the Secretaryship in June, the First Commissionership of the Admiralty in September, and the Privy Seal in December, as far as Harley was concerned, Nottingham had too many blemishes.[1] Most damaging was the fact that he was obnoxious to the queen who had never forgiven him his support of the invitation to the Electress, and who would now not hear of his appointment to high office.[2] Moreover, to Harley and his following Nottingham epitomized all that they deplored in the Tories' past. 'He is,' Poulet was to remind Harley a year later, 'party sense in person without respect to the reason of things...Nottingham has undone them [the Tories] once, and you have saved them; and if anything ever disturbs your government, it must be the taint of old courtiers.'[3] Thus Harley and Shrewsbury, though apprehensive that Nottingham might be dissatisfied, hoped that the inclusion in the ministry of his nephews by marriage, Dartmouth as Secretary and Sir Robert Benson as a Commissioner of the Treasury, the appointment of his friend Anglesey to the post of Paymaster of Ireland (with a seat in the Cabinet), and the gift of a prebend at Canterbury to his brother Edward would placate him.[4]

For his own part, Nottingham had lost none of his old suspicion of, and antipathy to Harley. Much as he desired to return to office,

[1] Dartmouth's note in Burnet, vi, 9; Salomon, *Geschichte des letzen Ministeriums Königin Annas*, p. 27; A. Boyer, *Quadrennium Annae Postremum, or the political state of Great Britain* (2nd edn. London, 1718–19), i, 5; Luttrell, vi, 633, 667; *Wentworth papers*, p. 167; BM Add. MSS. 17677DDD, fos. 592, 603, 679; *ibid.* 31143, fo. 571; *ibid.* Lansdowne MSS. 1013, fo. 134; NRO, Isham MSS. 2948.

[2] Dartmouth's note in Burnet, vi, 9; *Letters and correspondence, public and private, of Henry St John, Lord Viscount Bolingbroke, during the time he was Secretary of State to Queen Anne*, ed. G. Parke (London, 1798), i, 281; Swift, *Four last years of the queen*, pp. 15–16.

[3] *HMC Portland*, iv, 684.

[4] *HMC Bath*, i, 199. There were, however, reports that Harley was openly contemptuous of Nottingham, belittling him as an 'old woman' (BM Loan 29/152, Grey Neville to R. Harley, 1 Aug.; LRO, Finch MSS. Correspondence, box vi, bundle 23, Lady Roxburghe to Nottingham, 31 Aug.).

he avowed to Godolphin that he had 'ask'd for nothing' from Harley.[1] Nor had Nottingham's distrust been eased by Harley's failure to institute a thorough purge of the Whigs who still held office both at Court and throughout the country before the election of autumn 1710.[2] Though Lord Finch's candidacy (despite his absence abroad on the Grand Tour) was successful, Nottingham no doubt felt as little obligation to the new ministers on this count as did the successful Tories in Oxfordshire, since he, too, had to overcome the disadvantage of a hostile Lord Lieutenant and bench of justices.[3] Even the great Tory electoral successes did not incline the ministry further towards the Churchmen. As John Ward angrily informed Nottingham from London in mid-October, 'the elections about this town which have succeeded beyond all expectations seem not to have such an effect as I could wish but rather to promote such measures as may by other ways tend to a ballance'.[4] To counter such tendencies, Nottingham promised to come up to town before the meeting of parliament to concert tactics with Bromley, Ward, Hanmer, the new Lord Anglesey (whose predecessor had died suddenly in September), and other leaders of the high Churchmen.[5]

Tory dominance in the new House of Commons provided ample opportunity for Nottingham and his friends to exert pressure upon the ministry. No sooner did the Commons begin their consideration of Anne's opening address than Hanmer urged the House to represent to the queen the importance of 'discountenancing all persons of such principles, and avoiding all measures of such tendency, as might weaken her Majesty's title

---

[1] Blenheim MSS. E/27, A. Mainwaring to the Duchess of Marlborough, [Oct? 1710].

[2] Swift's opinion was that the Court 'had stopped its hands as to further removals' because it was 'afraid of too great a majority of their own side in the House of Commons' (*The correspondence of Jonathan Swift D.D.*, ed. T. Ball (London, 1910–14), I, 207–8).

[3] *HMC Portland*, VII, 22–3; NRO, Isham MSS. 2949, Nottingham to Sir J. Isham, 3 Oct.; LRO, Finch MSS. Correspondence, box VI, bundle 23, Nottingham to Lord Finch, 21 Oct.; *ibid.* Rutland papers 2, drafts of electoral addresses in Nottingham's hand.

[4] *Ibid.* Correspondence, box VI, bundle 23.

[5] *Ibid.* Ward to Nottingham, 21 and 28 Oct., 2 and 4 Nov.; *ibid.* Bromley to Nottingham, 2 Nov.

and government'.[1] The parliament was not more than a month old when interested observers such as Peter Wentworth and Swift were predicting that great numbers of the country gentlemen (many of them sitting for the first time) were 'resolved to proceed in methods of their own', to press for inquiries into the abuses of the former ministry and to provide ample security for the church.[2] And it was not long before the Tory zealots of the lower House banded themselves together, over one hundred and fifty strong, in the October Club in order 'to make the ministry in a great measure come in to us, instead of our depending upon them'.[3] Nottingham, who numbered his son-in-law Mostyn and his nephew Heneage Finch among the members of the club, did all he could to encourage the extremists.[4] He played a prominent part in the Lords' investigation of early 1711 into the conduct of the war in Spain, supporting Peterborough and condemning Galway once again, while persuading the hesitant Archbishop of York to vote in favour of a resolution placing the blame for allied defeats squarely upon the late ministry.[5] In addition he and his brother Guernsey vainly urged the passage of the Commons' bill to repeal the General Naturalization Act of 1709.[6]

By February 1711, then, Harley and Shrewsbury were deeply apprehensive of the prospect of disruption from the right and fearful that St John might be tempted to espouse the cause of the extremists.[7] Already the high Churchmen, in conjunction with

[1] PH, VI, 930.
[2] Wentworth papers, p. 161; Swift correspondence, I, 227–8, 231; Huddersfield Public Library, Whitly–Beaumont MSS., Sir A. Kaye to R. Beaumont, 3 Dec.
[3] Ibid. The first references to the October Club, organized in January, date from early February (Tullie House, Nicolson diary, 6 Feb.).
[4] Dartmouth's note in Burnet, VI, 41. For a partial list of the members of the October Club, see Boyer, Political state, III, 117–21.
[5] PH, VI, 936–98; BM Lansdowne MSS. 1024, fo. 252, W. Kennett's journal; LRO, Finch MSS., Political papers 148, draft of Nottingham's speech of 12 Jan.; ibid. Political papers 133, draft of the Lords' representation of Feb. 1711 in Nottingham's hand.
[6] BM Lansdowne MSS. 1024, fo. 265, 6 Feb.; Tullie House, Nicolson diary, 5 Feb.; LJ, XIX, 215.
[7] Harley's 'account of public affairs' printed in Tindal, XVIII, 269; Feiling, Tory party, p. 433.

some country Whigs, had pushed a Place bill through the Commons over the objections of Harley and the votes of the Court's supporters, and other projects—including the introduction of a bill for the resumption of grants—were being mooted.[1] It was apparently at this juncture that Harley, Poulet, Dartmouth, Rochester and Shrewsbury arranged a conference with Nottingham in the hopes of forestalling the schemes of the more violent Tories.[2] Dartmouth's account of the meeting amply documents the gulf between Nottingham and the ministers. Nottingham, he recalled,

desired to know what we designed to do, for as yet, he said, we had done nothing. I said, I believed at the conclusion of the last session he would have thought the dissolving the parliament, and turning out all the whig ministers, something. He said, that was nothing, if we did not make it impracticable for them ever to rise again. The duke of Shrewsbury desired to know by what means that should be accomplished. Lord Nottingham said, unless we prosecuted them, he should think we protected them; for it was plain, they had brought things to such a pass, that they could neither make peace nor war: and we were doing their work for them. I desired to know who he would have prosecuted: he said, lord Sunderland for one, and he was sure I could find matter enough in his office, if I pleased: I said, that should be some other body's work, not mine; and I knew the queen would never be brought into such measures. He got up, and as he went out, said, if we did not act in concert with the whigs, we should soon find the effects of our good-nature.[3]

Having failed to obtain any satisfaction from the ministry, the extremists—urged on by Nottingham—pursued a violent course. In spite of Harley's efforts, bills establishing a Commission of Accounts and a Commission for the Examination of Crown

---

[1] Boyer, *Political state*, I, 134; *Wentworth papers*, pp. 163, 180; *CJ*, XVI, 440, 471; *Private correspondence of Sarah, duchess of Marlborough, illustrative of the court and times of Queen Anne*, [ed. John Lord Russell] (London, 1838), II, 69; WSL, Kaye MSS., Sir A. Kaye's diary, 29 Jan.

[2] Though Dartmouth's account of this meeting does not record its date, Harley's reference to a conference of this nature in Feb. 1711, while it differs in several details from Dartmouth's report, suggests they were probably referring to the same meeting (Dartmouth's note in Burnet, VI, 41–2; Harley's 'account' in Tindal, XVIII, 269).

[3] Dartmouth's note in Burnet, VI, 41–2.

Grants were passed by the Commons.[1] The affiliations of the fourteen Commissioners elected by the House (at least ten were members of the October Club) left little doubt of the mood of the Commons, and it was only by exercising all his arts of persuasion that Harley was able to prevent the zealots from tacking the Resumption bill to a money measure.[2] Moreover, the October-ites, who complained that the ministry had not followed up the financial inquiries Harley had initiated in January, finally resolved to take the matter into their own hands.[3]

Late in March Nottingham drew up a detailed memorandum in which he outlined his views and set out the tactics he thought advisable in this situation. As an example of his style and as a record of his attitude towards Harley, it merits quotation.

There are some propositions [he began] so plain and evident that I need only mention them.

1 that a Coalition-scheme is impracticable.

2 that the attempt of it cannot be with a good designe because whatever tends to the interest of our Constitution in Church and State will be more faithfully pursued by friends than Enemies and because

3 that reason and experience shew that such a scheme must end in whiggism, and therefore it may be presumd that 'tis designd it should doe so and the rather because He [Harley] who projected the last union of parties is the onely person who can now carry on the like measures.

But whether he has such intentions is a doubt, his professions and all the present appearances are hard to be reconcil'd; But as it is difficult to determine what is to be expected from him so it is not necessary to my present purpose, For what I propose to be done, I take to be very proper in either case, that is, to establish the security and interest of the present Ministry if they are in earnest... or to render a medley-administration more difficult both by exposing the shameful proceedings of the late Ministers and by establishing in the Countrey

---

[1] CJ, XVI, 503, 529, 544, 588, 610–11; The Lockhart papers, ed. A. Aufrere (London, 1817), I, 325, 351–2; BRO, Downshire MSS., vol. LIV, R. Bridges to Sir W. Trumbull, 19 Feb.

[2] Boyer, Political state, III, 117–21; CJ, XVI, 562, 606; J. Swift, Some reasons to prove, that no person is obliged by his principles, as a Whig, to oppose her majesty or her present ministry, in Swift, Political tracts 1711–1713, ed. H. Davis (Oxford, 1951), p. 134.

[3] CJ, XVI, 446; Wentworth papers, p. 192; Swift correspondence, I, 249; J. Swift, Journal to Stella, ed. H. Williams (Oxford, 1948), I, 249.

the reputation and credit of the present members that they be chosen again in case of a dissolution of this Parliament which must be expected if the present measures should turn to Whiggism...

I know very well the cause of the delay of entring upon these matters; we have bin amus'd with promises of assistance herein from the Ministers and we have had continual assurances from day to day of great changes of officers; some perhaps have had too great faith in these assurances, and some have thought that if they had bin performd we had had sufficient Security against a relapse, in all which I can't help being of a different opinion, For I can't think that half the changes will be made that are expected or if there were a thorough change yet even this would not rivet the Ministers to us so much and so certainly as exposing the faults of their predecessors which would make them irreconcileable, whereas another change of the Toryes to whigs is a very Easy step and cancels all the disobligation of having turnd them out.[1]

Thus, Nottingham proposed the preparation of two addresses, while warning that it would be necessary to prevent the ministers from diverting the House. The first, he suggested, should be devoted to the fiscal abuses of the late ministry, the second to other grievances. Among these he mentioned the great loss of merchant shipping, the illegal imposition of a charter upon the Bewdley corporation, the invitation to the Palatine refugees, the inadequate preparations against the 1708 invasion, and the 'scheme of moderation, first invented by the Papists...and now again introduced by some who were in those Councils to divide and weaken our church under pretence of supporting it'.[2]

Nottingham's views found ready acceptance among his friends in the lower House. On 3 April Ward reported to him the outcome of a meeting with Bromley;

a Resolution [was taken] to bring on the Notice of the invasion, to force on the account of the Customs and Stamp office and what other mismanagements the Court can lay open without tedious inquiry and to make two representations the one of the money matters, the other of the Church and State, and in the latter to expose that mask of moderation by which we have so much sufferd and the triming measures we fear and this in the boldest lively colours.[3]

[1] LRO, Finch MSS., Political papers 150.   [2] Ibid.
[3] Ibid. Correspondence, box VI, bundle 24.

Though Nottingham did not remain in London until the end of the session, the bulk of his programme was carried out. On 31 May a lengthy representation castigating the financial mismanagement of the previous ministry as well as the grant of the Bewdley charter and the invitation to the Palatines was agreed to by the Commons.[1] Lack of time apparently precluded the presentation of a second address, but by including some of the other abuses and the denunciation of the 'wild and unwarrantable scheme of balancing parties' suggested by Nottingham, the memorial of 31 May can clearly be said to represent his own feelings with regard to Harley, as well as towards Godolphin and Marlborough.[2]

Extremist pressure on the ministry during the session of 1710–11 was not altogether unproductive. Once parliament had been prorogued, Harley (now Earl of Oxford) announced numerous changes in the administration. Among the new appointees were Nottingham's nephew Heneage Finch as Master of the Jewel House, his indigent cousin the Earl of Winchilsea as a Commissioner of the Board of Trade, his son-in-law Mostyn as Paymaster of the Marines, and John Ward as a Welsh judge.[3] Once again, Nottingham's claims to office were canvassed, in May for the Lord Presidency vacant by Rochester's death and in August for the Privy Seal upon Newcastle's demise.[4] But Harley had no intention of bringing Nottingham into the Cabinet, and the ministers continued to gamble that since his relations were now 'so well provided for' he would not rebel.[5] Though Bromley still continued to express his hope to Nottingham 'that you will again be pressed into the publicke Service', his repeated disappointments must have made it clear to Nottingham that he could expect little

[1] CJ, xvi, 683–5.
[2] Ibid.; Feiling, Tory party, p. 342.
[3] Boyer, History of Queen Anne, pp. 500, 514.
[4] Ibid. p. 515; Private correspondence of Duchess of Marlborough, ii, 67, 71; BM Add. MSS. 9119 (Coxe transcripts), fo. 164, A. Mainwaring to the Duchess of Marlborough, [May].
[5] HMC Portland, iv, 683–4; Bolingbroke correspondence, i, 281.

from Oxford.[1] To add to his dissatisfaction, he was no little suspicious of the peace terms now being negotiated by the ministry. Thus when Oxford, increasingly uneasy at the prospect of widespread opposition, wrote to him early in the autumn with assurances that the peace preliminaries were most advantageous to England, Nottingham did not trouble to conceal either his bitterness or his distrust.

I did not expect [he replied] that your Lordship should have taken the trouble of communicating to me an affair of so vast importance as the settling the preliminaries of a Peace, of which I am not a competent judge, not having for some time been acquainted with any matters relating to the public administration...I am very glad to hear from your Lordship so good a character of this treaty as your Lordship gives it, for I may conclude that the accounts of it in the prints must be very imperfect.[2]

Indeed, by the time Nottingham arrived in London late in November 1711, he was determined to oppose the peace 'though no Man else would, if Spain and the Indies were to go up to the Duke of Anjou'.[3] And this resolution was soon to lead him into uncharted waters.

[1] LRO, Finch MSS. Correspondence, box VI, bundle 24, 27 Aug.
[2] HMC Portland, v, 101.
[3] NRO, Finch–Hatton MSS. 281, Nottingham to his wife, 16 Dec. 1711.

CHAPTER II

PEACE AND THE PROTESTANT SUCCESSION

1711–16

The implications of Nottingham's decision to oppose the peace, whatever the consequences, were far-reaching; the security of the ministry itself was jeopardized. Reports that he and other high Churchmen were hostile to the peace preliminaries were already common gossip in London by November 1711.[1] Thus, when he arrived in London on 23 November, he immediately found himself the object of considerable attention and speculation. Emissaries from the ministry and also from the Whigs soon came to call on him. Although Nottingham tried to conceal his feelings from Lord Poulet, the Lord Treasurer's representative, he did not succeed. Indeed, Poulet reported to Oxford, after an interview of two and a half hours with Nottingham, that he was 'as sour and fiercely wild as you can imagine anything to be that has lived long in the desert'.[2] Alerted by Poulet, Oxford, already fretting over the delayed appearance of a number of the government's supporters in the upper House (particularly the Scottish peers), decided upon a prorogation until 7 December.[3]

The Duke of Roxburghe, the first of the Whigs sent to sound out Nottingham, had a more promising reception from his father-in-law. Though Nottingham would not 'expressly tell' him his opinion of the peace, it was, as Nottingham himself confessed, 'impossible to talk of this affair so as not to discover which way I

---

[1] BM Add. MSS. 17677 EEE, fos. 348, 377, reports of L'Hermitage of 26 Oct./6 Nov. and 27 Nov./8 Dec.; Bodl. Ballard MSS. 21, fo. 95, Dr Lancaster to A. Charlett, 8 Nov.; HMC Polwarth, I, 2.
[2] HMC Portland, v, 119.
[3] Tindal, XVII, 417; Swift, Journal to Stella, II, 421.

was inclined'.[1] Marlborough, the next to wait upon the earl, was also received favourably though cautiously, and a meeting between Nottingham, Marlborough and Godolphin was then arranged. Both the duke and the former Lord Treasurer fully declared themselves; the rejection of the proposed peace would, they stated, 'depend upon me, who might do what they cou'd not, that is persuade some Tories to concurre in this opinion, without which, this Matter must miscarry and we should be undone'.[2]

Nottingham's response to the advances of the Whigs and their allies was, by his own testimony, no less frank. He explained that while he was fully determined to oppose the peace, he had little hope of bringing over any of his friends since so many of them were already committed, either by conviction or by the Lord Treasurer's blandishments, to ending the war. In any case, he suspected that most Tories would be reluctant to oppose the ministry on so important a question lest the result be the supersession of Oxford by the Whigs. Certainly, more than professions of self-denial were needed from the Whigs; 'some real security' to ease Tory apprehensions would be necessary. Whig support for the long-sought measure against occasional conformity might, he thought, be the best token of their sincerity.[3]

While the Whigs were digesting Nottingham's proposal, he was again approached by the ministry, and this time by no less a personage than the Lord Treasurer. But Nottingham countered Oxford's assurances of the advantages of the proposed peace settlement with a single rhetorical query, 'whether Spain and the Indies were to be alloted to the duke of Anjou?' If this was what was intended, he declared that 'no terms whatsoever could make this a good Peace'.[4] After this rebuff, Oxford abandoned his efforts to sway Nottingham. In the meantime, the Whigs had resolved to accept his suggestion. Within two days after his

---

[1] NRO, Finch–Hatton MSS. 281, Nottingham to Lady Nottingham, 16 Dec.
[2] *Ibid.*   [3] *Ibid.*   [4] *Ibid.*

meeting with Marlborough and Godolphin, Townshend called on Nottingham to promise their full support for the Occasional Conformity bill.[1]

Although he had failed to prevent the conclusion of a working arrangement between Nottingham and the Whigs, Oxford decided not to postpone further the opening of the session. But when parliament did meet on 7 December, the government sustained a severe check. A vote of thanks was carried in the Lords for the queen's speech, but only after a proviso, supported by Halifax, Devonshire, Wharton, Godolphin and Marlborough, which condemned any peace that left Spain and the West Indies to a Bourbon prince, was carried by a single vote on the previous question. This rider was Nottingham's, moved by him in an oration of fully one hour in which he dramatically declared 'That though he had fourteen children, he would submit to live upon five hundred pounds a year, rather than consent to those dark and unknown conditions of peace' put forward by the ministry.[2] And on the following day, the address with Nottingham's amendment was approved by the House with only token opposition from the dispirited supporters of the ministry.[3]

Though pilloried by the ministry's propagandists as a traitor to the church and satirized as the 'orator dismal of Nottinghamshire', Nottingham allowed neither this abuse nor the dismay of erstwhile political sympathizers to sway him from his course.[4] One week later, he brought into the Lords a bill against occasional

[1] NRO, Finch–Hatton MSS. 281, Nottingham to Lady Nottingham, 16 Dec.
[2] Cunningham, History of Great Britain, II, 397; PH, VI, 1036–40; Bolingbroke correspondence, II, 49 n.
[3] BM Add. MSS. 22908, fo. 88, letter to Dr Colebatch, 11 Dec.; Wentworth papers, pp. 222–3.
[4] Besides the notorious advertisement in the Postboy of 7 Dec. and Swift's ballad 'An Excellent new Song, being the Intended Speech of a Famous Orator against Peace', at least one sham speech parodying Nottingham's oration of the 7th was printed. Nottingham seems to have been no little annoyed by the last, and instigated proceedings in the Lords against its author (HMC House of Lords, n.s. IX, 169, 368–9; M. J. Quinlan, 'Swift and the Prosecuted Nottingham Speech', Harvard Library Bulletin, XI (1957), 296–302; Wentworth papers, p. 225; NRO, Finch–Hatton MSS. 281, Nottingham to Lady Nottingham, 20 Dec.).

conformity, slightly tailored to fit Whig sensibilities.[1] Oxford, though he had discouraged its introduction when it had been proposed to him earlier in the autumn by several leading members of the October Club, could not openly oppose it, and it was quickly passed by the upper House.[2] However, the Lord Treasurer had not exhausted his resources. On the one hand, he tried to incite the dissenters to dissuade the Whigs from fulfilling their pledge to Nottingham.[3] On the other, he attempted to have clauses added to the bill in the Commons which might have caused the Lords to reject it. And when both these stratagems failed, he resorted to a trick which would have left the measure's enforcement to the discretion of the government.[4] But Nottingham, aided by Lord Anglesey, succeeded in alerting the Churchmen in the Commons to Oxford's manoeuvres, and thus forewarned they were able to secure its passage without amendment.[5]

The introduction and swift passage of the bill against occasional conformity confirmed the suspicion of many observers that Nottingham and the Whigs had struck up an 'unholy' alliance.[6] The most common opinion, reinforced by the wit of London punsters who designated him 'Nott-in-game', was that his disappointment at failing to obtain office in the Oxford ministry had prompted this step.[7] But Nottingham himself dismissed this insinuation with scorn. 'I should [wonder] at any that knew me', he declared to Lady Dorchester, 'if they cou'd think a place wou'd

[1] *HMC House of Lords*, n.s. IX, 168–9; NRO, Finch–Hatton MSS. 281, Nottingham to Lady Nottingham, 16 Dec.
[2] *Ibid*. Nottingham to Lady Nottingham, 26 Dec.
[3] BM Loan 29/160, bundle 8, Oxford to D. Williams, 21 Dec.
[4] By allowing the reward for informers to remain unspecified (NRO, Finch–Hatton MSS. 281, Nottingham to Lady Nottingham, 16 and 26 Dec.).
[5] *Ibid*. 26 Dec.
[6] BRO, Braybrooke MSS. F/23/2, C. Aldsworth to [Duke of Northumberland], 18 Dec.; BM Add. MSS. 22222, fo. 188, Lord Poulet to Lord Strafford, 20 Dec.; *HMC Polwarth* I, 3; *HMC Portland*, VII, 82.
[7] BM Add. MSS. 22908, fos. 87–8; BRO, Downshire MSS., vol. CXXXVI, bundle 1, R. Bridges to Sir W. Trumbull, 14 Dec.; NRO, Finch–Hatton MSS. 281, Nottingham to Lady Nottingham, 26 Dec.; J. Swift, 'An Excellent new Song' in *The poems of Jonathan Swift*, ed. H. Williams (Oxford, 1958), I, 142.

change my opinion'.[1] Though frustrated ambition may have played some part in his decision, it is probable that his opposition to the peace stemmed primarily from more disinterested motives. On the one hand, since the beginning of the war he had asserted at every opportunity his conviction that Spain and the West Indies must be secured to a friendly power. On the other hand, he had long distrusted Harley and he was now deeply suspicious of the loyalty of several of the ministers to the Hanoverian succession.[2]

But whatever the reasons for his defection, Nottingham—as he had feared—initially carried almost none of his former friends and associates with him. In the Lords' vote of 7 December, even his brother Guernsey voted with the ministry, while only one of the seven Tory 'rebels' in a similar division in the Commons (his son Lord Finch) had any close connection with him.[3] Indeed, his nephew by marriage Dartmouth was so far from agreeing with him that he accused Nottingham of accepting bribes from the Whigs, and the first reaction of his wife's uncles was equally outraged.[4] Thus, Somerset's efforts to convince peers who normally voted with the Court that the queen was dissatisfied with the peace terms contributed far more to the defeat suffered by the ministry in the Lords than did Nottingham's appearance on the Whigs' behalf.[5] And even the passage of the bill against occasional conformity did not retrieve Nottingham's interest among the high Churchmen. As he himself confessed,

[1] NRO, Finch–Hatton MSS. 281, Nottingham to Lady Nottingham, 26 Dec.
[2] *Ibid.* 20 Feb. 1712. He, himself, received the thanks of the Elector for his stand against the peace negotiations (Salomon, *Geschichte des letzen Ministeriums Königin Annas*, p. 162).
[3] *Bolingbroke correspondence*, II, 49 n.; BRO, Downshire MSS., vol. CXXXVI, bundle 1, R. Bridges to Sir W. Trumbull, 14 Dec.; G. Holmes, 'The Commons' Division on "No Peace without Spain", 7 December 1711', *BIHR*, XXXIII (1960), 227. Archbishop Sharp, despite rumours that he would follow Nottingham's lead, lodged his proxy with Bishop Dawes of Chester who voted with the ministry (BM Add. MSS. 17677 EEE, fo. 377; BM Loan 29/156, bundle 7, Sharp to Oxford, 28 Nov.).
[4] NRO, Finch–Hatton MSS. 281, Nottingham to Lady Nottingham, 26 Dec.
[5] BM Add. MSS. 22222, fo. 188; *Swift correspondence*, I, 312–14.

notwithstanding this their darling Bill which they could never had had but by me and that they know the Great-Man wou'd never have given it them nor suffer'd it if he cou'd have helpt it...yet there are such charms in the word Peace (for they know knothing more of it) or such inchantments in a white wand that though there be scarce any that believe him Sincere in their interests and they dont scruple to say so, Yet they are intirely govern'd by him and to such a degree that I am even rail'd at by 'em as a Deserter for opposing his Measures for Peace.[1]

None the less, by the beginning of January 1712 Nottingham's influence was beginning to make itself felt. Much to his despair, he could not bring his old friend Anglesey to modify his views about the peace, but Guernsey, Weymouth, Thanet, Carteret and Conway were wavering in their support of Oxford.[2] Yet, while Poulet lamented the queen's failure to declare herself forthrightly in favour of the ministry and reports spread that the Lords 'design to do strange things' when they met after the brief Christmas recess, the Lord Treasurer remained calm.[3] To the irresolute, he held out the promise of royal favour; Guernsey and Thanet were made Privy Councillors in mid-December and Weymouth joined them at the Board three months later.[4] At the same time, he finally succeeded in persuading Anne to dismiss Somerset from the Mastership of the Horse, though he could not dislodge the duke's red-headed wife from the queen's confidence.[5] Most important, Oxford prevailed upon Anne, roused by rumours that the Whigs were on the verge of proposing an invitation to a member of the Hanoverian family, to consent to the creation of a dozen new peers—enough to restore the ministry's majority in the Lords and

[1] NRO, Finch–Hatton MSS. 281, Nottingham to Lady Nottingham, 26 Dec.
[2] All the latter voted with Nottingham on 2 Jan. against the adjournment of the Lords requested by the queen (Bodl. Ballard MSS. 20, fo. 74, G. Clark to A. Charlett, 3 Jan.; BM Add. MSS. 17677FFF, fos. 19–20, L'Hermitage's dispatch of 4/15 Jan.).
[3] BRO, Downshire MSS., vol. cxxxvi, bundle 3, R. Bridges to Sir W. Trumbull, 28 Dec.; Swift, Journal to Stella, II, 444; BM Add. MSS. 22222, fo. 188; Feiling, Tory party, p. 445.
[4] Boyer, Political state, II, 707, and III, 170.
[5] Swift correspondence, I, 313; NRO, Finch–Hatton MSS. 281, Nottingham to Lady Nottingham, [late Jan.].

to snatch victory from the eager grasp of Nottingham and the Junto.[1] Despite these setbacks, Nottingham does not seem to have thought of going back on his alliance with the Whigs and the duumvirs. His hostility to the proposed peace was far too great for him to contemplate coming to terms with the Lord Treasurer, whatever his reservations were about Whig assurances of 'perpetual unalterable friendship'.[2] As he confided to his wife in February 1712,

You need not be afraid of my too great confidence in the persons you hint, so far as our way lyes together there is a necessity of trusting 'em, and in the present measures 'tis impossible to act without 'em: and if they shou'd deceive me in what they protest for the future, I shall be but where I was, and left to follow my own honest intentions.[3]

For the moment, the restoration of ministerial superiority in the upper House seemed to guarantee Oxford's continued predominance. Although Nottingham exerted himself to widen the breach within Tory ranks, he made little progress.[4] Even his appearance on behalf of the Scottish Toleration bill in February 1712 at Anglesey's request did not sway the high Churchmen who, he found, 'continue blindly to follow his [Oxford's] Dictates and Support his Measures'.[5] To be sure, there were minor successes in the Lords for Nottingham and the Whigs, most notably the approval of an address on 15 February denouncing the French refusal to recognize the queen's title and the rejection in May of a bill to resume crown grants. The latter was a particular blow to Oxford's prestige, since he had promised the October Club to obtain the bill's passage in the upper House if they would refrain

[1] BM Add. MSS. 22222, fo. 188; Swift correspondence, I, 313.
[2] NRO, Finch–Hatton MSS. 281, Nottingham to Lady Nottingham, 16 Dec.
[3] Ibid. 20 Feb. 1712.
[4] Original papers; containing the secret history of Great Britain from the Restoration to the accession of the House of Hannover, ed. J. Macpherson (London, 1775), II, 271; Holmes, 'No Peace Without Spain', pp. 230–1.
[5] NRO, Finch–Hatton MSS. 281, Nottingham to Lady Nottingham, 20 Feb. 1712; HMC First Report, p. 117; BM Add. MSS. 22908, fos. 89–90, J. Greenshields to [Dr Colebatch], 1 March.

from tacking it to a money measure.[1] Yet even the ignominious desertion of the allied forces in Flanders by the English contingent under the Duke of Ormonde failed to cure the Tories of their passion for peace. The Whig motion of 28 May that Ormonde be ordered to act offensively was rejected by the Lords by a vote of 68 to 40.[2] Nor were Nottingham's and the Whigs' denunciations of the peace terms, disclosed in the queen's speech of 6 June, any more effectual.[3] As Nottingham lamented to his wife, 'The World's grown mad and any Peace, any way will be approv'd of.'[4] Godolphin's death during the summer recess, coupled with Marlborough's departure for the continent despite Nottingham's efforts to persuade him to remain, only added to the opposition's dejection.[5] As Sunderland observed to Nottingham late in September 1712,

the present posture of our affairs...seem to be such that the quieter we are at present, the better, for these People have by corruption, and one way or other, gott such a Majority in both Houses, that till the Nation open their eyes, which will never be till the Peace is actually made...it seems to be running our heads against a wall, to hit any thing.[6]

However, the long drawn-out negotiations with France, coupled with the English abandonment of their allies in the field, would eventually produce, so Sunderland thought six weeks later, 'a great alteration in the minds of the People'.[7] And when the Houses finally reassembled in April 1713 after eleven proroga-

[1] NRO, Finch–Hatton MSS. 281, Nottingham to Lady Nottingham, 15 and 20 Feb.; Burnet, VI, 126–7; BRO, Downshire MSS., vol. CXXXVI, bundle 3, R. Bridges to Sir W. Trumbull, 14 and 21 May; *Bolingbroke correspondence*, II, 349–50.
[2] *PH*, VI, 1135–8. A strong protest, commonly ascribed to Nottingham, was entered by the minority and later printed and circulated publicly (BRO, Downshire MSS., vol. CXXXVI, bundle 3, R. Bridges to Sir W. Trumbull, 9 June).
[3] *PH*, VI, 1141–8. Their protest on this occasion, drafted jointly by Godolphin and Nottingham, was later ordered to be expunged from the *Journal* (LRO, Finch MSS., Political papers 136 and 137; *PH*, VI, 1148–51).
[4] NRO, Finch–Hatton MSS. 281, Nottingham to Lady Nottingham, 29 May.
[5] LRO, Finch MSS. Correspondence, box VI, bundle 24, drafts of Nottingham's letters of 20 Sept. to Marlborough and Sunderland.
[6] *Ibid*. Sunderland to Nottingham, 26 Sept.
[7] *Ibid*. Sunderland to Nottingham, 12 Nov.

tions, Nottingham could claim three important converts to his views about the peace—the Archbishop of York, Sharp's protégé Bishop Dawes of Chester, and Guernsey.[1] Furthermore, the impending settlement with France posed other problems for the ministry. The October Club once again began to press for the satisfaction of their demands, long postponed by Oxford on the grounds of untimeliness. Not only did they urge a halving of the land tax and the passage of a Place bill, but they also pushed through the Commons in May a malt tax which, in contravention of the Treaty of Union, was to be imposed on Scotland as well as England.[2] For the long-suffering Scots this was the final blow, and they now resolved to ally themselves with the Whigs in a show of independence.[3] The first, and only, product of their temporary agreement, in which Nottingham apparently acted as a mediator, was soon forthcoming.[4] On 28 May the Earl of Seafield moved the Lords for a day to consider the state of the nation. Four days later, the Scottish peers—ably supported by the Whigs, Nottingham, and Guernsey—elaborated on their grievances, and then sought permission to bring in a bill to dissolve the Union. However, after a long debate, confused by Whig desires to safeguard the Hanoverian succession in the event of the Union's repeal, leave to bring in such a measure was denied by a vote of 71 to 67.[5]

Although the revolt of the Scots proved abortive, the ministry did receive a severe check later in June on the second reading of the bill to implement the eighth and ninth articles of the Treaty of

[1] Both Dawes and Guernsey joined Nottingham in unsuccessfully opposing the address of thanks for the queen's opening speech on 9 April (*Wentworth papers*, p. 328; BRO, Downshire MSS., vol. xcviii, J. Bridges to Sir W. Trumbull, 13 April). For Sharp, see *Original papers*, ii, 562.
[2] BRO, Downshire MSS., vol. cxxxvi, bundle 3, R. Bridges to Sir W. Trumbull, 21 April; BRO, Braybrooke MSS. F/23/2, C. Aldsworth to the Duke of Northumberland, 20 May; Trevelyan, *England under Queen Anne*, iii, 241.
[3] 'It would make you spew', one disgusted Tory wrote to Sir Justinian Isham, 'to hear what fawning doings there is between 'em' (NRO, Isham MSS. 2976, 30 May).
[4] BRO, Downshire MSS., vol. xlv, R. Bridges to Sir W. Trumbull, [early June].
[5] Trevelyan, *England under Queen Anne*, iii, 242; Boyer, *Political state*, v, 348–53; BM Loan 29/45/J, bundle 12, an account in French of 2/13 June of the previous day's debate; Bodl. Add. MSS. A269, p. 23, E. Gibson to F. Nicolson, 6 June.

Commerce with France. Anglesey, always a firm Hanoverian and now disgruntled by his failure to obtain the Irish Lord Lieutenancy, and Lord Abingdon actively solicited against it, while the widely respected Sir Thomas Hanmer denounced this handiwork of Bolingbroke's henchman Moore on the floor of the Commons.[1] By a vote of 194 to 185, the bill was rejected on the previous question by a coalition of Whigs and Tory 'Whimsicals'. For a brief moment, it seemed the herald of opposition triumph; there were rumours that the Whigs would support the formation of a 'Whimsical' ministry in which Anglesey and Nottingham would hold key positions and it was reported that Nottingham now had 'great lords every day waiting on him'.[2] But Hanmer and Anglesey were not yet prepared for a total break with Oxford, and a temporary reconciliation between them was quickly effected.[3]

Although they were unable, for the most part, to obstruct the peace settlement during the 1713 session, the Whigs and Nottingham still had a trump to play—the question of the Hanoverian succession. This issue was to be the focus of English politics in the closing year of Anne's reign as a result of the widespread, if not wholly justified, suspicion of ministerial Jacobitism. Since the spring of 1713, Nottingham and the Whigs had unsuccessfully been urging the Elector to send his son to England to take his seat in the Lords and now, in the final weeks of the parliament of 1710–13, they moved and carried two addresses requesting the queen to press for the Pretender's removal from Lorraine.[4] Whig emphasis on the necessity to secure the Protestant succession and on the commercial disadvantages of the peace were also the key-

[1] Boyer, *Political state*, V, 388–9; *Original papers*, II, 495; BM Add. MSS. 31144, fo. 381, Sir H. Johnson to Countess of Strafford, 19 June; Bodl. Ballard MSS. 31, fo. 104, W. Bishop to A. Charlett, 20 June.

[2] BM Stowe MSS. 225, fo. 163, L'Hermitage to [Robethon], 14/25 July; BM Add. MSS. 31144, fo. 381.

[3] Tindal, XVIII, 90–2, 272; *HMC Portland*, VII, 146; Bodl. Ballard MSS. 31, fo. 106, W. Bishop to A. Charlett, 30 June; Bodl. North MSS. C9, fo. 5, T. Edward to Lord North and Grey, 22 June. But cf. *Original papers*, II, 496.

[4] *Ibid.* pp. 482–3, 489–94, 498; *PH*, VI, 1232–5.

notes of the electoral campaign that followed the parliamentary dissolution in mid-July. Nottingham, by dint of untiring campaigning and the aid of the Whig Duke of Rutland was able to secure the election of Lord Finch and his running-mate Lord Sherard.[1] But his brothers and Lord Barrymore failed in their efforts to defeat Sir Roger Bradshaigh and his ally George Kenyon at Wigan.[2] In all, General Cadogan estimated that one hundred and sixty Whigs were returned, though there was ample reason to fear that many would be disqualified by the House in its adjudication of disputed elections.[3] Thus, Whig hopes of overturning the ministry still depended on the conclusion of an understanding with the leading Hanoverian Tories, particularly Anglesey and Hanmer. As early as September 1713 Sunderland was anxiously pressing Nottingham to continue his efforts towards 'fixing' Anglesey in the anti-ministerial interest.[4] At the same time, Nottingham was also busy trying to bring over his brothers' friend Peter Legh, the patron of the parliamentary borough of Newton, Lancashire.[5] Moreover, his old protégé Richard Hill (the former envoy to Savoy) was doing his best to persuade Hanmer and the Bishop of Bath and Wells to take a stand against the ministry.[6] However, the courtship of the Hanoverian Tories,

[1] As early as the previous January, Lord Finch was already busy 'haranguing the freeholders, and spending liberally among them' (BM Loan 29/153, bundle 2, T. Peale to Oxford, 27 Jan. 1713). For a detailed account of the Rutland election, see LRO, Finch MSS., Rutland papers 2, Nottingham to W. Finch, 13 Sept.; ibid. Correspondence, box VI, bundle 24, Nottingham to Sunderland, [late Sept.].

[2] HMC Portland, V, 327; BM Loan 29/127, bundle 5, Sir R. Bradshaigh to Oxford, 6 Dec. 1713.

[3] BM Stowe MSS. 225, fo. 208, [Schutz to Robethon], 29 Sept./10 Oct. See also Speck, 'The House of Commons 1702–1714', p. 418.

[4] LRO, Finch MSS. Correspondence, box VI, bundle 24, 14 Sept.

[5] BM Loan 29/153, bundle 4, Auditor Harley to Oxford, 26 Sept. However, the long-delayed conferral of an office on Legh's brother Thomas in November seems to have kept the family loyal to the ministry though their friend, legal adviser and nominee at Newton, John Ward, was to vote with the Whigs the following April (John Rylands Library, Legh of Lyme MSS., letters of J. Ward to P. Legh, May–Sept. 1713; Boyer, Political state, VI, 293; BM Add. MSS. 47087 (no pagination), Lord Egmont to his brother, 17 April 1714).

[6] BM Loan 29/153, bundle 7, Lord Poulet to Oxford, 5 Oct.; BM Stowe MSS. 225, fo. 260, Schutz to Robethon, 27 Oct./7 Nov.

many of whom were high Churchmen, was no easy task. Fearful of a return to Whig domination and less prone to see Jacobitism in every ministerial corner, their conversion was long delayed.[1]

As the opening of the 1714 parliamentary session neared, the Whigs and Nottingham—spurred by the gravity of the queen's latest illness at Christmas and the hope that the arrival in England of a member of the Electoral family would induce wavering Hanoverian Tories to appear openly against the ministry— renewed their instances for the dispatch to London of the Electoral Prince.[2] In a long interview with the Hanoverian envoy Schutz in mid-February, Nottingham once again stated his and the Whigs' views. The ministers, he was certain, favoured the cause of the Pretender and would attempt to assist him either by invoking French aid or by tampering with the Act of Regency. Hence it was vital that the Elector be brought to authorize his representatives in London to demand from Lord Chancellor Harcourt the prince's writ of summons to the Lords as Duke of Cambridge.[3] Yet when parliament assembled on 16 February, nothing had been settled. The Elector, unconvinced of the urgency of the situation, still hesitated to take the decisive step, while Anglesey and Hanmer (elected unanimously as Speaker of the Commons) declined to act fearing that by doing so they would merely bring the Whigs back into power.[4] Consequently, the Whigs were constrained to virtual silence during the first month of the session.

However, Oxford's proposal of 17 March to make it treason to bring foreign troops into Great Britain, denounced by Nottingham as a threat to the Hanoverian succession and dismissed by Bolingbroke as superfluous, seems not only to have provoked a

---

[1] For an account of Anglesey's attitudes at this time, see LRO, Finch MSS. Correspondence, box VI, bundle 24, Nottingham to Sunderland, [late Sept.]. See also Schutz's letters in BM Stowe MSS. 225, fos. 208 and *passim; ibid.* 226, fos. 10, 45, 57, 176.

[2] *Original papers,* II, 572; BM Stowe MSS. 225, fo. 255, Schutz to Robethon, 23 Oct./ 3 Nov.

[3] *Ibid.* 226, fos. 171–4, Schutz to Robethon, 16/27 Feb.

[4] *Original papers,* II, 577–8.

crisis in the relationship between the Lord Treasurer and the Secretary but also to have persuaded the Hanoverian Tories of the necessity of joint action with the Whigs.[1] During the Easter recess, a series of conferences between the leading Tory 'Whimsicals' on one hand and Nottingham and Argyll (acting as spokesmen for the Whigs) on the other, finally produced agreement.[2] The adherence of Hanmer and Anglesey was won by Whig promises conveyed by Nottingham that they would renounce their pretensions to office provided the 'Whimsicals' would act '1. To secure the protestant succession: 2. To re-establish the alliances broken by the ministry: 3. To preserve the commerce of the kingdom'.[3]

When the Houses reconvened, after a temporary truce had been effected between Oxford and Bolingbroke, the Hanoverian Tories ranged themselves on the side of the opposition. With Anglesey, Abingdon, Ashburnham, Orrery, Carteret and Dawes (now Archbishop of York in place of the deceased Sharp) voting in the negative, a ministerial motion that the Hanoverian succession was not in danger 'under her Majesty's Government' was carried in the Lords by only fourteen votes on 5 April.[4] A week later, the ministry won what one observer described as a 'very Pyrrhic victory' in the lower House when a similar motion was approved on the previous question by a vote of 256 to 208, 'all my Lord Anglesea's Interest, with the Duke of Arguile's, the Earl of Abingtons and Sir Thomas Hanmers' being united against the government.[5] Nor was the attack on the ministry confined to parliament. Early in April, Schutz finally received what he

[1] *PH*, vi, 1330–1; Feiling, *Tory party*, p. 465.
[2] *Original papers*, ii, 585–9.
[3] *Ibid.* p. 589.
[4] *HMC House of Lords*, n.s. x, 274; *PH*, vi, 1333–7; BM Add. MSS. 47087, 8 April; BRO, Downshire MSS., vol. vii, newsletter of 5 April. Three days later, a Whig motion for an address against the Pretender, supported by Anglesey and Dawes, was carried without a division (*PH*, vi, 1338–9).
[5] BM Add. MSS. 47087, Lord Egmont to his brother, 17 April. See also *PH*, vi, 1346–8; BM Add. MSS. 31139, fo. 114, W. Bromley to Lord Strafford, 16 April; BRO, Downshire MSS., vol. xlv, R. Bridges to Sir W. Trumbull, 16 April.

thought was the Electress's authorization to ask for the issue of the prince's summons to the Lords. And on 12 April, on the advice of the Whigs and Nottingham, Schutz presented a formal demand for the writ to Harcourt.[1]

The issue now was plain, but Oxford, threatened with either the queen's displeasure or the prospect of Hanoverian hostility, strove manfully to escape his dilemma. Although the Electress's request was granted despite Anne's dismay and Bolingbroke's opposition, Schutz was advised not to appear at Court on the grounds that the queen was offended at his failure to inform her before taking so important a step. At the same time, Oxford made every effort to dissuade the Electress and her son from actually sending the prince.[2] Here he had some success. Though the Electress extended fulsome thanks to the leaders of the Tory 'Whimsicals' for their stand against the supposed Jacobite threat, the Elector refused to send his son to England and disclaimed Schutz's action.[3] When the opposition realized that their pleas were once again going to be ignored, they began to despair. As Nottingham gloomily predicted to Schutz late in May,

if the difficulties which you insinuate should prevail to disappoint our present expectations, the scene here would soon be chang'd; and putt an end to all our future hopes...to me and all who know our circumstances the case appears so very plain, so very terrible, that I wish I could flatter myselfe with any reasons to believe that the resolution, which seems to be taken, would not be irrecoverably fatal.[4]

But in spite of this setback, the 'Whimsical' leaders, the 'late converts, as they are called', seem to have remained firm to the Hanoverian interest.[5]

[1] Original papers, II, 592.   [2] Feiling, Tory party, p. 468.
[3] Original papers, II, 605, 610; W. Michael, England under George I, trans. A. and E. MacGregor (London, 1936–9), I, 33; LRO, Finch MSS. Correspondence, box VI, bundle 24, Schutz to Nottingham, 11/22 May (from Hanover).
[4] Ibid. draft of Nottingham's letter of 28 May to Schutz.
[5] BM Add. MSS. 47087, Lord Egmont to his brother, 14 June; BRO, Downshire MSS., vol. XLV, J. Bridges to Sir W. Trumbull, 13 May. But cf. Stowe MSS. 227, fo. 64, Gateke to [Bothmer], 18/29 May; Original papers, II, 615.

With the Electoral Prince's journey indefinitely postponed, the struggle between the ministry and the opposition took a back seat to the even fiercer contest raging at Court between Oxford and Bolingbroke, from which the Whigs hoped to derive some advantage. The Lord Treasurer's increasing estrangement from the queen prompted him to begin exploring the possibility of coming to some terms with the Whigs.[1] At the same time, Bolingbroke boldly staked a claim to the allegiance of the high Churchmen by bringing forward the Schism bill.[2] And neither Nottingham's outspoken strictures against this proposed curb on the freedom of dissenters to educate their children as 'barbarous', unseasonable, and an infringement of the Toleration Act, nor staunch Whig opposition could prevent its passage.[3] Indeed, Bolingbroke's bid for the support of the Church interest seemed likely to succeed, for Oxford did not dare to appear openly against the measure while Anglesey spoke and voted in its favour.[4]

However, the Lord Treasurer's counter-stroke—the issue on 23 June of the proclamation for the apprehension of the Pretender requested two months earlier by the Lords—brought to the fore once more the question of the security of the Protestant succession. On the 24th the Whigs and the 'Whimsicals' (with some Harleyite backing) joined in carrying a motion in the lower House to raise the price on the Pretender's head from £5,000 to £100,000 over the protests of Bromley and Wyndham.[5] Encouraged by intimations of assistance from Oxford, the Whigs also opened an offensive against Bolingbroke by undertaking early in July an investigation of the circumstances surrounding the conclusion of the Treaty of Commerce.[6] Nottingham raised the matter in the

---

[1] Original papers, II, 620; Feiling, Tory party, pp. 470–1.
[2] It was introduced in the Commons on 12 May by his follower Sir William Wyndham (PH, VI, 1349).
[3] Ibid. pp. 1351–8; Wentworth papers, pp. 385–6; LRO, Finch MSS., Political papers 145, notes for Nottingham's speech.
[4] PH, VI, 1351–8; LRO, Finch MSS., Political papers 161.
[5] PH, VI, 1358; Original papers, II, 630–2; BM Add. MSS. 47087, Lord Egmont to D. Dering, 24 June.   [6] Original papers, II, 633–4.

Lords on 2 July in an elaborate exposition of the disadvantages of the treaty, but before the attack against the Secretary reached its climax, parliament was prorogued on the 9th and Nottingham returned in disgust to Burley.[1] But the struggle at Court between the Lord Treasurer and the Secretary went on, and finally Oxford conceded defeat and resigned on 27 July. None the less, Bolingbroke's victory was only momentary. Four days later, the queen was dead, and Nottingham—hastily summoned from the country by Sunderland—was on his way to London to take his place among the Lord Justices appointed by the Hanoverian Court under the Act of Regency.[2]

The suddenness of Anne's death took both Jacobites and Hanoverian adherents by surprise. As a result, the proclamation of the Elector as George I on 1 August was received with enthusiasm in London and virtually without any incidents throughout the kingdom. During the month and a half before George Lewis landed in England, the country was governed by the Lord Justices, acting to a great extent on the advice of Baron Bothmer (the Elector's representative in London).[3] Apart from the seven *ex-officio* members of the Regency Council, most of its members were Whigs though Nottingham, Abingdon and Anglesey, in recognition of their services to the Hanoverian cause, were also included. Few major changes in policy or among the great officers of state, save for the dismissal of Bolingbroke, were made before the king's arrival, and the supporters of the old ministry vied with the Whigs during the brief parliamentary session in August in displaying their loyalty to the new régime.

However, by the time George I disembarked at Greenwich on 18 September, the struggle for the spoils of victory had already begun to divide the Whigs, and 'it was pretty publicly known that Lord M[arlborough], Lord T[ownshend], and Lord H[alifax], did

[1] *PH*, VI, 1361–2; BM Loan 29/8, bundle 3, newsletter of 3 July.
[2] LRO, Finch MSS. Correspondence, box VI, bundle 24, Sunderland to Nottingham, [30 July].
[3] Michael, *England under George I*, I, 52–9.

each of them aim at the whole power'.[1] To Halifax's great mortification, he soon found that the king, on the advice of Bothmer and Bernstorff, inclined to favour Townshend. While Halifax had to content himself with the First Commissionership of the Treasury rather than the Lord Treasurership he had coveted and expected, Townshend and his friend Stanhope were given the two Secretaryships and Walpole (Townshend's brother-in-law and adviser) was named to the lucrative post of Paymaster-General.[2] Marlborough, quick on his return to England to discern Townshend's new-found prominence, succeeded in coming to terms with the Norfolk Viscount, and by December 1714 knowledgeable observers were reporting that they, with Bernstorff and Bothmer, dominated the new ministry.[3]

Nottingham, who seems to have aligned himself with the Townshend wing early in the autumn, had no personal cause to complain about the distribution of places, for the Finches were amply rewarded for their loyalty to the Hanoverians.[4] He, himself, was made Lord President of the Council, while his brother Guernsey (soon to be raised to the Earldom of Aylesford) was named Chancellor of the Duchy of Lancaster.[5] In addition, his son Lord Finch was appointed a Gentleman of the Prince of Wales' Bedchamber, his son-in-law Mostyn—though deprived of the profitable Paymastership of the Marines—was compensated by being made one of the Tellers of the Exchequer, and his nephew Heneage was continued as Master of the Jewel House.[6] Further-

[1] Edward Wortley Montagu, 'On the State of Affairs When the King Entered', in *The Letters and Works of Lady Mary Wortley Montagu*, ed. Lord Wharncliffe (London, 1893), 1,135.

[2] For reports of Halifax's dissatisfaction, see Levens Bagot MSS., file A, John A [islaby] to Col. Grahme, 6 Dec.; Bodl. Add. MSS. A 269, p. 38, E. Gibson to F. Nicolson, 1 March.

[3] Bonnet's report of 24 Dec./4 Jan. 1714/15, printed in Michael, *England under George I*, 1, 374; 'Letters from James Brydges, created Duke of Chandos, to Henry St John, created Viscount Bolingbroke', *Huntington Library Bulletin*, IX (1936), 137–8.

[4] Montagu, 'On the State of Affairs', 1, 136; Bodl. Add MSS. A 269, p. 37, E. Gibson to F. Nicolson, [27] Nov.

[5] In addition to his salary of £1,500 as Lord President, Nottingham was given a pension of £3,500 'in consideration of good and faithful services' (*CTB*, XXIX, 250).

[6] Tindal, XVIII, 312; BM Add. MSS. 17677III, fos. 20–1, L'Hermitage's report of 4/15

more, Nottingham's favourite among the bishops, Dr Smallridge of Bristol, was continued as royal almoner on his insistence, and Nottingham was also offered the privilege of nominating Fleetwood's successor at St Asaph as compensation for the denial of his brother Henry's claims upon the bishopric of Ely.[1]

From the outset, Nottingham 'easily, and to all appearances heartily' agreed with the Whigs 'in the great lines of the Administration'.[2] Thus, in a memorandum he submitted to Bothmer early in September 1714 for transmission to the king, he frankly conceded to the Whigs—as the foremost supporters of the Hanoverian cause—a predominant role in the new ministry. At the same time, he urged a thorough inquiry into the conduct of the late ministers.[3] None the less, this memorandum also makes it clear that he was most anxious that places be found for the leaders of those Tory groups which had allied themselves to the Whigs during 1713 and 1714. He also thought that the king ought not to disturb Tory supremacy in the church.[4] Once the king had arrived, Nottingham exerted himself to bring home his views to the new sovereign. Just as he had tried to convert William at his accession, so now he endeavoured to persuade both George I and the Prince of Wales that the Tories, who would always support the crown's prerogative, were in principle 'likely to be the best subjects'.[5] Unfettered by departmental duties and possessing a

Jan. Halifax, at first, refused to admit Mostyn into his new post until the accounts of his previous office were made up, much to Nottingham's resentment (*Diary of Lady Mary Cowper, Lady of the Bedchamber to the Princess of Wales, 1714–1720*, ed. S. Cowper (London, 1865), pp. 29–30).

[1] Apparently his brother was offered but declined the Welsh bishopric, and it was finally given on Mostyn's suggestion to Dr Wynne (*Original letters illustrative of English history*, 2nd ser. IV, 286; HMC Portland, VII, 207, 209; Bodl. Ballard MSS. 31, fo. 129, W. Bishop to A. Charlett, 28 Sept.; Bodl. Add MSS. A269, p. 37).

[2] *Ibid.* p. 36, E. Gibson to F. Nicolson, 30 Oct.

[3] Nottingham's memorandum is summarized in Bothmer's diary which is partially printed by R. Pauli, 'Actenstücke zur Thronbesteigung des Welfenhauses in England', *Zeitschrift des Historischen Vereins für Niedersachsen*, 1883, pp. 66–7.

[4] *Ibid.*

[5] LRO, Finch MSS., Ecclesiastical papers, 6, p. 2. Lady Nottingham and the Duchess of Roxburghe, who seem to have been favourites of the Princess of Wales, took the same tack with her (*Diary of Lady Cowper*, pp. 16–18; *Wentworth papers*, p. 433).

fluent command of French, Nottingham took advantage of his easy access to the king to deliver him daily 'harangues' sometimes lasting an hour and a half.[1]

However, Nottingham's efforts were only partially successful. On the one hand, the king and his ministers did tread cautiously at first in matters ecclesiastical, and action on the dissenters' pleas for the repeal of the Occasional Conformity and Schism Acts was repeatedly postponed. On the other, Nottingham made little progress in his self-appointed task of familiarizing George I with the fundamentals of Anglicanism and the English constitution. His suggestion that services in the royal chapel be conducted in French or German for the king's benefit was not adopted.[2] Then, too, the commendation of the 'wisdom and happiness' of the constitution and the pledge to devote himself to a 'thorough study' of English interests, which Nottingham proposed to put in the king's mouth in his draft of George's initial speech to parliament, were deleted in its final version—an omen of the Elector's failure even to attempt to learn English.[3] Furthermore, Whig promises of office to the 'Whimsicals' with which he had personally associated himself were hardly fully honoured. To be sure, Anglesey was continued as one of the Vice Treasurers of Ireland and Sir Henry Bunbury was named one of the Commissioners for the Excise in Ireland, while Sir Thomas Hanmer was offered the Chancellorship of the Exchequer.[4] But Hanmer, as well as Bromley (who had been offered a Tellership of the Exchequer), declined to serve in offices which, though profitable enough, did

[1] *Diary of Lady Cowper*, p. 30. Even he, however, had linguistic difficulties, not to mention those of such as Walpole who spoke no French (Michael, *England under George I*, I, 374; Bodl. Carte MSS. 244, fo. 121, Mount Wood to Carte, 9 May 1717).

[2] Michael, *England under George I*, I, 375.

[3] Drafts in French of the royal speech which are attributed to Nottingham are in BM Stowe MSS. 228, fos. 23–4, and BM Add. MSS. 45680(I), and the latter is endorsed in his hand. Apart from the omissions noted above and a few verbal changes, the king's speech as delivered to parliament follows Nottingham's version almost word for word (*PH*, VII, 42–4).

[4] BM Add. MSS. 17677HHH, fos. 406–7, 415–16, L'Hermitage's reports of 28 Sept./9 Oct. and 8/19 Oct.; Boyer, *Political state*, IX, 5.

not carry with them Cabinet membership or the prospect of significant influence in the new ministry.[1]

Despite these disappointments, Nottingham was one of the ministry's leading spokesmen in the upper House during the first session of the Whig-dominated parliament which assembled on 17 March 1715. Both he and Aylesford defended the proposed address of thanks for the king's speech against opposition attempts to amend it, and they also vigorously supported the impeachments of Oxford, Bolingbroke, Strafford and Ormonde undertaken by the Commons.[2] Nevertheless, Nottingham was becoming increasingly disturbed by the growing evidence of dissatisfaction with the new régime among the Tories, including many of the former 'Whimsicals'. Thus, in a memorandum he prepared early in 1715, he stressed the folly of 'setting up a part of the nation in opposition to the whole'.[3] If Tories were to be disqualified even for places on the commissions of the peace solely because of their partisan sympathies, if no distinction despite Whig pledges was to be made between 'honest' Tories and those who had supported the late ministry to the last, there was danger of 'driving the majority of the Nation into despair' with possibly fatal consequences for the security of the kingdom.[4] To avert this threat, Nottingham once again advocated the filling of future ecclesiastical vacancies with men 'unexceptionable' to the Tories, and pressed the claims of Dr Smallridge to succeed Tenison (now seriously ill) as Archbishop of Canterbury.[5]

But for the moment, Tenison lingered on at Lambeth. Furthermore, Halifax's death in May 1715 and the temporary truce in partisan strife produced by the Jacobite rising the following autumn greatly lessened the value of so embarrassing an ally as Nottingham to Townshend and Walpole (now First Commis-

[1] Bodl. Ballard MSS. 31, fo. 129, W. Bishop to A. Charlett, 28 Sept.; BM Add. MSS. 47087, [late Nov.].
[2] PH, VII, 46; BM Add. MSS. 17677III, fo. 306, L'Hermitage's report of 12/23 July 1715.
[3] LRO, Finch MSS., Ecclesiastical papers 6, pp. 4, 8.
[4] Ibid. pp. 6-9.   [5] Ibid. pp. 9-10.

sioner of the Treasury), who were resolved to repress the rebellion ruthlessly. When Smallridge refused to sign a declaration of abhorrence of the rebellion in November, not even Nottingham's pleas on his behalf could prevent his summary ouster from the Almoner's post.[1] Even Nottingham's own position at Court was no longer secure. His colleagues were eager to rid themselves of this alien figure, and at the same time they were worried by the 'great Pains' he and his family took 'to insinuate the Tories into the Princess's Favour'.[2] By opposing late in February 1716, both in the Cabinet and the Lords, the execution of the Scottish peers convicted as adherents of the Pretender (though he had voted them guilty at their trials), Nottingham gave his former allies the opportunity for which they had been waiting, for the king was furious at his *volte-face*.[3] All his services to the Hanoverians were not sufficient to save him or his relations from dismissal after his successful intervention in the upper House on 22 February in favour of an address to George I asking him to show mercy to the condemned peers. Despite Cowper's desire to give the Finches one more chance, both Walpole and Bernstorff were adamant. As Bernstorff told the Lord Chancellor, 'it must positively be done now, for if they did not take this Opportunity, they, maybe, might not be able to do it when they would'.[4] Thus, on 27 February 1716 Nottingham's long official career, which had begun almost four decades before in 1679, came to an abrupt end with his ouster from the Lord Presidency.

[1] Bodl. Add. MSS. A269, p. 46, E. Gibson to F. Nicolson, 19 Nov.; Bodl. Ballard MSS. 31, fo. 154, W. Bishop to A. Charlett, 26 Nov. See also Smallridge's letter of 22 Nov. attempting to justify his refusal (LRO, Finch MSS., Ecclesiastical papers 7).

[2] *Diary of Lady Cowper*, pp. 65, 69, 98. As Lord Finch reminded Walpole, when Townshend and he sought Nottingham's aid in January 1718: '[we] had formerly helped them but afterwards they thought they could go alone' (LRO, Finch MSS. Correspondence, box VII, bundle 25, Lord Finch to Nottingham, 12 Jan. 1718).

[3] *Diary of Lady Cowper*, p. 82. For accounts of his efforts on behalf of the Scottish lords, see Tindal, XVIII, 545; Boyer, *Political state*, XI, 236; BM Add. MSS. 17677KKK, fos. 143–4, L'Hermitage's dispatch of 24 Feb./6 March 1716.

[4] *Diary of Lady Cowper*, p. 88. See also W. Coxe, *Memoirs of the life and administration of Sir Robert Walpole, Earl of Orford* (London, 1798), II, 51.

CHAPTER 12

THE CLOSING YEARS

1716–30

Nottingham's abrupt dismissal in February 1716 soon led to his partial retirement. Although he remained in London to oppose the Septennial bill in April 1716, during the following five years he attended the Lords only irregularly.[1] He was now almost seventy and the prospect of carrying on an active opposition against the ministry, particularly after the passage of the Septennial Act prolonging the life of the Whig-dominated parliament four more years, could have little appeal. As he announced in the Lords in his speech against the commitment of that measure, this may be 'one of the last times I shall ever trouble you, for after this bill is past into a Law, I shall think Debates will be to very little purpose'.[2]

Nottingham's reluctance to embark on a course of sustained opposition in the face of advancing years and the prolongation of a hostile Commons could only have been reinforced by his ambiguous political position.

On the one hand, he was completely at odds with his one-time Whig allies. Their differences, which had been temporarily submerged by the struggle against the Treaty of Utrecht and in favour of the Hanoverian succession, had come to the fore once again with the crushing of the 1715 rebellion. So great was the estrangement that when Nottingham in October 1716 sought to secure the removal of the names of several of his Rutland friends from the list of candidates for the burdensome office of sheriff, the only Privy Counsellor whom he was willing

---

[1] Drafts of two of his speeches against the Septennial bill are in LRO, Finch MSS., Political papers 152. See also *LJ*, xx, 332, 335; *PH*, vii, 303–5.
[2] LRO, Finch MSS., Political papers 152.

to ask for help was his successor as Lord President, the Duke of Devonshire.[1]

On the other hand, Nottingham was markedly reluctant to commit himself completely to the Tory opposition. Whatever his disagreements with the Whigs, he does not ever seem to have contemplated turning to the Pretender.[2] Moreover, he was unwilling even to act wholeheartedly with those Tories who were not tainted by Jacobitism but who had, none the less, supported or been members of Oxford's ministry. Hence his son Lord Finch, who was aware of his father's attitude, assumed that he would not entrust his proxy for the 1717–18 session to any Tory peer who 'might in some Questions...disown his own proceedings before the King came'.[3]

Nottingham was also disillusioned with the Prince and Princess of Wales, for his campaign to convert them to his views had not been as successful as Bernstorff and his former colleagues had feared. Though the princess complained of being deserted when Nottingham left London in June 1716 without seeing her, the prince seems to have done nothing to save him from dismissal.[4] As the prince himself admitted two years later when he sought Nottingham's aid in his quarrel with his father and the ministry, he was 'conscious he had not deserved so much service from you [Nottingham]'.[5] Thus, during the years between 1717 and 1721, Nottingham seems to have attended parliament only when he came up to London on private business.[6]

[1] National Maritime Museum, Southwell MSS., vol. xv, Nottingham to E. Southwell, 27 Oct. and 17 Nov.
[2] Despite his long anti-Jacobite record, the Earl of Mar did consider sounding him out on James III's behalf in 1717, but the proposal does not ever seem to have been implemented (HMC Stuart, iv, 233 and passim, and v, 416).
[3] LRO, Finch MSS. Correspondence, box vii, bundle 25, Lord Finch to Nottingham, 12 Jan. 1718.
[4] Ibid. box vi, bundle 24, Duchess of Roxburghe to Nottingham, 15 Sept. 1716.
[5] Ibid. box vii, bundle 25, Lord Finch to Nottingham, 12 Jan. 1718.
[6] What mainly brought Nottingham to London was a series of lawsuits concerning the estate of the late Marquess of Halifax and his wife, of which he was a trustee. He was absent for most of the 1717 and 1719–20 sessions and all of the 1717–18 session (LJ, xx and xxi, passim).

There was only one cause for which Nottingham was still prepared to exert himself, and not surprisingly it was that of the church. Although the king initially had abided by Nottingham's advice not to tamper with the English ecclesiastical structure, by 1717 the pressures on the Whig ministers to provide some relief of the disabilities imposed upon the dissenters were steadily mounting.[1] At the same time, the church was also threatened from another quarter. Whiston's propagation of Arian doctrines and Clarke's anti-Trinitarian study of 1712 had revived the dispute over the Trinity which had plagued the church during William's reign.[2] Moreover, Clarke's influence was not confined to Anglicans. His views were soon adopted by a number of prominent Presbyterians, most notably James Pierce of Exeter, and the controversy which broke out in 1718 among the dissenters of Exeter over the question of subscription to creeds of faith quickly spread to London.[3] To add to Anglican woes, the hierarchy itself was rent by a related dispute provoked by Bishop Hoadley of Bangor, who denied that the church had any temporal authority and questioned the whole concept of establishment. To be sure, Hoadley's notions were anathema to most of the bishops, not to mention the inferior clergy, but he had powerful patrons among the ministers, and when the lower House of convocation moved to censure him in May 1717 the convocation was quickly prorogued.[4] The attack on Anglican privilege reached its climax on 13 December 1718 when Stanhope—buoyed by the conclusion of the Quadruple Alliance, Byng's defeat of the Spanish fleet off Cape Passaro, and Cowper's resignation—suddenly introduced in the Lords a bill 'for strengthening the Protestant interest'.[5] This

---

[1] Michael, *England under George I*, II, 48–51; N. Sykes, *William Wake Archbishop of Canterbury 1657–1737* (Cambridge, 1957), II, 115–20.

[2] R. N. Stromberg, *Religious liberalism in eighteenth-century England* (Oxford, 1954), pp. 34–47.

[3] R. Thomas, 'The Non-Subscription Controversy Amongst Dissenters in 1719: The Salters' Hall Debate', *Journal of Ecclesiastical History*, IV (1953), 162–6, 180–6.

[4] Sykes, *William Wake*, II, 161–5; G. Every, *The high church party, 1688–1718* (London, 1956), pp. 165–6.

[5] *PH*, VII, 567–8.

measure, in addition to repealing both the Occasional Conformity and Schism Acts, also provided the means by which dissenters could legally evade the sacramental test for all offices.

Although the introduction of this bill surprised many, Cowper (always an opponent of further relief for the Nonconformists) and Nottingham may have had some advance warning. Not only did Nottingham, who had come up to town for a Chancery hearing in October 1718, remain in London for the session, but also Cowper and he proposed on 5 December that the judges be ordered to bring in legislation to remove the obligation of renouncing the Covenant imposed on all municipal officers by the Corporation Act of 1661.[1] This, as Dr Stratford reported to Charlett, 'is supposed to be done to prevent making any other alterations in the Corporation Act'.[2] But if this was Nottingham's and Cowper's intention, their tactic did not succeed. While their suggestion was unanimously agreed to, Stanhope merely seems to have waited until their bill had been read for a third time on 13 December before bringing forward his own far more sweeping plan.[3]

Stanhope's measure was heatedly debated by the Lords. The temporal peers divided on the question with Walpole's adherents siding with the Tories, and the ecclesiastical bench was also badly split with Wake vigorously opposing the bill.[4] Nottingham's speeches against Stanhope's proposals were directed mainly against the proviso to repeal the Act against Occasional Conformity, for it 'was his own framing, his own child I may say'.[5] When it was retorted that he had formerly sponsored schemes of comprehension in order to strengthen the Protestant interest, Nottingham replied with a detailed, if somewhat biased, account of the failure of the comprehension plan of 1689 emphasizing that 'after

[1] HMC Portland, v, 568; LJ, xxi, 17.
[2] Bodl. Ballard MSS. 35, fo. 151, endorsed '10 Dec.'.   [3] Ibid.; LJ, xxi, 24.
[4] Sykes, William Wake, ii, 125–7; PH, vii, 569–81.
[5] BM Add. MSS. 47028, fo. 523, Lord Egmont to Charles [Dering], Dec. Notes for his speeches are in LRO, Finch MSS., Political papers 153.

all had been offered that could be well parted with on our side, they [the dissenters] refused those offers and could never be brought even to say what they desired more...and showed that they were not by any means to be satisfied'.[1] He also took this occasion to attack the Bishop of Bangor and to lament the prorogation of convocation as well as the refusal to let it meet to transact business again.[2]

While the motley opposition in the Lords was strong enough to oblige the ministers on the 19th to agree to the deletion of the clauses dispensing with the sacramental test, a similar, though less far-reaching, clause was added by the Commons on the following day to Nottingham's and Cowper's bill 'for Quieting and Establishing Corporations'.[3] Conscious that the ministry had a majority sufficient to pass Stanhope's measure in its amended form, Nottingham resorted to another tack. When it was considered for the third time on 23 December, he first read a letter to the House which gave an account of the recent dispute over the doctrine of the Trinity among the Exeter Dissenters and then proposed an amendment which would have made subscription to the church's Articles of Faith, particularly those relating to the divinity of Christ and the Trinity, incumbent upon all office-holders.[4] His motion was supported not only by Anglesey and Oxford but also by both archbishops, and it was only by a margin of four votes that it was eventually defeated.[5] A similar proviso, moved by Nottingham's nephew in the Commons, was also rejected, and the lower House approved the measure on 10 January.[6]

Disheartened as he was by the ministry's success in securing the

[1] BM Add. MSS. 47028, fos. 523–4.
[2] LRO, Finch MSS., Political papers 153.
[3] LJ, xxi, 29–30; CJ, xix, 45. This development, taken with the failure of the opposition to attack the Commons' amendment when the bill was returned to the Lords, suggests that some form of compromise was agreed upon between the ministry and its opponents on the question of the sacramental test (see LJ, xxi, 37–8).
[4] Bodl. Ballard MSS. 20, fo. 119, note in Dr Charlett's hand; HMC Portland, v, 574.
[5] Ibid.
[6] PH, vii, 584–9; HMC Portland, v, 576.

repeal of the Occasional Conformity Act and in defeating his attempt to reserve offices to the doctrinally pure, Nottingham did not yet abandon the struggle against the anti-Trinitarians. Provoked by a tract of Whiston's addressed to him in 1719 as one of the foremost defenders of Anglican orthodoxy, he published a detailed refutation of Whiston's arguments two years later.[1] Nor did Nottingham content himself with rebuttal by way of the press. When he came up to parliament for the 1720-1 session to superintend the passage of a private act dealing with the Halifax estates, he took the occasion to try to win support for legislation on this issue.[2] Late in March 1721 he and Lord Trevor discussed a draft of a bill against atheism, blasphemy and profaneness with Wake, who approved its intent. However, the archbishop, after sounding out a number of his brethren, did not feel it advisable to bring in the measure himself as Nottingham had hoped he would.[3] Nevertheless, on 20 April Nottingham once again brought the problem of heterodoxy before the Lords. After some debate, Lord Willoughby de Broke then introduced a bill, 'substantially that' drafted by Nottingham, which would have provided penalties against any who denied the existence of God, the divinity of Christ, the doctrine of the Trinity or the validity of Christian revelation.[4] But though the archbishop did venture to speak out in its favour, the ministry marshalled its supporters against the bill and it was defeated by a vote of 60 to 31.[5]

This succession of setbacks to his efforts to maintain Anglican orthodoxy seems to have convinced Nottingham of the futility of struggling against the tide. Although he was greatly gratified by the enthusiastic response of many of the clergy to his tract against Whiston, he himself was too old and too weary to continue the

---

[1] He was encouraged to publish this reply by Dr Daniel Waterland, the author of a telling attack on Clarke, who carefully read his manuscript. Their correspondence is in LRO, Finch MSS., Literary papers 10.   [2] HMC Portland, v, 615.
[3] Sykes, William Wake, II, 135-6.   [4] Ibid. p. 136.
[5] PH, VII, 894-5. Brief notes for Nottingham's speech in favour of the bill are in LRO, Finch MSS., Political papers 154.

contest any longer.[1] As he explained in a letter he drafted to Lord Anglesey in 1723 to excuse his failure to attend the House of Lords,

though generally every man is the last that finds his own infirmities...I have had so many masters to teach me that lesson and I have so long and so often found by experience of how little value I am both to my friends and foes that I should be very vain indeed if I had not learnt that 'tis time for me to quitt the Stage and to betake myself to my owne little private affairs; and indeed since the Septennial bill...an old man may be allowed to despair.[2]

'Quitt the Stage' he did, nor did he ever stir himself to come to parliament again after the 1720-1 session.

During the last nine years of his life, then, Nottingham contented himself with his 'owne little private affairs'—the care of his estates and the marriage of his daughters.[3] These quiet years, spent mainly at Burley, did, however, give him ample time for reflections upon his career—reflections he was spurred into putting down on paper by the appearance of the first volume of Burnet's *History* in 1724.[4] Moreover, despite his retirement, he maintained an active, if disapproving interest in Westminster affairs, and at the age of eighty he even came to London to attend the coronation of George II.[5] But his attendance at Court in October 1727 was his last appearance on the stage upon which he had figured for so many years before death quietly overtook him at Burley little more than two years later on 1 January 1730.

[1] For examples of the clergy's expressions of approval of his reply to Whiston, see the correspondence in *ibid*. Literary papers 10.
[2] *Ibid*. Correspondence, box VII, bundle 28. This letter does not ever seem to have been sent to Anglesey.
[3] He had more success in the latter than the former, for one of his daughters was married to the Duke of Somerset and another (shortly after his death) to the Duke of Cleveland, while his estate at his death was still heavily burdened by family debts amounting to £22,000 and also £15,000 in dowry portions (Habakkuk, 'Daniel Finch', pp. 167–8).
[4] These included the narratives he prepared to aid Archdeacon Echard in his projected, but abortive, history of the reign of William III and the fragmentary memoir of his political conduct up to the Revolution which he drafted for the benefit of his children (*The conduct*, pp. 1–17, and *passim*; LRO, Finch MSS., Political papers 148).
[5] *Swift correspondence*, III, 424. See also LRO, Finch MSS., Political papers 155, headed 'pro Bishop Rochester's case, if I had been there' [Nov. 1722].

CHAPTER 13

CONCLUSION

The tale of Nottingham's long and contentious career in office and out has now been told; what remains is an attempt to explain and assess his part in late seventeenth- and early eighteenth-century politics. How did Nottingham come to play so prominent a role? What were the bases of his political influence? And how well did he justify the political leadership and high office that he attained?

Undoubtedly, Nottingham's birth and his father's official position were of considerable advantage in the successful launching of his career. It was thanks to the Finches' family ties with the Seymour ducal line of Somerset that he was first returned to the Commons in 1673. Furthermore, his appointment to the Admiralty Board in 1679 and his promotion to First Commissioner in 1680 owed no little to Charles II's esteem for his Lord Chancellor. Then, too, his father's death in 1682 left him as the head of his family at a relatively early stage in his career.

Nottingham's role as head of the Finch family carried with it both influence and responsibilities, and the latter were numerous. Not only was his inheritance charged with the portions of his surviving sister and four of his younger brothers totalling £15,000,[1] but he also felt an obligation to help smooth their paths in life. His first sister Elizabeth had died shortly after her marriage in 1670 to Samuel Grimstone (eldest son of Sir Harbottle Grimstone, Master of the Rolls under Charles II), but Nottingham took an active interest in the upbringing of her surviving daughter and helped to arrange her marriage in 1687 to William Savile, the first Marquess of Halifax's second son and eventual heir.[2] More-

---

[1] Habakkuk, 'Daniel Finch', p. 160.
[2] Foxcroft, Halifax, I, 490. Mary, the younger of Nottingham's two sisters, never married.

258

over, though two of Nottingham's five brothers, Heneage and William, had completed their legal training, had had their marriages arranged, and had been provided with official posts before the Lord Chancellor's death, he was put to some pains to further the careers of his three other brothers, Charles, Edward and Henry.[1] All three seem to have been intended for academic careers, but of the three only Charles ended his days in the universities as a Fellow of All Souls.[2] Henry, the youngest, proceeded to the M.A. at Cambridge in 1682, and was then nominated by Nottingham the following year to one of the new fellowships in Christ's College erected under the will of Sir John Finch.[3] As a member of Christ's, Henry took an active part in the University's resistance to James II's measures in favour of his fellow Catholics.[4] But by the early 1690s, Henry had grown restless within college confines, and thereafter Nottingham was busy in his behalf trying to secure for him the deanery of York to which he aspired. Yet it was not until Anne's accession that Nottingham was able to satisfy Henry's desire for a preferment where he would be close by his old tutor, Archbishop Sharp. Edward was even more difficult to settle. He had preceded Henry as a Fellow of Christ's in 1680, but he soon decided that his talents lay elsewhere. In 1684, he resigned his fellowship, and after an indecisive spell in the Inner Temple Nottingham made him one of his under secretaries and helped him to find a seat in parliament for Cambridge University in 1690.[5] However, Edward did not find 'the infectious heat' of politics to his taste either, and

[1] Heneage was married to Elizabeth Banks with a portion of £10,000 in May 1678 and William to a daughter of Sir William Hoskins with a portion of £3,000 in May 1681. By their father's death Heneage was Solicitor-General to the Crown, William Solicitor-General to Queen Catherine.

[2] Foster, *Alumni Oxonienses: 1500–1714*, II, 496. For an amusing, if scurrilous account, of a marital scrape of Charles's from which he escaped thanks in part to Nottingham's influence, see *Remarks and collections of Thomas Hearne*, I, 299–300.

[3] Malloch, *Finch and Baines*, p. 78; *HMC Finch*, II, 181, 188–9.

[4] Morrice, II, 79.

[5] J. and J. A. Venn, *Alumni Cantabrigienses* (Cambridge, 1922–54), pt. I, vol. II, 138; WSL, Dartmouth MSS. I, i, 1804, Lord Dartmouth to W. Legge, 10 Feb. 1690.

in the spring of 1693 he retired from Nottingham's office with a resolve to take orders.[1] Though for the time being he was content to live with his brother Henry, then rector of the lucrative benefice of Winwick (bestowed upon him by the Earl of Derby), Nottingham eventually had to consider how to find him church preferment, too. Eventually, he also was found a niche at York, as well as the richly endowed rectory of Wigan and a prebend in Canterbury Cathedral.

If on the one hand Nottingham was, in Burnet's words, 'the best brother I ever knew', on the other his brothers always sought and usually heeded his advice.[2] Even Heneage, closest in age and perhaps the ablest of all six brothers, for the most part followed Nottingham's lead.[3] Not merely did he seek Nottingham's aid in designing his new mansion at Albury and in educating his sons,[4] but also he skilfully took his brother's part as an influential spokesman of the Church party in the Commons from Nottingham's succession to his father's earldom until his own elevation to the peerage in 1703 as Baron Guernsey. Moreover, Heneage's marriage to Elizabeth Banks, the eldest daughter of the merchant financier Sir John Banks, was a rewarding family alliance for both brothers. Not only did Banks and his heir-apparent Caleb adopt as members of parliament in the Convention and later in William's reign the same political stance as did the Finches, but also the family tie with Sir John renewed and reinforced Nottingham's links through his mother's family, the Harveys, with London financial circles.[5] Again, the friendship struck up in the 1690s between the Finch brothers at Winwick and the Leghs of

[1] LRO, uncalendared Finch MSS., 1693, E. Finch to Nottingham, 1 Oct.; Luttrell, II, 464, and III, 81, 729.
[2] Supplement to Burnet's history, p. 290.
[3] For the opinion that Heneage was the ablest, see Swift, Four last years of the queen, p. 12; Onslow's note in Burnet, VI, 80.
[4] Althorp Savile MSS., box 7, Nottingham to Halifax, 1 May 1697; Chatsworth Finch MSS., Heneage Finch to his father Heneage, 14 July 1700.
[5] For the Banks' and their connections with the Finches, see D. C. Coleman, Sir John Banks baronet and businessman (Oxford, 1963), ch. VI and passim.

Lyme (kinsmen of Viscount Hatton) brought another widely related Tory gentry family within the Finch orbit, while still later Edward Finch's rectory of Wigan gave him some influence in parliamentary elections in that Lancashire corporation.

When Nottingham assumed his father's earldom, he succeeded not only to the headship of the immediate family, but also to the leadership of the Finch clan. Although the Earls of Winchilsea were the senior Finch line, from the Restoration onwards the Winchilsea branch was in a precarious financial position and was always eager to exploit the cadet line's access to governmental patronage. Not much love was lost between the two families even in the Lord Chancellor's day,[1] but dependency there was, and Nottingham was constantly bedevilled by the second and third earls' pleas for office.[2] So impoverished were they that, despite their Tory inclinations, the former voted in favour of William's bid for the crown in 1689 while the latter was compelled to offer his services to the duumvirs and the Junto in Anne's reign.[3] To be sure, as Lord Lieutenant of Kent and deputy Warden of the Cinque Ports under Anne, the third earl was able in 1702 to help further the parliamentary candidatures of a number of Tories,[4] but there can be little doubt that for Nottingham the deference he was accorded by his Winchilsea cousins was more troublesome than politically productive.

Of somewhat more value were the Finch family ties, mainly through the elder line, with the Thynnes of Wiltshire.[5] No doubt, it was the link by marriage that first brought Nottingham together

[1] KAO Dering MSS. U350, C2/121, Sir Heneage Finch to Sir E. Dering, 12 Aug. 1669; BM Stowe MSS. 745, fos. 111, 120, 124–5, Winchilsea to Sir E. Dering, 1 Feb. 1675, 20 June and 4 Aug. 1676.
[2] Chatsworth Finch MSS., 2nd Earl of Winchilsea to [Nottingham], 24 June 1689; *HMC Finch*, II, 221; BM Add. MSS. 29588, fo. 144, Weymouth to Nottingham, 28 Aug. 1702; *ibid.* fo. 163, 3rd Earl of Winchilsea to [Nottingham], 2 Sept. 1702.
[3] *LJ*, XIV, 113, 116; BM Add. MSS. 31143, fo. 313, P. Wentworth to Lord Raby, 1, March 1709.
[4] Horwitz, 'Parties, connections, and parliamentary politics', p. 51.
[5] The wife of Thomas Thynne, later first Viscount Weymouth, was Frances Finch, a daughter of the 2nd Earl of Winchilsea and granddaughter of the 2nd Duke of Somerset.

with Thomas Thynne, later first Viscount Weymouth, and Thynne's cousin George Savile, the great Marquess of Halifax. With both of these men, lifelong friendships grew up—friendships of political import as well. Weymouth usually followed Nottingham's lead until his death in July 1714 while Halifax—whose ties with the Finches were confirmed by the marriages of his son William, first to Nottingham's niece Elizabeth Grimstone and second in April 1695 to Nottingham's daughter Mary—and Nottingham steered parallel political courses during the Exclusion crisis and James II's reign, though diverging after 1688. After the Lord Chancellor, indeed, Halifax would seem to have exercised the greatest influence on Nottingham during his early years in politics, an influence climaxed at William III's accession when the Marquess strongly supported the new king's inclinations to appoint Nottingham to high office.

Other family ties of his parents, particularly their Kentish connections, were also of some value to Nottingham in the earlier stages of his political life. Thus, for instance, his Twysden cousins on his father's side, particularly Sir William Twysden (the third baronet), looked to Nottingham for a lead in the troubled years of James's and William's reigns.[1] But perhaps more important in Nottingham's growing political prominence in the 1680s than many of his parents' kinsmen were the clerical connections forged by his father. As a devoted churchman in a position of influence, he took good care during the 1670s and early 1680s to see to the advancement of a notable group of younger clergy. Among the more distinguished who benefited from his ecclesiastical patronage were his own chaplain John Sharp and Sharp's friends Edward Stillingfleet, John Tillotson, Thomas Tenison, John Moore, Simon Patrick, Richard Kidder and Humphrey Prideaux—all save the last to be made bishops after the Revolution.[2] It should not be surprising, then, that when the

---

[1] For Twysden, see BM Add. MSS. 33923, fos. 461, 468.
[2] Bennett, 'William III and the episcopate', pp. 110–11, 120–2.

London clergy in May 1688 sought the advice and assistance of a number of peers in their efforts to organize a concerted refusal to read James's second Declaration of Indulgence that their leaders—Tillotson, Stillingfleet, Patrick and John Fowler—should have turned particularly to Nottingham as the leading exponent of that loyal, but not rigid, churchmanship that the first earl had epitomized.

With Nottingham's own marriages, the Finch family circle was extended considerably further. His first wife, Essex Rich, was a kinswoman of the Earls of Warwick and Manchester, while her two sisters married into the Barrington and St John families. His second wife, Anne Hatton, was even more widely related: she, too, was a kinswoman of the extensive Montague clan and among her other relatives were the Tufton Earls of Thanet, the North Barons Guilford, the Bertie Earls of Abingdon, the Cecil Earls of Exeter and the Annesley Earls of Anglesey. And then there were the husbands of Nottingham's and Heneage Finch's daughters. Two of Nottingham's seven surviving daughters were married off before his final ouster from office in 1716. The eldest, Mary, was married in 1695 to William Savile, Lord Eland and later second Marquess of Halifax, and after his death in 1701 she married again, this time to the Scottish Duke of Roxburghe in 1708. Meanwhile, the next oldest of Nottingham's daughters, Essex, was wed in 1703 to Sir Roger Mostyn, a kinsman and friend of the Leghs of Lyme who had introduced him to Essex.[1] Furthermore, in 1700 Heneage's daughter Anne was married to William Legge, first Earl of Dartmouth, and in 1703 her sister Elizabeth was married to Robert Benson, created Baron Bingley ten years later. To add to this array of noble in-laws was Lord Bruce, himself a distant cousin of Nottingham, who in 1706 wed Anne Savile, the granddaughter of Nottingham's sister Elizabeth and the first Marquess of Halifax.

[1] John Rylands Library, Legh of Lyme MSS., box 44, Sir R. Mostyn to P. Legh, 6 July [1703].

What, then, was the political significance of Nottingham's extensive family connection? On the one hand, there can be no doubt that the influence and abilities of some of Nottingham's close relatives contributed no little to his own political career, particularly his father by virtue of his official position and his brother Heneage by virtue of his role in the Commons between 1685 and 1703. On the other hand, the burden imposed by his kinsmen's importunities for place and favour was no slight one. Moreover, the frequent indiscretion of some of Nottingham's Jacobite relatives such as Colonel Leslie Finch (a younger son of the second Earl of Winchilsea), Charles Hatton (Lady Nottingham's uncle), Henry Bulkeley (a cousin of Nottingham on his mother's side), and even Viscount Weymouth certainly lent some credibility to Whig charges that Nottingham himself was not loyal to William and Mary.[1]

Even more important, it must be borne in mind that ties of family were not the sole, or perhaps even the chief attractive force in the formation of a political following in the later Stuart period.[2] For one thing, though father and son, or older and younger brothers, tended to steer the same political course, there were some who did not, among them Nottingham's kinsmen the Harveys of Combe—the elder brother Edward was a Jacobite plotter while the younger Daniel was an army officer with Whiggish leanings.[3] Furthermore, political sympathy often preceded, rather than followed, alliance by marriage. Such was the case, for example,

---

[1] Luttrell, II, 38; BM Add. MSS. 29594, fo. 208, Nottingham to Hatton, 7 Aug. 1690; Foxcroft, *Halifax*, II, 246; *CSPD*, 1689–90, p. 485; *HMC Finch*, IV, 442.

[2] For a general discussion of the problems involved in trying to predicate political connections on the basis of kinship, see Horwitz, 'Parties, connections, and parliamentary politics', pp. 48–54.

[3] For Edward Harvey of Combe and his ties with Nottingham, see Chatsworth Finch MSS., Nottingham to Heneage Finch, 21 July and 4 Aug. 1701; BM Add. MSS. 47028, fo. 155, G. Berkeley to [Lord Percival], 26 Sept. 1715. Daniel, related by marriage to a host of Whig peers, voted as a member of parliament during Anne's reign for the General Naturalization Act and for Sacheverell's impeachment. Edward, also a member of parliament, supported Bromley's candidacy for the Chair in 1705, opposed the Sacheverell impeachment in 1710, and was a member of the October Club.

with the marriage of Lord Eland to Nottingham's daughter Mary and the marriage of Sir Roger Mostyn with Essex Finch.[1] Another significant consideration in weighing the import of family ties in the groupings of later Stuart politics is the fact that within the aristocratic élite of which Nottingham was a member almost everyone was related, more or less closely, to everyone else. Thus, even Nottingham and his one-time friend and later bitter foe, Admiral Edward Russell, were distant kinsmen.[2] And since most men were related, it was not only among one's followers but also among one's opponents that kinsmen—sometimes even close ones—were to be found. For instance, one of Sir William Twysden's competitors in the shire election in Kent in 1689 was another cousin of Nottingham, Sir John Knatchbull, who not only succeeded where Twysden failed in being elected to the Convention parliament, but also voted in favour of the Sach-everell clause in January 1690 despite the blandishments of office and favour held out to him by Nottingham.[3] Again, Henry St John—though a nephew of Nottingham's by his first marriage—was never reckoned one of the earl's followers by contemporaries, even in his early years in the Commons when he began to make a name for himself as a hotheaded Tory.[4] Later, of course, St John (created Viscount Bolingbroke) and Nottingham were the bitter-est of enemies. Clearly, ties of kinship were not of themselves sufficient to ensure or to account for political loyalty.

Somewhat more secure than the bonds of family loyalty in that day were the ties forged by the exercise of patronage and electoral influence. As First Commissioner of the Admiralty and later as Secretary of State, Nottingham had some voice in the

[1] Lord Eland voted against maintaining the Commons' resolution on James's abdication in 1689 under Nottingham's influence (Foxcroft, *Halifax*, II, 1, n. 2). Mostyn voted as a Tory from the time he entered parliament in January 1702.
[2] Anne Hatton, the second Countess of Nottingham, was the niece of Admiral Russell's sister. [3] BM Add. MSS. 33923, fos. 464–7.
[4] Algemeen Rijksarchief Heinsius MSS. 792, fo. 447, L'Hermitage to Heinsius, 6/17 Nov. 1702; BRO, Downshire MSS., vol. CXXXIII, H. St John to Sir W. Trumbull, 9 May 1704.

disposal of naval commands, diplomatic posts and colonial appointments. But most of those whose official careers in these spheres he helped to advance, whether kinsmen such as Captain Edward Dering or merely men whose abilities won his respect and whose views harmonized with his own such as Richard Hill or Francis Nicholson, were not destined to be members of parliament. There were, however, two spheres in which Nottingham's influence in the disposal of official patronage was of some political import. The first was parliamentary elections. During his tenure as Secretary of State, two general elections were held, those of 1690 and 1702. On both occasions, Nottingham did try to use the prestige of his office on behalf of some candidates, but the scale of his direct intervention was limited and the results at best mixed.[1] The second was the church, particularly during his first turn as Secretary, when he had a hand in the appointment of Sharp and several of Sharp's friends to the episcopate and hence to seats in the House of Lords. None the less, the political value of these appointments was considerably depreciated by the failure to achieve a comprehensive church settlement after the Revolution of 1688—a failure which kept the status of dissent alive as a political issue and helped not only to divide Nottingham and Sharp from many of their former clerical friends in the latter years of William's reign, but even worked to ruffle their own intimate relationship after Nottingham's break with Anne's other ministers in 1704.[2]

If Nottingham's use of official patronage did little to add to his political following, his electoral interest was of even less significance. His landed properties were not unusually extensive for a peer of his day, and furthermore the bulk of his holdings was concentrated from the mid-1690s onward in the tiny county of Rutland whose total parliamentary delegation consisted of its two knights of the shire. Not merely was his territorial influence in

[1] See above, p. 111, n. 4, pp. 183–4.
[2] Bennett, 'William III and the episcopate', pp. 120–31; Sharp, Life of John Sharp, I, 308–10.

other shires nugatory, but even in Rutland his electoral interest did not go uncontested by rival peers, among them Lord Gainsborough, the Earl of Exeter and the Duke of Rutland, although once his son and heir Lord Finch came of age he was always able to secure his election for the shire.

The narrow scope of Nottingham's own electoral influence, the limited political import of his official patronage, and the difficulties in transforming family ties into political bonds in the later seventeenth century all suggest that the chief source of his political influence and the basis of his parliamentary following still remain to be explicated. Contemporaries, at least, felt sure that they knew the explanation; and in their appraisals of his position what they most singled out for comment was the stance Nottingham had maintained throughout his career as the defender of the Church of England. Whether friendly or hostile, contemporary characterizations of Nottingham almost always emphasize, to quote the critical Swift, 'his Appearance of Religion and his seeming zeal for the Church'.[1] As a more favourable observer put it, 'In truth, no Man was thought to be a more able Defender of Church and State than the E--l of N-----m. His Commerces, his Familiarities, his Relations, his Acquaintances, were in a manner all that Way'.[2] Moreover, unlike his near-contemporary, sometime ally, and occasional rival for the 'Church interest', the second Earl of Rochester, Nottingham's devotion to the church was taken to be more than a mere exploitation of religious issues for political ends. As the Dutch agent L'Hermitage explained to Pensionary Heinsius, '*Ce Seigneur estant un Reputation destre attaché a l'eglise moin par esprit de parti que par principle de devotion s'il estoit persuadé qu'hors de eglise Anglicane il n'y a point de salut*'.[3]

[1] Swift, *Four last years of the queen*, p. 11. See also Macky, *Memoirs of the secret services*, p. 43; PRO, SP 8/2, pt. 2, no. 101, 'The Female Nine' [1690].
[2] *A vindication of the Earl of Nottingham from the vile imputations, and malicious slanders, which have been cast upon him in some late pamphlets* ([London, 1714]), p. vii.
[3] Algemeen Rijksarchief Heinsius MSS. 792, fo. 428, L'Hermitage to Heinsius, 23 Oct./ 3 Nov. 1702.

Again, unlike the libertine St John, his private life reflected his public professions of devout orthodoxy. In short, what appears most important in winning him a parliamentary following and, in turn, in appealing to successive sovereigns was the honest and sincere devotion to the interests of the church that he displayed throughout his public career. William thought Rochester a 'knave', but regarded Nottingham as an 'honest man', if too biased in favour of the Tories and the Anglican establishment.[1]

Because Nottingham's following in parliament was not primarily dependent on the bonds of kinship, official dependency, or electoral interest, it is difficult—indeed, well nigh impossible—to identify with precision all those peers or Commoners who were apt at any given moment to follow his political lead, much less to present totals for each succeeding parliament of the members who were enlisted in a 'Finch connexion'.[2] However, it does seem that his influence in parliament grew with the passing of time, not only because of the extension of the Finch family connection especially among the peerage, but also because his relationship with the leaders of the Church party in the Commons altered no little. During William's reign and even in the early years of Anne's, the chief spokesmen of the Churchmen in the Commons, overshadowing all others including Heneage Finch, were Sir Thomas Clarges (until his death in 1695), Sir Christopher Musgrave and Sir Edward Seymour—men somewhat older than Nottingham who had made their own political careers, men whom Nottingham might cajole by the promise of office or sway in personal discussion, but not men who would ever docilely follow Nottingham's lead. But with Musgrave's death in 1704 and Seymour's waning health after 1705, their places in the Commons were taken by younger men, above all William Bromley and Sir Thomas Hanmer, who sought and usually heeded Nottingham's

[1] Foxcroft, *Halifax*, II, 202.
[2] Walcott, *English politics*, pp. 53–60 and *passim*; Horwitz, 'Parties, connections, and parliamentary politics', pp. 48–54.

advice.[1] Moreover, though his brother Heneage had by this time been translated to the upper House, Nottingham also found in John Ward of Capesthorne (a lawyer who handled the Savile trust and who sat in the Commons for Newton, Lancashire, as a nominee of the Leghs of Lyme) an almost equally trusty agent for representing his particular views among the Churchmen in the commons.[2] Yet however great Nottingham's personal influence was over Bromley, Hanmer, and even Ward, the respect they and others accorded him was primarily as a champion of the church. Thus when Nottingham, in the autumn of 1711, allied himself with the Whigs, thereby seeming to repudiate a life-time's devotion to the defence of the Anglican establishment, virtually none of his former friends and followers (including his brother Heneage) could at first be induced to join with him in opposing Oxford and his ministers on the question of the Peace, even though the earl did secure Whig assent to the passage of the Act against Occasional Conformity.

If Nottingham's failure in 1711–12 to carry his erstwhile friends and followers with him in his open break with the Oxford minis-try defines the nature and limits of their loyalties to him, the episode also discloses much about his own qualities. Above all, it indicates that he was capable of taking a broad view of how the interests of the church could best be served in practice. Indeed, the devotion to the church as well as the loyalty to the crown in which Nottingham had been raised never blinded him to the need for translating these commitments into feasible lines of action in the repeated political upheavals of his lifetime. Thus, during his early years in parliament when the 'popish threat' seemed to pose the greatest menace to church and state, he became one of the leading exponents of reconciliation between Anglicans and dissenters by way of comprehension. Furthermore, during the

[1] Bromley's relations with Nottingham are best illuminated by the fragments of their correspondence surviving in LRO, Finch MSS. Correspondence, box VI, bundles 23 and 25, and see also HMC Portland, VII, 80.
[2] For Ward's influence over Hanmer, see HMC Portland, VII, 181.

Exclusion agitation, he figured as a sincere advocate of schemes to limit the powers of a Catholic successor, rejecting both the unprecedented step of disabling the heir to the throne and the unyielding posture maintained by the Duke of York's personal following who insisted that parliament could not alter the succession.

The great virtue, in Nottingham's eyes, of both comprehension and limitations was that while their adoption would involve major adjustments, it would at the same time preserve what he regarded as the essential features of the political and ecclesiastical order. Alterations in the ritual of Anglicanism, he felt, were but a small price to pay if English Protestantism could be secured against popery and the religious unity of the country could be re-established under the aegis of an all-embracing church. Again, a temporary diminution of the crown's powers might have to be accepted, but the principle of hereditary royal succession—which he believed to be vital for the maintenance of the existing political and social order—would be safeguarded. In this light, Nottingham's devotion to church and crown appears, then, not as an unyielding attachment to particular individuals or to specific ceremonies and forms. Rather, it was an adherence to what he conceived to be the essentials of those institutions, whose sanction he found not so much in divine ordinance as in historical tradition and legal precedent. Hence he was even prepared to countenance William's displacement of James II after the latter had demonstrated his readiness to rend the religious, political and social fabric of the kingdom in the cause of Catholicism, though he fought long and hard to clothe this drastic step in traditional garb, initially in that of a regency and later in that doctrine of *de facto* kingship which Francis Bacon and others had mistakenly read into the Treason Act of 1495. In short, as Nottingham himself stated in 1689 and as his anonymous vindicator of 1714 reiterated, 'it is Things, and Propositions, not men and Parties' to which he adhered.[1]

---

[1] *Vindication of Nottingham*, p. 46; and see above, p. 77.

To be sure, Nottingham was by no means above partisanship. Certainly, he was capable of altering his position on secondary issues as expediency demanded: he denounced the scheme to invite a representative of the Electoral family while serving as Anne's Secretary of State but supported it when in opposition; he condemned Marlborough for peculation when at odds with the duke but was prepared during the 1712–13 session to shift the burden of guilt to those still in office who had been parties to the disputed practices;[1] he opposed the adoption of the Schism bill in 1714 but argued against its repeal in 1718. More generally, it may be said that with the nearly simultaneous disappearance of Catholicism as a major danger and the enactment of toleration without comprehension in 1689, his championship of the church did gradually take on a more obdurate guise and a shriller tone. Indeed, the growth of dissenting political influence coupled with the increasing dissemination of heterodox religious views so alarmed him that from Queen Mary's death in 1694 he became one of the leaders of the high church reaction that reached successive climaxes in the agitation over his measure against occasional conformity, the Sacheverell trial, and Bolingbroke's Schism bill. Nevertheless, once Nottingham came to fear that the gravest danger to the established political and ecclesiastical order was posed by the Francophile and Jacobite propensities of those around Lord Treasurer Oxford, he again exhibited that readiness to compromise—even to the extent of allying with the Whigs and the duumvirs—that had characterized his career prior to 1694. And though this alliance did not long survive George I's accession, Nottingham was always careful not to take any step that could be construed as a repudiation of the measures he had pursued in opposition to the Peace of Utrecht nor did he ever waver in his loyalty to the new dynasty.

It was in large part because he adhered to 'Things, and Propositions, not men and Parties' that Nottingham never quite achieved

[1] LRO, Finch MSS., Political papers 134.

that distinction, in or out of office, to which he aspired. As an administrator, he was at best a qualified failure. His intentions were of the best and his diligence and industry unquestioned, but neither as Commissioner of the Admiralty nor as Secretary of State did he show himself to best advantage. To be sure, the burden imposed upon the inexperienced Admiralty Commission of 1679 was a heavy one; again, as William's Secretary he was allowed little initiative save in naval affairs where he ran afoul of Admiral Russell; and finally, in Anne's reign, when he at last felt free to put forward his own suggestions for the conduct of the war and the management of the alliance, Marlborough's pre-eminence hindered them from getting a fair hearing. None the less, it can not be doubted that Nottingham's stubbornness and his assurance of his own rectitude contributed no little to alienating his colleagues, thereby helping to frustrate his efforts in office.

As a counsellor and adviser of kings and queens, Nottingham had somewhat greater success. On the one hand, his repeated assertions that the Churchmen were the best support of the crown and its authority confirmed all of William's prejudices against the Whigs while his personal integrity, his industry, and his devotion to the church won him Mary's confidence and, after her death, that of Anne. But on the other, he later succeeded in forfeiting both William's respect for and Anne's trust in him by the vehement partisanship he exhibited once out of office. Given the opportunity once more in 1714 of frequent access to a new and foreign monarch, Nottingham did his best to convince George I and the Prince and Princess of Wales that the 'honest' Tories were the surest foundation upon which the new dynasty could build. And though he made little impression upon George I, he did seem to be succeeding with Princess Caroline. Ironically, it was his growing influence in that quarter that made his Whig colleagues and their German sponsors particularly eager to ease him out of office on the first plausible occasion.

Nottingham's record out of office was equally mixed. Though

he had a good sense of parliamentary tactics, he was not in Danby's, Wharton's or Harley's class as a parliamentary organizer or manager. Rather, he made his mark in the Commons and even more in the Lords as a speech-maker. However, his lengthy perorations—punctuated with biblical citations and legal precedents—were not always to the taste of his auditors some of whom like Ailesbury, found them more laborious than edifying.[1] Indeed, it was his penchant for elaborate set speeches, coupled with his dark complexion, that led hostile wits to mock him as 'Spintext' and as the 'Orator dismal of Nottinghamshire'.[2] More important, because his concern was with 'things' not 'persons', he often succumbed to the temptation of going his own way, regardless of others. As Feiling perceptively remarked, 'he was a man not exactly of tangents, but of corners; he consorted with his fellows, but his volubility was self-centred and did not react to common opinion'.[3]

Finally, though Nottingham had distinguished himself as the author of the Toleration Act, as the chief instrument in the reconciliation of the Churchmen to the Revolution settlement, and as one of the loyalest supporters of the Protestant succession, in his retirement at Burley in the last decade of his life he was often 'haunted' by 'anxious thoughts' about the new world he had helped to shape.[4] Nor was his uneasiness wholly unfounded. Although toleration had been carried in 1689, comprehension had foundered, and with it had perished his hope of re-establishing an united national church. Again, the Protestant succession had been preserved, but preserved in the person of an alien monarch who had made little attempt to come to terms with his new kingdom and who chose to honour and trust both in church and state not merely Whigs, but in Nottingham's eyes the worst sort of Whigs—not Lord Cowper or Archbishop Wake, but rather the

[1] *Memoirs of Ailesbury*, I, 232; *Supplement to Burnet's history*, pp. 290–1.
[2] It was Oxford who called Nottingham 'Spintext' (*Diary of Lady Cowper*, p. 18).
[3] Feiling, *Tory party*, p. 259.
[4] LRO, Finch MSS., Literary papers 10, draft of a letter to Anglesey, 30 Dec. 1721.

Earl of Sunderland and Bishop Hoadley. And if this were not enough to trouble him, Nottingham had also to confront the widespread acceptance of heterodoxy without and even within the church.

There was, indeed, cause for Nottingham to despair in his later years, but he also took pride in his own achievements. Thus, in the closing months of his life when his last Winchilsea kinsman died and the title of the elder Finch line descended to him, he refused to acquiesce in the disappearance of his own title. As he informed his son and heir Lord Finch (in his last extant letter) in September 1729,

I know very well that I cannot refuse the title of Winchilsea...but I am not debarred from using the Addition of Nottingham in all deeds and papers I shall signe...for this I certainly will doe to distinguish my branch of the family from the former.[1]

But Nottingham need not have been apprehensive; his own accomplishments in both public and private life had already set him and his family apart from the ill-fated elder branch of the Finches. Building upon the foundations laid by his father, he had established his family 'as one of those who are of the first consideration' by his own career, the prestigious marriages he made for his daughters, and the great house he erected at Burley-on-the-Hill.[2] At the same time, he had won for himself the reputation of 'a person of publick as well as private virtue'.[3] And if, as Speaker Arthur Onslow later remarked, his 'peculiarities did often subject [him] to some ridicule', 'no man in his own time was ever more known, or more in men's discourse, than this earl of Nottingham'.[4]

[1] BM Add. MSS. 29549, fo. 127, 30 Sept. 1729.
[2] Onslow's note in Burnet, vi, 80.
[3] *Letter-Books of John Hervey, First Earl of Bristol* (Wells, 1894), iii, 5.
[4] Onslow's note in Burnet, vi, 80.

GUIDE TO MANUSCRIPT SOURCES

A. NOTTINGHAM'S PAPERS

Nottingham's own surviving papers are, at present, divided into three main groups.

1. The Hatton–Finch manuscripts in the British Museum, especially Add. MSS. 29549, 29584, 29587–96.

2. The Finch–Hatton manuscripts owned by the present Earl of Winchilsea and Nottingham which have been deposited in the custody of the Northamptonshire Record Office.

3. The Finch manuscripts owned by Colonel James Hanbury of Burley-on-the-Hill. For some years, these papers were deposited in the London office of the Historical Manuscript Commission, and they have been partially calendared in *HMC Finch*, I–IV. Virtually all this collection has now been transferred to the Leicestershire Record Office.

Together these collections provide the bulk of the extant evidence concerning Nottingham's administrative work as Secretary of State under William and Anne, while his personal correspondence among these manuscripts sheds much light on Finch family history. However, all these collections are remarkably devoid of correspondence dealing with Nottingham's political activities, and this gap is only partly filled by an extensive series of documents—drafts of speeches, bills, and parliamentary protests—among the uncalendared Finch papers now deposited in the Leicestershire Record Office. Consequently, extensive recourse has been had to other collections relating to this period, both in public and private hands.

B. MANUSCRIPTS OWNED BY OR IN THE CUSTODY OF THE BRITISH MUSEUM

Four series of manuscripts in the Museum have been drawn upon frequently.

1. The letters of Charles Hatton and Sir Charles Lyttleton to Viscount Hatton in Add. MSS. 29571–9. These cover the years 1670–1706, and only a portion of them was printed by E. M. Thompson in the *Hatton correspondence*.

2. Transcripts of the reports of agents and representatives of the States General in London in Add. MSS. 17677 EE–KKK. These volumes cover the years from 1680 to 1716.

3. The Hanover papers in Stowe MSS. 225–8. Only a portion of these was

printed in *Original Papers*, ed. J. Macpherson, and the remainder is quite valuable for the years 1710–15.

4. The papers of Robert Harley, Earl of Oxford, in Loan 29, which have been deposited by the Duke of Portland. Only a small proportion of this immense collection is calendared (and then incompletely) in *HMC Portland*.

Other manuscripts of value include the following:

Add. MSS.: 4291, 7059, 7063, 7074, 7078, 7080, 9094, 9104, 9110, 19253, 22202, 22222, 22908, 24487, 25377, 28053–5, 28103, 29563–9, 30000 A–E, 31139, 31143–4, 32681, 33589, 33923, 34096, 34177, 34510, 34515, 34594, 35107, 36707, 36783, 37991–2, 38496, 41803, 42586, 45680, 47025, 47028, 47087, 47351, 52279.

Lansdowne MSS.: 193, 253, 773, 1013, 1024, 1034.

Egerton MSS.: 2617–18, 3345.

Sloane MSS.: 3929.

C. THE PUBLIC RECORD OFFICE

When Nottingham left office in 1693 and again in 1704, he did not take all of his administrative correspondence with him. However, most of the letters and letterbooks he left behind which dealt with domestic affairs have been calendared in the *CSPD*. Of his foreign correspondence which remains in the PRO in State Papers Foreign, volumes 84/225 and 87/2 have been particularly valuable.

Apart from Nottingham's own papers in the PRO, Baschet's transcripts of the reports of French envoys in London in PRO 31/3 have also been most useful, particularly for the years before 1689. Those consulted are PRO 31/3/129–201 which cover the period 1673–1714. Other manuscripts which contain relevant information include the following:

Admiralty Papers: 1/3550–3, 2/1749–54, 3/277–9.

State Papers Domestic: 8/1–12 (King William's Chest), 31/4.

Privy Council Registers: 2/68–73.

Manchester Papers: PRO 30/15/6, pt. 2, vol. XI.

D. THE BODLEIAN LIBRARY

Manuscripts which have shed some light on Nottingham's activities include the following:

Ballard MSS.: 3, 6–7, 10, 20–1, 31, 35, 39, 45, 48.

Carte MSS.: 39, 79, 81, 130, 180, 228, 233, 243–4.

Rawlinson MSS.: A 77, A 79, A 139 B, A 228, D 836, D 1079, Letters 98.

Tanner MSS.: 23, 25, 27–9.

Additional MSS.: A 269.

Clarendon MSS.: 90.

Top. Oxon.: C 325.

Locke MSS.: C 16.

North MSS.: C 9.

Willis MSS.: 15.

D. D. Ashurst: C 1.

E. OTHER ARCHIVES AND LIBRARIES

Algemeen Rijksarchief (The Hague): The resources of this great archive for the study of later Stuart political history have only been very partially explored. The correspondence of the Dutch agent in London, L'Hermitage, with Pensionary Heinsius has been used for the years 1694 and 1702—Heinsius MSS. 402 and 792.

All Souls College MSS.: Vol. 158 is an extremely detailed diary of Commons' debates for 1691–3 kept by Narcissus Luttrell, which both complements and considerably supplements Anchitell Grey's printed diary; vol. 273 contains papers of Owen Wynne who served as Secretary to the commissioners sent by James to negotiate with William in 1688; vol. 317 is a portion of Sir William Trumbull's diaries from the mid-1680s.

Berkshire Record Office: The Downshire and Trumbull MSS. deposited by the Marquess of Downshire are chiefly notable for the letters addressed to Sir William Trumbull in his retirement during the latter years of William's reign and throughout Anne's—they provide a mine of information about Tory attitudes and activities during this period; the Braybrooke MSS. contain a few interesting letters sent to the Duke of Northumberland in the latter part of Anne's reign.

Christ Church College: The Wake MSS.

Folger Shakespeare Library: Most valuable was the long run of newsletters addressed to Sir Richard Newdigate which covers the period 1674–1715 with occasional gaps.

Gloucestershire Record Office: The Lloyd-Baker MSS. deposited by Colonel Lloyd-Baker—the correspondence of Archbishop Sharp, including a number of letters from Nottingham.

Huddersfield Public Library: The Whitley-Beaumont MSS.

Hunterian Library: The Clarendon MSS.

Kent Archives Office: The Dering MSS. (U275 and U350) contain passing information about the Finch family.

Lancashire Record Office: The Kenyon MSS.

House of Lords Record Office: The Committee Books and MSS. Minutes contain material which supplements *HMC House of Lords*, and this material was of particular use in tracing the course of the 1689 Comprehension bill.

Middlesex Record Office: Jersey MSS.—the correspondence of the Earl of Jersey which is most useful for the years 1697–1704.

Morgan Library (New York): Autograph Collection.

National Maritime Museum: The Southwell MSS. contain the originals of many letters of Nottingham to Sir Robert Southwell in 1690 and also portions of Nottingham's correspondence with Edward Southwell.

Northamptonshire Record Office: The Buccleuch MSS. deposited by the Duke of Buccleuch and Queensberry contain the Shrewsbury–Vernon correspondence, not always fully or accurately edited by James in the *Vernon Correspondence*; the Isham MSS. contain a wealth of information about Northamptonshire politics and an occasional letter from Nottingham to Sir Justinian Isham.

Nottingham University Library: The Portland MSS. (PWa) deposited by the Duke of Portland—this portion of the Duke's manuscripts includes Bentinck's correspondence, which is especially valuable for William III's reign.

John Rylands Library: The Legh of Lyme MSS.

William Salt Library: The Dartmouth MSS.; The Kaye MSS.

Shropshire Record Office: The Attingham MSS.—the papers of Richard Hill.

Tullie House (Carlisle): Bishop Nicolson's diary—only entries of local interest from this diary have been published in the *Transactions of the Cumberland and Westmorland Antiquarian and Archaeological Society*, but it also includes detailed accounts of many Lords' debates, particularly for the years 1702–6.

Dr Williams' Library: The diary or 'Entring Book' of Roger Morrice, an ejected Presbyterian minister, who left a detailed account (partly in cipher) of dissenting activities from the late 1670s to the early 1690s. The diary also includes a great deal of information of general political interest for those years.

F. COLLECTIONS IN PRIVATE CUSTODY

Papers of O. R. Bagot, Esq., at Levens Hall: The correspondence of Colonel James Grahme, which is particularly valuable for the activities of the high Churchmen of Anne's reign.

Papers of the Marquess of Bath at Longleat: The Thynne MSS. which contain the correspondence of Nottingham with Viscount Weymouth.

Papers of the Duke of Devonshire at Chatsworth: This collection contains an interesting series of letters from Nottingham to his brother Heneage during William's reign. It also includes the 'Devonshire House Notebook' of the first Marquess of Halifax, which supplements the 'Spencer House Notebook' edited by H. C. Foxcroft in her *Halifax*.

Papers of the Duke of Marlborough at Blenheim Palace: Most valuable of this vast collection of the Churchill, Spencer, and Godolphin papers have been the unpublished letters between the Churchills, and between them and Godolphin, for the years 1701–5.

Papers of the Earl Spencer at Althorp: The Savile MSS. include much of the extant correspondence of both the first and second Marquesses of Halifax, and there is a sizable series of letters from Nottingham to his son-in-law, the second Marquess, for the years 1694–1700.

LIST OF PRINTED WORKS CITED

The following includes all such works except publications of the Historical Manuscript Commission and the Public Record Office.

Aiken, W. A. 'The administration of Daniel Finch, second earl of Nottingham, as secretary of state under Queen Anne, 1702–4', Cambridge University, M.Litt., 1933.

—— 'The Admiralty in conflict and commission, 1679–1684', *Conflict in Stuart England: Essays in honour of Wallace Notestein*, ed. W. A. Aiken and B. D. Henning. London, 1960.

—— (ed). *The conduct of the earl of Nottingham*. New Haven, 1941.

Memoirs of Thomas, earl of Ailesbury, written by himself, ed. W. E. Buckley, 2 vols. Roxburghe Club, London, 1890.

Ansell, P. M. 'Harley's parliamentary management', *Bulletin of the Institute of Historical Research*, XXXIV. 1961.

The epistolary correspondence of Francis Atterbury, D.D. Lord bishop of Rochester, ed. J. Nichols, 5 vols. London, 1799.

Correspondence of George Baillie of Jerviswood, 1702–1708, ed. G. Eliot (Lord Minto). Bannatyne Club, Edinburgh, 1842.

Barker, G. F. and Stenning, A. H. (eds.). *The records of old Westminsters*, 2 vols. London, 1928.

Baxter, S. B. *William III*. London, 1966.

Bennett, G. V. 'King William III and the episcopate', *Essays in modern English church history*, ed. G. V. Bennett and J. D. Walsh. New York, 1966.

Bindoff, S. T. 'Parliamentary history 1529–1688', *A history of Wiltshire*, vol. v, ed. R. B. Pugh and E. Crittal. The Victoria History of the Counties of England, London, 1957.

Bishop of Barrow-in-Furness, 'Bishop Nicolson's Diaries', pt. II, *Transactions of the Cumberland and Westmorland Antiquarian and Archaeological Society*, n.s. II. 1902.

Letters and correspondence, public and private, of Henry St John, Lord Viscount Bolingbroke, during the time he was Secretary of State to Queen Anne, ed. G. Parke. 4 vols. London, 1798.

Bourne, R. *Queen Anne's navy in the West Indies*. New Haven, 1939.

Boyer, A. *The history of King William the Third*, 3 vols. London, 1702–3.

—— *The history of the life and reign of Queen Anne*. London, 1722.

—— *Quadrennium Annae Postremum, or the political state of Great Britain*, 2nd edn, 8 vols. London, 1718–19.

The autobiography of Sir John Bramston of Skreens, ed. Lord Braybrooke. Camden Society, London, 1845.

Brown, P. H., (ed.). *Letters relating to Scotland in the reign of Queen Anne.* Scottish History Society, Edinburgh, 1915.

Browning, A. *Thomas Osborne earl of Danby and duke of Leeds 1632–1712*, 3 vols. Glasgow, 1944–51.

Browning, A. and Milne, D. 'An Exclusion Bill Division List', *Bulletin of the Institute of Historical Research*, XXIII. 1950.

Bryant, A. *Samuel Pepys, saviour of the navy.* London, 1957.

The Bulstrode papers, vol. I, Second Series of the Catalogue of the Collection of Alfred Morrison. London, 1897.

Bishop Burnet's history of his own time, 6 vols. Oxford, 1833.

Calamy, E. *Memoirs of the life of the late Reverend Mr John Howe.* London, 1724.

—— *An historical account of my own life with some reflections on the times I have lived in (1671–1731)*, ed. J. T. Rutt, 2 vols. London, 1829.

State papers and letters addressed to William Carstares during the reigns of K. William and Q. Anne, ed. J. M'Cormick. Edinburgh, 1774.

Campana di Cavelli, E. *Les dernier Stuarts et la château de Saint-Germain en Laye: documents inédits et authentiques*, 2 vols. Paris, 1871.

Churchill, W. *Marlborough his life and times*, 2 vols. London, 1947.

Clark, G. N. 'The Dutch Missions to England', *English Historical Review*, XXXV. 1920.

Clarke, J. S. (ed.). *The life of James the Second, king of England*, 2 vols. London, 1816.

Cobbett, W. *Parliamentary history of England. From the Norman Conquest in 1066, to the year 1803*, 36 vols. London, 1806–20.

Coleman, D. C. *Sir John Banks baronet and businessman.* Oxford, 1963.

The autobiographies and letters of Thomas Comber, ed. C. E. Whiting, 2 vols. Surtees Society, London, 1945–6.

Conway letters, ed. M. H. Nicolson. New Haven, 1930.

Coombs, D. *The conduct of the Dutch; British opinion and the Dutch alliance during the War of the Spanish Succession.* The Hague, 1958.

Diary of Lady Mary Cowper, lady of the bedchamber to the Princess of Wales, 1714–1720, ed. S. Cowper. 2nd edn., London, 1865.

The private diary of William, first Earl Cowper, lord chancellor of England (1705–1714), ed. E. C. Hawtrey. Roxburghe Club, London, 1833.

Coxe, W. *Memoirs of John duke of Marlborough; with his original correspondence*, 3 vols. London, 1818.

—— *Memoirs of the life and administration of Sir Robert Walpole, earl of Orford*, 3 vols. London, 1798.

Cunningham, A. *The history of Great Britain: from the Revolution in 1688, to the accession of George the First*, 2 vols. London, 1787.

Cunnington, G. E. 'The general election of 1705', *Bulletin of the Institute of Historical Research*, XVII. 1939–40.

Dalrymple, J. *Memoirs of Great Britain and Ireland*, 2 vols. London, 1771–3.

Davies, G. 'The seamy side of Marlborough's war', *Huntington Library Quarterly*, XV. 1951–2.

Davies, G. and Timling, M. 'Letters from James Brydges, created Duke of Chandos, to Henry St John, created Viscount Bolingbroke', *Huntington Library Bulletin*, IX. 1936.

Ehrman, J. *The navy in the war of William III 1689–1697*. Cambridge, 1953.

Ellis, E. L. 'The Whig junto in relation to the development of party politics and party organization from its inception to 1714', Oxford University, D.Phil., 1961.

Ellis, H. (ed.). *Original letters illustrative of English history*, 2nd series, 4 vols. London, 1827.

Essex papers, vol. I, ed. O. Airy. Camden Society, London, 1890.

The diary of John Evelyn, ed. E. S. de Beer, 6 vols. Oxford, 1955.

Everitt, A. *The community of Kent and the Great Rebellion 1640–60*. Leicester, 1966.

Every, G. *The high church party 1688–1715*. London, 1956.

Feiling, K. G. *A history of the Tory party 1640–1714*. Oxford, 1924.

Ferguson, J. *Robert Ferguson the plotter*. Edinburgh, 1887.

Finch, P. *History of Burley-on-the-Hill*, 2 vols. London, 1901.

Foster, J. *Alumni Oxonienses: 1500–1714*, 4 vols. London, 1891–2.

Fox, C. J. *A history of the early part of the reign of James the Second*. London, 1808.

Foxcroft, H. C. *The life and letters of George Savile, Bart., first marquess of Halifax*, 2 vols. London, 1898.

—— (ed.). *A supplement to Burnet's history of my own time*. Oxford, 1902.

Graham, J. M. *Annals and correspondence of the viscount and the first and second earls of Stair*, 2 vols. London, 1875.

Grey, A. *Debates of the House of Commons from the year 1667 to the year 1694*, 10 vols. London, 1769.

Gutch, J. (ed.). *Collectanea curiosa, or miscellaneous tracts relating to the history and antiquities of England and Ireland, the universities of Oxford and Cambridge, Etc.*, 2 vols. Oxford, 1781.

Habakkuk, H. J. 'Daniel Finch, 2nd earl of Nottingham: His house and estate', *Studies in Social History*, ed. J. H. Plumb. London, 1955.

Haley, K. D. H. 'A list of the English peers, c. May, 1687', *English Historical Review*, LXIX. 1954.

Hardwicke, earl of (ed.). *Miscellaneous state papers, from 1501 to 1726*, 2 vols. London, 1778.

Hart, A. T. *The life and times of John Sharp, archbishop of York*. London, 1949.

Correspondence of the family of Hatton being chiefly letters addressed to Christopher first Viscount Hatton A.D. *1601–1704,* ed. E. M. Thompson, 2 vols. Camden Society, London, 1878.

Haute, G. van den. *Les relations Anglo-Hollandaises au début du xviiie siècle d'après la correspondance d'Alexandre Stanhope 1700–1706.* Louvain, 1932.

Remarks and collections of Thomas Hearne, ed. C. E. Doble, 11 vols. Oxford Historical Society, Oxford, 1885.

Heim, H. J. van der (ed.). *Het Archief van den Raadpensionaris Antonie Heinsius,* 3 vols. The Hague, 1867–80.

The diaries and letters of Philip Henry, ed. M. Lee. London, 1882.

Letter-Books of John Hervey, first earl of Bristol, ed. [S. H. A. Hervey], 3 vols. Wells, 1894.

The diplomatic correspondence of the Right Hon. Richard Hill, ed. W. Blackley, 2 vols. London, 1845.

Holmes, G. S. 'The Commons' Division on "No Peace without Spain", 7 December 1711', *Bulletin of the Institute of Historical Research,* XXXIII. 1960.

—— 'The attack on "The Influence of the Crown", 1702–1716', *Bulletin of the Institute of Historical Research,* XXXIX. 1966.

Holmes, G. S. and Speck, W. A. 'The fall of Harley in 1708 reconsidered', *English Historical Review,* LXXX. 1965.

Horn, D. B. 'The diplomatic experience of secretaries of state, 1660–1852', *History,* XLI. 1956.

Horwitz, H. 'Protestant reconciliation in the Exclusion crisis', *Journal of Ecclesiastical History,* XV. 1964.

—— 'Parties, connections, and parliamentary politics, 1689–1714: Review and revision', *Journal of British Studies,* VI. 1966.

Howell, T. B. (ed.). *A complete collection of state trials and proceedings for high treason and other crimes and misdemeanors from the earliest period to the present time,* 33 vols. London, 1809–26.

[Humfrey, J.] *King William's toleration.* London, 1689.

Journaal van Constantijn Huygens, den zoon, van 21 October 1688 tot 2 Sept. 1696, 2 vols. Historisch Genootschap, Utrecht, 1876–8.

Correspondence of Henry Hyde, earl of Clarendon, and of his brother, Laurence Hyde, earl of Rochester, ed. S. W. Singer, 2 vols. London, 1828.

I'Anson, B. *The history of the Finch family.* London, 1933.

Jones, J. R. *The first Whigs.* London, 1961.

—— 'Shaftesbury's "Worthy Men": A Whig view of the parliament of 1679', *Bulletin of the Institute of Historical Research,* XXX. 1957.

—— 'Political groups and tactics in the Convention of 1660', *Historical Journal,* VI. 1963.

Kenyon, J. P. *Robert Spencer earl of Sunderland 1641–1702.* London, 1958.

Klopp, O. *Der Fall des Hauses Stuart und die Succession des Hauses Hannover*, 14 vols. Vienna, 1875–88.

Lauder, J. *Historical observes of memorable occurents in church and state, from October 1680 to April 1686.* Bannatyne Club, Edinburgh, 1840.

Lees, R. M. 'Parliament and the proposal for a Council of Trade, 1695–1696', *English Historical Review*, LIV. 1939.

A letter concerning the disabling clauses lately offered to the House of Commons, for regulating corporations. London, 1690.

A letter from a clergyman in the country to a dignified clergyman in London vindicating the bill for the better preservation of the protestant religion. London, 1702.

Lever, T. *Godolphin his life and times.* London, 1952.

Original letters of John Locke, Alg. Sidney, and Lord Shaftesbury, ed. T. Forster. 2nd edn, London, 1847.

The Lockhart papers, ed. A. Aufrere, 2 vols. London, 1817.

Luttrell, N. *A brief historical relation of state affairs from September 1678 to April 1714,* 6 vols. Oxford, 1857.

Macaulay, T. B. *The history of England from the accession of James the Second,* 5 vols. London, 1896.

Mackenzie, W. C. *Simon Fraser, Lord Lovat his life and times.* London, 1908.

Macky, J. *Memoirs of the secret services of John Macky, Esq., during the reigns of king William, queen Anne, and king George I.* Roxburghe Club, London, 1895.

Macpherson, J. (ed.). *Original papers; containing the secret history of Great Britain from the Restoration to the accession of the House of Hannover,* 2 vols. London, 1775.

Malloch, A. *Finch and Baines, a seventeenth century friendship.* Cambridge, 1917.

Manchester, duke of. *Court and society from Elizabeth to Anne,* 2 vols. London, 1864.

Mansfield, H. C. 'Party government and the Revolution of 1688', *American Political Science Review,* LVIII. 1964.

A selection from the papers of the earls of Marchmont, ed. G. H. Rose, 3 vols. London, 1831.

The correspondence 1701–1711 of John Churchill first duke of Marlborough and Anthonie Heinsius Grand Pensionary of Holland, ed. B. van't Hoff. The Hague, 1951.

Letters and despatches of John Churchill, duke of Marlborough, ed. G. Murray, 5 vols. London, 1845.

Private correspondence of Sarah, duchess of Marlborough, illustrative of the court and times of Queen Anne, ed. [Lord John Russell], 2 vols. London, 1838.

'Letters to John Mackenzie of Delvine Advocate, one of the principal clerks of session, From the Revd. Alexander Monro, D.D. Sometime principal of the University of Edinburgh 1690 to 1698', ed. W. K. Dickson, *Scottish Historical Society,* 3rd series, XXI (1933).

Mazure, F. A. J. *Histoire de la Révolution de 1688 en Angleterre*, 3 vols. Paris, 1825.

Memoirs of Mary, queen of England (1689–1693), ed. R. Doebner. Leipzig, 1886.

Michael, W. *England under George I*, trans. A. and E. MacGregor, 2 vols. London, 1936–9.

The letters and works of Lady Mary Wortley Montagu, ed. Lord Wharncliffe, 2 vols. London, 1893.

Morgan, W. T. *English political parties and leaders in the reign of Queen Anne 1702–1710*. New Haven, 1920.

Murray, O. A. R. 'The Admiralty, part three', *Mariner's Mirror*, XXIII. 1937.

Noorden, C. von. *Europaische Geschichte im achtzehnten Jahrhundert*, 3 vols. Dusseldorf, 1870–2.

The Norris papers, ed. T. Heywood. Chetham Society, London, 1846.

Lord Nottingham's Chancery cases, ed. D. E. C. Yale, 2 vols. Selden Society, 1957–62.

Parker, S. *Bp. Parker's history of his own time*. London, 1728.

Patrick, S. *The auto-biography of Symon Patrick*. Oxford, 1839.

Pauli, R. 'Actenstücke zur Thronbesteigung des Welfenhauses in England', *Zeitschrift des Historischen Vereins für Niedersachsen*. 1883.

Pinkham, L. *William III and the respectable Revolution*. Cambridge, Mass., 1954.

Powis, A. K. 'The Whigs and their relations with William III in the period 1689–98', London University, M.A., 1940.

The letters and the second diary of Samuel Pepys, ed. R. G. Howarth. London, 1932.

Pepys' memoirs of the royal navy, 1679–1688, ed. J. R. Tanner. Oxford, 1906.

Samuel Pepys's naval minutes, ed. J. R. Tanner. Navy Record Society, London, 1926.

Private correspondence and miscellaneous papers of Samuel Pepys 1679–1703, ed. J. R. Tanner, 3 vols. London, 1926.

The Tangier papers of Samuel Pepys, ed. E. Chappell. Navy Record Society, London, 1935.

A descriptive catalogue of the naval manuscripts in the Pepysian Library at Magdalene College, Cambridge, ed. J. R. Tanner, 4 vols. Navy Record Society, London, 1903–23.

Quinlan, M. J. 'Swift and the prosecuted Nottingham speech', *Harvard Library Bulletin*, XI. 1957.

Ralph, J. *The history of England during the reigns of K. William, Q. Anne, and K. George I*, 2 vols. London, 1744–6.

Ranke, L. von. *A history of England principally in the seventeenth century*, 6 vols. Oxford, 1875.

The Rawdon papers, ed. E. Berwick. London, 1819.

Memoirs of Sir John Reresby, ed. A. Browning. Glasgow, 1936.

The journal of Sir George Rooke Admiral of the Fleet 1700–02, ed. O. Browning. Navy Record Society, London, 1897.

The records of the Royal Society of London. 4th edn, London, 1940.

A relation of the proceedings at the Charterhouse &c, reprinted in T. Burnet, *The sacred theory of the earth*, 2 vols. London, 1719.

The letters of Rachel Lady Russell, ed. Lord John Russell, 2 vols. London, 1853.

Salomon, P. *Geschichte des letzen Ministeriums Königin Annas von England (1710–1714) und der englischen Thronfolgefrage.* Gotha, 1894.

Sharp, T. *The life of John Sharp, D.D., lord archbishop of York*, ed. T. Newcome, 2 vols. London, 1825.

Private and original correspondence of Charles Talbot, duke of Shrewsbury, with King William, Etc., ed. W. Coxe. London, 1821.

Diary of the times of Charles the Second by the honourable Henry Sidney, ed. R. W. Blencowe, 2 vols. London, 1843.

Simpson, A. 'The Convention Parliament 1688–1689', Oxford University, D.Phil., 1939.

—— 'Notes of a Noble Lord', *English Historical Review*, LII. 1937.

Smith, C. F. *Mary Rich countess of Warwick (1625–1678).* London, 1901.

Snyder, H. L. 'Godolphin and Harley: A study of their partnership in politics', *Huntington Library Quarterly*, XXX. 1967.

Somerville, D. H. *The king of hearts.* London, 1962.

Speck, W. A. 'The House of Commons 1702–1714: A study in political organization', Oxford University, D.Phil., 1965.

—— 'The choice of a Speaker in 1705', *Bulletin of the Institute of Historical Research*, XXXVII. 1964.

Straka, G. M. *Anglican reaction to the Revolution of 1688.* Madison, Wisc., 1962.

Stromberg, R. N. *Religious liberalism in eighteenth-century England.* Oxford, 1954.

The correspondence of Jonathan Swift, D.D., ed. T. Ball, 6 vols. London, 1910–14.

Swift, J. *The history of the four last years of Queen Anne's reign*, ed. H. Davis. Oxford, 1951.

The poems of Jonathan Swift, ed. H. Williams, 3 vols. Oxford, 1958.

—— *Political tracts 1711–1713*, ed. H. Davis. Oxford, 1951.

—— *Journal to Stella*, ed. H. Williams, 2 vols. Oxford, 1958.

Discourses concerning government by Algernon Sydney, ed. T. Hollis. London, 1763.

Sykes, N. *William Wake archbishop of Canterbury 1657–1737*, 2 vols. Cambridge, 1957.

The works of Sir William Temple Bart., 4 vols. London, 1770.

Thomas, R. 'The non-subscription controversy amongst dissenters in 1719: The Salters' Hall Debate', *Journal of Ecclesiastical History*, IV. 1953.

—— 'The seven bishops and their petition, 18 May 1688', *Journal of Ecclesiastical History*, XII. 1961.

Thomas, R. 'Comprehension and indulgence', in *From uniformity to unity 1662–1962*, ed. O. Chadwick and G. Nuttall. London, 1962.

Thompson, E. M. 'Correspondence of Admiral Herbert during the Revolution', *English Historical Review*, I. 1886.

Letters of eminent men, addressed to Ralph Thoresby, F.R.S., ed. J. Hunter, 2 vols. London, 1832.

Thoyras, Rapin de. *The history of England*, and N. Tindal, *The continuation of Mr Rapin's history of England from the Revolution to the present times*, 21 vols. London, 1757–9.

Trevelyan, G. M. *England under Queen Anne*, 3 vols. London, 1930–4.

Turner, F. C. *James II*. London, 1948.

Venn, J. and Venn, J. A. *Alumni Cantabrigienses*, 10 vols. Cambridge, 1922–54.

Letters illustrative of the reign of William III from 1696 to 1708...by J. Vernon, ed. G.P.R. James, 3 vols. London, 1841.

A vindication of those who have taken the new oath of allegiance to King William and Queen Mary. London, 1689.

A vindication of the earl of Nottingham from the vile imputations, and malicious slanders, which have been cast upon him in some late pamphlets. [London, 1714.]

Walcott, R. *English politics in the early eighteenth century*. Oxford, 1956.

Ward, A. W. *The Electress Sophia and the Hanoverian succession*. London, 1909.

Warner, R. (ed.). *Epistolary curiosities; consisting of unpublished letters of the seventeenth century illustrative of the Herbert family*, 2 vols. Bath, 1818.

Autobiography of Mary, countess of Warwick, ed. T. C. Croker. Percy Society, London, 1848.

The Wentworth papers, 1705–1739, ed. J. Cartwright. London, 1883.

Whitehead, G. *The Christian progress of George Whitehead*. London, 1725.

Letters addressed from London to Sir Joseph Williamson while Plenipotentiary at the Congress of Cologne in the years 1673 and 1674, ed. W. D. Christie, 2 vols. Camden Society, London, 1874.

Willis, B. *Notitia Parliamentaria*, 3 vols. London, 1715–50.

The life and times of Anthony Wood, ed. A. Clark, 5 vols. Oxford Historical Society, Oxford, 1891–1900.

INDEX

Abingdon, Earls of, 263; *see* Bertie
Abjuration, bills of, 114–15, 164–5, 186 n. 2
Admiralty, commission of 1679–84, 15–16, 20–2, 24, 25–8, 32–5, 36 and n. 2, 272
Admiralty, naval conduct *temps* William III, 101, 108, 109 and n. 4, 121–2, 136, 142–3, 144 and n. 2, 153
Admiralty, naval conduct *temps* Queen Anne, 202, 211
Ailesbury, Earls of, *see* Bruce
Algiers, relations with, 32, 34, 170
Allestree, Richard, 3
Almanza, battle of, 211, 212
Anglesey, Earls of, 263; *see* Annesley
Anne, Princess of Denmark and queen, 59, 79, 80 and n. 1, 81, 124, 165, 166, 167, 173, 180, 181, 182, 186, 188 and n. 5, 189, 191, 192 n. 6, 193, 194, 195, 196, 197, 198, 199, 200, 203 n. 3, 204, 206, 207, 210, 213, 214, 215, 218, 219, 220, 222, 223, 235, 239, 241, 243, 245, 272
Annesley, Arthur, first Earl of Anglesey, 41
Annesley, Arthur, fifth Earl of Anglesey, 223, 235, 236, 239, 240, 241, 242 and n. 4, 244, 245, 248, 255, 257
Annesley, John, fourth Earl of Anglesey, 205, 220, 221, 222
Argyll, Duke of, *see* Campbell
Arianism, 253
Arlington, Earl of, *see* Bennet
Arnold, John, 137
Ashburnham, John, Baron and first Earl, 242
Ashby, Sir John, 122
Assembly, of peers (1688), 64–5, 66–70, 70–3
Assembly, of commoners (1688), 70
Association, of 1688, 67
Association, of 1696, 156, 157, 160 n. 5, 164
Atholl, Duke of, *see* Murray
Atkins, Samuel, 184
Atterbury, Francis, 183
Aylesford, Earl of, *see* Finch

Baines, Sir Thomas, 3, 5
Bank, of England, 149, 152, 153
Banks, Caleb, 260

Banks, Sir John, 260
Bantry Bay, battle of, 95, 96
Barfleur, battle of, 130
Barillon, Paul (Marquis des Branges), 37, 45 n. 4
Barrington family, 263
Barry, James, sixth Earl of Barrymore, 240
Baxter, Richard, 185 n. 5
Beach, Richard, 132 n. 3
Beachy Head, battle of, 118
Beaufort, Duke of, *see* Somerset
Bedwyn (Great), 7, 15, 25
Belasyse, Thomas, Viscount and first Earl of Fauconberg, 68
Bennet, Earl of Arlington, 10, 11
Benson, Anne (Finch), 263
Benson, Robert, 222, 263
Bentinck, William, first Earl of Portland, 108, 113, 126, 133, 134, 144, 154
Berkeley, John, third baron, 67, 68
Bernstorff, Andreas Gottlieb, Baron von, 246, 250, 252
Bertie, James, first Earl of Abingdon, 151, 152
Bertie, Montague Venables, second Earl of Abingdon, 239, 242, 245
Bewdley, charter of, 227, 228
Bishops, petition of and consultations with, 50–1, 54–5, 71, 87
Blathwayt, William, 134, 143, 144
Bohun, Edmund, 137 n. 4
Bolingbroke, Viscount of, *see* St John
Bolton, Duke of, *see* Paulet
Bonrepaux, Marquis de, *see* D'Usson
Booth, Henry, Baron Delamere and first Earl of Warrington, 43, 65, 75, 83, 110
Booth (Captain), Sir William, 32 n. 2
Bothmer, Hans Caspar, Baron von, 245, 246, 247
Boucher, James, 193, 194
Boyle, Charles, fourth Earl of Orrery, 242
Boyle, Henry, 221
Boyle, Richard, first Earl of Burlington, 56
Bradshaigh, Sir Roger, 240
Bridges, George, 30 n. 2
Brisbane, John, Secretary to the Admiralty, 21, 24, 26 and n. 5, 27, 32, 33, 34
    and n. 5, 35 and n. 7, 36, 38
Bromley, William, 186, 201, 204, 210, 212, 215, 216, 217, 221, 223, 227, 228,
    244, 268–9
Brouncker, William, second Viscount, 26 and n. 4, 34, 36, 37
Bruce, Anne (Savile), 263

INDEX

Bruce, Charles, Lord Bruce and third Earl of Ailesbury, 263
Bruce, Thomas, second Earl of Ailesbury, 15, 71, 273
Buckingham, Dukes of, *see* Villiers, Sheffield
Bulkeley, Henry, 264
Bunbury, Sir Henry, 248
Burley-on-the-hill, building of, 145 and n. 3, 150, 157, 274
Burlington, Earl of, *see* Boyle
Burnet, Gilbert, Bishop of Salisbury, 62, 83, 84 n. 2, 85, 90, 94, 98, 100, 185 n. 5, 257, 260
Busby, Dr Richard, 2
Butler, James, first Duke of Ormonde, 14, 46
Butler, James, second Duke of Ormonde, 172, 177, 185, 218, 237, 249
Byng (Admiral), Sir George, 253

Cabal, the, 10 and n. 1
Cabinet (Cabinet Council, Council of Nine, Lords of the Committee), 116, 118, 119, 120, 121–2, 123, 124, 128, 130, 131, 132, 133 and n. 3, 134, 144, 169 n. 1, 171, 177
Cadogan, William (General), 240
Campbell, John, second Duke of Argyll, 219, 242
Canterbury, Archbishops of, *see* Sancroft, Tenison, Tillotson, Wake
Capel, Arthur, first Earl of Essex, 15, 25
Capel, Sir Henry, 16 and n. 2, 25–6, 83, 110
Carlisle, Earl of, *see* Howard
Carmarthen, Marquesses of, *see* Osborne
Caroline, Princess of Wales and queen, 247 n. 5, 250, 252, 272
Carteret, John, second Baron, 235 and n. 2, 242
Catholics, threat of and in office, 11–12, 13, 39–40, 44–6, 47–9, 55, 59, 61, 87, 271
Cavendish, William, first Duke of Devonshire, 41, 47 n. 3, 52, 74, 88, 112, 132, 152, and n. 2, 167, 182, 193, 194 and n. 1, 205
Cavendish, William, second Duke of Devonshire, 232, 252
Cecil, John, sixth Earl of Exeter, 267
Cevennois, rebels, 171 and n. 2, 173
Charles, Archduke of Austria, 175 and n. 1
Charles II, 16, 24, 26, 27, 30, 31, 32 and n. 2, 35 and n. 7, 36–7, 38, 44, 89, 258
Charlett, Dr Arthur, 202, 254
Charlton, Woodley, 47
Charterhouse, the, 46
Chesterfield, Earl of, *see* Stanhope
Chicheley, Sir John, 33 and n. 3, 109 n. 4
Chisnall, Sir Edward, 92

Christ Church College, 2, 3
Church, Anglican, 'in danger', 41, 181, 203, 206, 208, 219
Churchmen, 91, 94, 110, 111, 115, 155, 156, 210, 211, 215, 223, 230, 233, 268
Church party, 84, 87, 93, 98, 99, 102 and n. 6, 103, 105, 106, 107 and n. 6, 108, 116, 200; see also Churchmen, High Churchmen, Tories
Churchill, John, first Duke of Marlborough, 80 n. 1, 120, 123, 124, 132, 160, 163 n. 3, 166, 167, 168, 169, 170, 171, 173, 174, 175, 176, 177, 178, 179 and nn. 3 and 5, 180, 181, 182, 183, 184, 186, 187, 188, 189, 190, 194, 196, 197, 200, 204, 205, 207, 208, 212, 213, 214, 217, 218, 228, 231, 232, 236, 237, 245, 246, 271
Churchill, Sarah (Jennings), Duchess of Marlborough, 180, 188, 189, 197, 210
Churchills, the, 200, 218
Clarendon, Earl of, see Hyde
Clarges, Sir Thomas, 40, 73, 74, 91, 93, 97, 102, 104, 111, 112, 123, 129, 268
Clarke, Dr Samuel, 253, 256 n. 1
Cleveland, Duke of, see Fitzroy
Cochrane, Sir John, 119–20
Coinage, state of, 135, 152–3, 202
Commissions, of Accounts, 123 n. 5, 187, 225–6
Commissions, of the peace, alterations in, 44–5, 163, 188 n. 6
Comprehension, bills of and discussions concerning, 29, 87–93, 94, 100, 101 n. 3, 181 n. 3, 254–5, 269–70
Compton, Henry, Bishop of London, 40, 41, 44, 46, 52, 56, 67, 79, 101, 110
Convocation, of Canterbury, 92–3, 100–1, 181 n. 3, 187, 209, 253
Conway, Francis Seymour, first Baron, 235 and n. 2
Conway, Edward, first Earl, 10 n. 1, 11, 31
Cooper, Anthony Ashley, first Earl of Shaftesbury, 7 n. 7, 14, 15, 25, 33 n. 1
Cornwallis, Charles, third Baron, 132
Corporations, acts and bills concerning, 104–6, 108, 185, 254, 255 n. 3
Council of Trade, 155
Country moderates, 22, 23
Country party, 129, 140, 155
Country Whigs, 203, 206, 211, 213, 216; see also Junto Whigs, Whigs
Court Tories, 22, 32, 36; see also Tories
Coventry, Henry, Secretary of State, 35 n. 7
Cowper, William, first Earl, 207, 218, 221, 250, 253, 254, 273
Culpepper, Thomas, second Baron, 65, 68
Cunningham (Colonel), Richard, 95
Customs Commissioners, 110 n. 1

Danby, Earls of, see Osborne
Darien venture, 159 n. 3

Dartmouth, Baron and Earl of, *see* Legge
Davenant, Dr Charles, 173, 184
Dawes, Sir William, Bishop of Chester and Archbishop of York, 234 n. 3,
    238 and n. 1, 242 and n. 4, 255
Dean, John, 15 and n. 1
Deane, Samuel, 21 n. 1
'*de facto*' men, 137 and n. 4
Delamere, baron of, *see* Booth
Delavall, Sir Ralph (Admiral), 127, 132 and n. 3, 139 and n. 6, 144, 147, 148
Denbigh, Earl of, *see* Feilding
Derby, Earl of, *see* Stanley
Dering, Captain Edward, 266
Descents, amphibious expeditions, 129, 130–4, 135, 136–9, 142, 172, 175
Devil Tavern, meetings at, 91, 93, 107
Devonshire, Dukes of, *see* Cavendish
Dorchester, Countess of, *see* Sedley
Dorset, Earl of, *see* Sackville
Douglas, James, second Duke of Queensberry, 191, 192 and n. 6
Drake, Dr James, 203
Drummond, John, first Earl of Melfort, 78
Duncomb, Sir Charles, 157 n. 6
Duras, Louis, first Earl of Feversham, 65
Dutch, relations with, 13, 14, 45, 54, 96, 143, 161–2, 163, 167–80, 200, 203, 205
Dutch envoy, Arnout van Citters, 122
Dutch guards, 65, 159
D'Usson, Francis, Marquis de Bonrepaux, 21 n. 2, 45 n. 4
Dyckvelt, Sieur, *see* Weede

East India Company, 154
Ecclesiastical Commission (1686–8), 44, 55
Ecclesiastical Commission (1689), 90, 99–100
Echard, Laurence, Archdeacon, 257 n. 4
Elections, to Parliament, 14, 25, 73, 108, 111, 154, 155, 158, 159, 164, 183–4,
    203, 214 and nn. 2 and 4, 223, 240
Ely, Bishop of, *see* Turner, Moore
Empire, Austrian, relations with, 167 ff.
Erskine, John, sixth Earl of Mar, 252 n. 2
Essex, Earl of, *see* Capel
Eugene, Prince of Savoy, 169, 170
Exclusion, bills of, 24, 28; opponents of, 28; supporters of (Exclusionists), 16,
    26, 28, 32, 33
Exeter, Earls of, 263; *see* Cecil

Fanshaw, Charles, fourth Viscount, 74
Fauconberg, Viscount of, *see* Bellasyse
Feilding, Basil, fourth Earl of Denbigh, 184
Fenwick, Sir John, 157 n. 6
Ferguson, Robert, 119–20, 192, 193, 196
Feversham, Earl of, *see* Duras
Finch, family, 1, 258, 274; relations and political influence of, 26, 28, 30, 31, 32, 111, 261–5, 268
Finch, Anne (Hatton), second Countess of Nottingham, 42, 150, 151, 165, 183, 236, 237, 247 n. 5, 263
Finch, Charles, 259 and n. 2
Finch, Charles, third Earl of Winchilsea, 184, 205, 228, 261
Finch, Daniel, Lord Finch and second Earl of Nottingham: attacks upon and reputation of, 16, 50, 84, 85, 96–7, 103–4, 136–9, 143 and n. 6, 145, 147, 154, 173, 194–5, 232 and n. 4, 233, 267–8, 274; *de facto* views, 82, 83 and n. 1, 84, 112–16, 156, 164–6, 270; electoral activities and parliamentary following of, 40, 111, 136, 158, 183–4, 203, 214 and n. 2, 219–20, 223, 231, 234 and n. 3, 235 and n. 2, 238 and n. 1, 239, 240 and n. 1, 241, 242, 265–9; family affairs and marriages, 6–7, 30, 37–8, 41–3, 145 n. 3, 150, 154 and n. 1, 157, 159, 160, 214 n. 4, 257 and n. 3, 258–65; membership of the Admiralty Commission and conduct of naval affairs, 15–16, 21, 26 and n. 4, 27–8, 32, 34–5, 37–8, 96, 108–9, 118–19, 122, 130–2, 139, 143–4, 272; parliamentary activities, 8–13, 17–19, 23, 28–30, 40–1, 65, 66–70, 73–4, 75–8, 79 and n. 1, 80 and n. 4, 81 and n. 2, 82, 87, 88–9, 90, 93–4, 101, 103, 104–5, 111–15, 140, 147–8, 149, 150–6, 157 and n. 6, 159 and n. 3, 161–3, 164–6, 186–7, 196, 201 n. 1, 202–3, 204–6, 208–9, 211–13, 215, 216–17, 219, 224–8, 232–3, 235, 236 and nn. 2 and 3, 238–9, 241, 244–5, 249, 250–1, 254–5, 256, 273; relations with Anglican clergy and defence of the Church, 38, 50–1, 99–101, 125, 150, 182, 247, 249, 253, 254–6, 262–3, 266; relations with James II as Duke of York and king, 22–4, 26, 28, 30, 33, 39–41, 43, 44, 45 and n. 4, 46, 49, 55–9, 60–3; relations with William III as Prince of Orange and king, 46–7, 48, 52–4, 61, 65, 67, 83 and n. 4, 84 and nn. 2 and 3, 85, 97–9, 102 and nn. 6 and 7, 103, 104, 106–7, 116–17, 122–3, 124–5, 126–7, 145–6, 149–57, 160 and n. 5, 270, 272; relations with Anne, 166, 181, 197, 198 and n. 5, 199, 203 n. 3, 206–7, 222, 272; relations with the Hanoverians and support of their succession, 98, 165, 205, 234 and n. 2, 241, 242–3, 247, 248 and n. 3, 250 and n. 2, 252, 271, 272; support of limitations, 11–12, 22–4, 270; support of measures against occasional conformity, 185, 186 and n. 3, 187, 189, 202, 231–3, 254–5, 271; support of relief for Dissenters, 9, 11, 29, 87–95, 99–100, 101 n. 3, 269, 270; views on foreign affairs and war strategy, 31, 33, 108, 109 and n. 1, 130–2, 134–5, 167–8, 169 and n. 1, 170, 171 and n. 2, 173–4, 175 and n. 1, 176–80, 212, 229, 232 ff., 272; writings, 200 and n. 1, 203 and n. 4, 251 and n. 4, 256 and n. 1, 257 n. 1

Finch, Daniel, Lord Finch and third Earl of Nottingham, 219, 223, 234, 240 and n. 1, 246, 250 n. 2, 252, 267, 274

Finch, Edward, 111, 152 n. 2, 184, 222, 240, 259, 260, 261

Finch, Elizabeth (Heneage), Countess of Winchilsea, 1 and n. 3

Finch, Elizabeth (Harvey), 1, 2, 3

Finch, Elizabeth (Banks), 259 n. 1, 260

Finch, Essex (Rich), first Countess of Nottingham, 6–7, 37–8, 41 and n. 4, 263

Finch, Sir Heneage, first Earl of Nottingham, 1 and n. 3, 2, 3, 4, 5, 6, 7 and n. 5, 10 and n. 1, 11, 12, 13, 15 and n. 4, 23, 25, 28, 29 n. 4, 31, 32, 33 and n. 1, 34, 43, 258, 261, 262, 274

Finch, Heneage (father of first Earl of Nottingham), 1, 43

Finch, Heneage, second Earl of Winchilsea, 261

Finch, Heneage, Baron Guernsey and first Earl of Aylesford, 4, 15 n. 2, 31, 33 n. 1, 39 n. 1, 40, 43–4, 51, 66 n. 4, 73, 74 and n. 5, 84 n. 2, 91, 94, 105, 107, 108 n. 1, 111, 115, 123, 150, 151, 155, 156, 164, 179, 183, 185, 186 n. 2, 187, 211, 220, 224, 234, 235 and n. 2, 238 and n. 1, 246, 249, 259 and n. 1, 260, 263, 264, 268, 269

Finch, Heneage, second Earl of Aylesford, 224, 228, 246, 255

Finch, Heneage (son of second Earl of Nottingham), 42

Finch, Henry, 150, 152 n. 2, 160 n. 5, 182, 240, 247, 259, 260

Finch, Sir John, 3, 4–5, 6, 43, 259

Finch, John, 41

Finch, Leslie, 264

Finch, Mary (sister of second Earl of Nottingham), 258

Finch, Sir Moyle, 1

Finch, William, 25, 259 and n. 1

Fitzroy, Henry, first Duke of Grafton, 35

Fitzroy, William, third Duke of Cleveland, 257 n. 3

Flanders, war in, 131, 134, 168, 174, 175, 176, 179, 212, 237

Fleetwood, William, 247

Foley, Paul, 129, 136, 155

Fowler, John, 87, 263

Fox, Sir Stephen, 110

France, relations with and war against, 13, 30, 33, 62, 130, 167 ff., 178, 179 and nn. 3 and 5, 211–13, 217, 229, 230–1, 237, 238–9, 244

Fraser, Simon, 191, 192

Freeman, Ralph, 212

Gainsborough, Earls of, see Noel

Galway, Earl of, see Massue

General Naturalization, Act of, 216–17, 224

George, Prince of Hesse-Darmstadt, 185

George, Prince of Denmark, 59, 124, 186, 188, 211
George I, Elector of Hanover and king, 234 n. 2, 239, 245, 246, 247, 248, 250, 253, 272
George II, Electoral Prince and Prince of Wales, 241, 243, 247, 252, 257, 272
Gloucester, William, Duke of, 161
Godden vs. Hales, 16, 43–4
Godolphin, Sidney, Earl of, 31, 60, 61, 68, 83, 104, 124, 130, 142, 148, 152, 160, 161, 162, 163, 168, 176, 178, 181, 182, 183, 184, 185 and n. 3, 187, 188, 189, 190, 194, 195 and n. 7, 196, 197, 198, 200, 203, 204, 205, 207, 210, 213, 214, 217, 218, 220, 223, 228, 231, 232, 236, 237 and n. 3
Goodrick, Sir Henry, 137
Grafton, Duke of, *see* Fitzroy
Grahme, James (colonel), 189, 221
Grahme, Richard, first Viscount Preston, 78
Granville, George, 206
Granville, John (colonel), 158, 184, 187
Graydon, John (admiral), 178
Grey, Henry, Earl, Marquess, and first Duke of Kent, 220
Greye, Forde, first Earl of Tankerville, 156
Grimstone, Lady Anne, 42
Grimstone, Elizabeth (Finch), 258
Grimstone, Sir Harbottle, 258
Grimstone, Samuel, 258
Guernsey, Baron of, *see* Finch
Guilford, Barons of, 263; *see* North
Guise, Sir John, 111, 112
Gwyn, Francis, 154

Haddock, Sir Richard, 34, 108, 121–2
Hales, Edward, 16 and n. 3, 34
Halford, Richard, 214 n. 2
Halifax, Earl of, *see* Montague
Halifax, Marquesses of, *see* Savile
Hammond, Anthony, 158
Hampden, John, 91, 92
Hampden, Richard, 83, 84 n. 4, 88, 104, 108 n. 1, 111
Hanmer, Sir Thomas, 188 n. 6, 210, 212, 213, 223, 239, 240, 241, 242, 248, 268, 269
Hanover, electoral family of, invitations to England, 215, 235; succession to the throne of England, 165, 205, 234, 238, 239, 241, 242
Harbord, William, 92, 93, 97
Harcourt, Simon, first Viscount, 195 n. 7, 201, 202, 214, 215, 241, 243

Harley, Sir Edward, 47
Harley, Robert, first Earl of Oxford, 129, 138, 155, 159, 160, 167, 184, 185
and n. 3, 186 n. 5, 187, 190, 195 and n. 7, 198, 201 n. 5, 207, 210, 211, 213,
214, 215, 218, 220, 221, 222 and n. 4, 223, 224, 225, 226, 228, 229, 230, 231,
232, 233, 234, 235, 236, 238, 241, 242, 243, 244, 245, 249, 252, 255, 269,
273 n. 2
Harvey, Daniel, 2
Harvey, Daniel, of Combe, 264 and n. 3
Harvey, Edward, 264 and n. 3
Harvey family, 260, 264
Hatton, Charles, 264
Hatton, Christopher, first Viscount, 42, 43, 44, 60, 150, 151, 195, 261
Haversham, Baron, see Thompson
Hayter, Thomas, 26, 34
Hedges, Sir Charles, 160 n. 2, 164, 166 and n. 4, 176, 179, 182, 190, 191, 195
and n. 7, 207
Heinsius, Anthonie, Pensionary of Holland, 168, 169, 170, 173, 174, 175, 176,
177, 178, 179 n. 5, 267
Herbert, Arthur, first Earl of Torrington, 21, 24, 27, 28, 32 and n. 2, 33, 34,
35 and n. 7, 36, 37, 46, 95–6, 108–9, 118–19, 121, 123, 124, 152, 156
Herbert, Thomas, eighth Earl of Pembroke, 65, 67, 68, 72, 80, 82, 108, 113,
134, 159, 167, 219
High Churchmen, 201 n. 5, 203, 207 and n. 6, 220, 221, 224, 234, 236, 241, 244;
see also Church party, Churchmen, Tackers, Tories
Hill, John (colonel), 218
Hill, Richard, 172, 175, 176, 198, 200, 240, 266
Hoadley, Benjamin, Bishop of Bangor, 253, 255, 274
Holles, John, first Duke of Newcastle, 204, 207, 221, 228
Hooper, George, Bishop of Bath and Wells, 240
Hoskins, Sir William, 259 n. 1
Hough, John, Bishop of Lichfield and Coventry, 217
Howard, Sir Robert, 108, 127
Howard, Thomas, third Earl of Carlisle, 198
Howe, John, 95–6, 98, 104, 183, 190, 195 n. 7
Howe, John, dissenting minister, 185 n. 5
Humfrey, John, 185 n. 5
Hussey, Sir Edward, 137, 140
Hyde, Henry, second Earl of Clarendon, 41, 45, 50, 55, 56–7, 60, 61, 67, 68,
71, 72, 73, 74, 75, 80, 81 and n. 2, 82
Hyde, Laurence, first Earl of Rochester, 23, 30, 31, 36, 39, n. 1, 45, 50, 56–7,
59, 64, 73, 76, 80, 81, 102 n. 6, 127, 130, 132, 140, 141, 149, 152 and n. 3,
153, 158 n. 1, 160, 161, 162, 163, 166, 167, 177, 178, 181 and n. 3, 182, 183,

Hyde, Laurence, *cont.*
184, 186, 187, 188 and n. 5, 202, 203 and n. 3, 205, 206, 207 and n. 5, 208, 211, 212, 217, 218, 220, 221–2, 225, 228, 267, 268

Inchiquin, Earl of, *see* O'Brien
Indulgence, declarations of, 9, 46, 49, 50–1, 263
Ireland, war in, 95–6, 106–7, 123, 125
Isham, Sir Justinian, 158
Italy, war in, 168, 169, 170, 172

Jacobites, *see* James II, James III
James II, Duke of York and king, 13, 23, 24, 26, 27, 28, 30, 31, 33 n. 3, 34, 36–7, 39, and n. 1, 40–1, 43–6, 47–8, 49–51, 52, 54–5, 56 and n. 3, 58–60, 61, 62, 63, 64, 65, 66, 67, 68, 69, 74, 75, 76, 77, 78, 80, 83 n. 1, 87, 89, 259, 270; supporters of, 23, 33, 36, 67, 70 and n. 4, 71, 76, and n. 2, 98, 270
James III, Prince of Wales and the Pretender, 52, 69, 76, 77, 164, 166, 239, 241, 242 n. 4, 244, 252 and n. 2; supporters of, 239, 245
Jane, William, 100
Jeffreys, George, 41, 43
Jenkins, Sir Leoline, 22
Jennings, Sir Edmund, 40
Jersey, Earl of, *see* Villiers
Jones, Richard, first Earl of Ranelagh, 187
Junto Whigs, 156, 158, 159, 160, 163, 188, 190, 205, 207, 208, 210, 211, 212, 213, 214, 215, 216, 217, 218, 220, 236; *see also* Whigs

Kensington House, 43, 145 n. 3
Kent, Marquess of, *see* Grey
Kenyon, George, 240
Ker, John, first Duke of Roxburghe, 214 and n. 4, 230, 263
Ker, Mary (Finch Savile), Marchioness of Halifax and Duchess of Roxburghe, 41, 154, 214 n. 4, 221, 247 n. 5, 252 n. 6, 262, 263, 265
Keroualle, Louise, Duchess of Portsmouth, 34, 36–7
Kerr, Robert, first Marquess of Lothian, 126
Kidder, Richard, 99, 125, 262
Killigrew, Henry (admiral), 132 and n. 3, 139 and n. 6, 147, 148
King, Sir Peter, 204, 211, 213, 215, 216
Knatchbull, Sir John, 102 n. 6, 105, 265

Lancashire plot, 152, 153, 160 n. 5
Lee, Sir Thomas, 16 and n. 2, 25, 26 and n. 2, 33, 47
Legge, Elizabeth (Finch), 263

Legge, George, first Baron Dartmouth, 2–3, 30, 33, 35 and n. 7, 36 and n. 2, 47
Legge, William, first Earl of Dartmouth, 183, 207, 208, 209, 221, 222, 225, 234, 263
Legh, Peter, 152 n. 2, 240 n. 5
Legh, Thomas, 240 and n. 5
Legh family, 260, 263, 269
Leinster, Duke of, see Schomberg
Lenox, Charles, first Duke of Richmond, 184
Lexington, Baron, see Sutton
Limitations, on a Catholic successor, 12, 24, 29–30, 270
Lindsay, David, 191
Littleton, Sir Thomas, second bart., 26, 33
Littleton, Sir Thomas, third bart., 158
Lloyd, William, Bishop of St Asaph and Worcester, 53, 56–7, 100, 101, 182 n. 4
Lloyd, William, Bishop of Norwich, 101
Loans, sought by government, 110, 121
London, Bishop of, see Compton
London, 33 n. 1, 62, 139; lieutenancy of, 110, 163, 166
Lothian, Marquess of, see Kerr
Lowther, Sir John, first Viscount Lonsdale, 107, 110, 111, 112, 115, 127, 134, 137, 138, 140, 159
Lumley, Richard, Baron Lumley and first Earl of Scarborough, 46, 51, 194

Maclean, Sir John, 192, 193, 194, 196
Magdalen College, 46 and n. 2, 55
Manners, John, Earl and first Duke of Rutland, 240, 267
Mansell, Thomas, first Baron, 214
Mar, Earl of, see Erskine
Marlborough, Duke of, see Churchill
Mary, Princess of Orange and queen, 68, 70, 73, 78, 79 and n. 1, 80, 81, 82, 116, 117, 118, 120–1, 122, 123 and n. 2, 124–5, 127, 131, 141 and n. 2, 150, 151, 154, 272; supporters of ('Maryites'), 73, 77, 78, 79 and n. 1
Mary of Modena, queen of James II, 49
Masham, Abigail, 218
Massue, Henry de, first Earl of Galway, 130, 211, 212, 224
Max Emmanuel, Elector of Bavaria, 169, 170
Maynard, William, second Baron, 67
Mediterranean, fleet in, 152, 170, 171, 172
Melfort, Earl of, see Drummond
Meres, Sir Thomas, 16 and n. 2, 34
Methuen, John, 172, 173
Middleton, Charles (Secretary of State), second Earl, 61, 67, 191
Mitchell, Sir David, 178

Monmouth, Duke of, *see* Scott
Monmouth, Earl of, *see* Mordaunt
Montagu, Ralph, first Earl, 14, 68, 72, 75, 84 n. 4
Montague, Charles, first Earl of Halifax, 155, 159, 162, 187, 205, 207, 220, 232, 245, 246, 249
Montague, James (Solicitor-General), 211
Montague family, 263
Moore, Arthur, 239
Moore, John, Bishop of Norwich and Ely, 137 n. 4, 217, 262
Mordaunt, Charles, Viscount Mordaunt, Earl of Monmouth, third Earl of Peterborough, 41, 46, 52, 68, 75, 83, 110, 120 and n. 7, 121–2, 124, 141, 149, 156, 177 and n. 3, 212, 213, 224
Morrice, Roger, 111
Mostyn, Essex (Finch), 263, 265
Mostyn, Sir Roger, 188 n. 6, 224, 228, 246 and n. 6, 247 n. 1, 263, 265 and n. 1
Murray, John, first Duke of Atholl, 192 and n. 6, 193
Musgrave, Sir Christopher, 74, 91, 97, 102, 127, 129, 138, 141, 160, 185, 187, 190, 268

Nassau, Fredrick van, count Zuylestein, 48, 54
Navy, *see* Admiralty
Newcastle, Duke of, *see* Holles
Nicholson, Francis, 266
Nicolson, Francis, Bishop of Carlisle, 182, 213 n. 3
Noel, Baptist, third Earl of Gainsborough, 150, 267
Non-Jurors, 101, 108, 125
'No Peace Without Spain', 174 n. 2, 212, 232 ff.
Normanby, Marquess of, *see* Sheffield
North, Charles, fifth Baron, 68
North, Francis (Lord Chief Justice), first Baron Guilford, 34 and n. 5
Nottingham, Earls of, *see* Finch

Oates, Titus, 14, 97
Oaths, of allegiance, 76, 82 and n. 4, 84, 93–4
O'Brien, William, Earl of Inchiquin, 27
Occasional Conformity, bills and act against, 90, 91, 185 and n. 5, 186 and n. 3, 187, 189, 197, 200, 201, 202, 203, 231, 232, 233 and n. 4, 248, 254–6, 269
October Club, 224 and n. 3, 226, 233, 236, 238
Ogilvy, James, first Earl of Seafield, 238
Oldmixon, John, vii
Onslow, Arthur, 274
Onslow, Sir Richard, 109 n. 4, 211, 215

Orford, Earl of, *see* Russell
Ormonde, Dukes of, *see* Butler
Orrery, Earl of, *see* Boyle
Osborne, Peregrine, Earl of Danby, Marquess of Carmarthen, second Duke of Leeds, 96–7, 127, 214 n. 4
Osborne, Sir Thomas, Earl of Danby, Marquess of Carmarthen, and first Duke of Leeds, 10, 12, 13–14, 40, 46, 47 n. 3, 52, 53, 73, 75, 77, 78, 79, 82, 83, 84 nn. 2 and 3, 86, 88, 94, 95–7, 98, 101, 102, 103, 106 and nn. 1 and 6, 107 and n. 6, 110, 111, 112, 113, 114, 115, 116, 117, 118, 120, 121, 123, 124, 125, 126, 127, 128, 131, 132, 134, 139 n. 1, 140, 152 n. 2, 154, 156, 214 n. 4, 218
Oxford, Earl of, *see* Harley

Packington, Sir John, 186 n. 2
Paget, William, seventh Baron, 68
Palatines, invitation to, 227–8
Parliament, of 1661–78, 8–14; of 1679, 24, 25; of 1679–80, 24, 25, 26, 28–30; of 1681, 30, 33 n. 1; of 1685–7, 39, 40–1, 44, 45, 46; of 1689–90, 54, 57–8, 59, 60, 61, 73, 74–9, 80–2, 86, 87–94, 95–7, 98–9, 101–6; of 1690–5, 111–15, 121, 123 and n. 5, 124, 135–6, 137 and n. 4, 138–9, 140, 142, 147–8, 151–3, 154; of 1695–8, 155–7; of 1698–1700, 159, 160; of 1700–1, 161–3; of 1701–2, 164–5, 183; of 1702–5, 185–7, 189–96, 197, 200–3; of 1705–8, 204–6, 208–9, 210–14; of 1708–10, 217–19, 221; of 1710–13, 223–8, 230, 232–7, 237–9, 240; of 1713–15, 241–5; of 1715–22, 249, 250, 251, 253–5, 256
Partition, treaties of, 161, 162, 174
Patrick, Simon, 50, 87, 99, 262, 263
Paulet, Charles, Marquess of Winchester and first Duke of Bolton, 74, 81, 112, 121–2
Pedro II, of Portugal, 173, 174
Pelham, Sir Thomas, 110
Pembroke, Earl of, *see* Herbert
Pepys, Samuel, 20, 21, 35–6
Peterborough, Earl of, *see* Mordaunt
Petitions, for a free parliament, 57–8
Petre, Edward (Father), 49, 55
Philip V, of Spain, 173
Pierce, James, 253
Place bills, 11, 140, 187 n. 1, 206, 225, 238
Popish plot, 14
Portland, Earl of, *see* Bentinck
Portsmouth, Duchess of, *see* Keroualle
Portugal, alliance with and war in, 168, 172, 173, 174, 175, 176, 177, 180
Poulet, John, first Earl, 210, 222, 225, 230, 235

Powle, Henry, 111
Preston, Viscount, see Grahme
Price, Robert ('Robin'), 183
Prideaux, Humphrey, 182, 184, 262
Priestman, Henry, 109 n. 4
Privy Council, 15–16, 28, 32, 39, 144, 167
Pulteney, John, 173

Queensberry, Duke of, see Douglas

Ranelagh, Earl of, see Jones
Regency, proposal of in 1680, 30; proposal of in 1688–9 and supporters of
    ('Regencyites'), 68, 69, 70 and n. 4, 71–2, 74, 76 and n. 2, 270; act and council
    of, 205–6, 241, 245
Reresby, Sir John, 82
Rich, Mary, Countess of Warwick, 6–7
Richards, Solomon (colonel), 95
Richmond, Duke of, see Lenox
Right, declaration, bill, and statute of, 82, 98, 102, 113, 114
Rivers, Earl of, see Savage
Rochester, Earl of, see Hyde
Rooke, Sir George (admiral), 148, 171, 177, 185
Rupert, Prince, 35
Russell, Edward, first Earl of Orford, 46, 52, 53, 109 and n. 4, 116, 118, 120,
    122, 125, 127–8, 130–1, 132 and n. 3, 133 and n. 1, 134, 135–6, 137, 138–9,
    156, 159, 162, 265 and n. 2, 272
Rutland, Duke of, see Manners
Rutland, elections in, 158, 203, 214 and n. 2, 219–20, 223, 240 and n. 1, 266–7
Ryswick, treaty of, 158

Sacheverell, Dr Henry, 219
Sacheverell, Sir William, 83, 105, 108, 109 n. 4
Sackville, Charles, sixth Earl of Dorset, 80 n. 1, 132
Sackville, Edward (colonel), 28, 32 n. 2
Sacrament, receipt of as test for office, 88, 89, 90, 104, 209, 216, 254–5; see also
    Comprehension, Corporation, Occasional Conformity
St John, Henry, first Viscount Bolingbroke, 183, 186, 190, 198, 212, 214, 224,
    239, 241, 242, 243, 244, 245, 249, 265, 268
St John, family, 263
Sancroft, William, Archbishop of Canterbury, 44, 46, 50, 64, 67, 71, 73 and n. 4,
    83 n. 1, 99, 101
Saunière de L'Hermitage, Rene de, 267

Savage, Richard, Earl Rivers, 218

Savile, Elizabeth (Grimstone), 258, 262

Savile, George, first Marquess of Halifax, 6, 22, 23, 24, 25, 31, 32, 33, 35 n. 7, 36, 39–41, 46, 47 n. 3, 49, 50, 51, 52, 54, 56, 57, 58 and n. 1, 59–63, 65, 67, 73–4, 76, 77, 79, 81, 82, 83, 84 and nn. 2 and 3, 86, 94, 95–6, 98, 102, 104, 107, 113, 117, 121, 149, 151, 152 and n. 2, 154 n. 1, 156, 160, 262

Savile, Henry, 33 and n. 3

Savile, William, Lord Eland and second Marquess of Halifax, 154, 155, 157, 160, 252 n. 6, 258, 262, 263, 265 and n. 1

Sawyer, Sir Robert, 91

Scarborough, Earl of, see Lumley

Schism, Act of and repeal, 244, 248, 254–6, 271

Schomberg, Meinhard, Duke of Leinster and third Duke of Schomberg, 130, 137

Schutz, Ludwig Justus, Baron von, 241, 242, 243

Scotch plot, 190, 191–5, 196 and n. 3, 197, 200

Scotland, 126, 200, 202, 204, 211, 227; Jacobites in, 217, 249–50, see also Scotch plot; religious affairs, 126, 203, 208 and n. 2, 236; representative peers, 209, 214 n. 4; Security, act of, 193, 202, 209; Union with England, 165, 208 and n. 2, 209, 213, 238

Scott, James, Duke of Monmouth, 39

Seafield, Earl of, see Ogilvy

Sedley, Catherine, Countess of Dorchester, 233

Sedley, Sir Charles, 137

Septennial Act, 251, 257

Seymour, Charles, sixth Duke of Somerset, 67, 167, 182, 193, 194 and n. 1, 196, 197, 198, 213, 218, 219, 221, 234, 235, 257 n. 3

Seymour, Sir Edward, 10, 22, 23, 31, 32, 33, 102 n. 7, 104, 127, 130, 134, 136, 137, 138, 140, 141, 148, 152 n. 3, 157, 160, 167, 179, 185, 187, 188, 189, 190, 197, 198 and n. 4, 268

Seymour, Elizabeth (Percy), Duchess of sixth Duke of Somerset, 235

Seymour, Frances (Devereux), Duchess of second Duke of Somerset, 7

Shaftesbury, Earl of, see Cooper

Shales, John, 101

Sharp, John, Archbishop of York, 38, 42, 44, 50, 87, 99, 125, 149, 160 n. 5, 166, 182 and n. 4, 186, 202 n. 1, 217, 224, 234 n. 3, 238, 242, 262, 266

Sheffield, John, Earl of Mulgrave, Marquess of Normanby, first Duke of Buckingham, 114, 152, 157, 161, 162, 164, 165, 167, 182, 188, 189, 204, 205, 207 and n. 5, 208, 222

Sherard, Bennet, third Baron, 158, 240

Sheres, (Sir) Henry, 27, 28, 32 n. 2, 36

Shovell, Sir Cloudesly, 139, 171

Shower, Sir Bartholomew, 162

Shrewsbury, Earl and Duke of, *see* Talbot
Sidney, Henry, Earl of Romney, 52, 53, 124, 127, 132, 133 n. 2
Smallridge, George, Bishop of Bristol, 202, 247, 249, 250
Smith, John, 136, 137, 204
Somers, John, Baron, 108 n. 1, 129, 141–2, 160, 162, 163, 186, 194, 202, 205, 208, 212, 218, 220
Somerset, Dukes of, 7; *see* Seymour
Somerset, Henry, first Duke of Beaufort, 58 n. 1
Sophia, Electress of Hanover, 98, 205 and n. 4, 206, 222, 243
Southwell, Sir Robert, 14, 116, 121
Spain, war in, 168, 172, 177, 211–13
Spencer, Charles, third Earl of Sunderland, 194, 207 and n. 5, 208, 212, 218, 220, 225, 237, 240, 274
Spencer, Robert, second Earl of Sunderland, 15, 23, 24, 27, 28, 31, 34, 35 and n. 7, 36, 37, 46, 49, 50, 54, 127, 140, 144, 155, 158 and n. 1, 159, 163, 173, 183
Stanhope, James, first Earl, 191, 246, 253, 254, 255
Stanhope, Philip, second Earl of Chesterfield, 83 n. 1
Stanley, William George Richard, ninth Earl of Derby, 150, 260
Stepney, George, 175 n. 1, 196
Stillingfleet, Edward, 38, 50, 53, 87, 99, 262, 263
Stratford, Dr William, 215, 254
Strickland, Sir William, 194
Sunderland, Earls of, *see* Spencer
Sutton, Robert, second Baron Lexington, 219
Swift, Jonathan, 220, 223 n. 2, 224, 232 n. 4, 267

Tackers, 202, 203–4
Taff, John, 152 n. 2
Talbot, Charles, Earl and first Duke of Shrewsbury, 46, 51, 52, 54, 65, 79, 83, 84 n. 3, 86, 97, 99, 103, 105, 108 and n. 1, 110, 112, 114, 116, 118, 120 n. 7, 122, 140, 151, 156, 159, 218, 219, 220, 222, 224, 225
Tangier, 27, 35 and n. 7
Tankerville, Earl of, *see* Greye
Temple, Sir Richard, 78, 137
Temple, Sir William, 15, 25
Tenison, Thomas, Archbishop of Canterbury, 38, 87, 182, 198, 208, 209, 249, 262
Thanet, Earls of, 263; *see* Tufton
Thompson, Sir John, first Baron Haversham, 111, 112, 129, 202, 204–5, 208, 209, 211, 215, 217 and n. 3, 218
Thynne, Frances (Finch), 261 n. 5
Thynne, Sir Thomas, first Viscount Weymouth, 23, 25, 34, 57, 58, 65, 81, 83 n. 1, 154, 160, 165, 166, 182, 184, 201 n. 1, 235 and n. 2, 262, 264

Thynne, family, 261
Tillotson, John, 38, 50, 87, 99, 100, 125, 262, 263
Toleration, act and bills of, 29, 87–9, 92–3, 94, 183, 186, 244
Tollemache, Thomas, 152
Tories, 91, 102, 103, 106, 107, 108, 111, 112, 115, 121, 129, 155, 156, 162, 163,
    181, 182, 185, 190, 194, 201–3, 205, 210, 211, 214, 215, 217, 221, 237, 247,
    249, 252, 254; see also Churchmen, Church party, Court Tories, High Church-
    men, Tackers, Whimsicals
Torrington, Earl of, see Herbert
Townshend, Charles, second Viscount, 194, 212, 232, 245, 246, 249, 250 n. 2
Treason trials, act and bills of, 149, 151, 155
Tredenham, Sir Joseph, 91, 138
Trelawney, Charles (major-general), 142 n. 2
Trenchard, Sir John, 141, 143, 144 n. 2, 146, 148
Trevor, Sir John (1626–72), 5, 7
Trevor, Sir John (1637–1717), 105, 111, 134, 136
Trevor, Sir Thomas, first Baron, 141, 142, 160, 256
Triennial parliaments, act and bills of, 140, 141, 149, 150, 151
Trumbull, Sir William, 128
Tucker, John, 190
Tufton, Thomas, sixth Earl of Thanet, 154, 234, 235 and n. 2
Turner, Francis, Bishop of Ely, 64, 65, 68, 71, 75, 76 and n. 2, 101, 125
Twysden, Sir Roger, 6
Twysden, Sir William, 40, 262, 265

Vaughan, Edward, 16 and n. 2, 25, 26
Vernon, James, 159, 166 and n. 4
Verney, George, twelfth Baron Willoughby de Broke, 256
Verney, John, 195
Victor Amadeus, Duke of Savoy, 169, 170, 172
Villiers, Edward, first Earl of Jersey, 159, 160 n. 2, 167, 188, 190, 197, 198
    and n. 4, 207 n. 5
Villiers, George, second Duke of Buckingham, 145

Wake, William, Archbishop of Canterbury, 254, 255, 256, 273
Wallis, Dr John, 191
Walpole, Sir Robert, 246, 248 n. 1, 249, 250 and n. 2, 254
Ward, Edward, 141, 142
Ward, John, 223, 227, 228, 240 n. 5, 269
Warwick, Earls of, 263; see Rich
Waterland, Dr Daniel, 256 n. 1
Weede, Everard, heer van Dyckvelt, 46–7, 84 n. 1

INDEX

Wentworth, Peter, 224
Wentworth, Thomas, third Earl of Strafford, 249
West Indies, war in, 168, 174, 178, 208
Weymouth, Viscount, *see* Thynne
Wharton, Goodwin, 136, 137
Wharton, Sir Michael, 108, 109 n. 4
Wharton, Philip, fourth Baron, 67 and n. 3, 88
Wharton, Thomas, first Marquess, 108, 114, 116, 137, 159, 167, 194, 206, 211, 212, 220, 232
Wheler, Sir Francis (captain), 32 n. 2
Whigs, 92, 95, 98, 101–2, 103–4, 105–6, 107, 108 n. 1, 110, 111, 112, 116, 118, 125, 127, 128, 129, 136–7, 139 and n. 6, 140–1, 144, 147, 148, 151, 156, 158, 163, 164, 185, 189, 190, 191, 194, 196, 203, 205, 207, 216, 218, 220, 230–2, 233, 235, 236, 237, 238, 239, 241, 242, 243, 244, 245, 247, 251; *see also* Country Whigs, Junto Whigs
Whimsicals, 239, 240–1, 242, 243, 244, 248, 249
Whiston, William, 253, 256
White, Thomas, Bishop of Peterborough, 56–7, 82 n. 4
Wildman, Sir John, 120
William III, Prince of Orange and king, 30, 45–6, 47–8, 51–3, 56, 60–3, 64, 65, 66, 67, 69, 70, 73, 74, 76, 77, 78, 79, 80, 81, 82, 83–4, 86, 87, 88, 92–3, 98–9, 100, 101, 102, 103, 104, 105, 106, 107, 108, 109 and nn. 1 and 4, 110, 112 and n. 1, 113, 114, 115, 116, 117, 118, 119, 121, 122, 123 and nn. 2 and 5, 124, 125, 126, 127, 128, 129, 130, 131, 132, 133, 134, 135, 137, 138, 139, 140, 141, 142 and n. 4, 145, 146, 147, 148, 149, 151, 152, 153, 155, 156, 157, 158, 159, 160 and n. 5, 161, 163, 164, 165, 166, 174, 187, 247, 268, 272
Willoughby de Broke, Baron of, *see* Verney
Winch, Sir Humphrey, 16 and n. 3
Winchester, Marquess of, *see* Paulet
Winchilsea, Earls of, *see* Finch
Winnington, Sir Francis, 15 n. 2
Woodroff, Thomas, 7
Woodruff, Benjamin, 3, 4, 6
Wratislaw, Count, 169, 170, 185
Wright, Nathan, 160, 207
Wyndham, Sir William, 244 and n. 2
Wynne, Dr John, 247 n. 1

York, Archbishops of, *see* Sharp, Dawes

Zuylestein, Count of, *see* Nassau